The New Psychohistory

THE
NEW
PSYCHOHISTORY

Lloyd deMause,
Editor

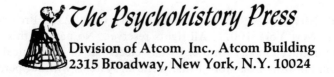 *The Psychohistory Press*

Division of Atcom, Inc., Atcom Building
2315 Broadway, New York, N.Y. 10024

Library of Congress Catalog Card Number: 75-14687

International Standard Book Number: 0-914434-01-2

Contents

The New Psychohistory

Foreword

Psychohistory, the first new discipline to be born in the social sciences in this century, had its beginnings in what used to be called "applied psychoanalysis," starting with the writings of Freud and his early associates. It remained pretty much confined to the back pages of the psychoanalytic journals for five decades, where it was used primarily as a way of illustrating clinical discoveries—so that when the Oedipus complex was new, leaders were found to have Oedipus complexes, and when ego psychology was developing, the same leaders were found to have had identity crises.

Psychobiographies of important people formed the bulk of these early studies, usually using the biographical information provided by traditional historians and attempting to guess at the childhood experiences which might have been responsible for their adult personalities. Since these were mainly psychoanalysts writing papers in their spare time, few were prepared to spend the years necessary to master the primary sources that would have provided them with accurate and detailed information on what childhood in the time of their subject might have actually been like. Therefore, if a tight, controlled, Puritanical character was encountered, say in a colonial American personality, and if psychoanalytic clinical theory at one stage of its development traced this "anal character" back to severe early toilet training, this was posited as true of the historical personality as well, little suspecting that children prior to the eighteenth century simply were not toilet trained early. These errors did not necessarily invalidate the initial psychoanalytic insight—psychoanalytic theory would itself on its own soon discover the "oral-retentive character"—but nevertheless the lack of empirical validation, and more important *invalidation,* was a crippling hindrance to any real expansion of psychohistory.

In the past decade, however, three new developments have combined to produce a vast expansion in psychohistorical writing, one which involved a methodological change sufficient to justify being called "the new psychohistory." The first development was the discovery that the history of childhood followed evolutionary patterns that were lawful, and that this new field of childhood history could form the basis for studying patterns of personality and behavior of both individuals and groups in history. The second factor was the development during the 1960's of psychoanalytic small-group process theory, as formulated by W. R. Bion, Philip Slater, Richard Mann, Graham Gibbard and John Hartman, a new experimental field which began to extend clinical psychoanalytic insight into larger group theory by identifying group fantasies, group defenses, and other shared needs on a strictly empirical basis, while avoiding the holistic reification of "society" which underlies traditional sociology.

The third factor leading to "the new psychohistory" has been a new attitude of radical empiricism by a new generation of psychohistorians, trained both in psychoanalysis and in one of the historical disciplines, and fully prepared to devote their lives to the development of a new science of historical motivation. This new group of psychohistorians soon began to center their activities around the new scholarly journal, *History of Childhood Quarterly: The Journal of Psychohistory,* from which the ten selections which make up this book were taken. They range in age from the young graduate student Dana Ward to 79-year-old Harvard Professor Emeritus William Langer, an astonishing example of continuously youthful scholarly activity, whose support and contributions to psychohistory began seventeen years ago with his Presidential Address to the American Historical Association giving historians their "next assignment"—which was to learn psychoanalysis. The authors of these articles were initially trained in many different disciplines, yet their articles show a continuity of purpose and unity of framework which is quite surprising considering the recentness of their collaboration.

The sequence of articles follows the three main divisions of psychohistory: (1) history of childhood, (2) psychobiography, and (3) group psychohistory. After the opening article on the independence of psychohistory, with its controversial suggestion of separate departments of psychohistory, come two articles on the history of childhood, the first examining family dynamics in one period, the Victorian, and the other surveying one aspect of this history, infanticide, in a broad evolutionary sweep. The next two articles are psychobiographies of Henry Kissinger and of the Russian revolutionary writer, Vissarion Belinskii, and because they are rooted at every point in original research in the sources they are able to demonstrate the development of their subjects step-by-step from childhood through adolescence to adult personality patterns. The next two articles are examples of group psychohistory, one on the sources of group symbolism, here French cinema, and the other on the group dynamics involved in Hitler's bond with the German people as each party to the wedding lived out traumas of their own, united only in historical action. The next two articles, one on Louis XIII and his state and the other on Theodore Roosevelt and Progressivism, attempt to combine all three levels into a unified psychohistorical analysis, drawing on general childhood patterns of the time, specific psychobiographical events, and group-psychohistorical formulations, all embedded in some of the most revealing source material thus far discovered by psychohistorians. The final piece, on psychohistory and psychotherapy, forms both a coda to the foregoing and a vision of the future of psychohistory as a true "history of the psyche," able to give causal analyses of patterns of historical motivation which we hope may yet enable us to understand and eventually to control our group actions. For psychohistory is a science in a hurry, racing against man's spiralling ability to destroy himself, and if our urgency sometimes comes through in our impatience with traditional narrative history, recognizing the source of this anguish may help explain what might otherwise appear excessive. Whether the promise of our new science of psychohistory will be fulfilled depends on whether psychohistorians such as those writing here, as well as the new generation of students who will read our work and be inspired to join us, feel this urgency with enough force to enlist their hearts and minds in the search for the causes of our shared psychoses.

Lloyd deMause

CHAPTER 1

The Independence of Psychohistory

LLOYD deMAUSE

It has been two years since the founding of the *History of Childhood Quarterly: The Journal of Psychohistory.* During that short time, it has attracted the attention of both the scholarly and mass media, being excerpted and attacked in the *New York Review of Books, Harpers, Commentary, Psychology Today, Human Behavior* and the *London Times Literary Supplement.*[1] Most of the attacks have used the arguments of historian Jacques Barzun in his recent book *Clio and the Doctors: Psycho-History, Quanto-History and History,*[2] in which he angrily opposes the notion that psychohistory is a division of history at all, since history, he says, is a narrative discipline telling *what* happened while psychohistory aspires to be a science focusing on *why* it happened. The book, and its earlier version as an article in the *American Historical Review,*[3] have been widely attacked by psychohistorians as containing too narrow a conception of the role of written history. Yet I wonder if Barzun might not in this instance be right and the psycho-historians wrong—if psychohistory is not quite a different enterprise from history, with its own methodology, its own independent tasks, and its own standards of excellence.

Ever since 1942 when the philosopher Carl Hempel published his essay "The Function of General Laws in History,"[4] it has been recognized by most philosophers of history that history cannot be a science in any strict sense of the term and that history can never regard it as part of its task to establish laws in the Hempelian sense. Written history may, in the course of its narrative, use some of the laws established by the various sciences, but its own task remains that of relating the essential sequence of historical action and, *qua* history, to tell what happened, not why.[5]

Psychohistory, it seems to me, is on the contrary specifically concerned with establishing laws and discovering causes in precisely the Hempelian manner. The relationship between history and psychohistory is parallel to the relationship between astrology and astronomy, or if that seems too pejorative, between geology and physics. Astrology and geology are disciplines seeking sequential orders in the sky and the earth, while astronomy and physics are not narrative at all, but are sciences attempting to establish laws in their own respective areas. Psychohistory, as the science of historical motivation, may concentrate on the same historical events that written history covers, but its purpose is never to tell what happened one day after another. When the first astronomers came along and found astrologers describing the positions of the stars day by day and trying to explain all the relationships between them, they created a revolution by saying, "Forget about the sequence of the skies. What interests us *qua* scientists is this one dot of light and whether it goes in a circle or an ellipse—and *why*. In order to find this out, we will have to drop the narrative task of astrology."

What is more, science never did pick up this task of narration—because it couldn't. Astronomy, even if it finally discovers all the laws of the universe, will still not narrate the sequences of skies, any more than psychohistory will ever narrate the events of this or that period. Psychohistory, as a science, will always be problem-centered, while history will always remain period-centered. They are simply two different tasks.

It does not, of course, follow that psychohistory simply uses the facts historians have narrated up to now in order to construct laws of historical motivation. Like astronomy and physics, psychohistory finds it necessary to conduct its own search for material peculiar to its own interests in both past and present society. Whole great chunks of written history are of little value to the psychohistorian, while other vast areas which have been much neglected by historians—childhood history, content analysis of historical imagery, and so on—suddenly expand from the periphery to the center of the psychohistorian's conceptual world, simply because his or her own new questions require material nowhere to be found in history books.

Now I am well aware that in claiming the field of historical motivation exclusively for the psychohistorian I immediately run up against the oft-repeated claim by historians that they work with motivations all the time, so there is nothing new in that. I had heard this claim so often in the two decades since I first studied the philosophy of history that I was finally moved to measure exactly how often historians actually do examine motivations in their works. I therefore kept a tally-sheet as I read 100 history books of varying kinds and recorded exactly how many sentences were devoted to any kind of motivational analysis whatsoever—not just psychoanalytic, but any level of attention at all. In no case did this motivational content reach as much as 1% of the book—so the field seemed to be ours by default. What wasn't pure narrative of one event after another turned out to be mainly the recitation of as many economic facts as possible in the hopes that their mere conjunction with the historical narrative would be mistaken for explanation.

Now anyone who has read any portion of the over 1,300 books and articles contained in the "Bibliography of Psychohistory"[6] will soon realize that psychohistory has reversed this 1-to-99 ratio, so that the bulk of psychohistorical writing is devoted to an intense concentration on motivational analysis while the physical events of history are necessarily given quite sketchy background treatment. There is, for instance, only one page at the beginning of Runciman's three-volume *History of the Crusades*[7] describing how the participants decided to begin four hundred years of wars, and then several thousand pages devoted to the routes, battles and other events which make up the "history" of the Crusades. A psychohistorian would *assume* the history, and spend his decades of research and thousands of pages in the most fascinating question for psychohistory—why so many set off on such a strange task as relic-saving. That the historian, when reviewing such a psychohistory, would accuse it of "ignoring" the full history of the Crusades should bother the psychohistorian as little as the accusation by the astrologer that Galileo "ignored" all the other stars in describing the path of one mere planet. It wasn't his task, and narrative history isn't ours.

This matter of psychohistory "ignoring" other fields when it specializes is a matter of some importance, since it is so often repeated by historians when criticizing psychohistorical works. In my own work, for instance, I have been accused of being ignorant of economics (although I am the founder and Chairman of the Board of a company which publishes seven professional economic newsletters), of being ignorant of sociology (although I am trained in sociology and was C. Wright Mills' research assistant at Columbia), of being unable to use statistics (although I earned my living as a professional statistician for five years) and of ignoring political factors (although all my graduate training was in political science). What seems not to have occurred to the critics of psychohistory is that we might choose to focus on the historical evolution of the psyche because only thereby can we reach the unsolved problems of precisely these same fields of politics, economics and sociology, fields which are shot through with unproven psychological assumptions and which have failed to become reliable sciences precisely because of the unsolved psychohistorical problems within them. Professionals in each of these fields recognize this quite well, and even admit it to each other in their journals—it is only historians, ignorant of the shaky psychological underpinnings of the fields from which they uncritically borrow, who imagine there can be "economic, political and social factors" which are somehow apart from "psychological" factors in history. As one instance, it is probably true that my own work on the evolution of childhood was at least partly a response to problems encountered in the theory of economic development, as set forth in such books as Everett E. Hagen's *On the Theory of Social Change: How Economic Growth Begins,* where the crucial link needed to produce a take-off in economic development is shown to be just the kind of personality which I was later able to trace in the history of childhood as the result of the "intrusive mode" of parenting. Just as surely is the study of class intimately tied up with evolving psychohistorical patterns of dominance and submission, and the study of power dependent upon an understanding of group-fantasy needs and defenses. The notion that psychohistory somehow "ignores" economics, sociology or political science is possibly the most ignorant charge that could be leveled against it.

When the *Times Literary Supplement* attacks the *Journal* for "seeing behind every action a hidden motive,"[8] all one can answer is "Of course! Action is simply behavior, and since only psyches can have motives, motivation, hidden or not, must be examined in and of its own right to give meaning to all action." Historians habitually skip this examination, as when A. J. P. Taylor describes why Hitler did not intend to go to war in 1939:

> Many however believe that Hitler was a modern Attila, loving destruction for its own sake and therefore bent on war without thought of policy. There is no arguing with such dogmas. Hitler was an extraordinary man; and they may well be true. But his policy is capable of rational explanation; and it is on these that history is built . . . In considering German armament we escape from the mystic regions of Hitler's psychology and find an answer in the realm of fact. The answer is clear. The state of German armament in 1939 gives decisive proof that Hitler was not contemplating general war, and probably not intending war at all.[9]

The sleight-of-hand involved in this way of writing history is never to examine the actor's actual motives at all, but simply to conclude from looking at material reality, here armaments, what his motives were. That this eliminates the possibility that Hitler might have intended war regardless of the state of his armaments is simply overlooked. Historians are presumed to be unable to "do psychology," which is "mystical" anyway, so they are forced to accept the most "rational" explanations . . . "and it is on these that history is built."

These and many other reasons integral to the logic of psychohistory lead me to believe that it will sooner or later be necessary for psychohistory to split off from history and form its own department within the academy in much the same way that sociology broke off from economics and psychology from philosophy in the late 19th century. As a matter of fact, there is a real sense in which psychohistory never was the exclusive or even the major possession of history departments: the majority of the books and articles in the "Bibliography of Psychohistory" were written by scholars who were not professional historians at all, and this is also the case for the articles written for this *Journal,* the contributing editors of which include psychiatrists, political scientists, educators, psychologists, psychotherapists, humanists and anthropologists as well as historians. Only a minority of the subscribers to the *Journal* are in fact historians. Courses in psychohistory are being offered today in many different departments, and even when offered in the history department they are likely as not conducted jointly by a historian and a psychoanalyst. Therefore my suggestion that separate psychohistory departments should be established is less a schismatic device than it is a move to unite the fractured parts of psychohistorical inquiry, so that all those who are really in the same field can communicate with each other, rather than their being minorities in separate departments and thinking of themselves as "political psychologists," "psychoanalytic sociologists," "applied psychoanalysts," and so on. The choice of *problems*—not the material studied—defines the discipline, and all these scholars are working on the same kinds of problems.

In uniting these many fields, psychohistory would, it seems to me, for the first time make some sense out of the crazy-quilt pattern of separate disciplines presently studying "the psychology of society." It would assume, of course, that "psychohistory" is not a narrower term than "psycho-social," and that in fact the term "psycho-social" is simply redundant, since the "social" is not "out there" but only "in here," in the head. The usual accusation that psychohistory "reduces everything to psychology" is philosophically meaningless—*of course* psychohistory is reductionist in this sense, since all it studies is historical motivations. Only when the "social" is admitted to being part of the "psychological" can the paradigm for psychohistorical study be recognized as follows:

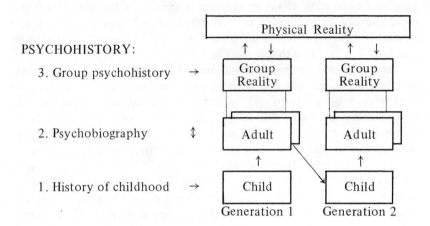

PSYCHOHISTORY:

3. Group psychohistory →

2. Psychobiography ↕

1. History of childhood →

Besides defining the three divisions of psychohistory, this paradigm does two things that distinguish it from the other social sciences, particularly sociology. First, it reverses the relationship between physical and psychological reality, so that instead of material progress setting the pace of history and somehow dragging behind the psyches of its actors, human psychology is made primary—setting Marx on his head and Hegel back on his feet—and material reality is viewed as primarily the outcome of man's decisions, past or present, conscious or unconscious. Secondly, the major basis for historical change is the *interrelations of persons,* not forgetting the relations between generations, and man is viewed for the first time not as *homo faber* but as *homo relatens.*

There are other differences in psychohistory that are only now becoming apparent. First of all, as a science, psychohistory proceeds not by patient accumulation of piles of facts, but by first defining problems interesting to its own internal development, then formulating bold hypotheses from available evidence to solve these problems, and finally attempting to test and *disprove* (not prove—proofs are for high school chemistry students) the hypotheses from new evidence now painstakingly acquired. In fact, psychohistory has a double burden of proof, for it has to conform not only to all the usual standards of historical research, but it must also be psychologically sound—unlike the usual shoddy psychology now found in every historical journal which makes one want to shout at every page, "But people just don't *work* that way!" This double burden of proof will require its own special kind of training, of course, with thorough grounding in the full range of tools of historical research and developmental psychology, since both are essential to the job of cracking open the clam-shell of historical motivation.

It is of course quite true, as historians have pointed out, that psychohistory has no special method of proof that is unavailable to the historian or to any other discipline for that matter. Like all sciences, psychohistory stands or falls on the clarity and testability of its concepts, the breadth and parsimony of its theories, the extent of its empirical evidence, and so on. What psychohistory *does* have which is different is a certain *methodology of discovery,* a methodology which attempts to solve problems of historical motivation with a unique blend of historical documentation, clinical experience and the use of the researcher's own emotions as the crucial research tool for discovery. Let me give a personal example to illustrate this.

For the past decade, I have been intensely interested in the small but growing literature on the causes of war which has begun to be produced by social scientists of many disciplines. I had long ago discovered that historians, wrapped up in the specifics of one particular war or period, were little interested in generalizing on their narrative. In fact, it seemed as though historians used the words "desire for power" as terminations of thought, as though the sight of millions of people organizing themselves for years in order to gobble up millions of their hostile neighbors at enormous sacrifice to themselves was the most transparent of human actions, requiring no explanation of motivation whatsoever. Those few historians who went beyond their narrative jumped immediately into economic "explanations," something not too difficult to do, since no war failed to have an economic dispute hanging around somewhere nearby. But they simply never got around to asking why war was the means by which this or that economic dispute was resolved. Neither did they seem to notice that the war was in fact never economically beneficial, and that when the leaders were deciding to go to war they simply never bothered to sit down and draw up a list of economic objectives, assign them a dollar value, subtract the costs of the war, and come up with a "war profit statement" (the very rationality of such an act makes it laughable). Yet the historians continued to pour out whole libraries describing economic conditions prior to wars, never bothering to examine the actual words and actions of the leaders who made the decision to go to war to see if all those economic factors actually had any causal effect on their motivations.

I was as little able to make any sense out of other kinds of historians' explanations for war, which were not only psychologically naive but often as not logically contradictory. Given "diplomatic" causes, opposite conditions were supposed to cause identical results, World War I having been caused by the "inflexibility" of the alliance system, so that when one little fight broke out all of Europe was dragged in, while World War II was caused by the "over-flexibility" of the alliance system, allowing Hitler to pick off one country after another without fear of bringing in others. Similarly, "social" causes were cited with contradictory results: the cause of France's going to war with Austria in 1772 was the revolutionary turmoil within her borders, while her war with England in 1803 was caused by the *end* of revolutionary turmoil, thus allowing her energies to be turned outward.

My own studies of the causes of war centered on the actual motivations of those who made the decisions, and of those around them who created the climate of expectation which allowed them to carry the decision into actuality. During the past year, I collected a large stack of photocopies and notes on the actual words of leaders and others during the times the decisions to go to war were being made—a task which is not as simple as it may sound, since historians generally remove from their narrative much of the most important material a psychohistorian needs to determine motivation, such as personal imagery, metaphors, slips, side comments, jokes, scribbles on the edges of documents, and so on, and these were not too easily recovered from their original sources in a limited time span. Still, at the end of the year I had accumulated a wide range of material, and had even learned from it a few new things about war.

The first thing I learned was that these leaders seemed to me to be less father-figures in the Oedipal sense than garbage-disposal directors, being expected by those around them to handle huge amounts of projected emotions which the individuals were unable to keep bound by means of the usual intra-psychic defenses. Large groups seem to present a different level of problem to the psyche than interpersonal relations, so that intrapsychic defenses become less effective and the psyche is thrown back on modes of relating that prevailed in pre-verbal infancy, when problems were handled by projecting them into the mother's body and re-introjecting them back into one's own ego. The individual relates to a large group with similar massive projection devices, and delegates leaders and other role-players to assist him in this task. This process is continuous throughout the history of all large groups, and requires specific *group-fantasies* to carry it out and to defend against the primitive anxieties that result. One group-fantasy leaders are expected to carry out is to find places to dump these huge quantities of projected emotions, what I took to calling external and internal "toilet-objects." That the emotions thus dumped were of infantile origin goes without saying, but to my surprise I found that they seemed to come from all levels of the psychic organization, so that in 1914 German leaders could call the Serbs not only "regicidal" (Oedipal), which one could understand, but also "poisonous" (oral), "filthy" (anal) and "licentious" (phallic).[10] Once the leaders had designated which countries were to be the toilet-objects for these projected emotions, the emotional dumping could continue as a regular part of the political system, and it was then the task of diplomacy to see to it that these now-dangerous objects were fully controlled, in the same manner that little children, favorite toilet-objects for adults, are controlled by being now "chastised," now "brought to their knees," now "taught a lesson," and so on. As long as these external toilet-objects did not threaten to get out of control, war could be kept at a distance, and "diplomacy" seemed to work.

But something always seemed to happen to disturb the delicate process of emotion-dumping, and a group-process began which inexorably led the way to war, even when all those concerned seemed to want to avoid it. This "helpless drift" toward war was the predominant emotional tone for every war I was studying, so that it seemed as though some extremely powerful group-fantasy was being acted out which even the most powerful of leaders was quite helpless to change once it got rolling. To use a German example once again, Kaiser Wilhelm II, who had been encouraging Austria-Hungary to go to war with Serbia, was so startled when Serbia agreed to virtually all of Austria's excessive demands that, having announced that "every reason for war drops away," he gave orders for Vienna to be told to be concilatory. But the pull of the group-fantasy was too great. His subordinates acted as though *they simply did not hear what he said,* and the war began anyway. As Bethmann-Hollweg remarked at the time: "All governments . . . and the great majority of their peoples are peacefully inclined, but the direction has been lost, and the stone has started rolling."[11] War seemed to be a group-psychotic episode, with patterns of thinking, levels of imagery, and degrees of splitting and projection that are usually only found in the limited psychotic episodes of individuals, but which are temporary and which sooner or later appear quite incomprehensible to those same people. The manic optimism and inevitable under-estimation of the length and severity of the war, the increase in paranoia as to the motivations of the enemy (an "index of paranoia" has even been constructed and graphed[12]), the total absence of awareness that in going to war real people would actually *die,* these and other seeming irrationalities are all indications that a powerful group-fantasy is being acted out. But just what this relentless group-fantasy was completely stumped me. Some controlling process held together all these images and insights that I had picked up from the material in front of me. But I had no idea what it was, and why it seemed so compelling to all the participants.

As in previous cases when I had been bewildered by the material before me, I was convinced that personal defensive reasons were behind my inability to find an answer, and I tried many ways to break my defenses down. I attempted to identify with those leaders on whom I had the most complete material, reading every biography from Napoleon to Hitler that I could get hold of, trying to listen to their "free associations" to the events around them. I immersed myself in the mass of material for weeks at a time and analyzed my dreams each morning for my *own* "associations" and defenses. Nothing seemed to work. I was completely stuck for several months.

In January of this year, I was reading *Business Week* and noticed the interview with Henry Kissinger in which he explained that he had learned that "it is easier to get into a war than to get out of it" and that the only case in which the U.S. would go to war again was "where there is some actual strangulation" occurring. This imagery struck me as familiar. It particularly reminded me of something Kaiser Wilhelm and those around him kept saying in 1914, that "the Monarchy has been seized by the throat and forced to choose between letting itself be strangled and making a last ditch effort to defend itself against attack," and that a "net has been suddenly thrown over our head, and . . . we squirm isolated in the net."[13] I remembered that when I initially read them I was struck by how inappropriate these feelings were, since Germany was in no way strangling and since England, who was accused of throwing the net over her head, was at that time quite friendly toward Germany. Since I was familiar with the many "encirclement" theories with which nations justified their going to war, I was once again tempted to pass off the imagery as rationalization when I stopped myself and said "No! Both Henry and Wilhelm seem quite sincere here. They are reporting to me that it *felt* as if they were being strangled and that consequently they had to go to war, and for once I ought to *trust* their feelings and see where they take me." I once again pulled out my pile of notes, and soon found that this had indeed been the controlling fantasy I had overlooked for so long—images of being "strangled" and "choked" leaped up from every page I had before me. What was more, the strangulation of war seemed to be caused by a fantasy of being in the birth canal, "unable to draw a breath of relief," "unable to see the light at the end of the tunnel," but nevertheless "against one's will" beginning "the inexorable slide towards war," starting with the inevitable "rupture of diplomatic relations," moving with "naked force" into "the descent into the abyss" and finally "breaking out" into the "war that is the price of one's freedom."

Needless to say, I was still extremely reluctant to accept the reality of such an unlikely, even bizarre group-fantasy as "war as birth." Yet even a provisional emotional acceptance of the basic birth thesis made all the difference in the world to how I proceeded with my research. For one thing, only now could I begin to use my knowledge of the psychoanalytic literature on common birth images in dreams, in which suffocation and claustrophobia always represent being trapped in the birth canal, facts which completely eluded me during the prior year while trying to make sense of the historical material. I had noticed, of course, that leaders said they felt "small and helpless" during the slide towards war, but had thoroughly blocked out the importance of the imagery. That there was a life-and-death struggle going on for "some breathing space" was apparent—as Bethmann-Hollweg told the Reichstag in announcing war on August 4, 1914: "He who is menaced as we are and is fighting for his highest possession can only consider how he is to hack his way through."[14] But there was also present all the imagery of birth-dreams familiar to psychoanalysts—choking, drowning, hanging, suffocating, being crushed in rooms or tunnels. In psychoanalysis, these images represent the patient's attempt to repeat and by repeating to master the fearful pressure of labor contractions and the gasping for air after birth. This reliving indicates that birth traumata are still very much alive in most adults, especially those whose regressive need to re-merge with the mother has been kept alive by inadequate parenting.[15] Not only have psychoanalysts traditionally found these images in dreams,[16] but more recently Arthur Janov has discovered that patients in Primal therapy regularly have "birth Primals" in which they re-experience their own births in great detail, and with enormous psychological and physical changes taking place after these re-livings.[17]

In somehow trying to make sense out of all these strands of thought, I noticed that it didn't seem as though *reality*—physical reality—was forcing leaders to feel like strangled babies. Henry Kissinger and the Kaiser were actually no more in danger of war when they began voicing feelings of choking in a birth canal than they had been a year earlier when they did not voice such feelings. What was actually "strangling" the American economy was more the effects of the 1.5 trillion dollars spent on war goods in the previous two decades than the current oil situation, and the notion that little Serbia was actually able to "strangle" central Europe was wholly fantastic. In fact, when I checked my material I found that nations who were *actually* surrounded, like Serbia herself, or Poland in 1939, did *not* voice such images, while countries which *do* say they feel encircled when going to war, like Germany in 1939, do *not* then say so when the war goes against them and they in fact become encircled (for instance there is not a single birth image in *Hitler's Secret Conversations,* running from July 1941 to November 1944). It is *group-reality,* a psychic reality, not material reality, which for reasons yet unknown causes nations to pour into their leaders feelings of being strangled in a birth canal, and which causes these leaders to then feel that only the extreme solution of going to war and hacking their way through offers the possibility of relief.

It was now not long before I became aware that wars proceed in the same sequence as birth. They develop out of a condition resembling pregnancy, the air heavy with feelings of great expectancy, what William Yancey, head of the Alabama delegation to the secessionist Democratic

Convention in 1860, before a hushed convention, referred to as "a dormant volcano" which threatened to become "a great heaving volcano."[18] Soon it seems that "every day is pregnant with some new event."[19] The nation's leaders find themselves in what Kaiser Wilhelm termed "the nervous tension in the grip of which Europe has found itself during the last few years,"[20] or what Admiral Shimada in a pre-Pearl Harbor meeting described as a "tight, tense, and trapped feeling" in the air. The nation soon found that it had to "relieve herself of the inexorable pressure to which he has been subjected . . . to extricate herself from the desperate position in which she was entangled . . . to at least gain a breathing spell."[21] The nation seems to be gripped, as Congressman Brinton said in 1917, in what felt like an "invisible energy-field." "There is something in the air, gentlemen," he told his fellow Congressmen, "something stronger than you and I can realize or resist, that seems to be picking us up bodily and literally forcing us to vote for this declaration of war . . ."[22] Shortly thereafter, diplomatic relations are "ruptured," "the past placed its hand on the shoulder of the present and thrust it into the dark future"[23] and the "descent into the abyss" begins as the nation starts its "final plunge over the brink."

When war is finally decided upon, the feeling is inevitably one of enormous relief. When Germany declared war on France in 1914, it came, said the Crown Prince, as a welcome end to the ever-increaisng tension, an end to the nightmare of encirclement. "It is a joy to be alive," rejoiced a German paper the same day; Germany was "exulting with happiness."[24] And in America, half a century earlier, when Fort Sumter fell, both North and South experienced the same relief that "something unendurable had ended." Crowds went wild with laughter, waving banners, being swept up in the excitement. "The heather is on fire. I never before knew what a popular excitement can be," wrote a Boston merchant, watching the jubilant crowds, and the *London Times*'s correspondent described the same thing in the South—"flushed faces, wild eyes, screaming mouths" outshouting the bands playing "Dixie."[25]

If the announcement of war was equivalent to the actual moment of birth, I wondered to myself how far this concreteness of detail could be carried. For instance, would it be too far-fetched to imagine that one might find in the historical material evidence of the actual explosive first gasp for breath of the newborn, usually accompanied by a slap on the back. I did not have to look far for confirmation of my hunch. Searching my notes once again for the actual feelings expressed by those present at the precise moment that war had been declared, I discovered several clear instances where an *actual birth explosion* had been hallucinated. For instance, when Lincoln issued his proclamation calling for troops to defend the Union, an action recognized by all as the beginning of the Civil War, he retired to his room alone, "and a feeling came over him as if he were utterly deserted and helpless . . . he suddenly heard a sound like the boom of a cannon . . . The White House attendants, whom he interrogated, had heard nothing . . . He met a few persons on the way [outside], some of whom he asked whether they had not heard something like the boom of a cannon. Nobody had heard anything, and so he supposed it must have been a freak of his imagination."[26] Similarly, when Chamberlain stood before the British Cabinet in 1939 and announced: "Right, gentlemen, this means war," one of those present remembered: "Hardly had he said it, when there was the most enormous clap of thunder and the whole Cabinet Room was lit up by a blinding flash of lightning. It was the most deafening thunder-clap I've ever heard in my life. It really shook the building."[27] The birth-explosion seemed to take place only after the emotional recognition that the birth crisis was terminated—it did *not* take place, for instance, upon the first actual shooting, at the siege of Fort Sumter. In fact, the birth-explosion could be hallucinated even if the message that war had started was in error. When Hitler in 1938 was handed the message that Czech forces were mobilizing, and it looked as though the long-avoided European war would begin, Paul Schmidt, his interpreter, said it seemed as though a "big drum-bang" had sounded in the dead silence of those few minutes.[28] This birth-explosion was so necessary, in fact, that leaders, including both Woodrow Wilson and F.D.R., always carefully delayed bringing their countries into wars until they could feel the exaltation (and exhalation) of the war-cry of birth. As Wilson put it, when one of his Cabinet told him in early 1917 that America would follow him if he led them to war:

> Why that is not what I am waiting for; that is not enough. If they cannot go in with a whoop, there is no use of their going in at all.[29]

The more I examined the words of leaders the more I recognized that all of them seemed to *realize* that war was a group-fantasy of birth against which one struggled almost in vain. During the Cuban missile crisis, for example, it was only after Khrushchev wrote to Kennedy pleading that the two nations not "come to a clash, like blind moles" battling to death in a tunnel[30] that war between them could be averted. Even more explicit is the code-word used by Japanese ambassador Kurusu when he phoned Tokyo to signal that negotiations had broken down with Roosevelt and that it was all right to go ahead with the bombing of Pearl Harbor. Forced to invent a voice code on the spot which Tokyo would recognize as meaning that war should begin, Kurusu announced that the "birth of a child" was imminent and asked how things were in Japan. "Does it seem as if a child might be born?" "Yes," came the reply, "the birth of the child seems imminent." The

only problem was that American intelligence, listening in, spontaneously recognized the meaning of the war-as-birth code.[31]

The imagery of war as birth seemed to reach back to earliest times.
Numa erected a bronze temple to Janus, the Roman god of doorways
and archways, and whenever Rome went to war the huge double doors
were opened, a common dream-image of birth. Thereafter, whenever a
war began, nations borrowed the Roman imagery and declared, as did
the *Chicago Tribune* the day Lincoln called for troops: "The gates of
Janus are open; the storm is on us." Certainly no American war has
seemed to lack birth-imagery, beginning with the American Revolution,
filled with images of birth and separation from the mother-country and
what Samuel Adams termed the fight for "the child Independence . . .
now struggling for birth"[32] right down to the Vietnam war, which began as "a swampy hole you got sucked into," soon turned into a "bot-
tomless pit" and a "tar baby" you couldn't let go of,[33] and ended with
a baby airlift.

While some of the symbolism of war is quite open and transparent
—it hardly needs a psychoanalyst to interpret the message General
Groves cabled to President Truman to report that the first A-bomb was
successful ("The baby was born") or to see the imagery of the Hiroshima bomb being called "Little Boy" and the plane from whose belly it
dropped being named after the pilot's mother—still some of the symbolism of war only becomes intelligible when one becomes familiar
with psychoanalytic clinical research into dreams of birth. Although I
was familiar with much of this literature, from Rank's essay on the
birth-trauma to Janov's extensive work on the re-experiencing of birth
during primal therapy, I discovered a whole new range of images once I
had sensitized myself by reading more extensively in the research on
birth dreams. For instance, I discovered a little-known book written 25
years ago by the psychoanalyst Nandor Fodor entitled *The Search for
the Beloved: A Clinical Investigation of the Trauma of Birth and Pre-
Natal Conditioning,* a book which was ignored at the time it was published only because it was so far in advance of its time. It includes, for
example, a complete description of the violence of "normal" birth
methods that anticipates at every point that of Frederick Leboyer,[34]
plus a proposal for psychotherapy to heal the birth trauma that spells
out in advance much of the work of Arthur Janov.

One of the birth symbols that Fodor calls attention to is the image—
or rather more often the nightmare—of fire. According to both Leboyer
and Fodor, the neonate's skin is extremely sensitive, and feels as though
it is burning up both during the long hours of labor and immediately
after birth, especially when the room is colder than 98°F. or when the
baby is wrapped in rough clothes.[35] Once this is realized, the historical
image of war as a "ravaging fire" is more easily comprehended. More-

over, just as in dreams birth can be symbolized by being caught in a burning house, much of warfare involves simply setting fire to people and things, even when it costs more to do so than the benefit involved, as in the case of the "strategic bombing" of Europe in World War II. War and burning seem so intimately connected that troops are driven to set fire to villages even when the latter belong to those who are supposedly allies, as in Vietnam. The impulse to set people and places afire seemingly transcends any other objective in war.

Similarly, Fodor's book contains many references to another dream image for birth—falling or jumping out of towers. This is, of course, a repetition of the moment of birth itself, which involves falling upside down and activates the baby's instinctual fear of falling and reflexive hand-grasping. Only if one keeps one's "inner ear" tuned for this imagery does it become obvious that leaders at crucial moments use the "jumping out of towers" theme to convey war-as-birth messages. For instance, just as Japan was deciding to go to war with America, its leaders were presented with a voluminous report containing well-documented evidence that Japan was outnumbered by America in every area of war potential and actuality by at least 10 to 1 and therefore couldn't possibly win. Since they were in the group-process stage that made the "slide to war" inexorable, Tojo looked at this overwhelming proof that Japan couldn't win the war and announced: "There are times when we must have the courage to do extraordinary things—like jumping, with eyes closed, off the veranda of the Kiyomizu Temple!"[36] Similarly, the French Foreign Minister, at the time of the Munich Agreement, referred to war as "jumping from the Eiffel Tower."[37]

By the time I had finished re-examining my historical material, it had become obvious that all the "innocent babies" killed—and sometimes rescued—during wars were not merely side issues, accidents of war, but rather that *babies were the heart of war's central fantasy.* Consider how often wars open with rumors of the enemy "disemboweling pregnant women," whether by Turkish bayonet or Khmer Rouge wooden stake.[38] Consider how often wars end with "baby-saving" missions, whether by American baby-lift from Vietnam or Nazi *Lebensborn* projects in Europe, where babies from occupied countries were stolen, measured with obstetrical-type instruments for racial fitness, and either killed as unfit or sent back to Germany for raising as Aryan. Consider how often the killing of babies—as in the Calley trial—becomes the emotional turning-point of a war, and how once it was recognized that *Americans were actually killing babies* (which of course they had been doing all the time) the public removed its support from the war. It soon becomes apparent that, as Fodor found in his birth-dream research[39] and as Melanie Klein discovered clinically,[40] breaking out of the birth canal involves simultaneously breaking *into* the mother's body, and that

the merging of these two fantasies is the essence of the war-as-birth
fantasy in which neighboring countries must be invaded to escape from
"encirclement" while at the same time the invader has the need to control and destroy the bad babies in the mother's body, the hated siblings,
the damaged contents of the womb. That foreign countries contained
infantilized bad-babies who had to be eliminated—or sometimes saved—
was indicated by far more than my Kleinian proclivities. The historical
material was full of such imagery. For instance, Hitler began World War
II not only because he felt Germany needed *Lebensraum,* "room to
live," but also because he had to save the good (German) babies in
neighboring states and kill the bad (Jewish, Polish, etc.) ones. The
blood-ties binding the mother to those babies who were to be saved
was clear in the imagery of the opening words of *Mein Kampf:*

> German-Austria must return to the great German motherland,
> and not because of economic considerations of any sort . . . *Com-*
> *mon blood belongs to a common Reich.* As long as the German
> nation is unable even to band together its own children in one
> common State, it has no . . . right to think of colonization . . .[41]

But aside from those few good babies who deserve to be saved, most
babies are hated occupiers of the mother's body, and must be eliminated. In fact, even the use of poison gas for genocidal purposes began
(in early 1939) with the gassing of mentally ill and deformed *children,*
and only two years later was extended to include Jews and others,[42] all
equally bad-babies, all made bad by the very same emotional dumping
described earlier in the section on external and internal toilet-objects.
For in the end the baby must die after all, and modern war has been
quite as effective in carrying out the filicidal impulses of humanity as
child sacrifice and infanticide used to be.[43]

   Now the point of this side trip into the methodology of psychohistorical discovery is that far more is involved in contributing to a specific
moment of discovery in psychohistory than the technical training of
the psychohistorian. Certainly both my historical and psychoanalytic
knowledge helped—I had to know how to get around in the literature
of both fields—but in a more profound sense every moment of my own
emotional development led to the breakthrough in recognizing the birth
imagery in war. This goes beyond my own obvious interest in the causality of war over the past two decades, and has nothing at all to do with
any theoretical bent toward birth trauma imagery, since I was neither a
Rankian nor a Janovian. Far more crucial were, for example, the long
hours somewhere around the seventh or eighth year of my personal
psychoanalysis when I struggled to re-experience and find meaning in
dreams of drowning and sinking in a whirlpool or quicksand, or, when
my son was two years old, those hundreds of hours I spent with him

pretending we were babies in mommy's belly, crawling around in the dark under the bedclothes and pretending to fall off the bed crying "Help! Save me!," because that was the endless game that seemed to give him a strong sense of the pleasure of mastery. Psychohistory, like psychoanalysis, is a science in which the researcher's *feelings* are as much or even more a part of his research equipment than his eyes or his hands. Like eyes, feelings are not infallible; they often introduce distortions, and so on, but since psychohistory concerns human motivation and since the discovery and weighing of complex motives can *only* be accomplished by identification with human actors, the usual suppression of all feeling preached and followed by most "science" simply cripples a psychohistorian as badly as it would cripple a biologist to be forbidden the use of a microscope. The *emotional* development of a psychohistorian is therefore as much a topic for discussion as his or her intellectual development. That it includes personal psychoanalysis as a foremost prerequisite goes without saying, as in the case of the psychoanalyst. But I think it goes beyond this formal requirement.

I must candidly report that as a result of my own personal contacts over the past decade with perhaps a thousand historians from all over the world, both in connection with the history of childhood project and in starting this *Journal,* I no longer believe that most traditional historians are emotionally equipped, even with training, to use their feelings as psychohistorical research tools, although there is a whole new generation of psychohistorians just now beginning to write who *are* able to do so. To expect the average historian to do psychohistory is like trying to teach a blind man to be an astronomer, so averse are they to psychological insight into themselves or their historical material from *any* school of modern psychology. There are complex historical reasons for this fact, having to do with the differential process of self-selection within the universities in recent decades and with the process whereby departments of history have lost so many emotionally open students to psychology. In light of this fact, whenever I speak to a scholar of the emotional development necessary to make a good psychohistorian and get a blank look of total incomprehension, I try to find a way to leave the subject of psychohistory altogether. My listener usually is in another world of discourse where emotional reactions are not considered crucial to the results.

A final illustration will further demonstrate this point. For many years I wondered why I, a radical and anti-nationalist, was nevertheless moved almost to tears when I stood with my son watching a parade with marching bands. The temptation was to shrug off the feeling or to give it a label that would deflect the discomfort, but I was so concerned with this feeling of being swept up by military music that I took to leaving my table at the New York Public Library each time I heard

music from a military band going down Fifth Avenue just to see if I
could catch my feeling and locate its power over me. If I seemed a bit
odd to associates who were with me at the time, so be it—I had to try
to answer this question, which was psychohistorical to its core. It was
only after the discovery of the war-as-birth thesis that my mind returned to the question of why the bands moved me so—I now had a
hunch that I knew the answer. I took a stop-watch out to the next
parade and timed the beats of the band. They occurred at about 110-
130 beats per minute. Then I timed some popular music, of the usual
soothing quality, on the radio—from 70 to 80 beats per minute. When
I checked with my wife's obstetrician, I found that the normal heart-
beat is about 75 beats per minute and that the elevated heart-beat of a
woman during a contraction in labor is between 110-150 beats per
minute. I obviously was a baby being born while watching the parade,
being picked up and carried along by my mother's heart-beat whether I
felt like it or not, and the tears in my eyes were for the impending
separation from my mother! Perhaps not the most important discovery
in the world, but one thoroughly psychohistorical—and though its
confirmation might be open to anyone using usual scientific canons of
truth, its *discovery* was only open to the psychohistorian with the quite
peculiar personality patterns and even lifestyle necessary for using one's
emotions as tools for the investigation of group reality.

All of which is not to indicate that I felt satisfied that I had found
the ultimate "cause" of war with the war-as-birth paradigm. Oddly
enough, science doesn't specifically aim at discovering causes—it tries
to solve problems interesting to its own internal development, and
causes are often the byproduct of this problem-solving. What I had done
by my research was, I think, something even more crucial to psychohistory than finding a cause: *I had changed the question I was asking.*
I had defined a new problem, embedded in a new theoretical structure
which I felt could be both fruitful and empirically testable, and I was
now able to ask a whole series of new questions such as: Why do nations project birth feelings into their leaders at some moments in their
histories and not at others? What means are used to communicate these
projections? Are these birth images defenses against other psychic conditions in the leadership group or in the nation? Were some wars exceptions to the war-as-birth paradigm, and if so what motivational imagery
did they substitute for it? Are there differential evolutionary patterns
of war imagery? Why do group-fantasies occur in such grotesquely
exaggerated slow-motion, taking months and years to act out events
that originally took hours, while exactly the same images in dreams are
condensed into minutes?

The ability to generate new questions is precisely the hallmark of a
science. Physical science expanded so rapidly in the seventeenth and

eighteenth centuries not because scientists were somehow brighter than those around them. In some senses, these early scientists were quite limited in their education and in a wide knowledge of the world around them. The same principle holds for psychohistorians, who hope to succeed where historians have failed by giving scientific explanation to historical motivation. Psychohistorians can achieve this, not because they are smarter than historians but because they conceive of their task in a wholly different way and have access to research tools and scientific models unavailable to the historian. Just as there was no way for even the most learned astrologers to understand the motions of the planets as long as they (1) conceived of their task as essentially narrative- rather than problem-centered, and (2) refused to use a telescope, so even the most learned historian cannot understand the causality of history as long as he (1) conceives of his task as narrative- rather than problem-centered and (2) refuses to use his own emotional-identification capacity in a scientific way at every step in the research process.

Other psychohistorians have, I believe, found ways similar to mine to intensity this emotional-identification and defense-stripping process. Rudolph Binion, in researching his psychobiographies of Lou Andreas-Salomé and Hitler, spent several years accumulating mountains of primary source material on their motivational patterns and then locked himself up for months with his evidence and read and re-read every detail until "the pieces . . . all fit together, with the facts all stacked up behind them: this alone carried final conviction."[44] Henry Ebel surrounds himself with his historical material and "Primals" for hours while free-associating to the material in front of him, in a concentrated effort to reach deeper levels of motivation than the usual reading reveals.[45] All these methods, like my own dream-interpretation to remove defenses against discovery, are attempts by psychohistorians to fashion research tools that, like microscopes and telescopes, give access to material hitherto denied them. For psychohistory is more a *rediscovery* than a discovery—*it is a process of finding out what we all already know and act upon.* Our discovery of exterior conditions is wholly dependent on how much we can strip away of our interior defenses against recognition of what we are doing all the time. Every person going to war speaks in birth imagery, responds to birth drumbeats, and communicates in birth symbols to others going to war, and every historian fills his books with writing that tells of "the pulse-beat of the coming violence growing louder and faster as the nation moves inexorably to the birth-pangs of war." We all know it—yet no one knows it. Only the psychohistorian who trains himself to use what is "in here" to discover what is going on "out there" can hope to succeed where so many have failed in understanding and bringing under control those group-fantasies we choose to call our history.

Lloyd deMause is founder and Editor of History of Childhood Quarterly:
The Journal of Psychohistory, *Director of The Institute for Psychohistory, Publisher of The Psychohistory Press, a member of the training faculty of the New York Center for Psychoanalytic Training, and Editor and an author of* The History of Childhood, Psychohistory: A Bibliographic Guide, *and* The New Psychohistory.

REFERENCES

1. Geoffrey Barraclough, "Farewell to Hitler," *New York Review of Books,* April 3, 1975, pp. 11-16; "Freud's Pop," *Harpers,* April, 1975, pp. 9-10 Gertrude Himmelfarb, "The 'New History'," *Commentary,* January, 1975, pp. 72-78; Lloyd deMause, "Our Forebears Made Childhood a Nightmare," *Psychology Today,* April, 1975, pp. 85-90; "The Baby Killers," *Human Behavior,* July, 1974, pp. 70-71; Elie Kedourie, "New Histories for Old," *London Times Literary Supplement,* March 7, 1975, pp. 2-4; Gertrude Himmelfarb, "Clio and Oedipus," *London Times Literary Supplement,* May 23, 1975, p. 565.
2. Chicago: University of Chicago Press, 1975.
3. "History: The Muse and Her Doctors," *American Historical Review* 77 (1972): 36-64.
4. Carl Hempel, "The Function of General Laws in History" in Herbert Feigel and Wilfred Sellars, eds., *Readings in Philosophical Analysis.* New York: Appleton-Century-Crofts, 1949.
5. Alan Donagan, "Explanations in History," in Patrick Gardiner, ed., *Theories of History.* New York: The Free Press, 1959.
6. Lloyd deMause, ed., *Psychohistory: A Bibliographic Guide.* New York: Garland Publishing, 1975.
7. Steven Runciman, *History of the Crusades.* 3 Vols. Cambridge: Cambridge University Press, 1950.
8. Kedourie, *TLS,* p. 3.
9. A. J. P. Taylor, *The Origins of the Second World War.* New York: Atheneum, 1968, pp. 216, 217.
10. Max Montgelas and Walter Schücking, eds., *Outbreak of the World War: German Documents Collected By Karl Kautsky.* Oxford: Oxford University Press, 1924, pp. 63, 307, 266, 161.
11. Montglas, *Outbreak,* pp. 250 ff. The inexorability of the movement to war, as well as most of the other irrationalities of the war process, is best summarized and adequately referenced in Geoffrey Blainey, *The Causes of War.* New York: The Free Press, 1973.
12. Ole R. Holsti and Robert C. North, "The history of human conflict" in Elton B. McNeil, ed., *The Nature of Human Conflict.* Englewood Cliffs, N.J.: Prentice-Hall, 1965, p. 166.
13. Luigi Albertini, *The Origins of the World War of 1914.* Vol. II. Oxford: Oxford University Press, 1952, p. 132; Imanuel Geiss, ed., *July 1914: The Outbreak of the First World War: Selected Documents.* New York: Charles Scribner's Sons, 1967, p. 295.
14. Ralph H. Lutz, *Fall of the German Empire 1914-1918: Documents of the German Revolution.* Vol. I. Stanford: Stanford University Press, 1932, p. 13.
15. For the various levels of parenting throughout history, see Lloyd deMause, ed., *The History of Childhood.* New York: The Psychohistory Press and Harper & Row, 1974 and 1975.
16. Nandor Fodor, *The Search for the Beloved: A Clinical Investigation of the Trauma of Birth and Pre-Natal Conditioning.* New Hyde Park: University Books, 1949, pp. 35-45.

17. Arthur Janov, *The Feeling Child: Preventing Neurosis in Children.* New York: Simon and Schuster, 1973, pp. 41-81.
18. Bruce Catton, *The Coming Fury.* Garden City, N.Y.: Doubleday & Co., 1961, p. 32.
19. William Eddis, *Letters from America.* Cambridge, Mass.: Harvard University Press, 1969, p. 151.
20. Max Montgelas and Walter Schücking, eds., *Outbreak of the World War: German Documents Collected By Karl Kautsky.* New York: Oxford University Press, 1924, p. 56.
21. Herbert Feis, *The Road to Pearl Harbor.* Princeton: Princeton University Press, 1950, pp. 293, 265.
22. Richard W. Leopold and Arthur S. Link, eds. *Problems in American History.* New York: McKay, 1965, p. 762.
23. Feis, *Pearl Harbor,* p. 293.
24. Barbara Tuchman, *The Guns of August.* New York: The Macmillan Co., 1962, p. 121.
25. Catton, *Fury,* p. 325.
26. Carl Sandburg, *Abraham Lincoln: The War Years.* Vol. 1. New York: Harcourt, Brace & Co., 1939, pp. 236-7.
27. Sidney Aster, *1939: The Making of the Second World War.* New York: Simon and Schuster, 1973, p. 387.
28. Paul Schmidt, *Statist auf diplomatischer Bühne 1923-45.* Bonn, 1949, p. 413.
29. Joseph P. Tumulty, *Woodrow Wilson As I Knew Him.* New York: Doubleday, 1921, p. 235.
30. Robert F. Kennedy, *Thirteen Days: A Memoir of the Cuban Missile Crisis.* New York: W. W. Norton, 1969, p. 89.
31. Toland, *Rising Sun,* pp. 174-5.
32. Henry Steele Commager and Richard B. Morris, eds., *The Spirit of Seventy-Six* Vol. I. New York: Bobbs-Merrill Co., 1970, p. 294.
33. David Halberstam, *The Best and the Brightest.* New York: Random House, 1969, pp. 249, 601, 617.
34. Frederick Leboyer, *Birth Without Violence.* NY: Alfred Knopf, 1975.
35. Personal communication with Dr. Leboyer at the Tarrytown Conference on Birth Without Violence, April 19, 1975; Fodor, *Search,* pp. 16, 93-103.
36. John Toland, *The Rising Sun: The Decline and Fall of the Japanese Empire, 1936-1945.* New York: Random House, 1970, p. 112.
37. Laurence Thompson, *The Greatest Treason: The Untold Story of Munich.* New York: William Morrow & Co., 1968, p. 112.
38. Robert Sam Anson, "Withdrawal pains," *New Times,* March 21, 1975, p. 25.
39. Fodor, *Search,* p. 253ff.
40. Melanie Klein, *Narrative of A Child Analysis.* New York: Basic Books, 1960.
41. Adolf Hitler, *Mein Kampf.* New York: Reynal & Hitchcock, 1939, p. 3.
42. Lucy S. Dawidowicz, *The War Against The Jews 1933-1945.* New York Holt, Rinehart and Winston, 1975, p. 132.
43. As I was writing up this article I found that I had encountered the essence of the baby imagery more than a year earlier in *The First Part of the Revelation of Moses the Son of Jehoshar* (Fort Lee, N.J.: Argonaut Books, 1973, pp. 58-9, 102, 106) in the brilliant aphorisms of Henry Ebel describing how "Dresden, Berlin, Hiroshima and Nagasaki were also made chokewomb hotwombs" and how "men wonder at the calm bestiality with which the Nazis murdered babies and infants and children. But that was the whole point. The helpless adults they butchered were equally 'children' to them. If they babyphagged as hard as they could, then perhaps they wouldn't be babyphagged themselves. If they pushed more babies into the chokewomb hotwomb, then perhaps Mama would spare THEM."
44. Rudolph Binion, "Hitler's Concept of *Lebensraum,*" *History of Childhood Quarterly: The Journal of Psychohistory* 1 (1973): 196; "My life with *Frau Lou*" in Perry Curtis, ed., *The Historian's Workshop.* New York: Knopf, 1970, pp. 293-306.
45. Henry Ebel, "Primal therapy and psychohistory" *History of Childhood Quarterly: The Journal of Psychohistory* 2 (1975): 563-70; and *The First Part of the Revelation of Moses the Son of Jehoshar.*

CHAPTER 2

Explosive Intimacy: Psychodynamics of the Victorian Family

STEPHEN
KERN

The myths of history, like the defenses of the psychoanalytic patient on the couch, are nowhere better revealed than in "official" versions of family life. Stephen Kern's examination of the underside of the myth of the solid Victorian family presents a picture which differs radically from traditional versions of nineteenth-century family interaction, in the same manner as a psychoanalyst's description of a schizogenic family differs radically from the family's own self-image.

Traditional studies of the Victorian period have repeatedly emphasized the stable, protective, peaceful nature of the family of the late nineteenth century. G. M. Young concluded that the family was one of the few institutions that "was not at some time or other debated or assailed." He viewed the family through the eyes of the Victorians as "a Divine appointment for the comfort and education of mankind." It provided "a stable and fortified centre."[2] Walter Houghton saw the family as "a rock in the midst of a rushing stream." And he concurred with Ruskin's evaluation of the family as "the place of Peace; the shelter, not only from all injury, but from all terror, doubt, and division."[3]

Some of the literature on the Victorian family in recent years has begun to explore some of the tensions and contradictions behind the calm exterior. Keith Thomas has traced the history of the double standard in England, and Peter Cominos has surveyed some of the hypocrisies that underlay Victorian "respectability."[4] Cominos viewed the family as "an immature association of dominance and submissiveness." The entire system, he argued, was finally challenged towards the end of the century. "The revolt, creating tensions, conflicts, deviant social characters, and incongruencies, plunged the Respectable Social System into a condition of crisis that reached a climax in 1894-5."[5] Steven Marcus has explored a secret underworld of the "other Victorians" where "a real secret social life was being conducted, the secret life of sexuality."[6] His interpretation challenges the traditional view of the Victorian family as stable and peaceful, and views it rather as one confused by a number of strange ideas about sexuality and threatened by a host of derivative fears about venereal disease, male impotence, and female sexuality. And recently Lloyd deMause has speculated that the Victorian period was a decisive turning point in parent-child relations when adult sexual exploitation of children, so freely indulged in until the late eighteenth century, came to be fully repudiated, and when parents began to punish the child for its sexual curiosity and sexual activity.[7]

In this essay I shall explore that other side of the Victorian family, and, in contrast with the traditional view, I shall argue that the European family of the late nineteenth century was not the unambiguous shelter from "all terror, doubt and division" that Ruskin eulogized, but was often a source of anxiety and conflict. However, I shall further argue that the explosive atmosphere that appears to have crept into so many Victorian families was a function of the excessive intimacy and interdependence that the family imposed upon its members. The family was indeed "fortified" against the pressures of the outside world, as Young argued, but that fortification, like neurotic defense mechanisms, often stifled more than it protected or comforted.

In the course of the nineteenth century, the emotional bonds within the European family mounted steadily, so that by the end of the century both parents and children began to seek refuge from the forces that held it together with such overbearing intensity. Medical literature on the parent-child relationship argued that the entire emotional history of the parents up to the moment of conception would somehow be transmitted to the child. The physical and mental condition of the parent during conception was of paramount importance, and, following conception, it was believed, the slightest shock or unpleasant thought would affect the future child. Pregnant women were frequently advised to refrain from sex altogether. If they engaged in excessive sex the child might develop some sexual anomaly, if they drank the child might become an alcoholic, and if they experienced any intense emotions the child might be demented. Of course the mother's responsibility for the mind and body of the child was believed to be the greater, but even the father's bad habits before his marriage, his youthful "excesses," and his slightest deviations from the strictest propriety would be imprinted indelibly on his children. Dominated by these ideas, the emotional tone of the Victorian family became one of explosive intimacy in which each of the members were held fast, bound by strong social, economic, and psychological ties. In this essay I shall focus particularly on the psychological dynamics that were operative in the Victorian family.

GERMS, GENES, AND IDEAS

In the latter half of the century the educated classes began to acquire bits and pieces of the discoveries in medicine and physiology that were being made with such impressive consistency. But the information that filtered into the marriage manuals and handbooks for the young was often worse than none at all. Confusion about the nature of cultural, infectious, and hereditary transmission from parent to child frequently added to the intensity of the psychological bonds between members of a family. Accordingly, it was believed that if a child's parent was insane, tubercular, or syphilitic, the child would inevitably inherit those problems. The nature of the three ways a parent can transmit its germs, genes, or ideas to a child was not precisely understood even in the higher circles of the medical world, and a bewildering tangle of ideas plagued the larger population. The confusion tended to produce a conception of the family as a biological unit in which the values, sex cells, and germs of parents worked in and upon the minds and bodies of children, leaving little room for individual development. Children came to feel trapped in their families, fated by the flow of mysterious substances through their bodies to repeat the same vices, catch the same diseases, and inherit the congenital weaknesses of their parents.

Weismann's theory of the immutability of the sex cells only began to appear in popular literature at the end of the century. For the most part, Lamarck's theory of the hereditary transmission of acquired characteristics was accepted. This view of heredity was elaborated by many others who frequently magnified the parents' sense of responsibility for their offspring. The American essayist Georgiana Kirby explained that the physical and mental experiences of the mother during conception and gestation determine the character of the child. The moment of conception is most important. "Never run the risk of conception when you are sick or over-tired or unhappy. . . . For the bodily condition of the child, its vigor and magnetic qualities, are much affected by conditions ruling this great moment."[8] Unpleasant experiences and thoughts are also communicated to the child during pregnancy.

Eduard von Hartmann (1895) believed that during pregnancy the father's blood, and with it his qualities, are permanently mixed with the blood of the mother, who then shares that mixed blood with the foetus. If she afterwards conceives with another man, the child will show the influence of her first husband. "The husband of a widow does not therefore find a clean page, but one written over by his predecessor, with whose hereditary tendencies his own must enter into conflict."[9] In *Sex and Character* (1903) the German essayist Otto Weininger expounded the same theory with a racist twist. "White women who have borne children to black men, and who then bear children with white men, are said to have retained enough of an impression from the first mate to show an effect on the subsequent children."[10] Strindberg dramatized this theory in *The Creditors* (1888) by having a woman's first husband return to haunt, and eventually destroy, her second marriage. Her second husband explains how "when the child was three years old it began to look like him, her former husband."

The German physicians, Wilhelm Fliess and Hermann Swoboda, believed that this transmission followed the rhythm of the cyclic movement of all life. In 1897 Fliess explained that the mother transmits her periodicity to her child. In his vast study *Der Ablauf des Lebens* (1906), he published hundreds of family tables illustrating a periodic unity in family life, in which attacks of enuresis and diarrhea, backache and headache, appear in the mother and her children according to varying combinations of 23- and 28-day cycles. Swoboda expressed the same idea that "the organism is subject to a rhythmic flux" transmitted to the child at birth.[11]

Samuel Butler's response to his own family experience alternately expressed two elements of a strong ambivalence. In his earlier studies of the psychological and biological mechanisms operative within the family in *Unconscious Memory* (1880), he described "the oneness of personality between parents and offspring"[12] without objecting to the intimate link between parent and child, whereas in *The Way of All Flesh* (1903) he reacted violently against the threatened imposition of that "oneness" between himself and his father. Many shared his later view that the tightly-knit family imposed itself excessively on the individuals in it

The most widely discussed aspect of heredity was degeneration—the transmission of destructive properties to the offspring. The lack of an accurate account of sexual reproduction led to the theory that acquired germs and vices remained forever locked into the germinal cells of the individual and accumulated from one generation to the next.

A popular source for the many theories of degeneration that circulated at this time was B. A. Morel's *Traité des dégénérescences* (1857). Morel outlined the sequence of four generations in which a family line is finally destroyed.

First generation: nervous temperament and moral depravity.
Second generation: tendency to apoplexy, neurosis, and alcoholism.
Third generation: mental disorders, suicide, and defective intellect.
Fourth generation: congenital idiocy or feeblemindedness, physical
                     malformations and sterility.[13]

Numerous variations on this sequence were suggested, and many attempted to observe its progress from generation to generation. Zola organized his novels about the Rougon-Macquart family according to such a sequence of family decline. Germs and vices as well as "internal secretions" were believed to be at work in the family, undermining health and morality in inscrutable ways. The French educator, Gabriel Compayré, argued that morbid phenomena are especially subject to the laws of heredity, and accordingly "the bad is transmitted much more easily than the good." The biological unity of family life reaches over the generations to carry the curse of ancestral sin and "unrestrained acts." "There has been some time—a day, an hour— in which the fate of an entire family has been cast, so that a mutual moral responsibility binds parents to children."[14]

The greatest source of anxiety was syphilis. It was mysterious and dangerous and at the same time connected with the most problematical of all human biological functions—sexual intercourse. No disease illuminated so clearly the responsibility of parents to their children. Not until 1905 was the syphilis spirochete observed under a microscope, and not until 1909 was a reliable treatment with salvarsan developed to replace the horrors and uncertainties of the mercury treatment, and even salvarsan had a highly toxic arsenic base. Suppression of open discussion of this "forbidden" subject led to countless family tragedies. Frequently husbands contaminated their wives who developed syphilis chancres soon after marriage and had numerous sexual problems and miscarriages, but who nevertheless believed themselves to be at fault and explained their problems as some inexplicable uniquely "female" reaction to married life. The existence of such a disease, widespread and uncontrollable, that affected the sex organs, minds, and bodies of parents and future generations was good reason for a man to restrict his sexual relations to one woman whom he knew to be a virgin. Victorian sexual morality had its reasons.

Syphilis was a disease ideally suited to bear out the admonitions of the zealous Christians who insisted that it was the divinely conceived wages of sin. It was an ideal Protestant disease, as well as an ideal Victorian disease. One transgression—a single sexual contact—could lead to a lifetime of suffering. There was no way of knowing for certain if one was contaminated or not, parallel to the Christian notion that man cannot ever be certain if he is destined to be saved or not. One was never certain of the cure, and of course none were deserving of cure. No precautions against it were sufficient, paralleling the Christian notion that no human works could possibly influence salvation. The diseased were truly condemned to "sickness unto death," and even beyond, through the infection of future generations. Like the Christian idea of sin, some are contaminated and others are not. Syphilis was known to attack fortuitously, and often the most blatant libertine contracted no symptoms, while one-time transgressors caught a heavy dose. Hence there was no way of understanding why some were condemned to suffer, while others were not. The ways of the disease, like the ways of God, were seemingly beyond the comprehension of man and subject to the fortunes of fate. The disease also had a mysterious and tormenting timing. After an initial contact a few superficial symptoms appear and then disappear spontaneously. After about eight weeks the secondary symptoms appear and may last for around nine months. Then the disease enters a period of latency from which it erupts three to fifteen years later with full force and attacks the vital centers—particularly the heart and nervous system. It was only in the late nineteenth century that physicians succeeded in ascertaining that these later symptoms are a direct consequence of the syphilis spirochete and not some general punishment for a life of debauchery, as was believed earlier in the century. Hence the progress of knowledge about the mechanisms of infection and transmission of venereal disease contributed at first to the fear of them. This is one instance where the progress of science intensified fears about sexuality and bodily processes, at least until that knowledge had progressed sufficiently to find a complete and lasting cure. The Victorians never found one.

Without mentioning the name of the disease, Ibsen in his play *Ghosts* (1881) explored some of the fears that syphilis produced. At first Oswald Alving believes that his weakness and loss of will were the consequence of his own debauched living, but in due course he learns that he has inherited the product of his father's recklessness. "The sins of the fathers shall be visited on the children," he says to his mother, who herself does not know the true cause of his illness. She believes that in some mysterious way the "ghosts" of the past remain alive in children and lead them to repeat endlessly the same life style as the parent. She pairs the physical with the mental heritage as she explains to her son: "It isn't just what we have inherited from our father and mother that walks in us. It is all kinds of dead ideas and all sorts of old and obsolete beliefs."[15]

In 1901 Eugene Brieux published a play about syphilis, *Les Avaries* (*Damaged Goods*), in which the disease is mentioned explicitly. Before the curtain the stage manager appears and warns the audience that the play concerns syphilis. George is told by his doctor that he must postpone his marriage for four years and undergo treatment for syphilis. Pride and social pressures make it impossible for him to comply. He marries too soon and produces a syphilitic child. In Act II the doctor fights with George's whole family to get them to dismiss the wet-nurse whose own health is threatened by the diseased child. Brieux points out not only the dangers of syphilis, but the hypocrisy which compels George to marry before he is cured, permits the wet-nurse to endanger her own life and that of other children whom she may nurse, and leaves the innocent mother a hopeless untouchable.

The spread of syphilis was widely believed to be but one of many problems leading to a degeneration of man and society. It was feared that the family was dying out—that, along with the destructive forces of disease and vice, social and economic changes were discouraging the continuation of the large family and of population growth.

Writers of fiction were also deeply concerned with the decline of the family. Hauptmann's *Before Sunrise* (1889) portrayed the advanced condition of degeneration of the Krause family. The children suffer from the parents' indulgence in incest, alcohol, and tobacco. A doctor observes of the family that "there's nothing but drunkenness, gluttony, inbreeding and, in consequence, degeneration along the whole line." The play concludes with the suicide of the most promising child, Helene, who is abandoned by her lover when he discovers that she may inherit her parents' alcoholism.

We have observed for the late nineteenth century a growing interest in the forces that hold the family together. We must assume that this intellectual development reflects historical fact, that these binding forces were deeply felt. At the same time many feared that the institution was falling apart. Partial knowledge of the mechanisms involved in infectious diseases and in hereditary and cultural transmission suggested that the members of a family were inextricably united by invisible chemical substances that flowed from one to another. While the evidence that children inherit their parents' vices and deficiencies abounded, there was far less to indicate that they inherited positive characteristics. Francis Galton concluded from his researches that children inherit a tendency for genius, but far more in keeping with the times was the belief that insanity was inherited. As social scientists observed and explained the process of cultural transmission more exactly, they adduced more evidence that family life determined the temperament and character of children. In response to the many social, economic, and cultural forces that held the Victorian family together as a sanctuary from the rest of the world, many attempted to break away from their families. The literature reflects this dialectical process: a growing sense of the biological and psychological unity of the family and a mounting tension between the members who sought independence from it.

THE MORAL EVALUATION OF THE FAMILY

The literature on the biological basis of the family agreed on one moral issue: the right of the child to physical and mental health. The manuals on heredity as well as the plays about syphilis agreed on this right of the child, but the larger question of the role of the child in the family, the dangers that beset him, and the rights that were his became the subject of extensive moral debate. Literature on child care around the turn of the century viewed with increasing alarm the physical and mental abuse of the child. Most of it focused on overt maltreatment: overwork in the factory and in the school, and neglect, brutality, and abandonment in the home. In addition to these gross material abuses, children were subjected to a more destructive psychological cruelty and emotional exploitation within the home.

The German home especially was often run in a military fashion. In several discussions of family life the term *"Hausordnung"* describes the ideal family arrangement. Sleeping and eating hours should be precisely established and followed. Each member should execute his particular duties with military exactness. Orderliness, punctuality, and obedience should always prevail. W. Spemann's book on etiquette defined *Hausordnung*. It includes the division of work in the family by weeks and months, the precise determination of the number and times of meals, and the exact stipulation of duties for each servant: "a complete ordering of the life of all."[16] The supreme importance of orderliness must be instilled in the child from the outset.

The exploitation of the child by parents was a popular subject for fiction. Tolstoy's *The Kreutzer Sonata* (1889) portrayed family life as a continuous battle between the parents with the helpless child in the middle. During a train ride, Pozdnyshev confesses how he came to kill his wife. She was a liar and fostered his jealousy until he was driven to kill her. Children, he explains, are a torment and a cause for dissension. "They were not only the object of our discord but the weapons of our strife. We used our children, as it were, to fight one another with."[17] The title character of Ibsen's *Little Eyolf* (1894) became a wall between his mother and father. In the course of the drama it is revealed that he was crippled as the result of an accident that occurred when he was left lying on the table while his parents were making love. The father tells the mother, "I forgot the child. In your arms. . . . In that moment you condemned little Eyolf to death."[18] The mother accuses the father in return. Eyolf drowns accidentally, and the play develops with the parents coming to understand and accept their responsibility in the sequence of events that led to his being crippled. The realization of their neglect and abuse of Eyolf becomes the basis of their attempt to save their marriage.

In a popular novel of 1895, Gabriele Reuter described the destructive force of a "good family" on a young girl. Agatha Heidling fears her mother, "before whom she became a little worm."[19] She begins to perceive that between parents and children there exists an unbridgeable gap, but her insight is of no use; she cannot act upon it. She falls in love with a young socialist, but is sickened when she observes him flirt innocently with a waitress. She cannot return to him, becomes terribly depressed, and eventually has a nervous breakdown. In the end she returns home, apparently destined to become an old maid. Parental exploitation in this story was most devastating. Through their efforts to lead their daughter to act according to the expectations of "good families," they made an emotional invalid of her.

The exploitation of a child by parents locked in battle with each other was the theme of Henry James's story of the eight-year-old girl in *What Maisie Knew* (1897). Masie is victimized after the divorce of her parents by having to live with each during alternate six-month periods. Under these conditions "the only link binding her to either parent was this lamentable fact of her being a ready vessel for bitterness. . . . They had wanted her not for any good they could do her, but for the harm they could, with her unconscious aid, do each other." She became "the little feathered shuttlecock they could fiercely keep flying between them."[20]

A number of writers criticized the quality of the emotional bonds between parents and children in this age of emotional austerity. Already in 1855 a popular handbook of etiquette complained that there is "too little affection in family relations," and that therefore "the springs of happiness are choked up in many homes."[21] By the turn of the century the emotional content of the parent-child relationship appears to have been observed with increasing concern. Elizabeth Blackwell (1884) emphasized the importance of trust and confidence accompanying parental love. To promote the most desirable developmental situation for the child, the parents must learn to employ "the formative power of loving insight and sympathy."[22] Bernard Perez (1896) and F. M. Wendt (1905) pointed out the element of fear in the child's love for his parents. Perez wrote that "the child's love is amplified by the fear which accompanies respect."[23] Wendt recommended the preservation of a "healthy fear" as a barrier against too close a relationship with the child.[24]

While most writers emphasized the goodness of love for children, some few focused on its dangers. The German physicians, Ludwig Strümpell (1892) and Adalbert Czerny (1908) warned against excessive love which can enfeeble the overprotected child, but Czerny also pointed out that the emotional development of children in foundling homes is retarded from the "lack of purposive stimulation from the environment."[25]

Paul Möbius developed a theory that parental love is the function of an *"Organ der Kinderliebe"*—certain lobes of the small brain which are larger in women. Möbius denied the instinctual or emotional basis of child love and explained it merely as the function of this special organ whose size alone determines the efficiency of its operation. Such massive denial of the emotional basis of family psychodynamics was, even at this time, unusual.[26]

Grant Allen affirmed the sexual basis of family love in "The New Hedonism" (1894), and in *Totemism and Exogamy* (1910) Sir James Frazer argued that there is a "natural instinct" for incest, but the idea that family relations have a sexual component was most clearly elaborated in discussions of the specific mother-child and father-child relationships.

Jules Dallemagne (1894) and Havelock Ellis (1903) characterized the mother-child relationship as sexual. Dallemagne reported observing one such relationship between a mother and her son in which a variety of sexual overtures were made.[27] Ellis offered an elaborate interpretation of the sexual nature of nursing and lamented the fact that civilization has worked against it:

> Some such [sexual] relationship does actually exist in the case of the suckling mother and her infant. The mother is indebted to the child for the pleasurable relief of her distended breasts; and, while in civilization more subtle pleasures and intelligent reflection render this massive physical satisfaction comparatively unessential to the act of suckling, in more primitive conditions and among animals the need of this pleasurable physical satisfaction is a real bond between the mother and her offspring. The analogy is indeed very close: the erectile nipple corresponds to the erectile penis, the eager watery mouth of the infant to the moist throbbing vagina, the vitally albuminous milk to the vitally albuminous semen. The complete mutual satisfaction, physical and psychic, of mother and child, in the transfer from one to the other of precious organized fluid, is the one true psychological analogy to the relationship of a man and a woman at the climax of the sexual act.[28]

While most writers focused on the positive elements of the mother-child relationship, some investigated the negative elements. Zola's novel, *A Love Affair* (1880) developed the theme of the jealousy of a young adolescent, Jeanne, as she discovers her mother's amorous relationship with her doctor. Her jealousy increases when she finally observes her mother and the doctor embrace. Her mother "averted her eyes before that twelve-year-old child's gaze, prematurely ablaze with adult passion." The child becomes the only obstacle to the couple's love, and at the same time provokes it. With Jeanne in bed, dying of tuberculosis, the doctor attempts to examine her. As he reaches to roll back the sheets she pulls them tightly over herself. "The twelve-year-old child was mature enough to understand that this man must not touch her, must not touch her mother's body through hers."[29] Her jealousy persists until her death and posthumously forces her mother to leave her lover.

The heroine of Hauptmann's *Rose Bernd* (1903) strangles her own fatherless child to spare it the suffering which she anticipates it will endure. This play shattered the picture of the idyllic mother-child relationship idealized in many short stories and family portraits of that time. A macabre mother-child relationship is explored in a short story by Thomas Mann, *Tristan* (1902). The mother enters a tuberculosis sanatorium ten months after giving birth to her son. For some unknown reason the child's increase in vigor debilitates the mother. In the end she dies and the child lives. It was also widely believed that parents can rob children of strength. This idea was popularized by the famous English gynecologist, William Acton, in a pathbreaking treatise on diseases of the sex organs. He argued that great men usually sire weak children, because their vital energies are exhausted by their own lives and somehow drain those unknown substances that go into the production of future generations.[30] Even married couples were counseled to guard against contamination and debilitation from each other. One manual for young husbands published in 1897 counseled married people to avoid "the absorption of the exhalations of each other's bodies, the weaker being injured by the fact that the stronger is likely to absorb vital and nervous force."[31] This kind of thinking is related to the popular notion that excess sexual activity, particularly the loss of semen by a man, drains his energies. The verb often used to describe a man's orgasm, "to spend," reveals to what extent the Victorians revered the virtues of thrift—economic and biological.

DYNAMICS OF THE FATHER-CHILD RELATIONSHIP

Discussions of the negative elements of the mother-child relationships were infrequent, while the negative elements of the father-child relationship were frequently explored, especially in fiction and autobiography. Another difference in the treatment of these two topics was the greater sexual specificity indicated for the father-child relationship. Accounts of the mother-child relationship only rarely distinguished between mother-son and mother-daughter relations, whereas studies of the father and the child varied more often according to the particular sex of the child. Motherhood was regarded as positive, supportive, and bisexual, while the father-child relationship was conceived to be conflict-ridden, with a special destructive sexual element in the father-daughter relation. The father, the more assertive parent, was more likely to engage in conflict with other members of the family, particularly with the son, who generally had more rights than daughters and who sought to challenge the father's supreme authority. The portrayal of the father-son relationship in literature and many of the reminiscences of it in autobiography focused on that conflict.[32]

Austin Harrison, son of the English jurist and historian Frederic Harrison, offered a sympathetic reminiscence of his father in which he mentioned some of the manifestations of his father's emotional conservatism which made communication between them strained, if not impossible. The Victorian child, he recalled, hardly knew either parent. Children lived apart and only "appeared" at stated times. "Respect was the injunction of the family; sons kept their distance and looked up."[33] His father's presence was a ceremonial, and he appeared always as if on a pedestal. Strindberg's memory of his father lacked Harrison's balanced judgment. Strindberg wrote that his father was the enemy of everyone in the family, and that all of his children hid from him.

The occurrence of father-son conflict among ancient and primitive cultures was noted by two English anthropologists, W. Robertson Smith and James Frazer. Smith's *The Religion of the Semites* (1889) offered evidence that the wish to kill the father is universal. Though he believed the mother-child relationship to be more often the source of feelings for the deity, he acknowledged that in some religions the father-child relationship is the model. The sacrifice of a deity, common in many of the early religions was a disguised form of matricide or patricide, and after the deed is accomplished, the clan makes efforts to expiate the feeling of guilt from any single member. Frazer also described a rite in which members of a community share in the guilt of a sacrificial murder. Each member of the community takes a hand in the killing of a sacrificial ox; a trial follows and does not blame any one person. Frazer's massive collection of religious practices, *The Golden Bough* (1890), offered numerous examples of father-son feelings having been projected onto the community's deity. Their sacrificial rites were an acting out of the conflict inherent in that relationship.

Samuel Butler returned to the subject of parent-child relations repeatedly during his literary career. In his utopian novel, *Erewhon* (1872), he envisioned a world in which the infant signs a "birth formula" which stipulates that the parents are in no way responsible for bringing him into the world or caring for him afterwards and by which he apologizes to the parents for intentionally and maliciously setting about to "pester and plague" them. In his philosophical essays of 1878 and 1880 Butler appears to have accepted the "oneness of personality between parents and children" that his theory of organic memory suggested. In *Erewhon Revisited* (1901) he described a situation in which father and son love each other. But in his autobiographical novel, *The Way of All Flesh*, published posthumously in 1903, he abandoned the satirical treatment of the parent-child relation of *Erewhon* and the positive acceptance of the relation argued for in his philosophical tracts, and turned on his father in what appears to have been a literary revenge.

Butler's novel marked the high point of criticism of the Victorian family. Today it appears to be a rather mild attack, and it is difficult to appreciate the pressures that compelled Butler to postpone its publication after its completion in 1885. He portrays his father with some affection, but as a man who simply did not understand, and did not like, children. The elder Pontifex knew only one way of relating to his son: with an unrelenting imposition of authority. "All was done in love, anxiety, timidity, stupidity, and impatience." Butler's critique was most persuasive because it was tempered and compassionate. He attributed his parents' domestic failure to stupidity and love as much as malice and selfishness. And when the break came, Ernest Pontifex made it without hesitation. After serving a short term in prison he emerged and found his parents waiting for him. "There, sure enough, standing at the end of the table . . . were the two people whom he regarded as the most dangerous enemies he had in all the world—his father and mother."[34]

The father-son relationship of Sigmund Freud and Max Weber provided the spark of conflict that triggered central insights in their thought. Both men were temporarily incapacitated by the death of their fathers, and for both that experience profoundly influenced that portion of their work which attempted to deal with problems created by the excessive imposition of paternal authority, which was particularly intense in Austria and Germany.

In 1896 Freud's father died. Soon afterwards he wrote: "I feel now as if I had been torn up by the roots." In 1908, remembering his mourning, he generalized from this experience that the death of a father was the most important event in any man's life. It certainly was in his, because in the following year, after an agonizing struggle with an anxiety neurosis, he initiated his self-analysis and began to understand the importance of family relations—he began to interpret his own Oedipus complex. In May of 1897 he wrote that one of his own dreams "of course fulfills my wish to pin down a father as the originator of neurosis." And he added, presumably from his self-analysis, that "hostile impulses against parents (a wish that they should die) are also an integral part of neurosis. . . . It seems as though in sons this death-wish is directed against their father and in daughters against their mother." He further speculated that "the horror of incest is based on the fact that, as a result of a common sexual life (even in childhood), the members of a family hold together permanently and become incapable of contact with strangers."[35]

The portion of Max Weber's work which attempted to characterize and explain different types of authority—charismatic, traditional, and legal—also derived in part from his own personal struggle with his father. In the summer of 1897, Weber defied his strongly authoritarian father for the first time and ordered him out of the house. Seven weeks later his father died, and shortly thereafter Weber had a nervous breakdown. He spent the next six years in and out of sanatoriums, nursing himself out of a severe melancholic depression and fighting a massive load of guilt. The price to pay for defiance of centuries of unquestioned and unchallenged paternal authority was high, even for a man of such enormous intellectual energy as Max Weber.[36]

In contrast with the formal studies and autobiographies which tended to subdue some of the more passionate and destructive elements of the father-son relationship, the imaginative literature often elaborated these elements in vivid detail.

The Brothers Karamazov (1880-1881) helped reduce whatever restraints might have held back earlier novelists depicting family conflict. The Oedipal theme in it prefigured Freud's later elaboration of the theory of the brothers of the primal horde who kill their father in order to possess his women. The four sons of Fyodor Karamazov work together, consciously and unconsciously, to destroy their father. Dimitry repeatedly expresses the wish to do so and engages in several battles with his father, in one of which he kicks him in the head while threatening to kill him. The hatred between Dimitry and his father was exacerbated by rivalry over a woman, Grushenka. Ivan supplies the bastard son, Smerdyakov, with the philosophical justification for crime. At Dimitry's trial Ivan explodes and projects the brothers' desire onto all mankind. "Who doesn't wish his father dead?" he screams. "My father has been murdered and they all pretend to be horrified. . . . Showing off before one another! The liars! They all wish their fathers dead."[37] Smerdyakov actually kills Fyodor, and the pious brother, Alyosha, does nothing as he sees the crime developing. The parricide portends the downfall of Russian society. The prosecuting attorney suggests to the jury that this is *the* crime which must be punished, however justified it may appear. Respect for the father is respect for authority, and that must remain inviolable if civilization is to continue.

Following *The Brothers Karamazov* there appeared a steady stream of literary works dealing with strained and tragic father-son relations. The son in Leon Bloy's *Le Désespéré* (1886) reflects, following the death of his father: "A father and a son are like two mute souls who look at one another across an abyss on either side of the mother, unable to speak or embrace."[38] In *Das Friedenfest* (1890) and *Michael Kramer* (1900), Hauptmann dramatized the conflict of the ineffectual son tormented by an ambitious father. Michael's father, like many of his fictional counterparts, only realized the destructive effect of his authoritarianism after his son's death. Similarly pressured sons are driven to suicide in Marie von Ebner-Eschenbach's two stories *Der Vorzugsschüler* (1897) and *Aus Spateherbsttagen* (1901).

If literature is an accurate index of historical fact, then the father-son relationship appears to have been acted out more violently at this time than in most other historical periods. The father-daughter relationship was also undergoing a change at this time. The themes of father-daughter incest and conflict were the subject of numerous important literary works. However, throughout this period the daughter remained of secondary importance within the family, and many general studies of the parent-child relation presumed that they need concern only the son.

Father-daughter incest, a recurring theme in literature, is injected into Hauptmann's *Before Sunrise* (1889) as just one more sign of the degeneration of the Krause family. The father's attacks on his daughter are a secondary consideration compared with drinking and smoking, which are given priority as *the* vices of the times. The intimate relationship between the thirteen-year-old heroine and her father in Lou Andreas-Salome's story *"Vaters Kind"* (1901) cools only after her father shoots the injured pet dog given to her by a young admirer. The father's possession of the girl's affection prior to that was extreme: "Ria's soul seemed to him to be a sweet little instrument that he alone knew how to play."[39] In George Bernard Shaw's *Man and Superman* (1901-03), Jack Tanner protested against paternal over-protectiveness which drives women to marry "because marriage is their only means of escape from these decrepit fiends who hide their selfish ambitions, their jealous hatreds of the young rivals who have supplanted them, under the mask of natural duty and family affection."[40]

Family conflict was most frequent between father and son and between husband and wife, but two works portrayed a bloody father-daughter relationship. In Schnitzler's *Der Ruf des Lebens* (1905), the dying father's hawkish possessiveness is matched in intensity by his daughter Marie's parricidal impulses. To the doctor who urges her to leave her father, she replies: "Not an hour goes by in which my fingers do not itch to strangle him."[41] She finally poisons her father but is too embittered to feel any relief.

The hatred of a ward for her guardian in Zola's *Earth* (1888) was so primitive that the final murderous act, no doubt one of the most brutal scenes in all of literary history, was executed with icy indifference. Old Fouan divides his land between two sons and a daughter. Trusting to the filial sense of his children for his keeping, he is disappointed and abused by each in turn, and in desperation settles with Buteau, who had married Fouan's ward, Lisa. The two quickly tire of caring for the old man and decide to murder him. Lisa thrusts a pillow over him during his sleep and breaks his nose. During the suffocation his face had turned black. To conceal their crime Buteau and Lisa decide to burn him. Lisa sets fire to the old man's beard. The burning momentarily revives him and, with his face blackened and his beard on fire, he gives them a dying look mixed with hatred and agony.

THE CONTROL OF CHILD SEXUALITY

The corporeal focal point of parent-child conflict in the Victorian period was child sexuality, in particular masturbation. Early masturbatory activity is a function of instinctual impulses, but as parental authority begins to turn upon this early manifestation of child sexuality, it becomes an expression of defiance, an assertion of independence. In a period when sexual morality was particularly severe and when the imposition of parental authority absolute, the playful self-indulgence of masturbating children was especially threatening to parents who were so anxious about suppressing their own sexuality. As soon as the child was able to acquire a moral sense, the parents sought to quash child sexuality with firm moral injunctions, threats of punishment, and, if necessary, physical restraint.

Conflict over the suppression of child sexuality was most acute in the father-son relationship. Perhaps the tyrannical father was partly acting out his anxiety from the loss of his own potency, jealous over the willful assertion of his son's seemingly abundant sexual energy. The combination of fear and jealousy may account for some of the intensity of this struggle in the mid nineteenth century, but these two factors are universal and not unique to this period. Several other factors may help explain why the effort to control child sexuality was so intense at this time.

The severely restrictive sexual morality of the nineteenth century was imposed by the newly triumphant bourgeoisie. Speculation about its repressive sex ethic by Lewis Mumford, Peter Cominos, and Norman O. Brown has concluded that the bourgeoisie was intent upon amassing great wealth, and consequently the virtue of thrift came to be extended to regulate all expenditure of energy.[42] Waste, whether financial or biological, came to be viewed as evil, and the class sexual morality called for ever more thrift in the sexual sphere. Child sexuality was a persistent reminder of the human tendency to squander, and parents sought to control it both to instill a proper morality in the child and to reaffirm the wisdom of their own self-restraint.

René Spitz has developed another line of reasoning about the probable causes of the sudden imposition of severe parental authority in curbing masturbation around 1850. From a survey of 559 works relating to the causes, effects, and controls of masturbation throughout history, Spitz concluded that in the late eighteenth century a decisive change of emphasis occurred as physicians began to abandon more moderate treatment involving bland diets and counseling and turned to more sadistic restraining methods. "While in the eighteenth century medical men endeavored to *cure* masturbation, in the nineteenth century they were trying to *suppress* it."[43] In the period 1850-1879 the most sadistic measures involving surgical operations (punitive circumcision, male and female infibulation, and clitoridectomy) were recommended more frequently than other procedures. From 1880 to 1904 various restraining apparatuses were the most frequently used control method, while after 1905 the spread of knowledge of psychoanalysis gradually began to reduce the incidence of surgical and physical suppression of child sexuality. Spitz suggests several historical factors which contributed to the particularly severe measures of the mid and late nineteenth century. The rise of Protestantism placed unprecedented responsibility upon the father to impose moral restraints upon himself and his family. The philosophy of the Enlightenment underlined the need for public health to be a major concern of the state. The connection between the familial responsibility of the father to watch over the morality of his family and the civic responsibility of the state to control public health and sexuality was realized in the early nineteenth century as the social problems created by the industrial revolution further illustrated the need for societal support of public health projects. By the early nineteench century, medical men began to accept the social responsibility of medicine.

The historical record confirms Spitz's conclusion that "the sadistic trend in anti-masturbationist therapy came at a period in history when people became aware of infantile sexuality."[44] Parents intruded their anxious moralizing into the most intimate biological and emotional processes of their children in order to curb possible sources of sexual excitation. They were counseled to keep their children to a strict sleeping regimen in order not to allow them to be in bed long either before falling to sleep or after awakening in the morning. Children's diets were carefully controlled to exclude any spicy foods which were believed to arouse erotic impulses. The bowels were carefully watched because constipation and piles were listed among the causes of masturbation. Clothing had to be specially designed. Suspenders should be loose to prevent pants from rubbing against the genitals, and one moralist advised carefully selecting boys' trousers with shallow and widely separated pockets. Horseback riding, prolonged sitting, and bicycle riding were to be curtailed because they too could generate masturbatory impulses from rhythmic friction. Of course the child's reading must be carefully regulated, and even many of the suggestive works of art found in museums were believed to be dangerous. Other moralists mention as possible exciting causes the easy accessibility of closets, perfumes, furs, or rocking chairs. Thus parents could meddle in every aspect of a child's life under the pretext of rooting out potential causes of masturbatory activity. The American psychologist G. Stanley Hall wrote as if in a final gasp of anxious frustration that the hand itself, that symbol of man's achievement over the animal world, may prove to be the cause of his ruin.[45] And for the child who persisted in masturbating in defiance of the more subtle preventative efforts of his parents, the Victorians resorted to force. Wandering hands were tied down at night, and a variety of elaborate restrictive devices were tried. Lafonde's elaborate corset restricted access by a metal cup over the genitals. Various kinds of rings were sold to be installed around the penis to prevent erection, and J. L. Milton described a gadget which awakened young men with an electric bell: "a ring placed on the penis is so made, that when expanded by erection it completes an electric circuit and so rings a small alarm bell placed under the sleeper's pillow." (See Figure 1). And for the incorrigible there were a number of surgical techniques: blistering of the penis, infibulation, and for female masturbators, surgical removal of the clitoris.[47]

By 1905, when Freud fully elaborated his family psychology and developed his theory of the Oedipus complex as the focus of the child's psychosexual response to family life, the Victorian family was exploding from unresolved Oedipal tensions. His early patients came to him on their hands and knees, emotionally crippled (sometimes physically) by pathological defense structures generated by severe sexual repression reinforced by familial pressure. His theory was a systematization of the ideas that had been explored by the Victorians who were living with, and trying to understand, the tense atmosphere of the Victorian family. Freud made a few striking additions. He insisted that these intense feelings exist from earliest childhood, sometimes with even greater force than later, and that they are present in all children and submerged under varying degrees of repression. He argued that the constellation of positive and negative feelings harbored by every child toward his parents and siblings forms a nucleus of ambivalence and conflict that determines later adult patterns of psychological and sexual relating. Underlying every adult dream, he boldly speculated, there was some repressed childhood wish, impulse, or memory, and the Oedipus complex itself was the nucleus for all adult neurotic or psychotic symptomatology. Perhaps Freud did exaggerate the sexual and familial determinants of adult mental life, but that exaggeration was a reflection of the extent to which those factors had governed family life of the late Victorian period.

CHILD SUICIDE

There is no more telling critique of the family than the suicide of a child, and in the 1890s child suicide appeared to many observers to be

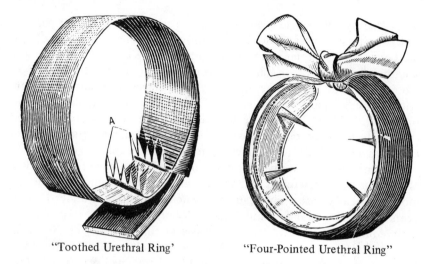

"Toothed Urethral Ring'   "Four-Pointed Urethral Ring"

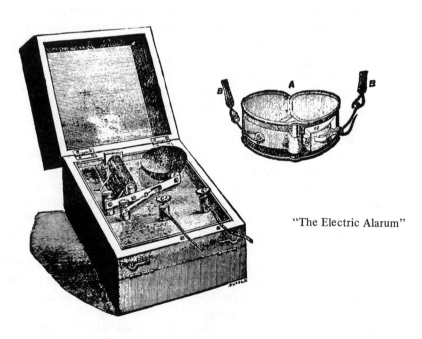

"The Electric Alarum"

Figure 1. Reproduced from J. L. Milton, *On the Pathology and Treatment of Gonorrhoea and Spermatorrhoea*, New York, 1887, pp. 397-401.

rising sharply. No single historical fact so urgently compelled parents and educators to re-evaluate their relationship with children. No doubt the largest single explanation for the apparent rise in suicides of all ages was the improvement of statistical techniques during the latter part of the century, but at the time, the rising percentages gave cause for much critical re-examination of school and home life in particular. Against the traditional dismissal of the suicide as a moral degenerate who succumbed to his hereditary endowment, observers began to study the particular psychological and social conditions of the suicide.

A comprehensive study of suicide by the Italian sociologist Enrico Morselli in 1879 concluded that shame and fear of punishment were the most frequently discernible causes of suicide in children under fifteen years of age. Mental illness and then family problems were, respectively, the second and third most frequent causes of child suicide. The German child psychologist and educator, Friedrich Scholz, in 1891 listed four environmental causes: misery of family life, shame, bad conscience, and fear of punishment. In an extraordinary pre-Freudian interpretation of the nature of the unconscious forces that drive a child to suicide, he wrote: "One ought not believe that suicide is really accidental, because it is consistently only the last link of a long chain of events that lead up to it, even if they are for the most part unperceived and unconscious."[48]

The most complete study of child suicide was by Abraham Baer, who criticized earlier studies, such as an article by a German doctor in 1870 which trivialized the motive that drove the child to suicide. Baer insisted that children have more intense feelings than adults. The most frequently recorded motives for child suicide he listed as remorse, shame, and bad conscience. Though he explicitly considered family life as a cause, he only mentions the effect of broken families and those in which the child is forced into excessive material suffering and deprivation. But the rate of child suicide, he warned, was increasing more rapidly than that of adults, especially because of the growing pressures of education and the encouragement of precociousness. He concluded: "Suicide in childhood is a product of our modern culture and social life. Degeneration and mental illness on the one hand, and bad education and precocity on the other explain the relatively frequent occurrence of child suicide and its increase in recent times."[49] Christian Ufer's review of Baer in *Kinderfehler* (1902) emphasized the role of the home and school in driving children to suicide.

A large number of fictional works on this period treated child suicide deriving from pressures of home and school, but school problems led to suicide only when parental attitudes reinforced them. Marie von Ebner-Eschenbach's *Der Vorzugsschüler* (1897) tells of fourteen-year-old George, frightfully driven by his parents, whose hopes for financial and social advancement rested solely on him. Though well qualified, George fails an examination, and, remembering his father's angry warning not to come home with a bad report, "goes the way of so many other unfortunate students—into the Danube."[50] In response to similar home-school pressures, the hero of Hesse's *Beneath the Wheel* drowns himself. The titular hero of Hauptmann's *Michael Kramer* (1900) buckles under his father's imposing ambition and expectations and commits suicide. The young heroine of Hauptmann's *Hanneles Himmelfahrt* (1893) throws herself into an icy pond while fleeing her brutal and drunken father. A most gruesome child suicide occurs in Thomas Hardy's *Jude the Obscure* (1895). Jude's plans to accomplish through his son what he could not achieve himself are repeatedly frustrated by the child's lack of ambition and morbid pessimism. One day Jude's wife thoughtlessly tells her son that it would be easier for the family to get lodgings if there were no children. The boy takes his mother's words to heart and hangs his two younger siblings, then himself. Jude consoles his aggrieved wife: "It was in his nature to do it. The doctor says there are such boys springing up amongst us—boys of a sort unknown in the last generation—the outcome of new views of life. They seem to see all its terrors before they are old enough to have staying power to resist them. He says it is the beginning of the coming universal wish not to live."[51]

The most commonly mentioned motive for suicide in childhood was fear of punishment, and shame ran a close second. Both problems derived from family life. As the Victorian family closed in upon the child the pressures upon the child mounted accordingly. The child of the Victorian period was subject to an extraordinary set of pressures particularly through the social ambitions of the family. Children were to inherit, and to enhance, the fortunes of the large middle class estates built up for over a century of aggrandizement that often included financially judicious marriages. The pressures brought to bear on many Victorian children were indeed of explosive intensity.

I would like to conclude with one long quotation that well illustrates the kinds of pressures that held the Victorian family together with a tenacity that eventually led to its undoing. It is from a marriage manual by the American phrenologist O. S. Fowler, *Love and Parentage Applied to the Improvement of Offspring*. The passage concludes a section on the nature of spiritual love in marriage and shows to what extent the Victorian parent was led to believe that the family unit was held fast by the innermost biological and psychological processes of man. The italics are Fowler's.

> While sexual love, as such, transmits the bodily organs and animal functions, it remains for this *spiritual* love to call forth into the most delightful and intense action possible, the entire *intellectual and moral* nature of parents, prepatory, and in order, to its conferring on man this boon of *angels*, this "image and likeness" of

God; besides purifying and sanctifying the animal by the ascendency of the moral, and guiding all by *reason*. And it is this *combined and concentrated*, as well as *high-wrought*, inter-communion of *every physical, every intellectual, every moral element and function of humanity* in generation as it is *by constitution*, which renders the pleasure attendant on this *double* repast so *indescribably* exalted and beatific to those who *spiritually love* each other, or in proportion thereto; besides being *the* ONLY means of augmenting and perfecting the intellectuality and morality of its product—redoubling more and more as its handmaid love becomes more and more perfect, and thereby enhances, and also unites, in this holy alliance, faculty after faculty, till finally, when both love and generation have their perfect, and of course *united,* work, they embrace within the wide range of their sanctified enjoyment, every animal, every intellectual, every moral, organ and function, and element of man's entire constitution![52]

The syntax of the passage forms a crescendo of the many themes Fowler had been developing and, laced with italics and prolonged as though the author could not bear to conclude each of its two sentences, strains to convey the enormity and totality of the marital union, culminating in offspring which are a product of *every* physical and mental attribute of the parents. Fowler is relentless in his apotheosis of the sanctity of the family. He implies that life outside of it is immoral, irrational, and base. The marital union is the center point of Victorian life, where all is "combined" and "concentrated" where "every intellectual, every moral element," every "organ and function" is *"united"* totally and for all time in view of the angels, in the "image and likeness" of God. In this world divorce is unthinkable—a rejection of God, an abandonment of the protective hand of religion, a violation of the natural forces of human biology, a corruption of the intellectual and moral qualities of mankind, and a serious threat to the well being of the state. There is a stickiness here that made family life as unbearable as it was vital to its members who had become so dependent on it. By the end of the century the Victorian family became an explosive unit, poised in a tenuous solidity that was already beginning to decompose as the very forces that held it together became too much for its individual members to bear.

Stephen Kern teaches European Intellectual History at Northern Illinois University, Dekalb. Trained in both history and psychiatry, he is currently working on a book on the history of attitudes towards the human body in European thought in the nineteenth and twentieth centuries.

REFERENCES

1. I am indebted to Rudolph Binion, Richard Price, and Lloyd deMause for critical suggestions for this article.
2. G. M. Young, *Portrait of an Age,* (Oxford, 1936), 150-153.
3. Walter E. Houghton, *The Victorian Frame of Mind,* (New Haven, 1957), 343-344.
4. Keith Thomas, "The Double Standard," *Journal of the History of Ideas,* April, 1959, 195-216. Peter T. Cominos, "Late-Victorian Sexual Respectability and the Social System," *International Review of Social History,* Volume VIII, 1963, 18-48, 216-250.
5. Cominos, *Ibid.,* 250.
6. Steven Marcus, *The Other Victorians,* (New York, 1964), 100.
7. Lloyd deMause, "Childhood and the Psychogenic Theory of History," in Lloyd deMause, ed., *The History of Childhood,* (Basic Books, Inc., in press.) See also Priscilla Robertson, "Home as a Nest: Middle Class Childhood in the 19th Century in Europe," in *Ibid.,* for an account of the Victorian parent-child confrontation over discipline, toilet training, and masturbation.
8. Georgiana B. Kirby, *Transmission; or, Variation of Character Through the Mother,* (New York, 1877), 11.
9. Eduard von Hartmann, *The Sexes Compared,* (London, 1895), 12.
10.. Otto Weininger, *Sex and Character,* (New York, 1906), 233.
11. Hermann Swoboda, *Studien zur Grundlegung der Psychologie,* (Leipzig, 1905), 33.
12. Samuel Butler, *Unconscious Memory,* (London, 1880), 19.
13. B. A. Morel, *Traité des dégénérescences,* Paris, 1857.
14. Gabriel Compayré, *The Intellectual and Moral Development of the Child,* (New York, 1896), 258.
15. Henrik Ibsen, *Ghosts and Three Other Plays,* (New York, 1966), p. 163.
16. W. Spemann, *Spemanns goldenes Buch der Sitte,* (Berlin, c. 1900), 71.
17. Leo Tolstoy, *Great Short Works of Leo Tolstoy,* (New York, 1967), 392.
18. Henrik Ibsen, *Hedda Gabler and Three Other Plays,* (New York, 1961), 433.
19. Gabriele Reuter, *Aus guter Familie,* (Berlin, 1908), 40.
20. Henry James, *What Maisie Knew,* (New York, 1954), 19, 27.
21. T. C. Leland, *The Illustrated Manners Book,* (New York, 1855), 255.
22. Elizabeth Blackwell, *Counsel to Parents,* (London, 1884), 86.
23. Bernard Perez, *L'Enfant de trois à sept ans,* (Paris, 1886), 232.
24. F. M. Wendt, "Zur Psychologie der Eltern und Kindesliebe," *Die Kinderfehler,* (1905).
25. Adalbert Czerney, *Der Arzt als Erzieher des Kindes,* (Leipzig, 1908), 5. See also Ludwig Strümpell, *Psychologische Padagogik,* (Leipzig, 1880).
26. Paul Möbius, *Geschlecht und Kinderliebe,* 1904.
27. Jules Dallemagne, *Dégénérés et Déséquilibrés,* (Brussels, 1894).
28. Havelock Ellis, *Analysis of the Sexual Impulse* (Philadelphia, 1908), 15.
29. Emile Zola, *Les Rougon-Macquarts,* (Paris, 1961), Vol. II, 944, 1062.
30. Marcus, *Other Victorians,* 27.
31. Sylvanus Stall, *What a Young Husband Ought to Know,* (London, 1897), 100.

32. In "Das Vater-Sohn Motiv in der Dichtung 1880-1930," *Stoff- und Motivgeschichte der deutschen Literatur,* XI (1931), the German critic Kurt K. T. Wais concluded from an extensive survey of the literature that the number of works dealing with the father-son problem between 1880 and 1930 is nearly equal to the number appearing in all of German literature before 1880. Wais argued further against Rank (1912), "who focused on the sexual impulse in father-son conflict," that the preoccupation with the conflict was a reflection of the social and political upheaval and reached a crescendo in the German Revolution of 1918.

33. Austin Harrison, *Frederic Harrison: Thoughts and Memoirs,* (London, 1926), 57.

34. Samuel Butler, *The Way of All Flesh,* (New York, 1960), 86, 278-279.

35. Ernst Kris, *The Origins of Psycho-Analysis: Letters to Fliess, Drafts and Notes: 1887-1902,* (New York, 1954), pp. 206, 207, 209.

36. Arthur Mitzman, *The Iron Cage: An Historical Interpretation of Max Weber,* (New York, 1969), offers an interpretation of the psychological and historical significance of this experience. "Weber's view of the world in the years before 1897 was shaped by his struggle to escape from and finally challenge the dominance in the Weber household of his father, a dominance which he identified subconsciously with the political hegemony of the Junkers over the landworkers in particular and the German people in general . . . His view of the world in the years after 1902 was structured by the lessons he drew consciously or otherwise, from the agonizing collapse which resulted from this struggle." pp. 6-7. See also Phyllis Greenacre, *The Quest for a Father: a Study of the Darwin-Butler Controversy, As a Contribution to the Understanding of the Creative Individual,* (New York, 1963), who also argues that the greatness of Darwin and Butler derived from conflict with their fathers. Each of them revolted against "God-given authoritarianism and stratified structure which characterized alike Victorian society and the Victorian family." p. 88.

37. Fyodor Dostoevsky, *The Brothers Karamozov,* (Middlesex, 1958), 807.

38. Quoted in Wais, *Stoff- und Motivgeschichte,* 1.

39. Lou Andreas-Salomé, *Im Zwischenland,* (Stuttgart, 1911), 127.

40. George Bernard Shaw, *Selected Plays,* (New York, 1948), Vol. III, 573-574.

41. Arthur Schnitzler, *Die Theaterstücke von Arthur Schnitzler,* (Berlin, 1922), Vol. III, 298.

42. A great number of historians have discussed this phenomenon. The specific sources I refer to are Lewis Mumford, *Technics and Civilization,* 1934, Norman O. Brown, "Filthy Lucre," in *Life Against Death,* 1959, and the Cominos article cited above.

43. René Spitz, "Authority and Masturbation," *The Psychoanalytic Quarterly,* (Vol. 21, 1952), 499.

44. For a demonstration of the growing awareness of child sexuality in the late nineteenth century see Stephen Kern, "Freud and the Discovery of Child Sexuality," *History of Childhood Quarterly,* Summer, 1973.

45. G. Stanley Hall, *Adolescence,* (New York, 1904), Vol. II, 438. For a good summary of the many causes and effects of masturbation that filled the medical literature of the period see Chapter VI, "Sexual Development: Its

Dangers and Hygiene in Boys," which is almost entirely devoted to "self-abuse."

46. John Laws Milton, *On the Pathology and Treatment of Gonorrhoea and Spermatorrhoea,* New York, 1887, 400.

47. The literature on this aspect of the history of medicine has focused on the clitoridectomy as a symbol of the extreme fear of sexuality that plagued the Victorians. A London surgeon, Issac Baker Brown (who later became President of the Medical Society of London) developed the operation of the clitoridectomy in 1858 to treat cases of what he judged to be excessive masturbation. The operation has a sporadic history—sometimes recommended, sometimes violently criticized—but was performed intermittently until sometime in the 1920's when it was performed for the last time in the United States. For a further discussion of the operation see Alex Comfort, *The Anxiety Makers,* (New York, 1967), John Duffy, "Masturbation and Clitoridectomy," *Journal of the American Medical Association,* (Vol. 186, 1963), pp. 246-248, René Spitz, *op. cit.,* and Stephen Kern, "Some Precursors of Freud's Theory of Castration Anxiety," to appear in *The Psychoanalytic Review.*

48. Friedrich Scholz, *Die Charakterfehler des Kindes,* (Leipzig, 1891), 171.

49. Abraham Baer, *Der Selbstmord im kindlichen Lebensalter,* (Leipzig, 1901), 73.

50. Maria von Ebner-Eschenbach, "Der Vorzugschüler," in *Ein Volksbuch,* (Berlin, 1909), 198.

51. Thomas Hardy, *Jude the Obscure,* (Boston, 1965), 226.

52. O. S. Fowler, *Love and Parentage Applied to the Improvement of Offspring: Including Important Directions and Suggestions to Lovers and the Married Concerning the Strongest Ties and the Most Sacred and Momentous Relations of Life,* (New York, 1846), 74.

CHAPTER 3

Infanticide: A Historical Survey

WILLIAM L.
LANGER

Professor Langer's overview of infanticide in the West was originally written as an introduction to a projected reprint of William B. Ryan's Infanticide: Its Law, Prevalence, Prevention and History *(London, 1862). Since the reprint did not materialize, he has revised and documented the essay for readers of the* Journal. *He reminds us, however, that it still makes no pretence to being more than a historical review of an important subject which is only now beginning to attract the attention it deserves.*

Infanticide, that is, the wilful destruction of newborn babes through exposure, starvation, strangulation, smothering, poisoning, or through the use of some lethal weapon, has been viewed with abhorrence by Christians almost from the beginning of their era. Although often held up to school-children as an abomination practiced by the Chinese or other Asians, its role in Western civilization, even in modern times, has rarely been suggested by historians, sociologists or even demographers.

Yet in these days of world population crisis there can hardly be a more important historical question than that of the chronically superfluous population growth and the methods by which humanity has dealt with it. Among non-Christian peoples (with the exception of the Jews) infanticide has from time immemorial been the accepted procedure for disposing not only of deformed or sickly infants, but of all such new-borns as might strain the resources of the individual family or the larger community. At the present day it is still employed by so-called underde-veloped peoples in the effort to keep the population in reasonable ad-justment to the available food supply. Among the Eskimos of Arctic Canada, for instance, many babies are set out on the ice to freeze if the father or elder of the tribe decides that they would be a continuing drain on the means of subsistence.[1]

In ancient times, at least, infanticide was not a legal obligation. It was a practice freely discussed and generally condoned by those in au-thority and ordinarily left to the decision of the father as the responsible head of the family. Modern humanitarian sentiment makes it difficult to recapture the relatively detached attitude of the parents towards their offspring. Babies were looked upon as the unavoidable result of normal sex relations, often as an undesirable burden rather than as a blessing. More girls than boys were disposed of, presumably to keep down the number of potential mothers as well as in recognition of the fact that they would never contribute greatly to the family income. In the seventeenth century, Jesuit missionaries to China were horrified to find that in Peking alone several thousand babes (almost exclusively fe-males) were thrown on the streets like refuse, to be collected each morn-ing by carriers who dumped them into a huge pit outside the city.[2]

The attitude of the ancient Greeks in this matter is well reflected in the pronouncements of Plato and Aristotle. The former favored the careful regulation of all sex relations, so as to produce the most perfect type of human being, while Aristotle was more concerned with the problem of population pressure. With its limited resources, ancient Greece, according to a modern authority, "lived always under the shadow of the fear of too many mouths to feed." Neglect of this prob-lem by many city-states was denounced by Aristotle as "a never-failing cause of poverty among the citizens, and poverty was the parent of revolution." He firmly contended that the size of the population should be limited by law and suggested that abortion might be preferable to exposure as a method of control.[3]

In Hellenistic Greece, infanticide, chiefly in the form of exposure of female babies, was carried to such an extent that the average family was exceptionally small. Parents rarely reared more than one daughter, with the result that there was an altogether abnormal discrepancy in the numbers of the sexes.[4]

The practice of the Hellenistic Greeks was continued under Roman rule and probably influenced Roman attitudes. After all, Rome itself was traditionally founded by the exposed youngsters, Romulus and Remus, who were saved from their certain fate by the nursing of a friendly wolf. Throughout the Republic and long after the authority of the father over his family had worn thin, unwanted children continued to be disposed of in the accepted way. It was thought altogether natural that proletarians, poverty-stricken and hopeless, should protect themselves from further responsibility. As among the Greeks, there was a marked disparity between the sexes, which suggests that many bastards and a substantial number of female infants were abandoned if not murdered by drowning.[5] Seneca saw nothing unreasonable in this procedure, while Pliny the Elder defended the practice on the ground that the size of the population must be regulated. Edward Gibbon, writing in the late eighteenth century on *The Decline and Fall of the Roman Empire*, denounced this exposure of children as "the prevailing and stubborn vice of antiquity," and charged the Roman Empire with being "stained with the blood of infants." Lecky, writing a century later, speaks of infanticide as "one of the deepest stains of the ancient civilization" and as "a crying vice of the empire."[6]

A decisive change of attitude came with Christianity. The Church fathers were undoubtedly, in this respect as in others, influenced by Judaic Law which, while it did not mention infanticide specifically in the discussion of murder, was always interpreted by Rabbinical Law as an equivalent.[7] Philo Judaeus, the eminent Jewish-Hellenistic philosopher, denounced the exposure of children and declared it a form of murder. Increasingly, Christian leaders thundered against infanticide as a pagan practice and insisted that all human life be held inviolable. Yet it was only with the triumph of Christianity that the Emperor Constantine in 318 A.D. declared the slaying of a son or daughter by a father to be a crime, and only at the end of the fourth century that the Emperors Valentinian, Valens, and Gratian made infanticide a crime punishable by death.[8]

While the contribution of Christian theologians to the adoption of a more humane attitude is obvious, it should be remembered that the later Roman Empire apparently suffered from progressive depopulation, due to devastating epidemics, recurrent famines and general disorder.[9] Under the circumstances there was clearly no need to limit population growth. On the contrary, increased fertility was desired. Hence the repetition of the exhortation of the Bible: "Be fruitful and multiply." Until the late eighteenth century at least, when the great upswing of the European population set in, large families were the fashion, being regarded as the blessing of a benevolent deity.

Yet there can be little doubt that child murder continued to be practiced, even in the most advanced countries of western Europe. Lecky, in his *History of European Morals* (1869), speaks of the popular distinction in the early Middle Ages between infanticide and exposure, the latter offense not being punishable by law: "It was practiced on a gigantic scale with absolute impunity, noticed by writers with most frigid indifference and, at least in the case of destitute parents, considered a very venial offence."[10]

Until the sixteenth century, and in some places until much later, the unenviable task of dealing with the problem was left to the Church authorities. In the hope of reducing the exposure and almost certain death of newborn children (especially girls), foundling hospitals were opened in the eighth century in Milan, Florence, Rome, and other cities. But these institutions proved to be ineffectual, since most of the children had to be sent to the country to be nursed, and the majority soon succumbed either through neglect or more positive action on the part of the wet-nurses.

Infanticide by out-and-out violence of various kinds was probably always exceptional. Throughout European history the authorities were baffled and frustrated primarily by the many cases of reputed suffocation, the "overlaying" or "overlying" of an infant in bed by its allegedly drunken parents. This could and surely did occur accidentally, but the suspicion, always present and unusually warranted, was that of intentional riddance of an unwanted child. Since it was impossible to prove premeditated crime, the authorities contented themselves with the imposition of penance in the case of married women, who were condemned to live for at least a year on bread and water. The unwed mothers and the presumed witches, however, were to bear the brunt as examples and admonitions. A girl known to have committed infanticide in any form might be absolved by pleading insanity, but was otherwise condemned to suffer the death penalty, usually in the most diabolical imaginable manner. Medieval sources tell of women being tied in a sack, along with a dog, a cock, or some other uncongenial companion and thrown into the river for a supreme struggle for life. This method was probably never in general use, and in any case seems to have been abandoned by the end of the Middle Ages.[11] A detailed analysis of the court and prison records of Nürnberg from 1513 to 1777 lists by name eighty-seven women executed for infanticide, all but four of them unmarried girls who had committed violent murder. Prior to 1500 the penalty in Nürnberg as in most of Germany was burial alive, often with gruesome refinements. During the sixteenth century the usual method was drowning, and after 1580 decapitation. Hangings were quite exceptional. It was hardly worse, however, than being buried alive, being drowned or decapitated, penalties which continued to be practiced, though less and less frequently, until the nineteenth century.

In any case, overlaying continued to be a vexing problem until modern times. In 1500, the Bishop of Fiesole set fines and penalties for parents who kept babies in bed with them. In the eighteenth century, a Florentine craftsman designed a basket frame (*arcuccio*) which would protect the child from smothering. An Austrian decree of 1784 forbade having children under the age of five in bed with parents, and Prussian legislation of 1794 reduced the age of the infants to two.[12]

Government authorities were apparently no more successful than the clergy in checking the practice of overlaying, at least among married couples. One may safely assume that in the eighteenth and nineteenth centuries the poor, hardly able to support the family they already had, evaded responsibility by disposing of further additions. But by the eighteenth century another form of infanticide became so prevalent that governments were at their wits' end in their efforts to combat it. For reasons too complex and still too obscure, there was a marked increase in sexual immorality, in seduction, and in illegitimacy. The evidence suggests that in all European countries, from Britain to Russia, the upper classes felt perfectly free to exploit sexually girls who were at their mercy. As late as 1871, Mr. Cooper, the Secretary of the Society for the Rescue of Young Women and Children, testified before a Parliamentary Committee that at least nine out of ten of the girls in trouble were domestic servants: "in many instances the fathers of their children are their masters, or their masters' sons, or their masters' relatives, or their masters' visitors." To be sure, lords of the manor often recognized the offspring as their own and raised them as members of the family. But in the new factory towns foremen favored amenable girls for employment. Young aristocrats, too, were much to blame. When traveling they expected to find relaxation with the chamber maids of the inn. It seems to have been taken for granted that the upper classes were entitled to the favors of pretty girls of the lower classes and that fornication was looked upon as an inevitable aspect of lower class life.

Yet if a girl became pregnant, she was left to shift for herself. She at once became an object of obloquy and might well be whipped out of the village by the more fortunate members of her sex. Many sought anonymity and aid in the cities, where professional midwives would, for a pittance, not only perform an abortion or deliver the child, but would also undertake to nurse and care for it, it being fully understood that the mother would not need to worry further about it. Starvation or a dose of opiates would settle the child's fate in a matter of days.

Naturally all girls in trouble were not willing to resort to so drastic a solution. There was always the possibility, admittedly slim, that if the unwanted baby were left on the steps of a church or mansion, it might stir the sympathies of a stranger and be adopted by him, as was Tom Jones by Squire Allworthy. Many young mothers therefore bundled up their offspring, and left them at churches or other public places. In the late seventeenth century, St. Vincent de Paul was so appalled by the number of babies to be seen daily on the steps of Notre Dame that he appealed to ladies of the court to finance an asylum for foundlings. His efforts soon inspired others to similar action, and before long most large towns in Catholic Europe had established similar institutions. In England a retired sea captain, Thomas Coram, was so depressed by the daily sight of infant corpses thrown on the dust heaps of London that he devoted seventeen years in soliciting support for a foundling hospital. Eventually a group of his supporters petitioned the King to charter a Foundling Hospital so as "to prevent the frequent murders of poor, miserable infants at their birth," and "to suppress the inhuman custom of exposing new-born infants to perish in the streets."[13]

The story of the foundling hospitals is too long and complicated to be more than sketched here. For a time they were the favorite charity of the wealthy and huge sums were expended in lavish construction and equipment. Although the London and Paris hospitals were the best known, the establishment at St. Petersburg, actively patronized by the imperial court, was undoubtedly the most amazing. Two competent western observers of the early nineteenth century agree in their enthusiastic praise. It was housed in the former palaces of Counts Razumovski and Bobrinski and occupied a huge tract in the very center of St. Petersburg. By the mid-1830s, it had 25,000 children on its rolls and was admitting 5000 newcomers annually. Since no questions were asked and the place was attractive, almost half of the newborn babies were deposited there by their parents. A dozen doctors and 600 wet-nurses were in attendance to care for the children during the first six weeks, after which they were sent to peasant nurses in the country. At the age of six (if they survived to that age) they were returned to St. Petersburg for systematic education. The program was excellent, but its aims were impossible to achieve. Despite all excellent management and professional efforts, thirty to forty percent of the children died during the first six weeks and hardly a third reached the age of six.[14]

The chronicle of the hospitals everywhere was one of devoted effort but unrelieved tragedy. The assignment was simply impossible to carry out. Everywhere they were besieged by mostly unwed mothers eager to dispose of their babies without personally or directly committing infanticide. Even so, actual child murder appears to have continued to an alarming extent, due to the fear of many girls of being identified at the hospital. Napoleon therefore decreed (January 18, 1811) that there should be hospitals in every departement of France, and that each should be equipped with a turntable (*tour*), so that the mother or her agent could place the child on one side, ring a bell, and have a nurse take the child by turning the table, the mother remaining unseen and unquestioned.

Although it is agreed that Napoleon's provision of *tours* helped to diminish the number of outright child murders, it meant that the hospitals were swamped with babies. It was impossible to find enough wet-nurses for even a short period, and most of the infants had to be shipped off to the country at once. Relatively few survived the long journey over rough roads in crude carts, and those happy few generally succumbed before long due to the ignorant treatment or the intentional or unintentional neglect of their foster parents. Small wonder that Malthus referred to the asylums as "these horrible receptables," while others spoke freely of "legalized infanticide." In the years 1817-1820, the number of foundlings in charge of the Paris hospital, many of them brought in from the provinces, and, interestingly, about a third of them children of married couples, was about equal to a third of all babies born in Paris in that period. Of 4779 infants admitted in 1818, 2370 died in the first three months. It would be unjust, no doubt, to put the entire blame for this situation on the foundling hospitals. Many of the infants were diseased or half dead when they arrived, and we may well believe that prior to the nineteenth century many newborn babies would in any event have succumbed to the methods of clothing and feeding then still in vogue.[15]

By 1830, the situation in France had become desperate. In 1833 the number of babies left with the foundling hospitals reached the fantastic figure of 164,319. Authorities were all but unanimous in the opinion that the introduction of the *tours* had been disastrous, that they had, in fact, put a premium on immorality. Thereupon the *tours* were gradually abolished until by 1862 only five were left. Instead, the government embarked upon a program of outside aid to unwed mothers. Presumably the growing practice of birth control and the advances made in pediatrics also contributed to the reduction in infant mortality.[16]

The story of the foundlings in England was no less tragic than that of France. The London Foundling Hospital (opened in 1741) was intended for the reception of London children only, but the pressure for admissions soon became so great as to give rise "to the disgraceful scene of women scrambling and fighting to get to the door, that they might be of the fortunate few to reap the benefit of the Asylum."[17] Under the circumstances Parliament in 1756 provided a modest grant on condition that the hospital be open to all comers, but that at the same time asylums for exposed or deserted young children be opened in all counties, ridings, and divisions of the kingdom. Parish officers promptly took advantage of the act to empty their workhouses of infant poor and dump them on the new hospices, while others had them shipped to London. By 1760, the London Hospital was deluged with 4229 newcomers, making a total of 14,934 admissions in the preceding four years. It was impossible to cope with the situation, and "instead of being a protection to the living, the institution became, as it were, a charnel-house for the dead."[18] In 1760, Parliament reversed itself by putting an end to indiscriminate admissions and returned the care of the provincial foundlings to the parishes. The London Hospital soon became more of an orphanage than a foundling asylum. By 1850, it had only 460 children and admitted only 77 annually.[19]

The parish officers were helpless in the face of the problem. A law of 1803 specified that charges of infanticide must be tried according to the same rules of evidence as applied to murder, while yet another law required that "it must be proved that the entire body of the child has actually been born into the world in a living state, and the fact of its having breathed is not conclusive proof thereof. There must be independent circulation in the child before it can be accounted alive." In other words, to kill a child by crushing its head with a hairbrush or hammer, or cutting its throat was technically not a crime, so long as its lower extremities were still in the body of the mother.[20] Since the required evidence was all but impossible to obtain, infanticide could be committed almost with impunity. In any case, juries refused, even in the most flagrant cases, to convict the offender, holding that capital punishment was far too harsh a penalty to pay when the real culprit was usually the girl's seducer. So infanticide flourished in England. Disraeli was only the most famous of several writers who maintained that it was hardly less prevalent in England than on the banks of the Ganges.[21] Dr. Lankester, one of the coroners for Middlesex, charged that even the police seemed to think no more of finding a dead child than of finding a dead dog or cat. There were, he asserted, hundreds, nay thousands of women living in London who were guilty of having at one time or another destroyed their offspring, without having been discovered.[22]

By the mid-century the matter had become one of public scandal. One doctor in 1846 commented on "the great indifference displayed by parents and others in the lower ranks of life with regard to infant life." Women employed in the factories and fields had no choice but to leave their babies in the care of professional nurses, sometimes called "killer nurses." who made short shrift of their charges by generous doses of opiates.[23]

Worse yet was the revelation that some women enrolled their infants in Burial Clubs, paying a trifling premium until, after a decent interval, the child died of starvation, ill-usage, or poisoning. They then collected £3 to £5 by way of benefit. Cases were reported of women who had membership for their babies in ten or more clubs, reaping a rich return at the proper time.[24]

The institution of "killer nurses" or "angel-makers" eventually became known as "baby-farming." By 1860, it had become the subject of lively agitation, both in lay and in professional circles. In 1856, Dr. William B. Ryan was awarded a gold medal by the London Medical Society for his essay on "Infanticide in its Medical-Legal Relations." He followed this two years later by an address on "Child Murder in its Sanitary and Social Bearings," delivered before the Liverpool Association for the Promotion of Social Science, presided over by Lord Brougham. He eventually published his findings in a book: *Infanticide: its Law, Prevalence, Prevention and History* (London, 1862), concluding: "We cannot ignore the fact that the crime of infanticide, as well as that of criminal abortion, is widespread and on the increase."

A survey of the British press in the 1860s reveals the frequent findings of dead infants under bridges, in parks, in culverts and ditches, and even in cesspools. The *Standard* in 1862 denounced "this execrable system of wholesale murder," while the *Morning Star* in 1863 asserted that "this crime is positively becoming a national institution." In Parliament an outraged member declared that the country seemed to be reveling in "a carnival of infant slaughter, to hold every year a massacre of the Innocents."[25]

In February, 1867, Dr. Curgeven, Dr. Ryan, and a formidable delegation of medical men from the elite Harveian Society called upon the Home Secretary with a lengthy list of specific recommendations for checking the increase in infanticide, with emphasis on the need for the registration of all child nurses and for annual reports on all "baby farms." The government acted with no more than its habitual alacrity, and it was only in 1870 that it was further pressed by the Infant Protection Society founded by Dr. Curgeven and when the country was shocked by the news that in Brixton and Peckham two women were discovered to have left no fewer than sixteen infant corpses in various fairly obvious places. The women were tried for murder and one of them was convicted and executed. Parliament at long last set up a committee to study the best means "of preventing the destruction of the lives of infants put out to nurse for hire by their parents." It can hardly have come as a surprise to the members that babies commonly died through being given improper or insufficient food, opiates, drugs, etc. In many baby-farms they were in crowded rooms, with bad air, and suffered from want of cleanliness and willful neglect, resulting in diarrhea, convulsions, and wasting away. The evidence was more than enough to induce Parliament to pass in 1872 the first Infant Life Protection Act providing for compulsory registration of all houses in which more than one child under the age of one were in charge for more than twenty-four hours. Each such house was required to have a license issued by a justice of the peace, and all deaths, including still-births, which had not previously been recorded, were to be reported at once. The penalty for violation of the law was to be a fine of £5 or imprisonment for six months.[26]

Less was heard or written about infanticide in the last quarter of the nineteenth and in the twentieth century. This was certainly a reflection of the beneficial results of the abolition of the *tours* in France, Belgium, and other countries, and of the increasingly stringent regulations in

Britain.[27] But credit must also be given to the growing public interest in maternity and child care, and to the progress in pediatrics which contributed to the reduction of the high infant mortality rate. Finally, consideration must also be given to the adoption and spread of contraceptive practices, even among the lower classes. Nonetheless, infanticide continued and still persists, albeit on a much lower scale. The ignorance and recklessness of many young people, and initially the expense and inconvenience of contraceptive devices made the unwed mother and the illegitimate child a continuing social problem. Only since the Second World War has the contraceptive pill, the intrauterine devices, and the legalization of abortion removed all valid excuses for unwanted pregnancy or infanticide. To the extent that these problems still exist, at least in western society, they are due primarily to carelessness, ignorance, or indifference.

William L. Langer is Archibald Cary Coolidge Professor of History, Emeritus, at Harvard University. The author of several books on diplomatic history, he is also the editor of the Encyclopedia of World History *(fifth edition, 1972) and of the twenty-volume series* The Rise of Modern Europe. *In recent years he has devoted himself chiefly to the furtherance of psychohistory and to the history of the European population.*

REFERENCES

1. Asen Balikči: *The Netailik Eskimo* (New York, 1970), chap. vii. I am indebted for this reference to my friend Professor Jerrold R. Zacharias of the Massachusetts Institute of Technology.
2. According to Dr. John B. Beck: "On infanticide in its relation to Medical Jurisprudence" (in his *Researches in Medicine and Medical Jurisprudence* second, revised edition, New York 1835) 13, this Chinese custom was still prevalent in the 1830s. Léon Lallemand: *Histoire des enfants abandonées et délaissés* (Paris, 1885), 606 ff. cites efforts of provincial governors as late as the 1870s to suppress infanticide. A basic work is P. Palâtre: *L'infanticide en Chine* (Shanghai, 1878).
3. Plato: *The Republic,* Books V and VII; Aristotle: *Politics* (Jowett Translation), II, 6-7; VII, 4, 16. The Greek attitude and practice is well discussed by A. R. Hands: *Aspects of Greek and Roman Life* (Ithaca, N.Y., 1968) 66 ff. Classical thought and attitudes were systematically discussed by M. de Gouroff (Antoine J. Dugour) in his *Essai sur l'histoire des enfants trouvés* (Paris, 1829), the first and only published volume of an exhaustive study the remainder of which was eagerly awaited by his contemporaries. See also Léon Lallemand: *Histoire des enfants trouvés et délaissés* (Paris, 1885) 71 ff.; William B. Ryan: *Infanticide: its Law, Prevalence, Prevention and History* (London, 1862), Part III. Recent studies are for the most part confined to medical and legal aspects of the problem, but see A. M. Carr-Saunders: *The*

Population Problem (Oxford, 1922), 256 ff.; John T. Noonan, Jr.: *The Morality of Abortion* (Cambridge, Mass., 1970).

4. For details, based largely on inscriptions, see W. W. Tarn: *Hellenistic Civilization* (third edition, 1952, 100-102); Hands: *op. cit.,* 68 ff. I am indebted for these references to my friend and colleague Professor Mason Hammond.

5. J. P. Balsdon: *Roman Women* (London, 1962), 196-197; Jerome Carpopino: *Daily Life in Ancient Rome* (New Haven, 1940), 77; Lallemand: *op. cit.,* 38, 53.

6. Beck: *op. cit.,* 11-12; John T. Noonan, Jr.: *Contraception* (Cambridge, Mass., 1965) 85.

7. Among the Hebrews, as among many peoples, the patriarch or head of the family had absolute power of life and death over members of his family, including the right to decide the fate of new-born babies. However, fruitfulness without limit was one of the very first commandments; hence infanticide was all but unknown. (Raphael Patai: *Sex and Society in the Bible and the Middle East* (New York, 1959), 136 ff. De Gouroff: *op. cit.,* 8, 12; Beck: *op. cit.,* 8, 12; Noonan: *op. cit.,* 86; Lallemand: *op. cit.,* 21 ff.

8. The attitude of the Christian Emperors was somewhat ambivalent. Constantine never explicitly forbade infanticide and the later Emperors did nothing to abolish exposure or the sale of exposed children as slaves. Not until the legislation of Justinian (529) was the subjection of foundlings to slavery forbidden. De Gouroff: *op. cit.,* 57 ff., 73 ff.; 85 ff.; Noonan: *op. cit.,* 86 ff.: Amédé Bonde: *Etude sur l'infanticide, l'exposition et la condition des enfants exposés en droit romain* (Paris, 1883).

9. A. E. R. Boak: *Manpower Shortage and the Fall of the Roman Empire in the West* (Ann Arbor, 1955).

10. William E. H. Lecky: *A History of European Morals from Augustus to Charlemagne* (London, 1869), II, 27.

11. H. Bode: "Die Kindestötung und ihre Strafe im Nürnberg des Mittelalters" (*Archiv für Strafrecht und Strafprozess,* LXI, 1914, 430-481). Y-B. Brissaud: "L'infanticide à la fin du Moyen Age, ses motivations psychologiques et sa répression" (*Revue Historique de Droit Francais et Etranger,* L. 1972, 229-256) concludes, on the basis of French records that this penalty, while it remained on the books as a deterrent, had disappeared by the fifteenth century.

12. Richard C. Trexler: "Infanticide in Florence" (*History of Childhood Quarterly,* I, 1973, 98-115). Mrs. Baines: "On the Prevention of Excessive Infant Mortality" (*Transactions of the Manchester Statistical Society,* 1868-1869, 1-20); Alfons Fischer: *Geschichte des deutschen Gesundheitswesens* (Berlin, 1933), II, 240; Arthur Thomsen: "Bankvavningen" (*Acta Reg. Societatis Humaniorum Litterarum Lundensis,* LVIII, 1960), with German summary, pp. 225 ff.; P. E. H. Hair: "Death from Violence in Britain" (*Population Studies,* XXV, 1971, 5-24).

13. The early history of the London Foundling Hospital was recorded by Jonas Hanway, an eminent philanthropist and one of the Hospital's governors. See his *Candid Historical Account of the Hospital for the Reception of Exposed and Deserted Young Children* (London, 1759), as well as the account of Hanway's biographer, John Pugh: *Remarkable Occurrences in the Life of Jonas Hanway, Esq.* (second edition, London, 1788). John Brownlow's *The History*

and Design of the Foundling Hospital (London 1868) is a basic treatment, but may be supplemented by M. Dorothy George: *London Life in the Eighteenth Century* (London, 1925) chap. v, and by the beautifully illustrated work by R. H. Nichols and F. A. Wray: *The History of the Foundling Hospital* (London, 1935).

14. See the glowing account of the eminent English physician A. B. Granville: *St. Petersburgh* (second edition, London, 1829), II, 290 ff.; and the enthusiastic observations of the well-known German traveler Johan G. Kohl: *Petersburg in Bildern und Skizzen* (second edition, Dresden, 1846), II, 72 ff. See also Bernice Madison: "Russia's Illegitimate Children" (*Slavic Review*, XXII, 1963, 82-95

15. The swaddling clothes, which generally equalled in weight that of the baby, were frequently too tightly wound. According to Dr. William Cadogan, chief physician of the London Foundling Hospital and author of one of the earliest handbooks of child care, the newborn babes were often "crammed with cakes, sweetmeats, etc. until they foul their blood, choak their vessels, pall the appetite, and ruin every faculty of their bodies." Cadogan: *An Essay upon Nursing and the Management of Children* (London, 1748; fifth edition, 1752), a book full of sane advice. Also Dr. John Theobald: *The Young Wife's Guide to the Management of her Children* (London, 1764).

16. The initial phase of the problem is competently treated in Shelby T. McCloy: *The Humanitarian Movement in Eighteenth Century France* (Lexington, Kentucky, 1957), 21 ff. and in Roger Mercier: *L'enfant dans la société du XVIIIe siècle* (Paris, 1961), 29 ff. Brief recent accounts may be found in the present author's articles: "Europe's Initial Population Explosion" (*American Historical Review*, LXIX, 1953, 1-17), and "Checks to Population Growth, 1750-1850" (*Scientific American*, February, 1972). The literature on the subject, now mostly forgotten, was generally by competent writers. The most important were:

Baron de Gerando: *De la bienfaisance publique* (Paris, 1829);
Jean Terme and J. B. Monfalcon: *Histoire des enfants trouvés* (Paris, 1837), a work crowned by the French Academy;
Bernard Remacle: *Des hospices des enfants trouvés en Europe, et principalement en France* (Paris, 1838);
Abbé Adolphe Gaillard: *Recherches administratives, statistiques et morales sur les enfants trouvés* (Paris, 1837);
Louis Benoiston de Chateauneuf: *Considérations sur les enfants trouvés dans les principaux états de l'Europe* (Paris, 1824);
F. S. Hügel: *Die Findelhäuser und das Findelwesen in Europa* (Vienna, 1863);
Ernest Semichon: *Histoire des enfants abandonnés depuis l'Antiquité jusqu'à nos jours* (Paris, 1880);
Léon Lallemand: *Histoire des enfants abandonnés et délaissés* (Paris, 1885).

The progressive abolition of the *tours* is analyzed in detail by Adolphe Baudon: "De la suppression des tours d'enfants trouvés" (*Le Correspondant*, XIX, 1847), 674-718.

17. John Browniow: *The History and Design of the Foundling Hospital* (London, 1868), 7.

18. Brownlow: *op. cit.*, 14.
19. Nichols and Wray: *The History of the Foundling Hospital*, 36 ff.; 47 ff., 56 ff.
20. Dr. George Greaves: "Observations on Some of the Causes of Infanticide" (*Transactions of the Manchester Statistical Society*, 1862-1867, 2-24) quoting Archbold: *Pleading and Evidence in Criminal Cases* (fourteenth edition, 529-530); William B. Ryan: *Infanticide: its Law, Prevalence, Prevention and History* (London, 1862), Part I. These provisions were not changed until enactment of the Infant Life Preservation Act of 1929, making "child destruction" a crime (Nigel Walker: *Crime and Insanity in England* (Edinburgh, 1968), chap. vii.).
21. Disraeli, in his novel *Sybil* (1846).
22. *Daily Telegraph*, September 10, 1862; January 21, 1863.
23. The most popular tranquilizer was Godfrey's Cordial, a concoction of opium, treacle, and a bit of sassafras. In Coventry 3000 children were treated to this remedy, of which ten gallons, enough for 12,000 doses, were sold weekly. In one Lincolnshire town of 6000 a single chemist sold 25½ gallons annually. (Testimony of the eminent physician Dr. John Curgeven, to a Parliamentary inquiry, 1871). See also C. Fraser Brockington: *Public Health in the Nineteenth Century* (Edinburgh, 1965) 225-226.
24. Joseph Kay: *The Social Condition and Education of the People in England and Europe* (London, 1850), I, 433 ff., who added (p. 447): "There can be no doubt, that a great part of the poorer classes of this country are sunk in such a frightful depth of hopelessness, misery and utter degradation, that even mothers forget their affection for their helpless little offspring and kill them, as a butcher does his lambs, in order to make money by the murder, and therewith lessen their pauperism and misery."
25. A thick volume of newspaper clippings in the Harvard Law School Library contains a wealth of evidence.
26. Further refinements were added by the supplementary acts of 1897, 1908 and 1932. See Dr. George F. McCleary: *The Maternity and Child Welfare Movement* (London, 1935), 84 ff.
27. Only in 1938 did Parliament enact the *Infanticide Act,* which recognized infanticide as a crime distinguished from murder. The courts have become increasingly less punitive. In 1961-1965 seventy-two women were convicted of infanticide, but 68.1% of them were put on probation and only one imprisoned for less than six months (Walker: *op. cit.*).

CHAPTER 4

Kissinger: A Psychohistory

DANA
WARD

I. INTRODUCTION

"Nixon, he is not fit to be President."

—Henry Kissinger

Just before Richard Nixon was elected President, the Institute for
Defense Analysis prepared a study of the bureaucracies responsible for
national security policy in the hope that the incoming President, who-
ever it would be, might be better prepared to deal with the demands of
formulating foreign policy. The study concluded: "Neither practition-
ers nor students of national security policy should over-emphasize the
importance of the process or the procedures of decision-making. In the
last analysis, the force of personality tends to over-ride procedures."[1]
With such an admonition from a knowledgeable group of analysts it is
indeed curious that political scientists have been so hostile toward psychohistorians who attempt to incorporate personality into their political
analysis. The teaching positions in most political science departments
are filled either with individuals who possess only a nodding acquaintance with the principles of psychology, or with a few social psychologists whose idea of psychology reminds one of sixteenth century tax-
onomists. The consequence of this attitude is a one-eyed vision of
politics.

We should likewise not attempt an explanation of political life from a solely individual, psychological point of view. Political action is the process by which individuals turn upon their history to transform their lives. There *are* givens in the world, forces, structures and belief-systems, that require specific responses. But the style of response, the personality factor, is as crucial as the imperative to respond. Political style, then, becomes a critical issue in studies which follow a psychohistorical approach: a method of study which takes into consideration both personal and collective motivation.

In this essay, which is a prelude to a more comprehensive study, I hope to demonstrate the impact of Henry Kissinger's personality on the foreign policy decision-making process. The political emphasis in this essay is primarily on the first administration. A discussion of the second administration up until resignation will be reserved for a later essay.

As will be demonstrated below, there are a number of basic tensions in Kissinger's psyche which influence the manner in which he perceives the world and consequently the actions which he recommends and undertakes. While on a personal, inner level Kissinger tends to have an undervalued sense of self which gives rise to depression, timidness, and lack of confidence, he presents a public figure of arrogance, strong will and competence. Kissinger has a tendency to use theoretical abstractions as a means of keeping people away, yet he exhibits a counter-vailing, excessive need for love and praise. Accompanying this tendency toward abstraction is a lack of concern for human considerations in his intellectual formulations. Most importantly, for our purposes, there seems to be a tension between the avoidance of, and compulsive confrontation with, risks. This tendency leads Kissinger to place himself in situations where he can publicly test his will and consequently prove his inherent "goodness" and "worth". An attempt also will be made to assess the role that Kissinger's attachment to historical and contemporary individuals has played in his attempt to resolve the inner tensions mentioned above. Finally, I will try to demonstrate that these various tendencies coalesce into a configuration of behavior typical of the depressive, or dysmutual, personality,[2] and that the patterns of behavior attendant upon such an organization of personality have combined to affect specific policy decisions such as the invasion of Cambodia, the mining of Haiphong, the secret peace negotiations, the peace settlement, and our relations with our "allies".

II. THE EARLY DAYS IN GERMANY

"One cannot escape the feeling that the President's advisor is a man who would like to be loved."
                                                    —*Look*, August 12, 1969

Fuerth, the town in which Alfred Heinz Kissinger was born early in the morning on May 27, 1923, was a South German industrial city with a population at the time of about 64,000. Fuerth was a natural settling place for many Jews who were not allowed to live in nearby Nuremburg. The city had a century-old reputation for religious toleration, and one of the families attracted to Fuerth was that of the Kissingers. But the Kissingers were not to enjoy the fruits of religious toleration. While Fuerth's reputation perhaps forestalled the effects of Hitler's rise to power, in the end Fuerth, too, would bear the scar of Hitler's terror. Through either emigration or extermination, "of Fuerth's pre-1933 population of 3,000 Jews, only 70 were on hand to attend the first postwar religious services."[3]

Obviously, life for Jews in Fuerth was not easy. With the passage of the Nuremburg laws in 1935, the somewhat stable middle class lives that, even through the depression, many were able to maintain were permanently disrupted. And among those families that suffered humiliation, privation and death at the hands of the Nazis were the Kissingers. Included among those who were killed by the Nazis were twelve relatives in Kissinger's family.[4]

Louis Kissinger was the head of the Kissinger household. In 1922, at the age of 35, he married Paula Stern, then 21 and his former student, who came from a middle-class Jewish family. A year later their first of two sons was born. The birth certificate listed the child's name as Alfred Heinz, but until fifteen years later when he changed his name to Henry, the Alfred was dropped and he would be called Heinz. Another year passed and in 1924 the second and last of the Kissinger children was born and named Walter Bernhard. Louis Kissinger, "a gentle, softhearted teacher in a girls' 'high school',"[5] was himself a son of a village school teacher. The home that he maintained for his wife and two children can be best described as middle class. The Kissingers lived in a five-room flat containing many books and a piano, and they were well enough off to be able to maintain a servant. Louis Kissinger was a deeply religious man, and the children were brought up accordingly. The elder Kissinger was a respected man in his community. In Germany, the position of *Studienrat* which he held at the Madchen Lyceum was of much greater social standing than the equivalent status of a high school teacher in the United States. A boarder who lived with the Kissingers in the early thirties has recalled: "Mr. Kissinger is a very serious, conscientious individual. Upper-most in his mind was providing for his family. And I think he felt he couldn't take too many chances."[6] To be deprived of his teaching position then would have had a devastating affect upon him and his family. That however, was precisely what occurred in 1935 when the Nuremburg laws forbade any Jew from holding a government position. Louis Kissinger lost his job and with it the economic security his family had enjoyed until then.[7]

But economic security was not all that the Kissingers were to suffer. In addition to the strictures on holding government jobs, the Nuremburg laws also required that Jewish children leave public schools to attend special, all-Jewish institutions. Thus Heinz was forced to attend the special school. Heinz was not a particularly bright student while in Germany—at least according to the usual indicators such as grades.[8] But in light of his brilliant performance in more favorable circumstances after he left Germany, we would not be totally off base if we assumed that Heinz's grades suffered as a result of the adverse conditions during this period.

One could hardly blame young Heinz if his mind were not on his studies. He would have had to be aware of the fragility of his father's status and his father's anxiety undoubtedly would have been transmitted to the children. But if somehow the situation at home escaped Heinz's attention, he became painfully aware of what it meant to be Jewish when he was on the streets of Fuerth. "Jewish children, when they ventured onto the streets or playground would be cornered and beaten up by Hitler Youth. Among the children getting this bloody lesson in politics was Heinz Kissinger."[9] In his later years, Kissinger would comment, "My life in Fuerth passed without leaving any lasting impressions. I can't remember any interesting or amusing incidents."[10] But the lessons of the street did leave a lasting, although hardly amusing, impression. One of the incidents that he does remember is that: "The other children would beat us up."[11] This was a painful reminder that he was not like the others. In his later life, while there were numerous other factors, his treatment at the hands of other children would be one contribution to Kissinger's anxiety about being left out and disliked.

Aside from a few references to soccer and to the beatings suffered on the streets of Fuerth, Henry Kissinger has been uniformly reluctant to attribute any significance to his early life, or for that matter, to even talk about it. While a member of the White House staff, Kissinger sloughed off reporters' questions about his life in Germany by saying that his life in Fuerth "left no lasting impressions", or "that part of my childhood is *not* a key to anything."[12] Even more strongly: "I was not consciously unhappy. I was not so acutely aware of what was going on. For children those things are not that serious. It is fashionable now to explain everything psychoanalytically, but let me tell you, the political persecutions of my childhood are not what control my life."[13]

If not to children, then to whom are "those things" serious? Kissinger was fifteen years old when he left Germany, an age when he simply could not have been unaware of what was happening around him. By 1938 Jews were being murdered on the streets, and that year marks the beginning of Hitler's systematic roundup of Jews after the murder of Vom Rath. It would seem that Kissinger's poor memory is a sustained effort to decrease the value and importance of his early life. This period in Germany was the "bad time"—it only served, in Kissinger's view, as a restraint, an obstacle to be overcome, and once overcome, forgotten.

A child three years older than Henry also lived for five years in the Kissinger household as a boarder, yet his memory of that period is somewhat less hazy: "The whole community was aware of what was coming. And maybe being so close to Nuremburg where they had the Party Congresses we got an earlier warning."[14] Living in the same household the young boarder received a very different, almost opposite, impression; rather than being unaware, the Jewish community in Fuerth seems to have received an earlier warning of the coming chaos.

Kissinger has devoted his entire life to trying to understand how such disruptions as Hitler's persecution of Jews and expansionary provocations arise, and how best to avert the pain and suffering attendant upon such disruptions, yet he refuses to make the connection that his own experience as an object of such chaos was important for his later pursuits. Throughout Kissinger's work is the theme of the opposition between the forces of chaos and the forces of order.[15] Kissinger's concerns for balance and chaos are not unrelated, but rather they form two sides of an almost arithmetic law in Kissinger's psycho-logic. As has been said, "The corollary of Kissinger's sense of the tragic is his passion for international order."[16] Indeed Kissinger has been described by close friends as possessing a "morbid preoccupation" with the contemplation of chaos. Thus it would appear that Kissinger's denial of the importance of his early years is somehow over-determined; rather than those years being unimportant as he would have us believe, they are the rock upon which his personality and life have been built.

In an article which attempted to describe the social origins of the depressive personality, Howard Rome has pointed to the tendency for such individuals to view the world as one in which chaos is the predominant characteristic. He says: "It is a world in which man's views of the universe—if he has any—offer little hope and less consolation, in which his view of his fellowmen is jaundiced and malign. It is a world whose predominant characteristic is chaos."[17] Kissinger is certainly not without his views of the universe. As will be shown in the latter discussion of his intellectual work and in the discussion of his identity, Rome's de-

scription of the "ideology" of the depressive personality is consistent
with Kissinger's view of the world and himself. We must assume that the
conditions of Kissinger's early life in Germany are the social root of
what will be shown to be a depressive personality. But the social origins
of the depressive personality are only half of the equation. To fully understand the development it is imperative that we look to early childhood family relations.

The depressive personality is a diagnostic category for a broad, but
specific range of behavior. It is not intended as a pigeon-hole, but
simply a conceptual tool for trying to understand the dynamics of an
individual's interaction with the world. The analysis of numerous case
studies has revealed that the depressive personality is the consequence
of a particular kind of family politics. The basic family alignment is
characterized by ambivalent parents and a favored sibling. The father
is often uninvolved with the children, and the mother may feel resentment toward her husband, may never really have wanted to be a
mother, or feels that the child is both a burden and an obstacle before
her escape from marriage. Lack of involvement or absence from the
family on the part of the parents leads to a sense of abandonment on
the part of the child; he feels alone. This feeling is reinforced if there is
a sibling who receives the attention of the parents. The sense that the
child derives from the parents' behavior is that one is not automatically
loved and accepted, nor is one automatically good. Acceptance and
goodness are earned, and love is the reward. The corrollary is that the
child feels basically worthless and bad.

It is this sense of worthlessness and the inability to elicit love which
is the root feeling of the depressive personality. The predominant feelings experienced by the child are weakness, inferiority, and a lack of
self-esteem. There is a tendency to withdraw from others, and an inability to form meaningful relationships for fear that the other will
discover one's worthlessness.

The behaviors which result from the familial politics and existential
experience of the self are many. "The dysmutual tries to overcome his
low self-esteem in many ways, one of which is through extreme ambition. Some dysmutuals, in milder stages of the disorder, rather than escape into manic moods, try to compensate for feelings of inferiority by
excessive work, long working hours and an over-all drive for supremacy."[18] In addition, "Dysmutuals are *insatiable* in love, sex, friendship,
glory, status or possessions."[19] They tend also to be tactless, alienating
their friends. "They are perpetually depressed and always on the defensive. Pleasant and friendly moods are like rays of sunshine that
break through the clouds."[20] There is in addition a tendency to be vulnerable to criticism. Finally, the dysmutual "repeats the pattern of his
childhood, forever trying to induce women to love him."[21]

It should be emphasized that the depressive personality can range from well integrated to psychotic depression. The purpose of classification is not to determine how neurotic an individual might be. The category simply represents an over-all pattern of behavior, world view, and values which are consistent regardless of the degree of personality integration. By matching the hypothesized behavior with the actual behavior we are able to assess the validity, or falsity, of the hypothesis. From there we can begin to understand the dynamic tensions and the reasons behind actions. To what degree then do the characteristics described above fit the family pattern in the Kissinger household?

The impression received by most people who knew the family and have commented upon it was that the Kissinger household was a harmonious one. Both parents were respected by the children and there seems to have been little conflict between the parents. Just as uniformly, the impression has been that Mrs. Kissinger was the dominant influence in the family. Based upon an interview with a man who as a child came to live with the Kissingers, it has been said: "While Louis was the authority figure in Fuerth, his wife dominated the family with her charm, a quality that became more significant later, in exile. 'He was the boss, but she was a strong woman, a very intelligent, aggressive woman.' "[22] Interviews that I had had with Kissinger's friends have also born out this impression. It is felt that the power behind the paternal throne lay with Mrs. Kissinger. As we will see below, it is Mrs. Kissinger who is the model for action and who in the early years in New York was the economic and social backbone of the family.

Louis Kissinger, in fact, was little involved with the children. And it may be this lack of involvement which was the most predominant characteristic of the father's role in the family. Even much later this attitude is reflected with respect to Henry's rise to power: "Louis Kissinger, now 87, had been a bit diffident about his eldest son's success, because it entailed so much travel on the Sabbath, a Washington Heights rabbi said. But with the Nobel Prize, Louis' joy was complete. 'Henry had made good to the nth degree.' "[23] This comment coming from a man close to Louis Kissinger may very well reflect the ambivalent atmosphere in which Henry grew up—one in which he was expected to make good in order to be loved. Indeed, one suspects that making good was by no means enough, given his father's "diffident" attitude even after so much success.

Every indication is that for the most part the children were the mother's responsibility. Louis Kissinger's most immediate involvement was as an administer of familial justice, although Mrs. Kissinger herself was not the least bit hesitant to assume that role. As the boarder in the family recalls: "From a disciplinary point of view, if she didn't like anything she didn't need Mr. Kissinger. If Walter or Henry did something wrong she took matters in her own hands and didn't burden her husband with the everyday events. She is a very resolute, energetic woman. A strong willed woman."[24]

The first pattern of behavior which emerges that may shed light on the significant events in Henry's early development is the difference between him and his brother Wally. His father recalls, "Henry was always the thinker. He was more inhibited than Wally. Wally was more the doer, more the extrovert."[25] The boarder in the family also recalled when I asked about the differences between the two boys, "Like night and day. Now remember, it was a long time ago, but Walter was the more out-going. . . . Henry was withdrawn, studious and a dreamer . . . I would say Henry takes after his father and Walter after his mother."[26]

The differences between Walter and Henry are an interesting comparison. All who knew the family in the German years recall that Henry was even then a loner, withdrawn and timid. Walter on the other hand seems to have impressed others with his ingenuity and his outgoing, aggressive manner. Surprise is often expressed by those who knew the family in the early years that it was Henry and not Walter who has emerged upon the public scene. But what is important is that there is a sharp contrast in personality between the two boys which would lead one to ask what is the source of that difference. Indeed it is not unusual for an active and expressive child to draw more attention than one who is withdrawn, reinforcing established patterns. But what was the initial source of the differentiation in personalities?

The difference between the two boys must lie much earlier in their development. Unfortunately there is no direct evidence. We can only postulate that with the arrival of the second child, Henry experienced a sense of loss as a result of his mother's need to devote attention to the new-born child. While it is highly doubtful that there was any frank rejection of Henry, the arrival of the new sibling could have led to a sense of neglect, followed by a withdrawal into the self and a sense of self-depreciation. Of course, without any direct source of verification this is simply speculation, but speculation which would begin to explain the earliest experiences which led to basic patterns of behavior in Henry's later years.

Frequently a child who is accustomed to the attentions of his mother interprets the diminished attention that comes with a new sibling as rejection. This sense of rejection is at the core of the depressive personality and its result is a withdrawal into the self. *If* this is what occurred in Kissinger's case it would begin to explain the differences between himself and Walter. And Kissinger's experience vis a vis his brother would be marked by a sense of unsuccessful competition which would reinforce the tendency to withdraw.

In the families of severely disturbed depressive personalities the familial relations are usually characterized by "a hostile mother, a disinterested or hostile father, and siblings favored by the mother."[27] But it is important to note that "parental rejection need not be associated with pathological hostility; an infant may feel rejected whenever his mother is sick, hospitalized, or unable to take care of him, when she is pregnant with another child, (or) when she works outside her home."[28]

To what extent then do Kissinger's parents fit this pattern which can lead to depressive anxiety? The evidence is agonizingly skimpy, but there is some nevertheless which would indicate that Kissinger felt a sense of rejection and ambivalence from his mother, disinterest from his father, and lived with siblings who were more favored. On this last point we have more substantial evidence upon which to base our judgment.

In 1930, when Henry was seven, another boy, Jack Heiman, came to live with the Kissingers. Jack was ten at the time, and because there was no Jewish school in his village he came to Fuerth to attend the Isrealitische Realschule where Henry was also going to school. Jack boarded with the Kissingers and moved into the boys' room. Today Heiman is a handicrafts dealer in Chicago and he recalls of his life then: "When I think of it today . . . they treated me like a third son. In fact they leaned over backward to be less strict with me. They never hit me, and they weren't bashful with Henry and Walter. They really got it. We were all in the same bedroom at night sometimes too noisy and rambunctious while Mr. Kissinger was grading papers. He'd come in and hit them—but not me, even though I was equally guilty."[29]

Here Henry was faced with the entrance of a "third" son who is obviously given preferential treatment. To make matters worse, it appears that Jack became closer friends with Walter than with Henry. "I was closer to Walter even though he was the younger."[30] Thus it would be understandable if Henry got the feeling that he was low man on the totem pole.

Jack's amnesty from corporal punishment was not the only special treatment afforded him by the Kissingers. "I remember that during the time I was there, every afternoon she spent her time tutoring me. She didn't have to but she did. And the boys didn't need it. I was the dummy. They treated me like a third son."[31] Heiman insists that the boys felt no resentment over the fact that their mother devoted her afternoons to him and not to Walter or Henry. But the attention given Jack could hardly have gone unnoticed.[32]

One form of behavior which may have been a means of overcoming this specific situation, but most certainly the more general milieu, was what seems to have been a highly competitive relationship between Jack and Henry. Jack recalls, "Henry always had a strong desire to win. Behind the house there was a little yard, and every free moment we went down and tried to play against one another. Henry was a very determined individual."[33] Henry was determined to win against the competitor for his mother's attention, perhaps thereby to win her love.

Mrs. Kissinger was described variously by Heiman as "very strong and astute", "very intelligent", "aggressive", "energetic", "resolute", and "strong willed". She was active in her community and "in addition to being a house wife had other intellectual interests."[34] The one characteristic which is particularly important is that "she just wasn't satisfied with housework."[35] It was this dissatisfaction which precipitated Jack's tutoring as a means by which she could exercise her mind and perform a useful function. At the same time however her dissatisfaction must have been communicated to the children. How would they interpret this communication? Were *they* the cause of her dissatisfaction?

There is one further comment by Heiman which might provide some insight into the atmosphere of the Kissinger household. In this case Heiman is speaking generally, and not in specific reference to the Kissinger household: "This kind of upbringing breeds bashfulness and insecurity. You don't have the opportunity to be on your own. Parents do not impose their will on kids as much now as then, and I think we matured later because of this."[36] The children obeyed the family laws and tried to live up to their parents' expectations, but they were hard tasks and great expectations. It is a situation in which it would be difficult to feel good about oneself and in which there was little one could do to change the situation. Thus we have the essential elements for the development of the depressive personality: an ambivalent attitude on the part of the parents, depreciation of self-esteem, and a sense of powerlessness.

Of course, none of these feelings were in any way so extreme as to border on the pathological. All I am trying to establish is whether there is any evidence for a familial base upon which the social repression experienced by Kissinger could build an edifice whose most prominent characteristic would be depressive anxiety and the patterns of behavior characteristic of such an organization of personality. Such a supposition is consistent with Kissinger's later personality patterns; all I can here show is that it is not inconsistent with what can be reconstructed of his childhood experience.

It is likely that it was with respect to religion that the greatest paternal expectations were placed upon the children. Until Henry went into the army he would be an extremely religious youth: "He put on tfillin (phylacteries for morning prayers) and went to synagogue regularly."[37] It also seems that Henry's rebellion against his father was in this most crucial area.

Louis's decline as the central figure in the family is the predominant change in the family relations, a change upon which many have commented. The man essential to Kissinger's own personal transformation, Fritz Kraemer, has said:

> You can do damage to the soul of a man and never touch his body. For five years, the most formative years (10-15), Henry had to undergo this horror. And the real horror is the breakdown of the world. Imagine what it means when your father, who was your authority, the father you admire . . . is suddenly transformed into a frightened little mouse."[38]

When the Kissingers left Germany, Louis' role in the family was even further undermined. "Louis Kissinger, a former teacher over 50 then and fated to end his working life as a bookkeeper, had to accept his changed status meekly."[39] We will discuss this process further below, but what happened in Kissinger's relation to his father was to set Henry on a search for strong individuals who would not accept things so meekly. The immediate form this process took was to renounce the role expectation that was most important to his father. "As his father's shadow diminished, Henry slipped out from beneath it, beginning his long rebellion against orthodox Jewishness."[40] This was Henry's way of saying "I will not accept things as they are."

What would the timid and withdrawn youth of Fuerth do with the resentment and hostility which he must have felt as a consequence of his familial and social experience? What would he do with the rage he must have felt over his treatment as a Jew? "In the 30's in the streets of Fuerth, he was powerless".[41] He could do nothing and his father could do nothing. About the only viable alternative for the young Heinz would have been to turn his rage inward and withdraw further into his protective shell. This would seem to be the path he followed, and his turning inward would have consequences in the formation of his self-image.

Kissinger was to learn many lessons in Fuerth that he would carry with him the rest of his life. He was to discover what it meant to be powerless, to be out of control of one's life, to see his heroes standing helpless, overtaken by events. As Kissinger moved out into the world, he would confront situations that would stir memories, perhaps unconscious, of the time spent in Fuerth. As he faced those situations he would often respond as he had learned to respond in the past. And, as he began to form his world view in more explicit terms, he would bring his past with him to be incorporated into his vision. At times, the responses that were adequate for the past would carry him through the present difficulty. But just as often the old ghosts would come back to haunt him—the insecurities, the fear of not being accepted—and his response, both for himself and, as special assistant to the President, for the nation, would confound his difficulties. It was in Fuerth that Kissin-

ger experienced the tragedy which he feels has given him an understanding of the world different from other Americans who, having "never
suffered disaster, find it difficult to comprehend a policy conducted
with a premonition of catastrophe."[42]

III. THE RETREAT ACROSS THE OCEAN:
THE SEARCH FOR A HERO

"Sooner or later, these states on the fringe of the Eurasian land
mass would be drawn into the Communist orbit. The source of
our culture and our values would then be alienated. Americans,
for the first time in our history, would live in a world where we
were foreign in the deepest sense, where people would share
neither our values nor our aspirations, where we might meet hostility everywhere outside of North America."
                                   —Kissinger, *Necessity for Choice*

When Heinz became Henry in New York, it would be some time
before he was comfortable with his new identity—the symbol of which
was his name change. The move to New York would not substantially
change his condition. His father still would find making a living extremely difficult, his mother would become the family's primary financial support, and, most of all, Henry would still be different from the
majority. Like in Fuerth, there would be other refugees who shared his
differentness, but to the majority he was still unacceptable, and this
feeling would continue to activate his earlier depressive anxieties.
    The most immediate symbol of his differentness was his accent.
" 'I was terribly self-conscious about it (his accent)' he says, 'I finally
lost my self-consciousness over it, I'd say about 1957 or so.' "[43] The
date at which he attributes his loss of self-consciousness is by no means
arbitrary. It was in 1957 that Kissinger was to be finally "accepted".
This was the year that the public recognized Kissinger's worth, for his
book *Nuclear Weapons and Foreign Policy* was published and stayed on
the best seller lists for fourteen weeks. However, his acceptance was not
total, particularly in the intellectual world.[44] And Kissinger's fear that
he would not be accepted stayed with him. It is still one reason that until the last year of the first administration he did not allow his heavily
accented voice to be recorded in most news conferences.[45]
    Kissinger's chief of staff in the first administration, Brigadier General
Alexander Haig, has remarked that Kissinger "is not always sure he'll be
accepted. He doesn't really believe anybody likes him."[46] It is this trait
that is the most prevalent vestige of his life in Fuerth and the early days

in New York. His uncertainty is what led some of his colleagues at Harvard to characterize him as a "damp-handed" professor. And it was this uncertainty about his self that led Kissinger to turn inward and retreat into the seeming safety of his inner world. If he never confronted other people, then the world he had maintained within his self would not be disrupted.

Kissinger never really gave anyone the chance to reject him. He placed himself in a sort of exile after he left Germany that was not simply political. As before, the manner with which he dealt with the threatening environment of New York "was to go deep in his shell. From 1939-43 when he was going to George Washington High School in New York, Kissinger seems to have made no friends—hence the survival of the German accent."[47] Thus his fear of being unacceptable inadvertently insured that the mark of his difference would not leave him. Perhaps on one level Kissinger was afraid of being swallowed up by the majority. In that case his retreat might be an attempt to maintain what little vestiges of his self he still retained.

As was mentioned, when the Kissinger family left Germany for New York, young Henry's position in the world was not fundamentally changed. True, there was no longer an imminent fear of death, but Kissinger was still the outsider, still in his own mind unacceptable because of his differentness. For youth, such a cultural position can be just as threatening to the psyche as the political persecutions in Germany were to the person. So in a strict sense, Kissinger was right in saying that the political persecutions of his youth were not what control his life. But the implication that there are no answers to Kissinger's adult life to be found in his youth is utterly wrong. Many of the cultural obstacles in front of social acceptance that Kissinger found in Germany, he would also find in America.

His years in New York passed without any great crisis or turning point. During his days at George Washington High School he worked after school in a shaving brush factory squeezing acid out of the brush bristles for the Leopold Ascher Co., and after a while he was promoted to delivery boy. For the most part Henry remained uninvolved with others and withdrawn.

Accompanying Kissinger's tendency to withdraw into himself was a tendency to avoid confrontation with others. He recalls that "if he was walking down the street in New York and saw a group of boys approaching the other way, he would cross to the opposite sidewalk."[48] This may have been an appropriate response given his experience in Fuerth, but nowhere do we have evidence of Kissinger testing his courage and walking through the crowd. Nowhere do we see his willingness to "contemplate the abyss, . . . as a challenge to be overcome—or to perish in the process," which he now advocates.

This tendency to retreat in the face of confrontation however is a trait which intellectually Kissinger dislikes strenuously. Behind his severest criticisms of historical figures and one of the major criticisms of the Kennedy Administration was his abhorrence of a "wait and see" attitude or of a policy that avoided confrontation. For example in *The Necessity for Choice* Kissinger argues:

> History for Communism is an incentive for action, a guarantee of the meaningfulness of sacrifice. The West, on the other hand, has a tendency to use evolutionary theory as a bromide. Waiting for history to do its work for it, it stands in danger of being engulfed by the currents of our time.[49]

Failing to act in the face of the historical imperative is the major sin in Kissinger's international catechism.

Like many of Kissinger's likes and dislikes, this particular idiosyncrasy also has its roots in Fuerth. While Kissinger's father was a respected man in his community, he was not a forceful man. He was the "gentle and soft-hearted" man whom Kissinger has described as "a man of great goodness in a world where goodness had no meaning."[50] In other words, his father was a man whose qualities were irrelevant in the real world. "His father was stripped of his post and humiliated . . . he had been broken in spirit."[51] "In Manhattan, of course, his erudition was irrelevant and he had to fall back on drearily unskilled clerical work."[52] Louis Kissinger was not a man who would, or could, stand up against the wave of history. Rather, he would wait things out, wait to see what would happen. Like many other intellectuals "he waited hopefully for Germany to come back to its senses."[53] Finally he was convinced that waiting was not the answer; but it was not through great deliberation that he came to this conclusion. It was forced upon him by his wife. It was Mrs. Kissinger who was responsible for getting the family out of Germany in 1938. She was the model of action. She made arrangements with relatives in England, took English lessons, and the family escaped from Germany.

Kissinger's mother, like many other refugee women, must have possessed a strong sense of self, for she adapted very well to her new role in America. She was not used to menial labor and in New York where the only work she could get was as a cook, she would have needed a strong sense of self to accept the change in status. The change was generally a difficult thing to handle in most of the German-Jewish refugee families who came to America, particularly for men. It was difficult for men in the family to carry on as they had been able to do in Germany. This was the case in the Kissinger family. And "the change in status is something which the children (Henry and Wally) were conscious of."[54] Although Louis Kissinger had been less of a forceful figure in the family than his wife while they were in Germany, he was still the primary provider and deserving of the children's respect. But in America even this position was undermined.

Kissinger respected and loved his father, but there was that wish that his father would act, that he would stand up and confront history. Kissinger in the midst of the "bad times" was looking for a hero, and he was to be disappointed that it was not his father.[55] A long-time personal acquaintance of Kissinger has said, "About the deepest things in one's life one can say nothing. Imagine the horror of life in Nazi Germany, imagine seeing a father whom one has loved and revered being made to give up a job, being humiliated. And all this when one is young and defenseless, and so impressionable."[56] Kissinger eventually found men both in history and among his contemporaries who preached the gospel of action and the necessity of confronting history, and it was to these men that he attached himself. But like his father, these men too would ultimately be irrelevant to their times.

Kissinger's search for a hero gave him a version of understanding that he could use in the days of turbulent uprisings by America's youth in the sixties and seventies. On several occasions he has remarked that the youth of today are looking for heroes. After a march in 1969, when Kissinger consulted with a few of the demonstrators, he remarked to a reporter: "I can understand the anguish of the younger generation. They lack models, they have no heroes, they see no great purpose in the world."[57] One must wonder if it is not Kissinger's own anguish in Fuerth, when he needed a model of action, a hero to look to and when there was no purpose in the world, that provides the basis of his understanding. And in a more revealing statement he says:

> I find quite chilling the similarities between the revolutionary romanticism of some of our more radical students today and the young German intellectuals of the 1930's—and I don't mean the Nazi thugs but those idealistic students who were looking for commitment for its own sake. My primary feeling about our students is sadness over the conditions that produced them. They are looking for heroes—not brothers, but for fathers.[58]

Yet if the rhetoric of the youth movement is to be believed, it is not fathers for which youth is looking. The paternalistic patterns of the past are the targets of youthful dissent. The youthful vision of the future is a world not marked by paternalism, but by brotherhood. If anything, the youth movement could be interpreted as an oedipal rebellion in which the fathers are to be struck down and the brothers are to share the power once concentrated in the person of the father. Kissinger's mistake in his interpretation of the youth movement is that he attributes to the young the same need for a hero which he felt as a child. In

Kissinger's mind, hero is father. But in myth, the hero was always a peer, a son, and in the group-process literature it has been found that the heroic figure always emerges from peers and not from leaders.

It is interesting that what Kissinger would like to see established in American foreign policy is a heroic vision. He would hope to provide the "great purpose in the world", or what he calls the Administration's "unifying principle". What he finds distasteful is what he regards as an unheroic policy. For instance, in *Necessity for Choice* he states:

> There was a time when the West believed that an overwhelming economic superiority guaranteed its triumph over Communism— without ever being able to describe just how. Though this attitude was fatuous, it is no less fatuous to draw so much comfort from the hope that when the Soviet Union equals our economic performance it will become as consumer-oriented and bland as we are. This is hardly a heroic attitude, nor one likely to appeal to a world where millions strive for a new sense of direction.[59]

Just as youth need heroes and heroic visions, so do other nations. In order to solve the problems of the world we must rally round our hero. In the following revealing quote Kissinger lays out what role the Presidency must play in providing this heroic figure. The introductory words are Landau's:

> Kissinger's outburst in response to antiwar demonstrations . . . are the haunted dreams of a child of Weimar, the dread specter of revolution and political anarchy, the demise of all recognizable authority: "When you look around the world you see student riots in Berlin, which have co-determination with the universities. You have student riots in Paris which do not have co-determination. You have student riots in the United States which has a race problem, Vietnam and slums. And you have student riots in Holland which has no race problem, no slums and no Vietnam.
>
> "Therefore, you could conclude that what we are facing in this world is not capricious students—I will not say anything as pat as this—but a resolve against a condition of modern society which is much deeper than any policy issue—a state of mind which, precisely because it will not grapple with specific issues, and just with a mood, is very hard to deal with—which leads to rebellion against authority of any kind, not just the authority of this President, but the authority of any President, whether he be president of a university or the President of the United States.
>
> "What we have to attempt to do, really, all of us, is to preserve some vestige of authority in this country, if we are ever going to move with confidence and competence toward a better future. What we have to do in Vietnam inevitably has some elements of ambiguity.

"We have to convince the American people that we will pull
out our troops, but we have to convince Hanoi that the withdrawal is not independent of their actions, so that they have an
incentive to negotiate. We have to do many things which cannot
be done unless the intermediary leadership in this country ...
will at least support the proposition that there is only one man
who can bring peace in Vietnam, and that is the President of the
United States. If confidence in him and in all institutions is systematically destroyed, we will turn into a group that has nothing
left but a physical test of strength and the only outcome of this
is Caesarism."[60]

It would be some time after coming to America that Kissinger's quest
for a hero would be fulfilled, and once fulfilled his ambitions would also
be significantly altered. Before he went into the army to his fateful
meeting with Fritz Kraemer, Kissinger held the modest ambition of becoming an accountant. While at George Washington High School, Kissinger was a straight-A student and upon graduation he began to study ac-
counting at night sessions at the City College of New York, following
his father's adopted profession. But after a short time he was drafted in
1943 and would soon go off to war and the turning point of his life.

The most significant aspect of Kissinger's life in New York was his
failure (or success) at not becoming assimilated to the American culture.
He would always be German. He always maintained a sense of regret at
having had to flee from Hitler. "He was not among those refugees from
Hitler Germany who could look back on their birthplace only with discomfort and bitterness; he was instead one of those refugees who re-
gretted having to leave their country behind."[61] And, "Kissinger would
feel an overwhelming affinity for the greater historical and cultural
tradition into which he had been born."[62] We are unable to know what
the sources of this affinity are, but a good guess would be the influence
of his family life. In his parent's apartment it was Germany. Since he
never established real roots in America until much later, his experience
even in New York was German. And when in time he became interested
in intellectual pursuits, it was not American writers that he would read,
but Europeans. Thus the fundamental pillars of his identity are German,
but since he was no longer in Germany, his adjustment to his new environment was forestalled. He would find a means of entering the
American world and acquiring some form of American identity through
that great leveler and Americanizer, the U.S. Army. The army would
thrust the stamp of America on the young unformed Kissinger.

IV. THE ARMY: A NEW IDENTITY

"Our Generation has succeeded in stealing the fire of the gods
and it is doomed to live with the horror of its achievement."
                                                          —Henry Kissinger

In order to understand the significance of Kissinger's army experience,
it will help first to look at the task facing him in his adolescence.[63] Adolescence is the period in an individual's life during which he gradually
enters the adult world and takes on roles for which life in the family has
prepared him. This period begins at about age twelve and can, under
special conditions, continue on into the late twenties and early thirties.
Emancipation from the family and the establishment of a place in the
greater culture are the goals of adolescent development. It is the time
when the abstract social order and the subjective, inner, familial world
become integrated. All the preparation for adulthood which should
take place during the earlier years is called upon as a guide to the individual's entrance into the greater society. "To enter history each generation of youth must find an identity consonant with its own
childhood, and consonant with an ideological promise in the perceptible historical process."[64] Hopefully there is a continuity between the
childhood experience and the ideological and concrete structure of the
greater culture. When this continuity is lacking, the normal development of adolescent identity formation is disrupted and in many cases
prolonged. And it is just such a discontinuity which Howard Rome argued provided the sociological contribution which, along with the
familial foundation, contributes to the depressive personality.

Erikson has described this period of prolonged adolescence in the
following manner:

The libido theory offers no adequate account of a second period
of delay, namely, prolonged adolescence. Hence the sexually matured individual is more or less retarded in his psychosexual
capacity for intimacy and in the psychosocial readiness for parenthood. This period can be viewed as a psycho-social moratorium
during which the young adult through free role experimentation
may find a niche in some section of his society, a niche which is
firmly defined and yet seems to be uniquely made for him.[65]

Kissinger has shown just the sort of reduced capacity for intimacy
of which Erikson speaks above, and which is characteristic of the depressive personality. His inability to make friends, his problems with his
marriage, and his relations with women can be viewed partially as the
consequence of the historical disruptions which played upon earlier
feelings of disorder and rejection. Kissinger, unsure of who he was, was
unable to give of himself to others for fear of having nothing left for his

own. Kissinger would not find his secure niche until he moved out of his familial world and found a new structure which would provide the necessary roles and role models with which he could identify and in which he could integrate himself.

The role experimentation of adolescence took on a completely different light in view of his new environment. The turning point came with his entrance into the United States Army. In the Army, Kissinger was able to become an actor, although in a circumscribed sense, rather than an object of history. While army life required submission to a hierarchical order, it also provided channels for action far beyond the scope Kissinger had experienced previously. This partial transformation from object to agent is particularly crucial, for accompanying it is a change in Kissinger's character. The balancing factors which form the dynamic tension of his personality are developed during this period.

The army performed three functions in this process: first, it provided the first stable, structured, environmental order outside the family circle; secondly, it provided for his encounter with Fritz Kraemer, the man who was his first heroic model; and thirdly, it provided Kissinger with a means of retribution, an outlet for action against those who had manipulated his earlier life. As Beloff puts it: "It seems that the real transformation from the oppressed and teased foreigner Heinz, to the successfully and proudly integrated American Henry, came during his army service in WWII."[66] It was in the army that Kissinger was able to find the compromise between his conflicting identities. Kissinger gathered his forces and came to terms with himself through an environment in which lines of authority were clearly drawn, roles were explicitly understood, and where he could be reasonably sure of what to expect from day to day. In the army Kissinger could have faith in his environment and the men of authority to whom he could look for guidance.

One of these men would stand up above all and would come to play a role in Kissinger's life up to the present. Kissinger had been sent, after he had been found to have an exceptionally high IQ, to a special training program composed of draftees the army was using as insurance, if they needed special skills later in the war. After six months the program was dropped because of its "undemocratic" character, and Kissinger was transferred to the 84th Division stationed at Camp Clairborne, Louisiana. It was there that Kissinger met Private Fritz Kraemer. Kraemer was a refugee from Prussia where he had been trained as a lawyer and received two PhD's. Kraemer, according to Landau, was:

> fiery and flamboyant and yet indisputably old-world, a capricious European adventurer . . . Kraemer was a highly intelligent man, winning and captivating in his brilliance, yet his was an intelligence that could not be duplicated by schooling and academic

training alone; it was an intelligence filled with eccentricity and high drama, an intelligence that bemoaned the limitations of impotent scholarly thinking and pulsated with the electricity of Kraemer's own life.[67]

While Landau might have been a bit carried away in his description, it is clear that Kraemer was an eccentric. Today Kraemer works in the Pentagon and is unique for being the only monocled individual there.

Kraemer had asked the commanding general of the 84th if he might be allowed to address the troops on the reasons the U.S. was fighting the war against Germany. The gospel Kraemer preached to the college recruits was "that it was their duty to engage in combat as well as in intellectual exercise because after all, one needed soldiers as well as thinkers to fight a war."[68] This eccentric European had impressed Kissinger with his speech. Kissinger wrote him a note which read: "Dear Pvt. Kraemer: I heard you speak yesterday. This is how it should be done. Can I help you somehow? Pvt. Kissinger."[69] Kraemer responded to the note asking for a meeting and so began their friendship.

"Kraemer took Kissinger under his wing and used every trick in the book to get him made an interpreter in the 84th Division."[70] And as the war progressed and the division moved to Europe, Kraemer would do much to advance the career of the young Kissinger.

When the division took the city of Krefeld, it found the city government had vanished along with the fleeing Nazi troops. Something had to be done to provide for the city's nearly 200,000 people. Kraemer suggested, in his matchlessly persuasive way, that since this young Kissinger spoke German, and had an extraordinary intelligence besides, he should be put in charge of re-organizing Krefeld's government.[71]

As preview to a later government re-organization, Kissinger proved extremely efficient and capable. Within three days the government was functioning again.

In recognition of his ability, within a year Kissinger would be head of the district of Bergstrasse. "He had complete power to arrest anyone for anything, lived in a castle, and when he was transferred, the people of Bergstrasse begged to keep him there."[72] In contrast to his last stay in Germany, he had certainly become recognized and valued by others.

It was also at Bergstrasse that Kissinger took on his first mistress: "He appropriated a villa, commandeered a Mercedes and took his first mistress—the young widow of a Wehrmacht officer."[73] But one of the characteristics which seems to emerge in this period is the manipulative manner in which he operated. He had many girlfriends, and was "relaxed and casual in his approach."[74] A friend at the time has commented that when talking about women Kissinger "would conceptualize about the phenomenon of power in an occupied country like Germany. He told complicated stories about how he would get the women who wanted to ingratiate themselves to those in authority . . . He always talked in manipulative terms. He was the man with the gun, the Jeep, the coffee, stockings, chocolate."[75] Although this appears to contrast sharply with the shy and timid boy of Fuerth, in the shallowness of the relationships there is a string of continuity. It has been found by psychoanalyst Frieda Fromm-Reichman that the typical depressive personality "seeks and quickly forms superficial relationships and tends to be clinging and exploitative."[76] The behavior is in response to the feeling of rejection and is an attempt to induce others' love as a substitute for the feeling of lovelessness as a child. The depressive personality is forever in search of a greater love because he is never convinced that anyone could really love him, a theme which we will discuss below in Kissinger's other relations to women.

After his duty in Bergstrasse, Kissinger, through Kraemer's intervention, was appointed to the faculty of the European Command Intelligence School as a 22-year-old sergeant instructing officers up to the rank of lieutenant colonel. In the end the disparity of rank became too embarrassing and he was discharged from the army and hired for a short time at $10,000 a year. Kissinger had come a long way. From the shy, withdrawn refugee, he had come to be a man of means and influence—however limited it might be.

Kissinger had found the outlet for action against those who had manipulated his earlier life. While the army had provided a structured environment, it had also given him a more meaningful vehicle for resolving his inner confusion. The army had provided Kissinger with the means of his return to Germany as the triumphant liberator. It was in the Army that Kissinger could prove his worth to those, including himself, who had doubted it.

The military was well suited to meet Kissinger's needs. As Erikson has said, the army is: "one of the social institutions which undertake to channel as they encourage initiative and to provide atonement as they appease guilt."[77] The army, then, for Kissinger was on one level a means of appeasing his own guilt at blaming his father for not acting against Hitler. By his own role in the occupation, he could give to his father's life some relevance since his father sired a son who was part of the group of men united together against the wave of history. In effect, Kissinger completed the life which his father left unfinished. Kissinger was able to submit to the authority of an ordered life as a compromise "toward sanctioned ways of action", a compromise which worked as support for him on both sides. Kissinger found in the army the symbols that would represent the consolidation of his earlier inner conflict, a channelling of inner dynamic conflicts into useful and culturally accepted modes of expression.

It was also a means by which he could express inner hostility in a socially accepted manner. Remembering that repressed hostility is considered to be at the core of the depressive personality, the outlet for aggression provided by the army helped to unblock some of his inner tension and allow the confident and competent Kissinger to emerge. Here is the source of the transition from the oppressed Heinz to the proud Henry.

Fritz Kraemer's contribution to this consolidation was not simply material advancement. He played a central role in Kissinger's cosmos of symbols. This flamboyant, eccentric German may have seemed a bit odd to the young draftees, but not to Kissinger. In the American desert Kissinger had found a German oasis which would quench his thirst for a link between his old and new worlds. But this oasis was part mirage. Kraemer, like Kissinger's father, was an irrelevant man. He lived in an age that had passed him by. Kraemer, like Kissinger's later patron "Wild Bill" Elliot, was a man who longed for the days of aristocracy. He held nothing but contempt for the present and its absurd worship of technical achievement and hence lack of appreciation for personal eminence. Thus his attitude was of almost pure cynicism. He recently remarked when speaking of Kissinger: "The medium brilliant can be overawed by their own or somebody else's brilliance. The truly brilliant will understand that brilliancy means nothing."[78] Without action, brilliance is impotent. Here was a man that saw the world as something to be manipulated. Principles are meaningless unless acted upon and brilliance irrelevant unless used. Thus here was a man who would represent to Kissinger what he would have liked his father to be—a man of action who was willing to stand up against the forces of history. The irony, of course, was that Kraemer too was an outsider, a man who really did not fit his times, and in a sense he too was irrelevant to the world in which he lived. But most importantly, Kraemer represented the means by which Kissinger could consolidate his inner chaos, and rather than retreat from the world as he had done in the past, turn upon it and act.

Kraemer's importance in Kissinger's development is best shown by the role he played in the young man's decision to change his occupational goals. It can be assumed that it was the groundwork laid by his teacher-father that led to the ease with which Kraemer, the intellectual, became a father-figure. Kraemer's age, his German origin, and intellectual background, combined with Kissinger's search for an actor, provided the basis for this identification and opened him to being molded, in some degree, by Kraemer's philosophy.

> What Kraemer evoked in Kissinger himself was important in shaping the younger man's future: a profound interest in learning and in the intellectual process, and an almost obsessive desire to grasp the roots of man's historical experience. . . . The constant company of a man like Kraemer accentuated something far more important: the *impulse* to learn.[79]

And so rather than becoming an accountant, Kissinger decided to be an intellectual.

What must have been a turning point was an exchange that Kissinger recalled some time later. Soon after Kraemer's speech to the troops, Kissinger recalls, "He told me I had a good political mind. It was a thought that had never occurred to me."[80] Suddenly somebody of short acquaintance says point blank that he was "unbelievably gifted" (which were the words according to Kraemer)[81] and it was a thought that had never occurred to him. It would not be too far-fetched to say that this exchange marked the beginning of the transition from the inward-turning Heinz to the outward-turning Henry. Kissinger had embarked on the road to what would become his adult identity.

V. HARVARD

> "The relationship between a woman and a man of my type is unavoidably very complex. One must be cautious. Oh, how hard it is for me to explain these things."
> —Henry Kissinger in the *New Republic,*
> December 16, 1972

Carrying out his decision to follow an intellectual career, Kissinger won a New York State Scholarship and was admitted to Harvard. He left his $10,000-a-year job and went to Harvard in September of 1946. Going to Harvard was a major turning point in Kissinger's own expectations. He consciously saw it as a real chance to do something with his life. "It was a raising of expectations and he viewed Harvard as *the* big decision in terms of family, friends, and army experience."[82] Kissinger would go to Harvard thinking of himself as a G.I. Bill man who might not otherwise have been able to go if it were not for the army.

Kissinger entered Harvard then, after having just experienced both the security of an ordered environment and the horror of two holocausts—the German and the American in Japan. For the first time a sense of an integrated self seems to have come to Kissinger, even though there was still much doubt about his past. Yet there is quiet. For the time the turbulance and fear of the preceeding years had subsided and calm had taken its place, but a calm that had a mushroom cloud hanging over it. The years spent studying at Harvard were years of reflection, a time when Kissinger was able to try to make sense of what lay behind.

Little is known of Kissinger's years at Harvard. But there are at least two significant sources of data. The first, as might be expected, is another of the flamboyant, out-dated men to whom Kissinger attached himself. William Yandell Elliot, affectionately and sometimes not so affectionately known as "Wild Bill", was a professor of Government at Harvard. He had been all-American tackle and a Rhodes scholar at Vanderbilt, and had written a book in 1924 describing the forces that would result in fascism in the next ten years. From those pillars of success Elliot never went much higher. Although he was considered to be one of the powers of the Harvard faculty, he was always more than a little annoying to his students and fellow faculty members. One of Kissinger's contemporaries at Harvard has compared Elliot to the "Big Daddy" in "Cat on a Hot Tin Roof". Elliot, who comes from a small town in Tennessee, was known for throwing students who disagreed with him out of his office. He was a man who, like Kraemer, held disdain for the common man. Elliot

> had attended Balliol College, Oxford, at a time in the 1920's long after the place had been over-taken by the spirit of Benjamin Jowett, the notion that societies trained their elites—and senior scholars prepared their young disciples—for positions in government and other public service . . . It was this apparition, this tattered image of a by-gone age that Kissinger latched onto while a Harvard undergraduate, and the experience would be lasting.[83]

Thus there is a marked similarity in the two men who played such an important role in Kissinger's young life. This role is best described in Joseph Kraft's article on Kissinger in *Harpers:*

> To shock Henry Kissinger out of the depths, to charge him with purpose and ambition required men who were themselves outsiders—a couple of flamboyant personalities nostalgic for vanished features of an aristocratic life they presumed to embody and full of snobbish contempt for present times . . . They delivered to him an antidote against the quietude of his early life, a reason for not being the victim he had been. They taught the principle and embodied the practice of struggle against anarchy . . . It was that do or die credo which struck fire with Kissinger. He had known the time when there was "no place for goodness". He made it his life's work to show that force could be used to avert tragedy and catastrophy.[84]

The second source of data is the product of his Harvard years: Kissinger's PhD thesis, subsequently published as *A World Restored,* is a testimony to his past and the blue-print for Kissinger's own philosophy. His study of Metternich and Castlereagh in the nineteenth century and their battle against Napoleon's revolutionary tide was, as he himself admits, an attempt to help solve some of the parallel problems faced by the modern Western powers in stemming the tide of the East. But before we look in depth at the significance of *A World Restored,* let us bring Kissinger through Harvard.

The most significant event of Kissinger's undergraduate years was his marriage. After a seven-year courtship, Kissinger married Ann Fleischer on February 6, 1949. He and Ann had met while Henry was working his way through high school back at the shaving brush factory. Ann was also of a refugee family and shared the same sort of cultural background, although she was not particularly motivated to excel academically. "The men who knew her as boys invariably describe Ann Fleischer as 'reserved' or even 'introverted'."[85] While they were at Harvard she worked in a furniture store and seemed to enjoy being out of the academic world and doing something different. While Ann has been said to have developed toward a more independent personality since the divorce, at the time she was, as a very close friend described her, "gentle and dependent. She has a slight taste for martyrdom, but she is generous and warm-hearted, giving and fearful. She needs to serve and this need is accompanied by dependence."[86] In other words, Ann, in marked contrast to Kissinger's mother, was hardly the type of person who would dominate a relationship.

Ann did not share Kissinger's intellectual world with him, and if she took an interest in what he was doing it was largely because it was Henry that was doing it. There was a pretty clear boundary between their private life and Kissinger's professional life. This boundary was even maintained to the extent of Kissinger later building a study over his garage which had a separate entrance. "Ann was proud of the study, but one Cambridge friend recalls a day when Kissinger 'invited me up there to see it, and have a drink, and Ann came up to sit with us. He told her to get out—he didn't want her there'."[87]

They led a very traditional life in their domestic arrangement. Ann was loyal and serving and Kissinger expected her to perform her wifely duties. Later on in the marriage when Kissinger was writing the book on nuclear weapons for the Council on Foreign Relations, she was still not expected to interfere with his work. As one commentator described the situation: "He worked with single-minded concentration on it (*Nuclear Weapons and Foreign Policy*). He lived with his wife in a New York apartment, and when he came home at night he forbade her to talk to him because it would interrupt his train of thought."[88] From what is said about their relationship by friends, Kissinger was hard on her and was not particularly supportive or understanding. He was not at all patient with her and would tell her in no uncertain terms when he was irritated. "Henry didn't think Ann was intelligent and he had a tendency to be cruel to her in public. Knowing that she was sensitive he would deride her and criticize her telling her that what she was talking about was absurd and unimportant."[89]

The main problem was that Kissinger would have liked her to have been more independent, but at the same time he expected her to maintain a subordinate position in the relationship. Ann herself contributed to the problem in that "she bent excessively and this did not enlarge Henry's respect for her or his patience."[90] The marriage seems to have occurred largely because it was expected; after such a long time the courtship was naturally expected to end in marriage. "Ann certainly expected it for some time and this was the major quality about it. Henry doesn't like to commit himself in many ways. She needed commitment and Henry stood away from it."[91]

It was the kind of marriage where the man gets involved with his profession and leaves the wife behind. They were basically not compatible and finally they grew apart. The break was not immediate and clear-cut. They would spend weekends together, on the surface because of the children, but also because he too found it hard to let go. Even after the divorce he would have Ann sew buttons for him and perform other "wifely" tasks.

The significant characteristic of Kissinger's relationship to Ann was his continuing assault upon Ann's value as a person. In Kissinger's eyes Ann was an unintelligent, unimaginative, unimportant individual and he never lost an opportunity to let her, and those around him, know that this was his opinion. If indeed it was the case that Ann was the zero Kissinger treated her as, it would hardly seem necessary to engage in such a frontal assault upon her being.[92] But on the contrary, Kissinger found that it was necessary to berate Ann even though it does not seem that Ann was the nothing which he made her out to be. Ann, if anything, had the seeds of a more independent personality since "there were aspects which now have become more marked and visible since she has been on her own."[93] What seems to be at work here is yet another aspect of Kissinger's projective system which places on others the qualities which he fears are his in an attempt to rob his "bad" self of the power over him. Laing's comment on such a person is particularly cogent. He states: "By destroying in his own eyes, the other person as a person, he robbed the other of his power to crush him."[94]

This type of behavior is a basic characteristic of the depressive personality. Feelings of powerlessness and rejection are behind it. The depressive personality is "forever trying to induce women to love him. As long as he is involved in pursuit he is submissive and over-affectionate but when his courtship has been accepted, he rejects the woman and looks for another mother-substitute who will love him more."[95] This flight from rejection and powerlessness, the root of depressive anxiety, will manifest itself through most of Kissinger's adult life.

Kissinger's life in Germany and later New York must have been an important contribution to his characteristic insecurity and mistrust because it was an environment which was unpredictable and out of control. The corollary of the renunciation of relationship with others is the need to be in control. An environment which is out of control can cause an individual to retreat into the boundaries of the self. Kissinger's withdrawal and problems with interpersonal relationships is the psychological foundation of the fundamental axiom of his political philosophy: "if it [society] cannot master the environment it will become its victim."[96] The characteristics of mistrust and insecurity can still be seen as definitive of his relationships throughout his years at Harvard and even after his student years.

Kissinger majored in philosophy as an undergraduate and was particularly interested in Spengler. "One of Kissinger's closest colleagues, Stanley Hoffman, made the remark that Henry 'walked, in a way, with the ghost of Spengler at his side.' "[97] But his concern with Spengler was not a whole-hearted embrace. As one commentator states:

> The unending decay and death of successive civilizations that seemed inevitable to Spengler was a notion that the young Kissinger rejected. His experience in Germany had taught him that one must never accept inevitability, and that one must do everything in one's power to wrest balance and order from chaos and destruction.[98]

Landau commits a fundamental error in his analysis of Kissinger's philosophy in the above quote. Kissinger did indeed accept the inevitable decline of civilization. What was important to Kissinger was that the change in the system is ordered. Kissinger's acceptance of the inevitable is predicated on the belief that one must do everything possible to slow or contain its progress. But Landau is correct in pointing to the influence of Kissinger's past on his academic pursuits. It can hardly be a coincidence that Spengler, the philosopher of gloom, found a place in the heart and mind of the serious and gloomy Harvard undergraduate. As a youth Kissinger had witnessed one of Western Civilization's most agonizing moments. It would only be natural for the young man to seize upon Spengler's concept of decline as one of the factors in his ideological simplification of the universe. In Spengler he found one of the building blocks for the "identity consonant with his own childhood" of which Erikson speaks.

Kissinger wrote his undergraduate thesis on Spengler, Toynbee and Kant. The quiet, withdrawn Kissinger of Fuerth and New York had found enough words by the time he got through his undergraduate work to write a 350-page paper that resulted in the school setting a limit of 150 pages on all undergraduate theses in the future. In his thesis, "The Meaning of History", Kissinger criticized Kant and Spengler because their philosophies left little room for human action and will. According to Spengler and Kant, civilization was moving toward its predestined end and nothing man could do would stop it. Kissinger's past experience had shown him the necessity for human choice and action. His father's passivity, Kraemer's gospel of action, and Elliot's preaching of that gospel kept Kissinger searching for the fit between his past and his future.

Kissinger earned his BA in three years, graduating *summa cum laude* in 1950, and went on to graduate school in the Government Department. In those days, if one had been a *summa* as an undergraduate, you were not required to take the oral examinations for your higher degrees. So this set Kissinger apart from the other students both in his own perception of himself and the perception of him by his fellow students. But Kissinger seems to have been able to use this separateness as an integrating factor, a source of the proudness he now has for his acting alone; while the others were studying for their orals, Kissinger was working with professors on their books. The others looked upon him as something special. He was probably the most talked-about graduate student at the time, although scarcely the best liked. "People saw him as arrogant and argumentative. He was moody, unhappy and sour. It was a cause to remark if Henry was in a good mood. He was very sharp with people, and stubborn."[99]

Kissinger looked to older men for his close relationships with but a few notable exceptions. One of the few close friends of his peer group at Harvard was Klaus Epstein, and Kissinger spent a great deal of time together with him discussing history and international politics. Epstein read and criticized every page of Kissinger's piece on Metternich and it is said that he was influential in Kissinger's view of history. Even at this early date Kissinger had begun to be identified by his classmates as the guy who was always talking about the balance of power. One of his classmates has commented, "Balance was seen as Henry's thing. He was preoccupied with balance and order."[100]

In the debates of the time about the Soviet Union, the bomb, and the partition of Europe, Kissinger always took a hard line and had a tendency to couch his arguments in black and white terms. He would often become the center of a discussion at parties but generally it was a discussion between himself and one other person with several others listening in but not participating. Kissinger gravitated toward pontification in such situations. He was much more comfortable in a "discussion that was not personal but dealt rather with political, historical or other academic questions. He was not spontaneous, flexible or playful."[101] His discussions then reflected another typical depressive characteristic. His pontification in discussions and also in his writing are like the expressions of depressive neurotics who "are full of tabloid wisdom and express their cliché statements as if they were great and original ideas."[102] Thus Kissinger tended to be heavy-handed in his social discourse and uncomfortable dealing with peers on a personal basis.

Kissinger was one of the few students who got along with both of the poles of power in the Government Department—Carl Friedrich and Elliot. Most students didn't get along with both men but Kissinger had a good rapport with the two. They were awe-inspiring figures in the department and Kissinger "always seemed to like powerful personalities who bring together not only the academic world, but the world of the present and participation in that world."[103] Kissinger at one point was so close to Friedrich that he was identified as *his* professor. Kissinger was struck by both men but did not seem to be over-powered by them. "He was not a 'little Elliot" or a 'little Friedrich'."[104] It was Elliot with whom he maintained the most lasting friendship, and Elliot was the most influential of the two in Kissinger's own thinking.

It was in the two years after he finished his undergraduate work that Kissinger found the philosophical framework which would unite history's progress and man's will. He fell upon Hegel's dialectic of history to fill the gap in his personal philosophy. Hegel's philosophy accepted the progress of history but left the end of its path open to speculation. There was room in the dialectic for heroic human action. Man's will could steer civilization away from one obstacle and another as man careened down the hill of history. Hegel's philosophy:

> maintains only that in each epoch, there will arise a civilization
> and, more rarely, an individual, whose duty it will be to guard and
> transmit the historical spirit and transmit it without ever attaining
> a full comprehension of all the implications it bears in the context
> of mankind's final destination.[105]

But history's final destination is left open for great men to exert their will. Hegel's philosophy of the "rare" individual would fit nicely Elliot's Oxford training. Under Elliot, Kissinger would be trained for the role Hegel postulated.

Kissinger continued to wrestle with the meaning of history and for his master's paper he dropped Kant and substituted Hegel, who took his place beside Spengler and Toynbee in Kissinger's philosophical cabinet. Kissinger got his master's degree in 1952 and under Elliot's tutelage would go on to his PhD degree in 1954 as well as winning the Sumner Prize for outstanding work on the prevention of war.

In his PhD thesis, Kissinger traced the role of one of Hegel's rare historical individuals who transmit the spirit of an age. Kissinger studied Metternich as he adjusted the fulcrum of Europe's balance of power.

VI. THE ROAD TO WASHINGTON

"The intricate web of destiny in which we, both as individuals
and as nations, are called upon to function, has caused most of us
to become obsessed with personal and national insecurity."
                                    —Howard Rome, "Depressive Illness:
                                        Its Socio-Psychiatric Implications"

The man to whom *A World Restored* was dedicated, William Elliot,
continued to play the central role in Kissinger's life for the next few
years until Nelson Rockefeller emerged on the scene. But Rockefeller
never did occupy a position of such closeness to Kissinger as Elliot had
during and after the graduate years. Elliot played a role much like that
of Kraemer. Elliot, like Kraemer, was much older than Kissinger. Both
men had a flare and style which was unmistakable. Their style was, to
Kissinger, a mark of confidence backed by a tradition of intellectual
order. Both longed for a more aristocratic age and possessed fiery and
flamboyant personalities which made them stand out among their seemingly more placid contemporaries. Both attempted and succeeded with
varying degrees to put their own personal stamp on Kissinger's thinking.
Elliot was looking for a disciple and Kissinger was looking for someone
to follow. And it was Elliot who began to build the contacts Kissinger
needed as he climbed his ladder of success.

When Kissinger received his PhD it was assumed by most, including
Kissinger himself, that he would naturally be offered a teaching job
at Harvard.

But although his name was seriously considered and well supported, the decision went against him. Details of the argument are
of course academic secrets, but according to one of the members
of the faculty at that time, he was not only judged personally a
difficult colleague (he had the reputation of being much nicer to
his superiors than to his subordinates) but still more important
the professors suspected that he was less interested in the university or in teaching and research than in making a career in public
service.[106]

There was another offer at the same time at the University of Chicago
and at the University of Pennsylvania. Chicago did not generally make
offers that they thought would be turned down. According to one reporter,[107] Kissinger had led the University of Chicago to think that he
would accept their offer. Even though Chicago offered him a higher
position, when Harvard came up with a part-time teaching position in
the Department of Government, he accepted the Cambridge offer. His

reason for taking the lesser position was based primarily upon the fact that he would be closer to Washington both geographically and in terms of his personal contacts.

During his year as an instructor, Elliot and Kissinger founded and directed the International Seminar which would later serve Kissinger as a major source of international contacts.[108] Again with Elliot's help, Kissinger founded and edited *Confluence* which was a scholarly journal used to debate policy issues.

Then came Kissinger's biggest break up until then. In the winter of 1954-55 a job as the managing editor of *Foreign Affairs* opened. The editor, Hamilton Fish Armstrong, solicited some of his friends at Harvard to see if they had any young prospects for the job. Arthur Schlesinger, Jr. suggested Kissinger, and Armstrong asked Kissinger to come to New York for an interview. Armstrong didn't give him the job but thought Kissinger might be useful in another capacity. The Council on Foreign Relations had been conducting a study group on the question of nuclear weapons and their effect on foreign policy. Armstrong was associated with the group and suggested that Kissinger apply for a spot as the writer of the study group's findings. Kissinger sent in his credentials, including recommendations from Elliot, Schlesinger, and McGeorge Bundy. He was offered the job and accepted. The study group had been meeting for some time to discuss problems of nuclear strategy and by the time Kissinger joined the group, most of the work had been done. What the group needed was a fresh mind to put their work together into a book. The result was Kissinger's best-selling, *Nuclear Weapons and Foreign Policy*.

The book is the cornerstone of Kissinger's popular reputation in the academic world, and for a while his reputation went beyond the confines of the ivy-covered buildings. The book stayed on the best-seller lists for fourteen weeks. What his personal contacts could not do for him, the popularity of his book would. Indeed, Richard Nixon, then Vice-President, was photographed with a copy of Kissinger's book sticking out of his suit. His later books would never attain the popularity that *Nuclear Weapons* did. But the book, while hailed for its originality, was an editing job more than anything else.[109] Of course, Kissinger put his own stamp on the ideas and contributed a few of his own, but here we have an example of Kissinger's greatest asset—his ability to present and order arguments. Jeane Davis, secretary for the NSC staff told me that the key to Kissinger's relationship with Nixon was Kissinger's ability to organize and present the options to the President in a clear and coherent manner. Ms. Davis has said, "Nixon is a lawyer and he is influenced by hard factual material. At certain points the President's instinct might point in one direction, but when he sees the options objectively laid out, he's enough of a lawyer to be influenced."[110] Kissinger's ability to synthesize arguments, as demonstrated in *Nuclear Weapons,* has been a key factor in terms of his ability to influence presidential decisions.

The central thrust of *Nuclear Weapons and Foreign Policy* is a criticism of the defense establishment for not creating a place in its planning operations for anything other than full-scale nuclear war. The book is an attempt to offer an alternative approach in which nuclear weapons could be used in limited war. Kissinger argues that through diplomacy the U.S. would be able to make its intentions not to engage in full-scale war known to the other side. Presumably this knowledge would insure that the "enemy" would not respond out of proportion to the threat. Thus there is a great reliance upon persuasion in his formula. He feels that if the opponent is adequately informed, then their response will be appropriate should limited nuclear war "become necessary".

But there is an internal contradiction in Kissinger's logic on this point. In Landau's words:

> How did Kissinger ever think that diplomacy could settle questions of such strategic importance when he himself proclaimed in what was probably the most pronounced internal contradiction in his thinking, that "the emphasis of traditional diplomacy on 'good faith' and 'willingness to come to an agreement' is a positive handicap when it comes to dealing with a power dedicated to overthrowing the international system."?[111]

Kissinger came to repudiate in part the position taken in *Nuclear Weapons.* In an article entitled "Limited War: Conventional or Nuclear? A Reappraisal", Kissinger stated:

> Several developments have caused a shift in my view about the relative emphasis to be given conventional forces as against nuclear forces. These are 1) the disagreement within our military establishment and within the alliance about the nature of limited war; 2) the growth of the Soviet nuclear stockpile and the increased significance of long-range missiles; 3) the impact of arms-control negotiations.[112]

As can be seen, the reasons he gives for his change of position are purely tactical. Because the practical obstacles in front of the type of co-ordination necessary are too great, it would be unadvisable to attempt limited nuclear war. There is no reason to believe that if the problems of control could be overcome that Kissinger would have been unwilling to use tactical nuclear weapons. For instance, if somehow Kissinger could have gained the assurance of China and the Soviet Union that they would not view the use of nuclear weapons in Vietnam as a threat to their national security then Kissinger would have been perfectly willing to use such weapons. Indeed something approaching this is what occurred in the mining of Haiphong harbor. The possibility that a foreign ship would be sunk in such an action has carried with it many of the fears of confrontation with the big powers as has the use of nuclear weapons in the past. This remains true even though Kissinger reduced some of the risks involved through his talks with the Chinese and Russians.[113]

In 1956 while Kissinger was working with the Council on Foreign Relations and writing *Nuclear Weapons,* the Rockefeller Brothers' Fund had organized a series of panels to discuss foreign and domestic policy. Kissinger became the director of these panels and was responsible for writing their reports. "The national security panel report of the Rockefeller Brothers' Fund, billed as 'the answer to Sputnik', became a public document of enormous prestige and influence; Kissinger was its author."[114] The paper followed fairly closely the lines of *Nuclear Weapons,* arguing for a strategy based upon limited war and the use of tactical nuclear weapons.

However, it was not the paper which was the most important product of his association with the Fund. It was during this period that Kissinger began to cement his ties to Nelson Rockefeller. Kissinger had met Rockefeller in the early fifties at a military conference in Quantico, Virginia. They continued to keep in contact, but primarily on a business basis. Kissinger was an expert and Rockefeller needed advisors. And as Kissinger's reputation began to grow, Rockefeller would call upon Kissinger more and more as an advisor.

"The two men (Kissinger and Rockefeller) were dauntless interventionists, men who believed that the U.S. had the responsibility to show its muscle in every area of the world and they felt strongly that America must live up to its destiny."[115] Most importantly, both Rockefeller and Kissinger shared a concern for the establishment of order and the necessity to stand up against those forces which would disrupt that order. Once again we find Kissinger attaching himself to a man who is a staunch interventionist and who possessed a willingness to be tough. "Kissinger, like his hero Metternich, put his great talents at the service of a rickety and anachronistic order. 'The willingness to engage in nuclear war when necessary' said the Rocekfeller report, 'is part of the price of our freedom.' This, the ferocious conventional wisdom of the Pentagon, runs like a leitmotiv throughout his work."[116]

Like that theme, the type of men he associates himself with also form a certain continuity. "The rungs on Kissinger's ladder to success have a common characteristic. At each major step upward he has been the protegé of men who believed in military strength, and, if necessary, war, and who were obsessed with the postwar struggle for hegemony between the U.S. and the USSR, and fearful of the revolutionary tide in the poorer countries."[117] In Rockefeller we see a man whose personal style is a toned-down version of Kraemer and Elliot but whose intellectual maxims fall into the same sort of willingness to confront the forces of history. By the time Kissinger began to associate with Rockefeller, his own ideas were fairly well established. He was ready to make a commitment to a man not so much because of the man's person, although still important, but upon the basis of the congruity between the man's ideas and his own. Twelve years later Kissinger would commit himself to the ideas of Nixon, a man for whom he had no personal respect. Perhaps because of his growing confidence in his own ability and his own ideas, Kissinger became able and willing to accept the challenge of trying to put his ideas into action even if the man who would make the final decision was not a man who Kissinger particularly admired.

As a result of his connections, Kissinger was given a job as a consultant to the Kennedy Administration, and it was then that he encountered the frustration of trying to do battle against the Executive Bureaucracy. He had extremely painful experiences while working for Kennedy. "It would be difficult to underestimate the sense of injury Kissinger suffered at the hands of the slick, fast-talking Kennedy White House aides who sloughed him off as a quirksome academic trying to peddle his bag of silly ideas."[118] From Landau's account of Kissinger's days as a Kennedy advisor it appears that the stumbling block before his success centered around jealousy of access to the President. Kissinger's old colleague and friend, McGeorge Bundy, was angered at Kissinger's attempts to circumvent him and see the President directly. Bundy gave Kissinger the choice of either becoming a full-time consultant or going back to Harvard. Kissinger was not yet willing to leave the security of a tenured position at Harvard simply to be stuck at a low level of influence, so Kissinger stopped making the trip down to Washington. "From all of these encounters, Kissinger suffered a feeling that he would not blithely forget in later years."[119]

There is another version of the Kennedy days which also throws light on Kissinger's personality. According to an article in *Newsweek* that appeared almost a year into the first Administration, " 'It was less Henry's views than his style that hurt him,' recalls a sympathetic colleague who served with him at the time, 'he simply wasn't light-footed enough for the Kennedy circle."[120] A story in *Time*[121] tells of Kissinger's pursuit of exerting influence on policy to the point that Kennedy himself was said to be a bit annoyed with the professor's insistence. In short, Kissinger was just in the way of the fast-moving knights of Camelot. The glamour and smoothness of the slick Kennedy aides simply overshadowed the pedantic German and his rather stuffy views. What strange irony that it would be the stodgy professor who would become the glamour figure of the Nixon Administration.

Ultimately, Kissinger would resort to submitting anonymous reports through a friend at State in an attempt to have his views expressed. For the most part however, Kissinger's association with the Kennedy Administration was minimal. All told, Kissinger's service was less than 18 months. "His departure was expedited after he took his wife, Ann, on a personal tour of India, Pakistan, and Israel—identifying himself at each stop as a White House consultant, thus giving the trip an official imprimatur and annoying some Kennedy people."[122] Again, both the self-inflated importance and the anonymous, unsolicited advice are basic behavior patterns of the depressive personality: "distortion of truth to please people or to impress them, exaggeration . . . (and) the offering of unsolicited guidance," are processes of compensation for depressive anxiety. Unfortunately, such characteristics often seem to be part of the necessary qualifications for political office.

Kissinger made a couple other forays into the executive arena before his assignment as Special Assistant for National Security Affairs. Johnson had begun looking for a way out of Vietnam when Kissinger mentioned to Averill Harriman that he had an informal channel to Ho Chi Minh through a French acquaintance. Johnson decided it might be helpful to relay some information on U.S. policy to Ho through Kissinger's informal contact. Kissinger was sent to Paris to open up the flow, but the talks seem to have had little effect. At any rate, Kissinger got a taste of the kind of secret negotiations he would carry on during the Nixon years.

By far the more important association than his governmental service was his role as an advisor to Rockefeller in the '64 and '68 campaigns. From the first association back in '56, Kissinger would continue his relationship with Rockefeller. He maintained his position as head of the Study Fund, and while he published four more books elaborating and updating the basic principles established in *A World Restored,* he would also enjoy a close association with Rockefeller as he made his bid for power. It was as a result of his work for Rockefeller that Nixon once again became aware of the professor who writes about nuclear weapons and had some pretty good ideas about foreign policy.

VII. A TWO-ACT COMEDY OF ERRORS

> The opening to China has been an important element in the
> mechanics of my success. And yet this is not the main point . . .
> The main point comes from the fact that I have acted alone. The
> Americans love this immensely. The Americans love the cowboy
> who leads the convoy, alone on his horse, and nothing else. Per-
> haps not even with a gun, because he does not shoot. He acts, and
> that is enough, being in the right place at the right time.
>
>   —Henry Kissinger, *New Republic,*
>   December 16, 1972

Thanks to Freud, modern man has a greater appreciation for the
seemingly lesser events of an individual's life. Often the most minor occurrences can be tied into the broader totality and can be seen as representative of fundamental aspects of the psychic structure. Slips of the
tongue or pen, and dreams are among the seemingly insignificant aspects of our lives that Freud brought to the forefront of psychological
inquiry. There are two such seemingly minor incidents in Kissinger's
relations with his colleagues which shed light on an evaluation of Kissinger's personality. While the two events are neither slips nor dreams,
Freud's work should remind us that what seems insignificant is not
necessarily meaningless.

The first incident is related by Landau:

> His initial clashes and rivalries in Cambridge were not nearly so
> tied to animosity as they were to his almost total degree of per-
> sonal insecurity. One close colleague remembers an occasion on
> which he and Kissinger attended an academic conference outside
> Cambridge, but accidently saw little of each other during its
> course. The colleague returned home to find a long, impassioned
> note from Kissinger accusing him of failing to nod hello or other-
> wise offer greetings at certain times during the conference, and ex-
> claiming that unless he could offer Kissinger some explanation for
> this conduct, their friendship would have to come to an end. The
> colleague responded not with an apology, but with a straight for-
> ward explanation of why Kissinger's assertions were uncalled-for
> and somewhat silly, and Kissinger apologized for the outburst.
> Such episodes reinforced the feeling that Kissinger's occasional
> difficulty relating to his colleagues was not that he was personally
> indecent, . . . but that he was . . . a man who saw himself disliked
> or persecuted far more often than was the case.[123]

The second encounter is of a similar character. This incident, once
again, involves a fellow faculty member. Kissinger was at a conference

with another Harvard professor with whom he had planned to have dinner in order to discuss some problems that were related to the conference. When the friend suggested that they dine together in a hotel room so they could talk without interruption, Kissinger accused his colleague of not wanting to be seen in public with him.[124] The man pointed out how absurd the accusation was and they went on to have dinner in the room.

Kissinger's central fear in both of these incidents is that of rejection. His perception of both encounters was wholly out of proportion to what was called for by the occasions. It would appear that this anxiety has been a life-long characteristic and is what led to Haig's reference to Kissinger's "uncertainty" about being accepted. Both these incidents are clear evidence of Kissinger's lack of self-esteem. The clinical evidence seems to indicate that in a high percentage of cases these characteristics, fear of rejection and lack of self-esteem, point to basic insecurity from infancy with corresponding reinforcement of insecurity in social relations. The usual result is the constellation of characteristics which make up the depressive personality.

I have tried to show that the basic dynamics of Kissinger's personality generally fit the outlines of the depressive character. While the behavioral and social data is fairly clear, the familial data is less so. Certainly Kissinger's family experience provides the foundation upon which the broader culture placed its stamp.

I postulated a feeling of rejection on Kissinger's part as a result of the arrival of his brother Walter as the initiating experience. This was followed by the entrance of the "third son" who receives preferential treatment, and is allied with Walter, creating a familial situation of rivalry in which Kissinger perceived himself as the loser. His parents' ambivalence further contributed to the familial basis of his depressive anxiety.

In terms of behavior patterns, Henry's withdrawn nature, lack of involvement with others, his treatment in Fuerth and New York, his "moodiness" at Harvard, treatment of his wife and women in general, his tendency to be solicitous to superiors and hostile to inferiors, his self-enhancing distortions in India, his unsolicited advice to Kennedy — are all further behavioral substantiation of our judgement of his personality as depressive.

Other characteristics which were not fully elaborated upon are the frequent humorous references on Kissinger's part to his "megalomania" and what others have described as his self-depreciating humor. Since "megalomania is a defense against feelings of inferiority",[125] his humor would also seem to provide further substantiation of the analysis. Kissinger has also evidenced a tendency to over-work and over-eat (once remarking that when he negotiates, he eats, and will probably gain 300 pounds over the Middle East). These again are characteristics of depressive anxiety. "People who are given to this kind of depression feel defeated, lack self-confidence, blame themselves, feel isolated and forsaken, have a pessimistic outlook on life . . . over-eat or under-eat, and dwell on past events."[126] All of these characteristics belong to Kissinger's repertoire.

Even his success is part of the picture: "The dysmutual [depressive] tries to overcome his low self-esteem in many ways, one of which is through extreme ambition. Some dysmutuals, in milder stages of the disorder, rather than escape into manic moods, try to compensate for their feelings of inferiority by excessive work, long working hours, and an over-all drive for supremacy."[127] These characteristics are evidenced in Kissinger's behavior in the First Administration when he literally exhausted scores of aides on the National Security Council with his long and intensive hours.

His emotional threat to resign last June is again a consequence of his fear of rejection. The typical depressive is "exceedingly sensitive and vulnerable to criticism."[128] His public threat to resign came as a result of the criticism of his role in the taping of his subordinates on the Security Council Staff. This was not the first, only the most dramatic, threat of resignation. Aside from much talk about resignation during the Vietnam period, when Kissinger was on Rockefeller's staff, whenever Kissinger's access was blocked by veteran staff members, his *"habitual* solution was to march into Rocky's office and 'resign' ".[129]

An aspect of this constellation of behavior which has had significant ramifications for American foreign policy is the tendency toward personal isolation. As the opening quote in this chapter indicates, Kissinger's "acting alone" has been elevated to the highest significance in his conduct of policy. This is in marked contrast to his fear of being unacceptable, rejected and alone. What was a private experience and fear of being alone in his youth has been transformed into a value in his intellectual formulations. As in his "cowboy" statement it is the actor standing alone who is supposedly loved by the Americans, and, as Kissinger argues, the policy-maker must be willing to stand alone if his accomplishments are to be of value. Thus it is the ability to stand alone and face the abyss which is the primary value in Kissinger's estimation of a policy-maker's greatness. What we must assume was the beginning of Kissinger's reformulation of being alone into a virtue was his relation to Kraemer and later being singled out from among his student contemporaries at Harvard as an exceptional individual. Rather than being isolated as one of the unacceptables, Kissinger was set apart and above the other students at Harvard. He must have experienced some of his being separate and different as being better and in a sense greater than his contemporaries. And this also fits the depressive's compensating feeling that he is unique and superior. It must have been then that the negative aspects of being alone—the separateness, unacceptability, and unattachment—were counter-balanced by the attributes and advantages of being singled out. Although being alone, as Kissinger himself states has always been a part of his style, it has not always carried with it the positive connotations he now attaches to it. One distinctive advantage of being alone, as Kissinger may have discovered in his youthful withdrawal, is that being alone, one cannot be easily rejected.

What Kissinger has done is transform the anxiety-producing condition of being alone in the everyday world into a positive requisite in the world of statesmanship. What Kissinger saw as Metternich's and Bismarck's most important characteristic has become the significant aspect of his image in the American public. Although not a Prince, but a cowboy, Kissinger sees himself as the loner, a hero standing before the unresistable forces of history.

Kissinger was motivated to take up his "lonely" profession in part by the fact that the solitude of the statesman is seen as noble. First Kissinger experienced the pain of isolation which was then followed by the pleasure of singular achievement at Harvard. He would follow upon this theme by writing about the profession of statesman, characterizing it as a lonely undertaking, and then go on himself to take up the noble occupation.

Consonant with his self-image as the loner, Kissinger is not the type to seek out the advice of others. And if he does attempt to gather opinions from others, as his early reputation in the NSC seems to indicate, it is largely for appearance sake. This same process has been replicated in the conduct of relations between the U.S. and its allies. The complaints by Europe, Japan, Taiwan, and Thieu, over their neglect or superficial consultation is not unlike Kissinger's personal relationships. Remembering that one reason given for not initially granting him a position at Harvard was the judgement that he tended to be solicitous towards his superiors and hostile to his inferiors, we can begin to appreciate the failings of his personal diplomacy. In recent years, Kissinger's personal experience has had a major effect upon our national experience. His inability to empathize with others, his compulsion to face risk in order to prove his worth, and his tendency to act alone have in fact become significant components of American public policy.

VIII. A WORLD AND SELF RESTORED

> The statesman is . . . like one of the heroes in classical drama who
> has had a vision of the future but who cannot transmit it directly
> to his fellow men and who cannot validate its "truth".
>
> —Henry Kissinger,
> *A World Restored*

In this part of the paper I will attempt to draw upon the themes developed in the previous section in order to offer some partial explanations of American foreign policy, primarily in the first Administration. I emphasize "partial" because I will look at a limited number of issues, focusing on one dimension—that of personality. What follows is a look at Kissinger's writings, particularly *A World Restored,* in relation to the style of Kissinger's operation, the handling of the peace negotiations, the invasion of Cambodia, and the mining of Haiphong harbor.

In the words of I. F. Stone, "The best clues to Kissinger as a diplomat still lie in his study of Metternich."[130] While Harvard has placed the actual PhD on "restricted circulation", the public can view a slightly revised version of his thesis in his book *A World Restored,* which although written first, appeared after the success of his first book, *Nuclear Weapons and Foreign Policy.* In *A World Restored,* we see Kissinger first flexing his intellectual muscle and we can trace the development of his later philosophy from the foundations established here. Indeed it could be argued that there has been no basic change in Kissinger's outlook from then until now. The same principles he culled from his study of Metternich have been systematically applied to the modern world situation. The China policy, the Pakistan debacle, the State of the World Messages, all reflect the principle of balance and the role diplomacy plays in the control of this balance, all of which Kissinger first elaborated in *A World Restored.*

In addition to the importance of the book in terms of public policy for foreign affairs, the book is a personal testament of Kissinger's own life. He does not disguise the true focus of his study. He states:

> Napoleon is not exactly equivalent to Hitler or Castleraugh to
> Churchill. Whatever relationship exists depends not on a precise
> correspondence, but on a similarity of the problems confronted.
> And the conclusions will reflect—just as with any other generalization—the ability to abstract from the uniqueness of individual
> experience.[131]

While Kissinger did not intend "the uniqueness of individual experience" to refer to himself, the evidence indicates that the lessons of his youth were incorporated in his understanding of history.

Reading through *A World Restored,* one cannot help but be struck by the parallels between Europe after Napoleon and the world after Hitler. Kissinger makes a conscious attempt throughout the book to lead the reader to make comparisons between the two historical periods. And if the reader failed to see the similarities, the final chapter reveals explicitly the reason for the author's concern for the period. Kissinger went back into history to discover the connections of the past with the present. It is an attempt to place in perspective the chaos from which the world had just escaped and that had touched the personal lives of so many like Kissinger himself. The book is both an ordering into a logical continuum of the forces of history and an attempt to identify the problems which those forces will generate—the problems which must be confronted by an America emerging onto the world stage after WWII. In addition, Kissinger's personal life merges with the task he sees facing the U.S. He must resolve the inner chaos and uncertainty of his earlier life in order to achieve a maturity capable of sustaining himself as he assumes his adult role and moves out into the world. *A World Restored* is the testament of a youth's struggle to achieve an identity that the world until then had denied him. The work describes not simply a world restored, but a self restored.

One of the more interesting aspects of *A World Restored* can only be appreciated looking back with a view of Kissinger's own period of statesmanship. It is difficult to know to what extent symbols become models of action or are simply appropriate to developments which preceeded the attachment. Certainly both are a function of symbolic representation; but whatever the case, much can be learned of predictive value by looking at a political actor's model of action.

The similarity between the picture that Kissinger paints of Metternich and the image of Kissinger as statesman is astounding. A comparison of the two reveals the pervasiveness of the identification. One of the more remarkable aspects of the public Henry Kissinger has been his newsworthiness. Not just his value as a headliner for the *Washington Post,* but his ability to capture the covers of Hollywood's gossip magazines with his "between-the-covers" escapades. Of course, the secrecy in which he has enveloped himself is a primary source of intrigue, but much of the "hot" news value lies more in his playboy image—an image that somehow fits like a suit two sizes too large. There is something of a contrived air about this image, and it would be impossible to place all the blame on over-zealous journalists. Few other public officials had date-books like Henry Kissinger. When questioned about his proclivity for dating Hollywood starlets and beautiful models, Kissinger tries to disclaim any personal responsibility. He says that the young ladies are simply attracted to his position and not to his person: "I find the playboy image very amusing",[132] "I am their celebrity of the hour, the new

man in town. I don't kid myself."[133] Aside from the lack of self-value
which lies beheath the statement, it is curious that he bothers carrying
out the ruse. Indeed, he enjoys his role, and it has proved useful in the
past as during the secret Paris negotiations, when he could use his dates
as a front. However, it appears more as if Kissinger is living up to an
image, an image provided by his role model, Prince Metternich. Kissinger writes of Metternich:

> His conversation brilliant but without ultimate seriousness, equally
> at home in the salon and in the cabinet, graceful and facile, he
> was the beau-ideal of the eighteenth century . . . He would have
> moved through the drawing rooms of the fashionable world with
> his undeniable charm and grace, subtly and aloofly conducting his
> diplomacy with the circuitousness which is a symbol of cer-
> tainty.[134]

It is as if the nineteenth century has come alive with the dashing statesman flitting between salon and high level negotiation. Kissinger in Paris
is the epitomy of Metternichian style. Kissinger, here, has almost written
his own history.

In addition, there is a striking parallel of language in his article on
Bismarck which sheds light on the importance of personal style in
Kissinger's hero-matrix. He writes of Bismarck: "Proud in bearing, self-
confident in expression, the speaker represented the *beau-ideal* of the
Junkers, the large landholders who had built up Prussia."[135] Kissinger is
particularly attracted to those individuals who in his eyes possess a
proud certainty and sense of self. These men are the "beau-ideals"
whom everyone admires. These are men who are rooted in an environment in which they received positive reinforcement on all fronts; it is
to men like these that Kissinger looks for models.

In order to balance a fear of inadequacy, Kissinger has turned to symbols of power, action, assuredness, or vitality. Metternich's and Bismarck's style, along with that of Kraemer and Elliot, all share to some
degree a flamboyant assuredness which Kissinger's insecurity kept him
from having. He had a certain confidence, but confidence is more an
attribute than a fundamental form. Confidence is tacked on, learned as
it were, after the establishment of the basic form of security or insecurity. The style of Metternich, Bismarck, Kraemer and Elliot was an
attribute which Kissinger incorporated as a means of identifying with
the security which he thought was inherent in their style. It is significant that before his appointment as special assistant for national security affairs "Kissinger's major qualm about Nixon, it appears, was
the President-elect's lack of individual assertiveness."[136] Thus it seems
that individuals who display an outward confidence and assertiveness
are extremely attractive to Kissinger.

Metternich grew up in an age described in *A World Restored*, in which "nobody who lived after the French Revolution would ever know how sweet and gentle life could be. And the certitude of the time of youth never left Metternich."[137] It was precisely this "certitude of the time of youth" that Kissinger is lacking and which formed one of the corner stones of his attraction to Metternich. It is most revealing that Kissinger focuses on the tranquility of Metternich's youth as the source of his confidence, for it is this tranquility which Kissinger would most have desired as a substitute for his "bad times". Thus lacking the inner calmness of certainty, Kissinger reacts with a front of arrogance in the hope that his inner chaos will go undiscovered by others and so that he might convince himself in his moments of doubt.[138]

Kissinger has admitted of himself that "living as a Jew under the Nazis, then as a refugee in America, and then as a private in the army isn't exactly an experience that builds confidence."[139] Elsewhere he has said of the Harvard period: "I was completely unsure of myself. I had gotten out of the Army and I felt like an imigrant again."[140] The first half of his life was marked by extreme uncertainty. Today however, Kissinger can look back on his life and be satisfied that he overcame the barriers of his youth. Indeed, he can even say that the "bad times" were unimportant. But as a graduate student at Harvard, because of his admitted lack of confidence, he would have needed examples of men who overcame great barriers and survived to make history. Metternich then as one such man is even given a fantasized origin[141] in order to make him better fit Kissinger's need for symbols of identification, symbols which would aid him in his effort to understand his past and to consolidate a sense of self.

If we look at Kissinger's modern heroes, DeGaulle and Chou En Lai for instance, they are men who also have overcome incredible obstacles, men who have always faced adversity and won—men who have stood alone and passed the test. Kissinger has even talked recently of Nixon's "heroic" qualities. Nixon too is a man who overcame incredible obstacles and came back to shape history. Kissinger himself acknowledges his preference for such individuals. He has said that "the models he would prefer are those 'to whom it is given not only to maintain perfection of order but to have the strength to contemplate chaos, there to find material for fresh creation'."[143]

But the positive identifications are not all that are present in his treatment of Metternich. Those who stood idly by against Napoleon are subject to extreme criticism. In his discussion of Prussia in 1806, there appears a criticism which would be reverberated in his critique of the past American foreign policy. Kissinger remarks:

It is the nature of statesmen conducting a policy of petty advantage to seek in vacillation a substitute for action. A policy which lets itself be influenced by events—which in the formal phrase 'awaits developments' is likely to seek the remedy against a decision recognized as erroneous in adopting its extreme opposite without considering the intermediary solutions.[144]

This is the other side of Kissinger's hero coin; the side which includes his father. Those who vacillate, those who are indecisive, those who do not act in the face of the imperative to act, are apt to be overcome by events which pass them by. At every point in which Kissinger confronts inaction he is negatively critical. In his article on Bismarck for instance, he says; "a policy that awaits events is likely to become their prisoner." If we remember Kissinger's reluctance to leave Germany, his father's vacillation, Louis's wait-and-see attitude, followed by the sudden reversal into flight, Kissinger's four years of intransigence in Vietnam is given added meaning.

IX. THE VIETNAM TEST

"The United States cannot accept a military defeat, or a change in the political structure of South Vietnam brought about by external military force; once North Vietnamese forces and pressures are removed, the United States has no obligation to maintain a government in Saigon by force."
                                        —Henry Kissinger, *Foreign Affairs,*
                                        January, 1969

Throughout Kissinger's writing and speaking there is a pervasive tendency to place his truths of statesmanship in the context of a test. In *A World Restored,* for example, among several other such tests: "The test of a statesman, then is his ability to recognize the real relationship of forces and to make this knowledge serve his ends."[145] In reading any of Kissinger's books, one cannot help but notice this grammatical structure. Usually the "test" is linked to some form of "adequacy", "strength", or "ability". For example, "the test of statesmanship is the adequacy of its evaluation before the event."[146] The pervasiveness of this choice of terms in Kissinger's writings and statements would seem to indicate that the root of Kissinger's testing lies in his own doubt about himself and his environment. Taken with what we already know of Kissinger's personality it is reasonable to conclude that "the test of" is a means of dealing with his doubt about his own personal reception by his environment. His tests are tools in organizing the world. By testing for the existence of certain desirable qualities, he knows when to advance and when to retreat, when he is strong and when he is weak.

The significant aspect of this mode of perception is the doubt which is inherently attendant upon such ambiguity. What one needs is the courage to face that doubt, or in Kissinger's terms, contemplate the abyss. Therefore, courage is transformed into the primary value, for you need courage to confront the uncertainty. Kissinger castigates those policy-makers and intellectuals who lack this courage: "The corrollary of the tentativeness of most views is an incurable inward insecurity. Even very eminent people are reluctant to stand alone and they see in concurrence one of their chief tests of validity."[147] This very evaluation of courage, acting alone, and certainty is the consequence of Kissinger's formulation of his own life. Kissinger's past doubts and fears of confrontation have been projected onto others, while being alone is raised to a virtue. But there is, inherent in the view that courage, assertiveness and certainty are the primary values of a statesman, a perpetuation of uncertainty since you must also always be testing your will.

This, then, is the process by which personal motives are transformed into political action. We generally look simply at the rationalizations or political prescriptions of a political actor. That is, if a political actor feels that even ambiguous threats to American power such as "communist aggression" in Vietnam must be met with force, then that formula is usually viewed as the reason for an action taken or the reason for supporting such action. Rarely do we ask ourselves why a certain principle is believed or valued. Let us then take a closer look at the private motivation in Kissinger's testing process as manifested in Vietnam.

The most significant and confusing aspect of the manner in which Vietnam was handled in the Nixon Administration is two-fold: on the one hand is the congruity between the *form* advocated by Kissinger to end the conflict before his appointment as assistant to the President and the actual execution of the negotiations; and on the other hand, the almost absolute disjunction between the actual *substance* of the settlement and Kissinger's pre-appointment prescriptions.

The essential form of Kissinger's plan for negotiation was his two-track formula whereby the United States and Hanoi would hammer out the military questions, leaving the settlement of the political questions to the Vietnamese themselves. Of course the major obstacle before the accomplishment of this split was the North's insistence that the political questions be resolved before they even began to talk about the ending of military actions. But Kissinger countered in his *Foreign Affairs* article that if the United States got bogged down in negotiating explicit details of the political question, then U.S. interests would be squandered. He argued that if the U.S. attempted to negotiate a political settlement it would have to be on the basis of tacit bargaining rather than a formal agreement. In other words, Kissinger felt that if the war were to be resolved, the major issues would have to be left formally unresolved. Ambiguity was the order of the day. And it remains the most curious aspect of the final agreement. On the surface, everything political still remained to be resolved, but in fact the die had already been cast.

Two of the substantive quagmires which Kissinger warned the United States to stay away from are central to the final settlement. And it was the fact that these two factors were included that lay behind the North's willingness to settle. As Kissinger warned:

> Negotiating a ceasefire may well be tantamount to establishing the preconditions of a political settlement.... A tacit defacto ceasefire may prove more attainable than a negotiated one. By the same token, a formal ceasefire is likely to predetermine the ultimate settlement and tend toward partition. Ceasefire is thus not so much a step toward a final settlement as a form of it.[148]

The reason for this assessment is that in Vietnam there are really no symmetrical lines of engagement. The "enemy" cannot be driven back to an imaginary front-line because there is no front line. The "enemy" is everywhere. So if a ceasefire was negotiated, the only way to insure the political viability of the South would be to insure the withdrawal of enemy troops. Thus Kissinger's first warning was that enemy troops could not be allowed to remain in the South or the peace would be lost.

The second warning was closely tied to the first. In this instance Kissinger argued that the United States cannot be a party to negotiating a coalition government. "The issue is whether the United States should be party to an attempt to *impose* a coalition government. We must be clear that our involvement in such an effort may well destroy the existing political structure of South Viet Nam and thus lead to a communist takeover."[149] The reason that a coalition government will lead to a communist takeover is illustrated by one of Kissinger's examples of difficulties a coalition would bring about:

> Communist ministers would be foolhardy in the extreme if they entered Saigon without bringing along sufficient military force for their protection. But the introduction of communist military forces into the chief bastion of governmental strength would change the balance of political forces in South Viet Nam.[150]

Obviously, the ambiguity with regard to enemy troop withdrawal in the terms of the final agreement was a substantial departure from Kissinger's original position; and since the ceasefire has taken place, as Kissinger warned, the communist troops are acting very much like an occupation force. South Vietnam has now become a partitioned country: there are communist territories and government territories, and again as Kissinger argued, the military partition will inevitably lead to, at a minimum, a political division of power.

While it is not the United States which *imposes* the coalition government on the South, it is the United States which agreed to the conditions which, after a "suitable interval", will result in its equivalent. Such
is the nature of Nixon's "honorable peace". The disengagement from
Vietnam proved to be similar to a local town father straightening his tie
as he emerges from the local house of prostitution.

This of course raises the question of why we spent four additional
years fighting for the South to determine its own future when in the
end the terms of the agreement foreclose that future. It is a question
which will never have an adequate answer.

A partial answer, however, would be that Kissinger and Nixon simply
spent four years testing our strength and will, and ended by failing the
test. The U.S. steadily increased the level of violence in its test of
strength but, unlike a weight lifter, kept adding to the weight even after
it became apparent that the weight could not be lifted. If Vietnam had
not been viewed as a test, the United States never would have dragged
out the war for so long.

The war was a test on many levels. In one sense it was seen as a test
of credibility. As Kissinger argued,

> However fashionable it is to ridicule the terms credibility or
> prestige, they are not empty phrases; other nations can gear their
> actions to ours only if they can count on our steadiness. The
> collapse of the American effort in Viet Nam would not mollify
> many critics; most of them would simply add the charge of unre-
> liability to the accusation of bad judgement. Those whose safety
> or national goals depend on American commitment could only be
> dismayed. In many parts of the world—the Middle East, Europe,
> Latin America, even Japan—stability depends on confidence in
> American promises.[151]

But confidence and trust are of little value when the end result is a
worse position than what was started with. If the other countries,
which are supposedly looking at Vietnam as a test of the American
word, looked at the hard reality they would realize that the United
States cannot guarantee internal security with any sort of effectiveness
short of destroying the country in order to save it. Those nations would
do better to direct their attention to the ills in their own society that
give rise to instability than to hope for salvation in the form of American military might.

In general, American conduct in Vietnam was a series of test probes
designed to demonstrate purposefulness and strength. The Cambodia invasion for example was a test probe which was designed, among other
things, to demonstrate to the Soviet Union and Hanoi that the United
States was willing to stretch the limits of the war to the extent necessary
to end the conflict. In Kissinger's words, the Soviets will judge the U.S.

according to "the general purposefulness" of U.S. performance in Vietnam. We must demonstrate a willingness to face up to the risks of global diplomacy or the Soviets will be encouraged to step up pressures elsewhere. As Nixon said in his speech announcing the Cambodia invasion: "It is not our power, but our will and character that is being tested tonight."[152] Presumably, if we were to fail the test, the communists would look upon the United States as a paper tiger.

The dynamics of the Cambodia invasion are remarkably similar to the way the decision to mine Haiphong, which is discussed below, came about. The communists in both situations were conducting successful military operations, the U.S. military evaluation of the possibility for success in both instances was dubious at best, in both instances the reasons given for the moves were not necessarily military, but political and psychological, and in both instances the decisions were made in the face of substantial disagreement within the highest levels of the U.S. national security system.

Kissinger's role in the decision was central. It was Kissinger who spent the entire day alone with Nixon the day before the decision was made. On the day of the decision Nixon and Kissinger compared a set of pluses and minuses each had worked out for the operation. "Nixon glanced at Kissinger's list, Kissinger at Nixon's. The lists were almost identical."[153] The only people in the entire NSC system who were in favor of the decision were Nixon, Kissinger, and, predictably, the Joint Chiefs of Staff. For the most part, the "formalized machinery of the NSC was largely bypassed and . . . there were frequent direct contacts between White House officials [read Kissinger] and members of the JCS, with Secretary Laird feeling at times inadequately informed."[154] Rogers also opposed the action, and at one point Kissinger had a meeting with five of his brightest aides to get their views; all were against.[155] Nixon and Kissinger were truly alone.

The Kalbs tell us that during this period, "Kissinger's innate conservatism surfaced. His old fear of America's going the way of the Weimar Republic . . . obsessed him."[156] Kissinger, as he told a group of editors, felt that "what was at stake here was the problem of authority in this society altogether."[157]

It looks, then, as if we have most of the necessary ingredients to activate Kissinger's most fundamental psychological tensions. Here was a perfect opportunity for a test of "character" (as specifically stated by Nixon). There was the necessity to stand alone against great opposition and there were the unavoidable risks—both domestic and foreign—involved in carrying the war beyond the boundaries of Vietnam proper. That these factors were a part of Kissinger's position is difficult to refute in light of the terms used by Nixon to announce his decision—a decision in which Kissinger was the closest and most influential collaborator, and undoubtedly had a hand in the wording of the announce-ment. The mood of the announcement was reported by the *New Yorker* in much the same manner as described here. They reported: "According to the President and members of his Administration, the invasion was intended not simply to do something, but also to *prove* something—something about America's 'character' and 'courage' ".[158] Thus the Cambodia invasion is one of the best examples of the role Kissinger's testing and risk-taking played in our Vietnam policy. Had an individual been in Kissinger's place who was not "obsessed" with the prospect of America's decline, who did not view the situation as a crisis of authority, who did not feel compelled to demonstrate his willingness to face the abyss alone, who did not need to prove his strength, then it is likely that a different path would have been followed. The question remains, if Kissinger had said no, would Nixon have gone ahead totally alone?

Cambodia is another example of Kissinger's tendency to rely on no other person's judgement but his own. It would seem that this is a fur-ther manifestation of Kissinger's self-righteousness (which permeated his relationships from the time at Harvard when he was judged a "difficult colleague" to his management of the NSC staff where he is said "to bully and berate those underneath him") in collusion with Nixon's needs. This is further evidence that the "all-or-nothing" quality in Kissinger's moral and intellectual judgements remains.

But it is particularly at this point that the importance of a psycho-logical understanding of Kissinger is best revealed. Erikson has dis-cussed the characteristics of self-righteousness in these terms:

> It is the all-or-nothing quality of the super-ego, this organ of moral tradition, [that] makes moral man a great potential danger to his own ego—and to that of his fellow man. . . . The resulting self-righteousness can later be most intolerantly turned against others. . . . Moral Man's initiative is apt to burst the boundaries of self-restriction, permitting him to do to others in his or in other lands, what he would neither do nor tolerate being done to his own home.[159]

We have discussed the danger to his own ego in the tendency of Kissin-ger to treat himself with a certain self-contempt. But the tendency to direct this contempt outward, as in his bullying of his subordinates, his wife, and colleagues, takes on a new character once Kissinger is Special Assistant. It would not seem to be a coincidence that the tactical nuclear weapons advocated for use by Kissinger would take place in underde-veloped countries, nor is it a coincidence that the willingness to engage in limited war is largely restricted to those countries. Likewise, it was Kissinger, who in his wisdom declared that Vietnam simply is not a moral issue[160] and proceeded to orchestrate the violation of the boundaries of Cambodia, doing to others what he would not tolerate being done to himself. It is the distinction of such "moral men" that morality is posited solely in their person, to be distributed according to their view of what deserves to be considered a moral issue. Rather than bullying subordinates or his wife, he became a principle actor in the bullying of North Vietnam in an attempt to force them into a settlement on American terms.

Another of the more important choices in this process was the decision to mine Haiphong. The decision to mine Haiphong Harbor can be set in perspective by looking at *National Security Study Memorandum #1* (NSSM#1) which was the first task assigned to the NSC staff when Nixon came into office. It was an over-all study of the Vietnam situation and one section was devoted to the feasibility of cutting off the shipment of war materials to the North by mining Haiphong and submitting overland routes to intensive bombing. The 548 page report was secret until released by Senator Gravel and printed in part by several newspapers and journals, including the *New York Review of Books.*[161] This study was to provide the basis for Nixon's secret plan to end the war; the major feature, as Whalen reported,[162] was the Haiphong move. Interestingly enough, nowhere in the report was there mention of Vietnamization, the path ultimately chosen. In addition, with regard to the effectiveness of the blockade against Haiphong, the report ranged from doubtful to strongly negative. The CIA flatly stated that

> All of the war-essential imports could be brought into North Vietnam over rail lines or roads from China in the event that imports by sea were successfully denied. . . . Almost four years of air war in North Vietnam have shown that . . . air strikes . . . can not successfully interdict the flow of supplies.[163]

The State Department was more disposed to the operation, but the Defense Department felt the operation would be unsuccessful unless "the air campaign would be conducted in such a manner as to be free of the militarily confining constraints which have characterized the conduct of the war in the North in the past."[164] But the DOD admitted that the lifting of such restraints necessarily "would accept high risks of civilian casualties in order to achieve destruction of war supporting targets."[165] Although State and the DOD were somewhat positive in their responses, the answers were hedged with all sorts of "ifs" that ended up saying that if the North was willing to devote sufficient man power to their transportation operations, they would be capable of overcoming the obstacles American actions would place before them.

Nixon himself realized that even if the operation could be successful it would involve great risk of bringing the Soviets directly into the picture in a confrontation that could lead to the apocalypse. He said before his election, "We can't invade North Vietnam. The only thing left is Haiphong and that involves risks with the Soviets."[166] So apparently, because of the uncertainty that the operation would achieve what it was intended to achieve, and therefore involve too substantial a cost for such minimal returns, the plan was put on the shelf for three years. In the meantime Nixon tried his Vietnamization policy.

But what happened to force Nixon into falling back on this dubious plan? There were several pressures which led to the decision. First, it could be argued that the decision to mine Haiphong was simply part of a calculated negotiating process in which increased levels of force alternate with periods of negotiation, until the costs for the enemy become too great to sustain. Certainly this interpretation fits the Nixon-Kissinger formula for negotiation and at some level provides one of the base lines from which the decision was made. However, the second line of argument deserves greater credibility. This argument is that Nixon was forced into a corner by the North Vietnamese offensive which shattered the image that Vietnamization had succeeded. And directly related to the second line of argument, a third would be that with the domestic situation in poor shape, an apparent failure overseas would dash Nixon's hope for victory in the up-coming elections and revitalize the war as a political issue. Let us look then at the implications of these arguments.

As election time grew nearer and all the efforts to end the war seemed futile, the last thing Nixon could have afforded would have been a major failure overseas. On top of the resentment of workers over wage control, the frustration of consumers over rising prices, the anger at the inequality of the tax structure, and the burning fuse beneath the busing bomb, a washout in Vietnam would have been more than the American voter could have taken.

However, just after Easter in 1972, the North Vietnamese offensive shattered the image of progress so painstakingly created by the Nixon Administration. While the North Vietnamese troops began to overwhelm the half-hearted resistance of ARVN, it looked as if Nixon's Vietnam policy would join the long list of Administration failures. It became apparent that the progress reported by Nixon like the progress reported by Johnson before him, was but an image. Thus Nixon began to look in desperation for a new image that would conceal the shattered pieces of the old.

What Nixon needed was an action that would be so dramatic as to cause enough commotion to draw attention away from North Vietnam's advances, thereby not compounding the embarrassment on the domestic front. Thus in an effort to win votes at home, Nixon pulled his trump card. Called on to do double duty, his unrevealed plan of 1968 was pulled out from the bottom of the secret National Security Memorandums in an attempt to renew his lease on Pennsylvania Ave.

NSSM#1 makes clear that the plan which Nixon improvised in a moment of off-the-cuff questions and answers during the 1968 election campaign was the plan to confront the Soviets with a blockade of Haiphong. And as indicated by Nixon's cancelled speech on Vietnam,[167] the President felt that Vietnam could only be settled by confronting the Soviet Union's role in supporting North Vietnam. Nixon's plea in his cancelled speech was to bring the Soviet Union to the bargaining table, but, to use his own words, "in the language of realism that the Soviets understand". The speech is littered with similarly veiled military threats, and Nixon cites John Kennedy's action in the Missile Crisis as the type of realism the United States needs to make "a fresh start."

The North Vietnamese offensive in 1972 was embarassing Nixon and was a direct affront to American strength. The only answer was to come back with something stronger than anything that had been tried before. The North's offensive had darkened the abyss and it became necessary to face up to the risks "or perish in the process". Nixon had stated that he would not "be driven into the sea", and was therefore ready to make the decision which in I. F. Stone's words at the time, was "potentially the gravest decision ever taken by an American President for it sets off a slow fuse that could ignite World War III."[168]

But aside from balancing the threat to American strength, the blockade would serve an extremely useful political function. By painting a picture of crisis, Nixon had hoped to rally the American people behind the Presidency as they had rallied so often in the past in times of crisis. He succeeded according to a Harris poll late in May of 1972. Nixon obviously is a man not unaware of the impact of foreign crisis and summit trips on domestic popularity. As Whalen describes Nixon, "He conceived the Presidency almost entirely as a foreign policy making office. He also had a lively appreciation of the potential domestic political rewards of personal diplomacy. Whenever Johnson's Glassboro meeting with Kosygin came up, Nixon noted with amazement that nothing had happened there, yet Johnson's poll-rating jumped sharply."[169] We can be sure that the lesson did not go unlearned.

But what of Kissinger's part in the decision? There have been conflicting reports on Kissinger's position, and the variance stems largely from Kissinger's attempt to keep his image as the administration's dove intact among intellectuals. I was in Washington at the time of the Haiphong crisis and spoke with a number of people working on the NSC staff. It was clear from these interviews that Kissinger was in favor of the move, even though later some of the sources bought Kissinger's later "doubts" story. After the event, Kissinger let loose with a few hints that he was not one hundred percent behind the President's decision. I must agree with the Kalbs that it is highly possible Kissinger was simply manipulating the press and as an aide put it, "agonizing about his image with the liberal community."[170]

It is almost certain Kissinger took an active and supportive role in the decision. He had secretly gone to the Soviet Union and as an aide told me "felt out the Communists". The Kalbs tell us that "Moorer and Kissinger were the strongest advocates of B-52 strikes against North Vietnam's capital and its major port."[171] Kissinger needed a "signal" that the U.S. would not tolerate being humiliated by the communist offensive at any cost, including the upcoming summit.

The costs however could have been much greater than a cancelled summit. How far could the Soviet Union and China go in ignoring the destruction of their own ships in Haiphong?[172] Certainly the risks of big power confrontation were great even with the secret consultations. Not only were the risks great, but militarily the move was thought to be at best dubious. Once again risk and being alone were central to the dynamics of decision-making.

Both Kissinger and Nixon felt that the North's offensive was an affront to American power and that, therefore, we would have to respond or be embarrassed militarily—a condition which Kissinger had stated was unacceptable (see opening quote to this chapter). We must conclude that the decision to mine Haiphong was heavily colored by psychological proclivities which forced Kissinger not to run away from risks, not to allow himself to be embarrassed, and not to allow the situation to get out of control.

The decision to mine Haiphong is important in pointing up the most dangerous aspects of the Nixon-Kissinger doctrine in both its intellectual rationalizations and psychological mind-set. The Haiphong incident is an excellent example, as was the Cambodia decision, of the basic presuppositions of global diplomacy. In I. F. Stone's words:

> It is now clear that Nixon took the gamble on Vietnamization in the hope that if this failed, a bigger gamble would succeed. The bigger gamble . . . was either to buy off Moscow and Peking or, if that didn't work, to use the threat of nuclear confrontation to make them stand by while we destroyed North Vietnam from the air. In other words, if his gamble failed he was and is prepared to gamble America's future and the world's. This is the reality behind Nixon's proclaimed "search for a generation of peace."[173]

Had an administration been in office that did not view Vietnam as a test and which did not feel the need to demonstrate strength and face risks, there is a great probability that the war would not have lasted an additional four years.

X. UP FROM THE TEST

"To cooperate without losing one's soul, to assist without sacrificing one's identity, to work for deliverance in the guise of bondage and under enforced silence, what harder test of moral toughness exists?"

–Henry Kissinger,
A World Restored

Consistently Kissinger has shown that "it is the strong opponent that counts."[174] His concern in the peace negotiations were so exclusively centered upon Le Duc Tho that he over-looked Thieu, which resulted in the December blood bath.[175] "Allies are tiresome necessities, but adversaries pose a challenge that can be capped with the sweet triumph of a hard bargained deal."[176] It was Kissinger's need as a youth to organize the chaos which surrounded him that sent him in search of strong figures. That search may have ended, but its lessons for Kissinger remain.

In a review of the Kalb's book, Ronald Steel summarizes the impression one receives after reading their account. I invite the reader to compare this summary with the characteristics of the depressive personality with which we began this essay:

one sees his hypersensitivity to criticism, his insistence on personalizing any disagreement, his self-pity and much-advertised paranoia, his lack of self-confidence (which may explain his fear of appearing 'soft' and his hard-line position on military policy), his insensitivity to those serving under him, and his obsequiousness toward those of higher standing. These are not unique traits, and are not more contemptible than those of many great men. But they are important if we are to understand the person Kissinger is.[177]

Kissinger did not stay in his youthful cocoon. He would come back from total non-involvement with others to the point of being the center of world attention, involved in all our lives. There was a point in Kissinger's life when he quit "crossing to the other side of the street."

Today Kissinger continues to view his own performance in terms of uncertainty and as a test, as in his remarks about his own period of statesmanship. He has said, "The great danger of any policy is to project the present into the future. You have to base your bet on a judgement which cannot be proved true. This takes inward strength. It takes someone who is not worried by being alone a while."[178] A bet is another form of test. There is the same uncertainty and in effect a bet is simply a test of intuition, or, in the sense implied by Kissinger, of knowledge of the situation. The policy-maker does not base his *decision,* but his *bet,* on a judgement which cannot be proved.

When there is a bureaucratic structure in which all information is funneled through one channel, and responsibility for decision-making is a "lonely process", this tendency toward risk-taking increases the possibility of losing the bet or failing the test. It is refreshing to have leaders who at least tacitly recognize their fallibility, but when all the chips are in the pot it would be best to *avoid* risks than to have to always confront uncertainty. Brodine and Selden summarize this tendency toward risk-taking in their admirable analysis of the Nixon-Kissinger doctrine entitled *The Open Secret.* In their words:

> Kissinger's entire system minimizes the opportunity for those who would avoid risk to affect the final outcome of a decision. . . . When wise and humane counsel is needed we may anticipate instead a confrontation called for by those 'strong nerves' characteristic of the Kissinger ideal of statesmanship, that willingness to 'fact up to the risks of Armageddon' in the hope that the other side will back down.[179]

Brodine and Selden's statement turned out to be prophetic in the case of the "Red Alert" initiated by Kissinger in October of 1973. Here was a clear case in which the crackpot realism of the Kissinger-Nixon Doctrine brought us into a direct and, by most unofficial accounts, unnecessary confrontation with the Soviet Union.[180]

Thus Kissinger, backed by American fire power, has offset his past avoidance of risks, behavior for which he severely castigated others, with a need to place himself in situations where he could demonstrate his courage, strength, adequacy or ability. His entire philosophy as expounded in *Nuclear Weapons and Foreign Policy* is based on the "willingness to face up to the risks." This is in marked contrast to the young boy who ran to the other side of the street to avoid the risk of an oncoming threat. Unfortunately, today his personal tests become meshed with national tests. The danger of course is that in an attempt to prove his worth, Kissinger is apt to attempt to pull something off, the resources for which he lacks.

There is a second aspect to this sort of behavior. As emphasized in his cowboy statement, and his bet statement, and his statement referring to the lack of courage on the part of intellectuals and policy-makers, the political actor is viewed as one who must act *alone.* Kissinger made a revealing comment on the subject when he said: "This romantic and surprising character suits me because being alone has always been part of my style, or, if you wish, of my technique."[181] If we remember Kissinger's lauding of Metternich's technique which was a "symbol of certainty" then it would seem that Kissinger views himself in much the same romanticized manner in which he viewed his "beau-ideals". But somehow Kissinger decked out in chaps and spurs, riding his horse with a briefcase tucked beneath his arm is a tragically ridiculous figure.

"Being alone" was the symbol of the Nixon Administration. Decisions were not cooperative and consultative decisions, but "lonely" decisions. Nixon's retreat to Camp David or to Key Biscaine before major decisions had an air of deliberativeness about them. But there is another side to the coin. If one makes decisions alone there is no one present who can sense or see doubt. No one to turn to and admit uncertainty, no one to see weakness. Neither is there anyone to suggest alternatives. Psychologically, being alone is one means of protection from a world perceived as hostile and is a protection against a self which is experienced as unembodied or dismembered in the presence of others. To what extent this is the motivation behind both Nixon's[182] and Kissinger's retreat into isolation has yet to be investigated; but from what we know of Kissinger's past and his personality, being alone serves as a means of protection against revealing doubt or uncertainty and is felt as a "safe" and "strong" condition. Thus a personal, psychological characteristic became a public, governmental method of operation. Decisions became personal tests; national pride was tested in Vietnam and our willingness to stand up and fight was tested in Haiphong and reflected in Red Alerts.

If we take Kissinger's marked intellectual preference for facing risks and his belief that leaders must stand alone on certain issues against public opinion, we can begin to understand his psychological readiness to escalate the level of violence in Vietnam. The four years of Nixon's first administration far exceeded the boundaries of violence set by President Johnson. It was after Nixon's election that the United States moved into Cambodia, mined Haiphong Harbor, bombed Hanoi, and, to an extent not matched in any other period, exported violence in the form of "protective reaction strikes" outside the area of Vietnam proper. All of these actions involved steadily increasing risks of big-power confrontation.[183] In terms of magnitude, the actions taken during this period far exceed the level of violence and destruction of other post WWII brinksmen. While the Berlin Crisis and the Cuban Missile Crisis were equally tense moments in our history, they were in no way equal in terms of actual death and destruction attendant upon U.S. actions in Vietnam. Measured in actual human suffering, the bellicosity of Dulles or Kennedy brinksmanship is more than equalled by the Nixon-Kissinger version of Global Diplomacy.

It may well be the "loneliness" theme which provides for the increased readiness to ignore the human costs of violence. One aspect of the depressive personality that is an important component of this style is the tendency toward withdrawal and lack of involvement or empathy with others. It is significant that Kissinger's concerns are largely with the abstract; with women in occupied countries, not specific individuals; with women as a hobby, not in their uniqueness; with order and chaos, and not individual lives and individual deaths. When extended to the actual conduct of decision-making, this tendency results in the abstract pursuit of empty phrases like "peace with honor" or "a generation of peace". It was largely as a result of the consultative nature of Kennedy's handling of the Cuban missile crisis that a blockade was settled upon rather than the more violent "surgical air strikes" which were Kennedy's first instinctive reaction.[184] The pressure of others who were involved in the actual decision-making was one of the reasons why an alternative was settled upon. In Kissinger's "lonely road" there is no opportunity for those who would exercise caution to have their views heard.[185]

There can be little doubt that at the bottom of Kissinger's political action are his private motivations. In a later work I will go more into the political issues, but for the moment, I hope I have established the psychological beginning to an understanding of Kissinger's role in American foreign policy.

Kissinger is searching for an external order that can substitute for his inner chaos. Uncomfortable with ambiguity, he responds with a pervasive moral certainty. Countering internal threats to his being, he projects his anxiety onto appropriate objects in the real world and invests them with an affect that indicates an intensity much greater than might seem appropriate. The displacement is then transformed into an intellectual rationalization in an attempt to tame and strip the fears of their power over him. As a political actor he attempts to transform his intellectual rationalizations into political reality.

How much of this political reality is the product of Kissinger's actions and how much is Nixon's, is the most unsatisfactory aspect of the analysis. Their compatibility makes this task particularly difficult. Indeed, the compatibility of the two men is reminiscent of Wilson and Colonel House in which House played upon Wilson's needs to satisfy his own ambition.

William Appleman Williams once commented on the Nixon-Kissinger relationship in much the same manner. Williams describes Nixon as a man fleeing forward from a lack of a sense of self. As Nixon has said, "Any person tends to vegetate unless he is moving on a fast track."[186] Thus when Nixon and Kissinger met, Kissinger's desire for control of his environment overcame a strong personal dislike of Nixon and combined with Nixon's need for a new frontier. "Kissinger understood (or sensed) ... [that] for a man fleeing forward the last frontier is the world. There is the virgin land where a man can find and fulfill himself (see H. N. Smith's *Virgin Land*). And no doubt about it, the making of foreign policy within *that* idiom *is* the fastest track of all."[187] But like all tracks, it is circular and the race becomes an endless repetition. Unfortunately, as Marx pointed out long ago, the second time around is a farce.

Dana Ward was educated at the University of California, Berkeley, and the University of Chicago. Presently, he is completing work towards his doctorate at Yale.

REFERENCES

I would like to express my gratitude to Marvin Zonis, Susanne Rudolph and Ted Wysocki who read and criticized the paper at an early stage in its development, and to Lloyd deMause for his suggestion of the concept of the depressive personality and for his skill and thoughtfulness as an editor.

1. *The President and the Management of National Security,* Clark and Legere, eds., (New York: Praeger, 1969), p. 8.
2. The analysis of the depressive personality is based upon Wolman's account in *Call No Man Normal,*Benjamin B. Wolman, (New York: International Univer-
3. sities Press, Inc., 1973).
3. *Chicago Daily News,* Gaylord Shaw, May 2, 1972.
4. *Harpers,* J. Kraft, January, 1971.
5. *New York Times,* November 14, 1971.
6. Interview on August 28, 1974 with Jack Heiman.
7. From talks with friends of the family, there is some reason to think that Louis Kissinger had believed in the pre-Nazi myths of the German culture, and that to a large extent he held an assimilationist attitude. For that reason the shock of Hitler must have been that much more distressing and unbelievable to him. This would account for his stunned reaction to Hitler's rise as will be discussed below. However, I should caution the reader that there is no direct evidence of this assimilationist attitude, only inferences made by old friends.
8. *Atlantic Monthly,* "Professor Bismarck goes to Washington", by Nora Beloff, December, 1969.
9. *Chicago Daily News,* Gaylord Shaw, May 2, 1972.
10. *Ibid.*
11. *Time,* Feb., 14, 1971.
12. *New York Times,* Nov. 14, 1971.
13. *Ibid.*
14. Heiman interview, August 28, 1974.
15. For more on this subject see my master's thesis at the University of Chicago: *Kissinger: A Study in Personality.*
16. *Reader's Digest,* October, 1969.
17. Howard Rome, "The Social Origin of the Depressive Personality", *Psychiatric Annals,* June, 1974.
18. Wolman, *op. cit.,* p. 244.
19. *Ibid.,* p. 233.
20. *Ibid.,* p. 234.
21. *Ibid.,* p. 238.
22. Heiman interview, August 28, 1974.
23. *New York Post,* series ran between June 3 and June 15, 1974, hereafter cited as *Post* Series.
24. Heiman interview, August 28, 1974
25. *Chicago Sun Times,* October 24, 1971, "He's President Nixon's Brainchild", by Lloyd Shearer.

26. Heiman interview, August 28, 1974.
27. Wolman, p. 231.
28. *Ibid.*, p. 230-1.
29. *Post* series.
30. Heiman interview, August 28, 1974.
31. *Ibid.*
32. The question of course is what was Walter's response? Perhaps because of his special relation to Jack, his more secure sense of self, or a closer relation to his mother (which must be investigated further) Walter may have been better able to deal with the situation. Naturally this is a major gap in the data which we hopefully will be able to fill later.
33. Heiman interview, August 28, 1974.
34. *Ibid.*
35. *Ibid.*
36. *Ibid.*
37. *Post* series.
38. *Ibid.*
39. *Ibid.*
40. *Ibid.*
41. *Chicago Daily News,* May 2, 1972, Gaylord Shaw.
42. Henry Kissinger, *A World Restored* (Grosset & Dunlap: New York, 1964), p. 83.
43. *New York Times,* November 14, 1971.
44. See David Landau, *Kissinger: The Uses of Power* (Boston: Houghton Miflin, 1972), p. 75-77 for details of the intellectual reaction.
45. Based on two interviews with ex-members of the National Security Council Staff. Another reason of course has to do with the White House relationship with the press and other political considerations.
46. *Harpers,* January, 1971, article by J. Kraft.
47. *Ibid.*
48. *Ibid.*
49. Henry Kissinger, *The Necessity For Choice* (New York: Harper and Row, 1960), p. 8.
50. *Harpers,* January, 1971, article by J. Kraft.
51. *Ibid.*
52. *Atlantic Monthly,* Beloff, December, 1969.
53. *Ibid.*
54. Interview with the author, December 16, 1972.
55. I use the term "hero" because even though "hero" is a word which tends to brind faint smiles and visions of knights and damsels in distress, the word is used repeatedly by Kissinger in his own conversations and writing. To Kissinger, a hero is a specific sort of individual who acts alone in the face of overpowering obstacles.
56. Landau, *op. cit.,* p. 15.
57. *Look,* August 12, 1969.
58. *Time,* December 22, 1969, p. 23.
59. Kissinger, *Necessity for Choice, op. cit.,* p. 290.
60. Landau, *op. cit.,* p. 130-31.
61. Landau, *op. cit.,* p. 16.
62. *Ibid.,* p. 16.
63. For the theoretical foundation of what follows see Erik Erikson; *Identity: Youth and Crisis, op. cit., Young Man Luther* (New York: Norton, 1962), *Childhood and Society,* (New York: Norton, 1963), and *Insight and Responsibility* (New York: Norton, 1964).
64. *Identity: Youth and Crisis, op. cit.,* p. 257.
65. *Ibid.,* p. 156.
66. *Atlantic Monthly,* Beloff, December, 1969.
67. Landau, *op. cit.,* p. 18-19.
68. *Ibid.,* p. 19.
69. *New York Times Magazine,* November 14, 1971, p. 107.
70. *Ibid.*

71. *Ibid.*
72. *Ibid.*
73. *Post* series.
74. *Ibid.*
75. *Ibid.*
76. Wolman, *op. cit.,* p. 228.
77. Erikson, *Identity: Youth and Crisis, op. cit.,* p. 184.
78. Landau, *op. cit.,* p. 20-21.
79. *Ibid.,* p. 20.
80. *Chicago Daily News,* Gaylord Shaw, *op. cit.,* May 2, 1972.
81. *Ibid.*
82. Interview with a friend of Kissinger's from the Harvard days, December, 16, 1972.
83. Landau, *op. cit.,* p. 40-41.
84. *Harpers,* Jan., 1971.
85. *Post* Series.
86. Interview by the author with a close friend during and after the Harvard years on December 16, 1972.
87. *Post* Series.
88. *New York Times,* November 14, 1971.
89. Interview, December 16, 1972.
90. *Ibid.*
91. *Ibid.*
92. An alternative interpretation might be that Kissinger cared about what the "public" thought of his judgement. In that case his assault upon Ann would be a public advertisement that he too knew she was no credit to him. But I feel this interpretation has less validity than that which is developed in the body of the paper; for if he cared about what the public thought of his judgement then it would seem that he would not want to call attention to his "mistake".
93. Interview with one of Kissinger's old friends on December 16, 1972.
94. R. D. Laing, *Divided Self,* (Middlesex, England: Penguin Books Inc.; 1971), p. 48.
95. Wolman, *op. cit.,* p. 238.
96. Kissinger, *Necessity for Choice, op. cit.,* p. 303.
97. Charles Ashman, *Kissinger: The Adventures of Super-Kraut* (Secaucus, New Jersey: Lyle Stuart, 1972), p. 59.
98. Landau, *op. cit.,* p. 21.
99. Interview on December 16, 1972 with an old friend.
100. Interview, Dec. 16, 1972.
101. *Ibid.*
102. Wolman, *op. cit.,* p. 247.
103. Interview December 16, 1972.
104. *Ibid.*
105. Landau, *op. cit.,* p. 22.
106. Beloff, *op. cit.*
107. *Ibid.*
108. An interesting sidelight to the International Seminar is that in April of 1967 "The summer school International Seminar at Harvard which Professor Kissinger directs was identified as the recipient of funds used by thirteen foundations as conduits for the CIA. He denied any knowledge of the origin of the money and said that the program had not been influenced by it." *New York Times,* December 4, 1968.
109. As Landau has written, "The great bulk of his writing contains ideas that have originated elsewhere. His first publications on limited nuclear war drew heavily from earlier work by Bernard Brodie, James Gavin, and Edward Teller . . . His ideas about negotiation and tacit communication depended almost entirely on the writings of Thomas Schelling and Herman Kahn . . . To say that Kissinger was an intellectual pioneer in any of these areas would be a gross overstatement." Landau, *op. cit.,* p. 56.

110. Interview on May 10, 1972.
111. Landau, *op. cit.*, p. 48, quoting Kissinger in *Nuclear Weapons and Foreign Policy*, (New York: W. W. Norton, 1969), p. 37-8.
112. Kissinger, in *Arms Control, Disarmament and National Security*, ed. Brennan, 1961, p. 143.
113. Interview with a member of NSC staff, May 11, 1972, and below.
114. Landau, *op. cit.*, p. 55.
115. *Ibid.*, p. 53.
116. I. F. Stone, *New York Review of Books*, November 2, 1972, p. 22.
117. I. F. Stone, *New York Review of Books*, October 19, 1972, p. 14.
118. Landau, *op. cit.*, p. 81.
119. *Ibid.*, p. 81.
120. *Newsweek*, December 22, 1969.
121. *Time*, February 14, 1969.
122. *Post* Series.
123. Landau, *op. cit.*, p. 84-85.
124. J. Kraft, *Harpers*, January, 1971.
125. Wolman, *op. cit.*, p. 248.
126. *Ibid.*, p. 225.
127. Wolman, *op. cit.*, p. 244.
128. *Ibid.*, p. 235.
129. *Post* Series.
130. I. F. Stone, *New York Review of Books*, November 2, 1972, p. 23.
131. *A World Restored, op. cit.*, p. 331.
132. *Chicago Daily News*, Shaw, May 2, 1972.
133. *Chicago Sun Times*, Shearer, October 24, 1971.
134. *A World Restored, op. cit.*, p. 8-9.
135. Kissinger, *Daedelus*, Spring, 1968.
136. Landau, *op. cit.*, p. 134.
137. *A World Restored, op. cit.*, p. 8.
138. A critic has argued that Kissinger's arrogance may simply be a cultural characteristic and not a peculiarity of Kissinger's personality. I feel that Kissinger's arrogance may well be supported by German cultural traditions which lean toward the arrogant, but that given the language in the preceeding quote I doubt that culture was, in this respect, the determining factor. The language romanticizes the tranquility of the pre-revolutionary world and emphasizes the impossibility of attaining certitude after disruption. Kissinger knew what it was like to live through revolution and would attempt to incorporate the certitude of pre-revolutionary life by copying Metternich's style—but lacking the certitude of youth, his behavior results in arrogance.
139. *Harpers*, J. Kraft, *op. cit.*, January, 1971.
140. *Post* Series.
141. See my masters' thesis for details, *op. cit.*
142. See Beloff, *op. cit.*, p. 87, and a television interview on CBS's *60 Minutes*, November 18, 1972.
143. Beloff, *op. cit.*
144. *A World Restored, op. cit.*, p. 16.
145. *Ibid.*, p. 325.
146. *Necessity for Choice, op. cit.*, p. 3.
147. Kissinger, "Policy Maker and the Intellectual", reprinted from the *Reporter*, March 5, 1959, in Selected Materials from Senator Jackson's report of the subcommittee on Government Operation, *Organizing for National Security*, 1960, p. 256.
148. *Foreign Affairs*, January, 1969, "The Vietnam Negotiations", Henry Kissinger.
149. *Ibid.*
150. *Ibid.*
151. *Ibid.*
152. *U.S. News & World Report*, May 11, 1970.
153. Marvin and Bernard Kalb, *Kissinger* (Boston: Little Brown & Co.), 1974, p. 161.

154. *New York Times*, June 14, 1970.
155. *Harpers, op. cit.*, January 1971.
156. Kalb and Kalb, *op. cit.*, p. 164.
157. *Ibid.*, p. 169.
158. *New Yorker*, May 9, 1970.
159. Erikson, *Childhood and Society, op. cit.*, p. 257.
160. *Look*, August 12, 1969.
161. *New York Review of Books*, June 1, 1972.
162. Richard Whalen, *Catch the Falling Flag* (New York: Houghton Miflin Co., 1972).
163. *New York Review of Books*, June 1, 1972, quoted from NSSM #1.
164. *Ibid.*
165. *Ibid.*
166. Whalen, *op. cit.*, quoted in I. F. Stone, *NYRB*, June 1, 1972.
167. *Ibid.*
168. *NYRB*, June 1, 1972, *op. cit.*, p. 11.
169. Whalen, *op. cit.*
170. Kalb and Kalb, *op. cit.*, p. 301.
171. *Ibid.*, p. 290.
172. There were reports, unacknowledged by China or the Soviet Union, that at least one ship was damaged. See *Facts on File*, May 1972.
173. *NYRB, op. cit.*, June 1, 1972.
174. *NYRB*, September 19, 1974, p. 25.
175. For details see Kalb and Kalb, *op. cit.*, and "Behind the Cease Fire Agreement, by Tad Szulc, *Foreign Policy*, Summer 1974.
176. *NYRB*, September, 19, 1974, *op. cit.*, p. 26.
177. *Ibid.*, p. 29.
178. *Newsweek*, August 21, 1972.
179. Brodine and Selden, *The Open Secret: The Kissinger-Nixon Doctrine in Asia* (New York: Harper and Row, 1972), p. 7.
180. For details see: Roger Morris, "Kissinger and the Brothers Kalb", *Washington Monthly*, July/August, 1974.
181. Fallaci, *op. cit.*, December 16, 1972.
182. For evidence of Nixon's retreat see a similar approach to mine in Bruce Mazlish's *In Search of Nixon* (New York: Basic Books, Inc., 1972).
183. The most risky being the mining of Haiphong Harbor with the possibility of damaging foreign ships.
184. See Graham T. Allison, *Essence of Decision: Explaining the Cuban Missile Crisis* (Boston: Little Brown and Co., 1971).
185. And I am not holding the Kennedy system up as a model of decision-making, but simply saying that the increased circle of decision makers changed the flow of the process and helped, to a small degree, to balance some of the personality factors—a balance which was lacking in the Nixon Administration.
186. William Appleman Williams, *New York Review of Books*, February 24, 1972, quoting Nixon.
187. *Ibid.*

CHAPTER 5

Fathers and Sons Revisited: The Childhood of Vissarion Belinskii

PATRICK P.
DUNN

In the first issue of this Journal, *the experiment of Bronson Alcott in attempting to bring up his children without physical punishment was described. At about the same time, early in the nineteenth century, a Russian father was trying to do much the same thing, but in an atmosphere of even greater social disapproval. Professor Dunn describes the results in his fascinating study of the family origin of personal autonomy, and speculates on broader trends in Russian childrearing which may have helped create the conditions for later revolutionary action.*

". . . you weren't treated harshly as a child?"
"You see the kind of parents I have: not at all strict."
"Are you fond of them, Yevgeny?"
"I am Arkady!"
"They're very fond of you!"

—Turgenev, *Fathers and Sons*

. . . [Grigorii Belynskii] was the only father in the city who understood that in raising children it is not necessary to treat them like cattle."

—D. P. Ivanov

For a variety of reasons Ivan Turgenev's *Fathers and Sons* has long been recognized as a great novel: in it Turgenev creates his first strong masculine hero, Evgenii Bazarov; it has become a symbol of generational conflict; and it occupies a central position in Russian intellectual history, marking simultaneously the emergence of the term "nihilism" and the split between Turgenev and the leaders of the radical tradition in Russian literary criticism. Bazarov, the central character in the novel, was modeled on the life of the noted literary and social critic, Vissarion Belinskii (1811-48). Both fictional Bazarov and real Belinskii were commoners, sons of military doctors who had retired to the provinces after the Napoleonic Wars; both made their way in the world by their intelligence rather than by inherited wealth or position; both hastened their death through their own carelessness about their health; and both were revolutionaries, seeking to destroy (through ideas and persuasion rather than violence) the very foundations of mid-nineteenth-century Russia.

Rarely noticed, however, is the unusual relationship between Bazarov and his father. The warm, nurturant attitude of the elder Bazarov stands in stark contrast to the cold, distant, even hostile attitude characteristic of Russian fathers in the nineteenth century. But this fictional relationship too had its reference in reality, in the relationship of Belinskii and his father. In this article I will explore Belinskii's unusual childhood and how it influenced his later career as literary and social critic.

Vissarion Belinskii was born in Sveaborg, Finland, apparently in May of 1811. His father, Grigorii (1784-1835), was a physician assigned to the Russian Baltic Fleet stationed in that city; his mother, Mariia Belynskaia (1788-1834), was the daughter of a ship captain whom Grigorii had met the previous year when assigned to the Kronstadt naval base. Both Belynskii and his father-in-law were sons of priests who, because of wartime needs, now found themselves in military rather than clerical garb. Grigorii and Mariia were married less than six months after they had first met; their son followed nine months later, and then in the fall of 1811 Grigorii left for sea duty until 1813.[1]

Vissarion's first year was a difficult one.

> I remember the history of my mother. She loved to roam about like a scandal-monger, to make idle chatter. As an infant I was left to a nurse, a hired wench; so that I would not disturb her with my cries, she smothered and struck me. . . . of course I was not given the breast; I was a sickly infant, near death, and did not take the breast, did not know it (although now I love it doubly), I sucked on a nursing bottle and even then, if the milk was soured or spoiled—I was not able to get fresh milk.[2]

There is no additional account of these early events which might confirm or disconfirm Belinskii's recollection, but it would be unfair to doubt the honesty of these words, to doubt that this at least is what Belinskii believed occurred. Further, as I shall show later, the inability of Mariia Belinskaia to comprehend and satisfy her children's psychological needs can be substantiated. Vissarion's memory of infancy either genuinely or symbolically indicates the early extreme oral deprivation which was to influence his adult life.

Mariia Belinskaia, however, was not an unusual mother. The traditional Russian mother was detached from her children, restrictive rather than permissive in handling their spontaneous behavior, and understood only the basic material needs of her children. Although I have dealt with this topic elsewhere,[3] for proper perspective it should be pointed out that the use of wet-nurses was widespread in Russia, as was swaddling children and then entrusting them to the care of older children or old women. Mothers simply were not greatly involved with their children; indeed in the 1780's when the mother of Sergei Aksakov personally put her infant daughter to the breast of the wet-nurse and personally rocked her child to sleep, a relative warned that "such exaggerated love was a crime against God, and he would surely punish it."[4] Mariia Belinskaia did not commit such a crime. She emerges from the recollections of friends and relatives as a "fiery and irritable" woman who was unable to relate to her husband "in a loving and trusting manner," and "all of her concern, as with the majority of provincial mothers, was concentrated on clothing her children properly and especially on feeding them satisfactorily."[5] Her concern with feeding children is not inconsistent with Belinskii's memories of infancy; a hired girl with a bottle would be satisfactory in the mind of an adult who had no realization of the significance of the mother-infant relationship at feeding.

In 1816 Grigorii Belynskii resigned from service for reasons of health (further details unknown) and took a government position as the district doctor in Chembar, located in his home province of Penza. He had excellent connections in Chembar; the Secretary of the District Court, Petr Ivanov, had married one of Belynskii's cousins, and Vissarion was to become very close to the Ivanov children, especially Ekaterina and Dmitrii; the wealthiest landowner in the district, Nikolai Vladykin, was also related by marriage to the family of the new doctor. With his profession and these social ties Belynskii might well have become a popular and respected member of society; instead he became alienated, lonely, and bitter.

What differentiated Belynskii from the rest of society and led to his alienation were his experiences in the years 1805-11. The son of an Orthodox priest, at an early age he had begun formal preparation for the traditional career of the family. But in 1805, at the age of 21, he left the seminary, somehow made his way to St. Petersburg, and enrolled in the Imperial Medical-Surgical Academy which, since its establishment near the end of the Wars of the French Revolution, encouraged the enrollment of seminarians with a good knowledge of Latin. The details surrounding Belynskii's decision are unclear, but the consequences were enormous. It broke the tradition of sons of priests following the careers of their fathers, it removed him from the controlling influence Russian parents, especially fathers, traditionally exercised over the lives of even their adult sons,[6] and it replaced the comparatively sterile cultural climate of the provinces with the fertile one of the capital. In these conditions Belynskii was able, if not forced, to develop a sense of personal autonomy, to exercise his powers of discrimination and to control his own actions, rather than merely adhering to tradition and traditional authority. His career was unlike his father's; in Petersburg, Kronstadt, Sveaborg, and at sea he moved in and out of situations for which his previous experiences as the son of a provincial priest were inappropriate. He had to make his own decisions, form his own opinions, and act on them; the results were untraditional. He chose his own wife, for example, and Voltaire and Masonic writings formed his attitudes toward authority and religion. Even the medals he won for valor, although traditional awards, indicate his personal courage to do what he felt necessary, to act alone, under adverse conditions. And returning to Chembar, he did not change. He horrified local residents by rarely attending church services, and was given the nickname of Ammos Fedorovich, the free-thinking character in Gogol's *Revizor*. He spoke out on current issues and would not yield to the traditional power of the nobility. The most notable example of the latter involved the apparent suicide of the maid of Princess Kugusheva, wife of the district police captain; after examining the girl Belynskii reported to the District Court that the girl had died of injuries sustained during a beating administered by the Princess, who then shoddily staged the suicide. Outspoken and showing no deference to superiors, Belynskii watched his practice dwindle and his circle of friends shrink.[7]

Alienated from Society, Belynskii turned to his family. His wife offered little solace. Illiterate, but with hopes of rising in social circles, she continually criticized her husband's carefree attitudes toward religious and social obligations. Her criticism and demands became more insistent as the physician's practice, reflecting social opinion, dwindled. He usually answered her criticism with cold silence or caustic wit, the latter reply often sparking heated quarrels which frequently drove their children to refuge in the Ivanov home. One relative even believed that one source of conflict was that Belynskii failed to show proper deference to his wife, daughter of a shipmaster, while he was but the son of an impoverished priest.[8] Alienated from society and having little in common with his wife in terms of education and attitudes, Grigorii Belynskii turned to his eldest son, Vissarion, developing with him a warm, nurturant relationship uncharacteristic of nineteenth-century Russian fathers.

Russian priests traditionally become involved with their sons early in life; it was under his father's direction that the future priest probably first studied Latin, first read the scriptures. So to Belynskii, the son of a priest, it probably seemed natural that he become involved in his son's education. He taught Vissarion Latin, but there the traditional content ended. Along with scripture, Vissarion read Voltaire;[9] along with interpretations of scripture, Vissarion listened to his father's interpretations of past and current events. His father's involvement did not end when Vissarion entered the district school at the age of eleven. For example, one of the teachers at the school was a devotee of the birch as an instrument of discipline and a method of hardening young bodies, justifying his actions in terms of both the Spartan educational system and the accepted practices of seminaries. The young Vissarion, although not himself beaten, but unaccustomed to physical discipline, was indignant and turned to his father. Belynskii, who considered birching "barbarian," intervened in his capacity as district doctor and through the school Inspector put an end to the practice. Dmitrii Ivanov, Vissarion's cousin, summed up the father-son relationship by saying that there existed "a true empathy between them, which was preserved forever and acted nobly on both during the harsh events of life."[10] There was a negative side however; even as a child Belinskii shared his father's social alienation. In 1829, upon his acceptance into Moscow University, Belinskii wrote to his father: "I suppose that in the well-known city of Chembar people are amazed that I have been accepted into the Imperial Moscow University. Of course I care very little for the opinions of the citizens of Chembar. I was not appreciated in Chembar, but I have been recognized in Moscow."[11]

Such a father-son relationship was truly unusual in nineteenth-century Russia. The father was a significant figure in the child's world, but as an awesome antagonist who demanded strict obedience rather than as a teacher who nurtured and empathized. In 1783, for example, the French influence publicist N. I. Novikov pleaded with Russian fathers to spend at least one hour a day with their children and warned that control of children through "strict rules, severe punishment . . . and angry deeds" would breed filial contempt rather than love.[12] Yet over and over again one finds in memoirs memories of paternal detachment and hostility. Filial love, when mentioned, is usually coupled with fear, so that it resembles identification with an aggressor rather than empathy between individuals. Again, although I have dealt with this topic elsewhere, a few examples help place the Belynskii family in perspective. Of his childhood years in the first decade of the nineteenth century, Aleksandr Deliaev remembered of his non-noble father:

We children were very much afraid of him, since he was very strict, but simultaneously we also loved and respected him immeasurably. When he rested after dinner, we all had to go about on tip-toes . . . It was not I alone, but also all the servants in the house and on the estate loved and feared him at the same time.[13]

Alexander Herzen (b. 1812) in describing his father wrote:

Mockery, irony, cold, caustic, utter contempt, were the tools which he wielded like an artist; he employed them equally against us and against the servants. . . . until I went to prison I actually was estranged from my father, and joined with the maids and men-servants in waging a little war against him.[14]

Of his childhood in the 1840's N. Levakovskii recalled that "Our father's treatment of us, beyond providing the means of material existence, can be formulated in one word 'strictness'," and in the home where "affection was considered impermissable," any show of it was met with a "cuff on the nape of the neck."[15] When one finds warm, involved parents, they are also recognized by their contemporaries as being somehow different, as being "sinful" as the mother of Aksakov, or alienated like Grigorii Belynskii, or odd like the father of V. Lebedev:

His idea concerning the upbringing of children was that their primary education as well as their preparation to social life . . . was a duty of the parents. His ideas about childrearing, as well as those about social events, both of which were the result of observation and thought . . . earned for him . . . the reputation of an eccentric.[16]

The unusually warm relationship with his father, like the early extreme oral deprivation, was to have a profound effect on Vissarion's character.

Belinskii left no memoirs, and references in his letters to his childhood are rare. But there are two sources dating from his early years in Moscow (1829-34) which yield evidence both of the domestic drama in the Belynskii household and its effect on the children. The first of these is the correspondence among Vissarion, his parents, brothers, and the Ivanovs. The second is *Dmitrii Kalinin,* a play Vissarion completed in 1831 (at the age of 19).

The correspondence can be divided into two phases. From the fall of 1829 through 1831 the central concern is Vissarion's difficulties at the university and Belynskii's encouragement, advice, and prodding of his son; the family remained relatively stable. From 1831 until Belynskii's death in 1835 the letters reveal the family's growing disappointment with Vissarion, the heightening of its internal conflicts, and the deterioration of the health of both parents.

Grigorii Belynskii expected two things of his son: that he pursue his own interests and that he eventually obtain a position in teaching or civil service which would then enable him to help his younger brothers follow his path. Belynskii's letters to his son contained advice and money. For example, when it appeared that Vissarion might have to wait a year before formally enrolling in the university, his father cautioned him not to squander the year but to "attend the lectures in those subjects you wish to study" even if it would gain him no credits. When Vissarion needed money his father cautioned him to be more provident, but sent the funds in order that his son "learn to value such a sum through its application to necessities." When Vissarion contemplated leaving the university in 1831 because of what he felt to be intolerable living conditions and the tyranny of administrators, his father reminded him that such an action would preclude fulfillment of both the youth's own dreams and those of the family. He cautioned his son to hold his tongue, but especially to "obey authority, for without this you will never become what you wish to be; if you ignore this, then farewell!. . . God preserve you! Believe your father who desires only good for you."[17] Although his advice was heeded, Belynskii was losing his influence with his son; in late 1830, as cholera closed the university, students quarantined to the dorm began forming circles. In one of them Vissarion found a source of encouragement and ideas more immediate than his father. In January of 1831 Belynskii conceded to Ekaterina Ivanova that "we are no longer necessary to him [Vissarion], he needs only money, and if I would send him a hundred rubles or so, he'd surely remember about us."[18] Late that same month Vissarion used lines from the minor poet I. M. Dolgorukov, to announce that he was embarking on "the great, spacious sea" of literature, that he was submitting the play *Dmitrii Kalinin* to the censorship committee for permission to publish it. Both Ekaterina Ivanova and Belynskii had read drafts of the play and both wrote, warning Vissarion to reconsider his decision; Belynskii even quoted to his son lines of the same minor poet, Dolgorukov, that he "watch out—lest woe come to you."[19] But Belynskii's university friends, the so-called "Literary Society of [Dorm room] #11," urged the aspiring playwright on in hopes of performing the play at the university, and he submitted it; it was banned and its author put under special surveillance by the inspector of students. Relations between father and son cooled rapidly, the former feeling forgotten by his son, the latter increasingly widening his contacts in Moscow. Belynskii now turned his attention to his third son, Nikanor.

The letters to Vissarion from home after 1831 came mainly from his brother Konstantin and his mother. The central concerns became Vissarion's search for a position, his father's increased drinking, and the "problem" of the youngest son, Nikanor. Nikanor (b. 1821) seemed to be the focus of the problems. Like Vissarion, he was intelligent and close to his father, who encouraged his literary aspirations, even sending

some of his writings to Vissarion for submission to the censorship committee. Nikanor shared his father's disdain for religion and his caustic
wit, and Belynskii considered this son to be gifted and destined to follow in the footsteps of Vissarion. This infuriated Mariia Belinskaia who
favored her second son, Konstantin, who "lives the life of a virgin, never
missed Holyday or Sunday matins, tolerates his poverty, does not drink,
is frugal, orderly, quiet . . ." The differences between the two boys was
clearly revealed in one of their mother's letters to her eldest son: "It is
noon, Nikanor is completely engrossed in reading a book on Russia in
1812 which father bought for him yesterday, while Konstantin is smear-
ing butter on flat cakes and eating heartily with one hand and churning
fresh butter in a carafe with the other." In his mother's view, Vissarion,
too, should reform his life, become like Konstantin, and she explained
all his difficulties by his failure to be a devout Christian. When Vissarion
was expelled from the university in 1832, primarily for reasons of
health (he had been hospitalized several times for respiratory difficulties, forerunners of the T.B., which, at the age of 37, was to cause his
death), his mother wrote that this was the result of the fact that "you
did not have true faith in God, hope in the Creator, and did not be-
seech the Mother of God; turn to God more, have faith, pray, go to
church oftener. . ."[20] But Vissarion snapped back that "childish toys
such as religious ceremonies" could do him no good.[21] And he asked
his father not to judge him too harshly, not to condemn him, for "only
when the curtain falls do they call an actor back with cheers and hisses,
only when he has finished his performance."[22] Vissarion was beyond
his mother's control, but Nikanor was not. She tried to enforce his
obedience, even striking him; and her use of physical discipline guaranteed an angry explosion by her husband.[23] Perhaps, a few years earlier,
her attempts to bring Vissarion into line had fueled the fires of the
heated parental arguments that drove the children from the house. In
short, the correspondence reflects a family split into two camps; Vissarion and Nikanor lined up behind their father who encouraged his sons'
non-traditional behavior and judged by performance, while Konstantin
and his mother tended to traditional obedience and religiosity. This reveals much of the conflict within the family.

   Dmitrii Kalinin is an angry play about incest, murder, and suicide, but
written by a frail, gentle young man who was paralyzed by fear at the
sight of physical violence. It is a fantasy, a release of repressed emotions
and attitudes. The plot is simple. Dmitrii is a young man, raised as a ward
of a landowner named Lesinskii, who detests his wife and their sons but
spends much time reading and talking with his ward. Dmitrii falls in love
with Lesinskii's daughter and asks for her hand, but Lesinskii dies suddenly and his wife opposes the marriage because she plans to marry off
Sophia to a Prince for purposes of social prestige. Further she reveals that
Dmitrii's parents had been serfs, hence Dmitrii is a serf, and will become

a household servant; Dmitrii later finds out that Lesinskii had freed him from serfdom, but that Lesinskaia and her sons had destroyed the legal document. When Andrei, Lesinskaia's favorite son, calls Dmitrii a slave [rab], a fight ensues and Andrei is killed; Dmitrii then stabs Sophia in the heart, fulfilling her request to die rather than live the life her mother had charted for her. Finally Dmitrii takes his own life, but not before learning that he is Lesinskii's illegitimate son; hence in his death scene he denounces his father and condemns himself as guilty of incest and murder.

Belinskii's conscious purpose in writing the play was to gain a bit of fame and enough money to ease his economic need; unconsciously it expressed his deepest personal resentments and conflicts. The Lesinskii family is clearly modeled on the Belinskii family; both husbands had little in common with their wives and turned most of their attention on their eldest son. The members of #11 knew that "the hero of the drama we read was the author himself, and the scenes depicted were taken from his family life."[24] If Vissarion and his father shared an empathy, then Lesinskii and Dmitrii are described as "akin in heart and soul." Like Belynskaia, Lesinskaia is an uneducated woman who craves social status; the second sons of both fathers were obedient and close to their mothers. Sophia, an intelligent, sensitive young woman who was raised outside the household by an aunt, is modeled on Ekaterina Ivanova, Vissarion's intelligent, sensitive cousin (henced also raised outside the household by an aunt). Finally, the correspondence between Belinskii and his family discussed above revealed quarrels between his parents over the behavior of their children; in the play Dmitrii recalls "there were often disagreements between her [Lesinskaia] and her husband because of me, even quarrels and fights."[25] Thus, *Dmitrii Kalinin* is really a drama about the Belynskii household, a vehicle for Vissarion's expression of emotion.

The emotions which found expression in the play were Vissarion's hatred of his mother, ambivalence toward his father, and frustration with a society which did not conform to his childhood expectations, which blocked the development of the personal autonomy encouraged by his father's guidance and support.

When Dmitrii describes Lesinskaia as "from the first day of my life ... a perpetual enemy," Belinskii is venting more than his feelings toward a mother who abandoned him to an inconsiderate hired girl; he is denouncing a woman who never understood his personal needs. One key to the play is the use of the word "slave" (rab) to describe Dmitrii who was not technically a slave but a serf (krepostnoi). N. M. Mikhailovskii traced Belinskii's use of the words slave and slavery in letters, articles, and recorded conversations and concluded that slavery was the subjugation of the human personality to authority, be it political authority or the authority of custom, tradition, or social opinion.[26] To do or believe anything because such actions or beliefs are dictated by authority, tradition, or even an intellectual system, was to be a slave; belief and action must spring from personal conviction. Both Lesinskii and Belynskii encouraged their sons to develop autonomy, to live by their convictions; Lesinskaia's attempt to rob Dmitrii of the freedom his father had given him symbolizes Vissarion's reaction to his mother's efforts to convince him that his difficulties in life proceeded from his failure to observe social and religious traditions. Like Lesinskaia, she is the "superstitious female-snake," the "constant tormenter"[27] who never understood her son's need to believe and act from conviction, who taunted him because he was neither obedient nor religious—like her Konstantin or Lesinskaia's Andrei. Vissarion's attraction to his mother as a woman was deflected to Ivanova and emerges in the play in the intense, incestual relationship of Dmitrii and Sophia. But it was an inadequate substitute for the fullness of the missing mother-son relationship.

Belinskii's ambivalence toward his father and his frustration in society are bound together, the realization that his childhood was disfunctional reinforcing what "natural" ambivalence he might have felt. His upbringing prepared him for a world in which individual effort and merit brought recognition, and instead he found himself in a world where birthright and wealth outweighed, almost crushed, effort and merit. On the journey to Moscow in 1829, for example, the nobles in the party objected to traveling with him; he almost failed to gain entry into the university because the noble assembly of Chembar was slow in forwarding certification of his free birth; while he lived miserably in a dormitory, sons of nobles lived well, even had servants; cholera confined commoners to their quarters, while sons of nobles went home. Students were told what they could do, where they could go, what they could read; nowhere was merit and effort recognized, everywhere was "slavery," the subjugation of personal autonomy to social and governmental authority. The play was Belinskii's protest. Sophia, for example, argued that "rights by birth . . . are an insult to humanity, that only the worthiness of a person must grant rights in honor and glory."[28] Dmitrii argued that:

> When laws are contrary to the rights of nature and humanity, to reason itself, then man can and should violate them. Do I not have the right to love a girl because her father is wealthy and carries the empty title of nobleman, while I am poor and without title? She loves me; here is the source of the inalienable right with which I answer.[29]

The most famous passage in the play is Dmitrii's denunciation of serfdom:

> Could it be that these men were born into the world only to serve the whims of such men as those [landowners]? . . Who gave them this fatal right—for one man to enslave by force the wills of other creatures like himself, to take from them their holy treasure— freedom? Who gave them permission to violate the laws of nature and humanity?[30]

That Belinskii was protesting serfdom is undeniable; but his protest is broader, it is against anything—law, tradition, or custom—which is placed in value above the human personality. As Mikhailovskii pointed out, the play, like all of Belinskii's work, "is permeated by this struggle with slavery in the cause of the value of the human personality."[31] But upholding the human personality meant transgressing social, legal, and religious mores, involved suffering and guilt. It was not a fate Belinskii would wish on anyone and he warned his brothers not to follow his lead; but he could not live otherwise, there was no turning back from the path on which he had set out under his father's direction. And Belinskii's hatred for his father, the other side of their warm relationship, is expressed by Dmitrii just before his suicide: ". . . damn you [Lesinskii] and this terrible gift, this life of guilt for which I am indebted to you."[32] The incest theme developed in the play makes it possible, of course, that this is also an expression of father-son Oedipal rivalry; still, the stronger theme here is the ingratitude of the son for the gift of an unhappy life.

Belinskii's experiences in childhood dominated his adult life by pre-disposing him to certain types of behavior, certain modes of thought and feeling, which, because of social factors and the "intellectual climate" were relevant to (or at least tolerated in) nineteenth-century Russia. The impact of childhood is most evident in two areas—his constant need for oral gratification and his lifelong struggle for the worth and dignity of the individual.

Belinskii's career as a literary critic was consistent with his early childhood interest in literature; as early as 1824, at the age of 12, he impressed the curator of his school with his knowledge of literature, and one of his teachers at the *gimnaziia* wrote that "I do not recall talking so sincerely about literature and education with anyone else in Pensa."[33] So it is natural that he seek a job dealing with literature. Further, "the time was ripe"; literary journals were an established fact in Russia by 1830 (although the existence of any specific publication was precarious), yet journalism was not yet a socially acceptable career for a nobleman. Hence Belinskii, competent in literature but not of the nobility,[34] was ideally suited for such a career. Finally, chance played a part; N. I. Nadezhdin, editor of the *Teleskop,* was a professor at the university and turned to students for the help he needed in publishing the journal. In early 1833 he asked Belinskii to join the staff. Hence Belinskii's career as a literary critic was a result of training and circumstance. But literature had a deeper meaning for Belinskii: it was a leading component of that part of his personality shaped by oral and maternal deprivation. In 1835 Belinskii wrote a stirring tribute to woman, as man's "guardian-angel, whose solicitous gaze greets man on his entry into the world, toward whom the child turns his first smile, through whom noble passions are aroused in man eventually leading to a life of reciprocal love with a woman," but, the essay concludes, what is the fate of a man "if death or the circumstances of life do not allow him to drink of this cup of bliss or, if instead of the cup of shared love he tastes the pain of rejected love? . ."[35] For Belinskii oral needs were displaced from the physical to the intellectual sphere, and interaction with friends replaced the maternal interaction usually accompanying oral gratification. Books and ideas were clusters of nutrients to be taken in and restructured into personal, usually unique, ideas and attitudes. Consistent with this, Belinskii was little concerned with what he ate or with his physical appearance; he always seemed to lack the "feminine attention" that kept clothes mended, cheeks rosy. Not that he was pitiable, for he always acted proud and bold and people realized his unconcern for his physical appearance reflected his concentration "on other, more important, interests."[38] Belinskii's writing abounds with oral metaphors; for example Dmitrii Kalinin says "blessed is he who experiences the enchantment of love, who *tastes* its joy," "love *filled* my being," and again "the right to *nourish* love and enjoy it."[37] [Italics mine.] "To drink of the bitter cup of fate" was one of his favorite phrases. The social interaction accompanying oral gratification was furnished by circles of friends; a book, an idea, was not something to be devoured alone, but to share with others. In Chembar Belinskii had the Ivanovs, in Penza Popov and a group of seminarians, at the university the "Literary Society of #11," and after the university the Stankevich circle; the emotional impact of the circle can be gauged by Belinskii's letters. Through the summer of 1833 he found Moscow boring and applied for a teaching position in Belorussia, but in a letter in September he told of his joining the Stankevich circle and wrote of Moscow:

> O Moscow, Moscow! To live and die in this city of white stone is my greatest desire. I confess to you, brother, that to leave Moscow would be to leave paradise. If I am sent to damn Belorussia, then I shall stay but a year, two at most—then back to Moscow, beloved Moscow.[38]

In his published reviews, which probably reflect a displacement of the need to experience gratification to the need to give it verbally, the critic always tried to establish a personal relationship with the reader, speaking to them directly, often using the familiar "ty" rather than the formal "vy." For example, the third installment of Belinskii's first major publication, "Literary Reveries," begins:

> "How, now, what is this? Not a review, surely?" the alarmed
> readers ask me.
>   Yes, dear sirs, though perhaps not quite a review, but some-
> thing like that. And so—*silence*! But what do I see? You make a
> wry face, you shrug your shoulders, you shout at me in chorus:
> "No, sir, that's an old trick—you cannot fool us. . . . We have not
> yet forgotten the previous reviews, they made us feel bad
> enough! . . ."
>   What can I say to this unavoidable greeting? Really, I am com-
> pletely at a loss .. . Well then . . . read it, if merely to beguile
> the time—there is nothing to read nowadays, you know, so this
> might prove a stop-gap . . . .[39]

When Belinskii was cut off from contact with others, he became dis-
couraged and depressed. Undoubtedly the most severe instance of this
was the period immediately following his move from Moscow, the center of intellectual life in the 1830's, to St. Petersburg, the city of practical men and bureaucrats. Cut off from friends, from the excitement of
literary and philosophical gatherings, and mired in deep depression,
Belinskii, in a letter to his close friend Botkin, had the clearest insight
into his own needs. He recalled how as an infant he had not been given
the breast, confessed that he now desired it strongly, and admitted that
lately in the company of women, whether he was acquainted with them
or not,

> I am on fire. I feel everything felt by a man who has, for a long
> time, been chasing a woman who inflames his passions, a man who
> is making his final assault on her. Were I in this position (let us
> suppose it for a joke), it seems to me that blood would gush
> from my mouth, nose, ears, and I would fall upon her breast like
> a dead body. . . . I am ill, friend, very ill—pity me. I shall talk no
> more about this subject which fascinates me against my will. . . .[40]

Finally, it appears that in his marriage Belinskii sought to reestablish the
elements of his own childhood and through his son resolve more favor-
ably his childhood crises. He married a woman with the same name as
his mother, Mariia; he named his children Vladimir and Ol'ga. In all the
drafts of *Dmitrii Kalinin* prior to its submission to the censors, Dmitrii
and Sophia were named Vladimir and Ol'ga. Thus, symbolically, Belinskii's wife represented his own mother, his son represented himself as a
child, and under his guidance the warm mother-son relationship he himself craved could now symbolically be established. But even here Belinskii was frustrated; Vladimir died shortly after his birth.

      On the one hand, then, Belinskii's choice of a career, his personal re-
lationships, and his marriage, were influenced by his relationship with

his mother; on the other hand, the major themes of his literary and social criticism were influenced by the warm, interactive relationship with
his father. The amount of freedom coupled with advice and support allowed to Belinskii by his father allowed the son to learn to regulate his
own actions and through this to develop a certain sense of pride and
autonomy.[41] Belinskii's pride in self was noted by his teachers in the
gimnaziia, reflected in his correspondence to his parents, and symbolized
in Dmitrii Kalinin's protests against "slavery," against anything which
limited a person's right to determine his own actions. For a brief period
in late 1837 Belinskii almost capitulated to a reality which failed to appreciate him, almost succumbed to Hegel's "beautiful and holy world"
where "in order that my existence be necessary, I be the piece of trash
that I am." By June of 1838, however, Belinskii was demanding of his
Hegelian friend, Michael Bakunin: "respect my individuality, my sub-
jectivity."[42] By July his acceptance of reality was severely strained: "To
hell with it! You accept everything here, you bear everything, take everything upon yourself if only to live; to hell with it, to live![43] But he
clung desperately to Hegel, it was the tie to his friends, to Stankevich,
the central figure in the circle of men and ideas that nourished his being.
And then Stankevich died; Belinskii tore into Hegel's Absolute: "What
is this Universal (for the perception of which Stankevich lived and died
alone)? A Moloch devouring its own, a Saturn eating its children?"[44]
"This Universal," he finally realized, "is the executioner of human individuality,"[45] and must be abandoned. By early 1841 Belinskii reaf-
firmed that "the fate of a subject, an individual, a personality is more
important than the fate of the world. . . ."[46] From 1841 on Belinskii
wrote against the slavery he had protested in *Dmitrii Kalinin,* whether
the agent of enslavement be intellectual systems, the government, or the
church. For example, in his most famous work, a letter of 1847 to
Gogol protesting the latter's defense of serfdom, he wrote:

> That you base such teaching on the Orthodox Church I can un-
> derstand: it has always served as the prop of the knout and the
> servant of despotism; but why have you mixed Christ up in this?
> What in common have you found between Him and any church,
> least of all the Orthodox Church? He was the first to bring to
> people the teaching of freedom, equality and brotherhood and set
> the seal of truth to that teaching by martyrdom. And this teach-
> ing was men's *salvation* only until it became organized in the
> Church and took the principle of Orthodoxy for its foundation.
> The Church, on the other hand, was a hierarchy, consequently
> a champion of inequality, a flatterer of authority, an enemy and
> persecutor of brotherhood among men—and so it has remained to
> this day.[47]

The belief in the value of the human personality remained his central concern throughout his life; even his acceptance of socialism was merely to affirm this belief. Socialism, he wrote Botkin in 1841, "has become for the idea of ideas . . . the alpha and omega of belief and knowledge." But he revealed later in the letter his understanding of socialism: "Sociality, sociality—or death. That is my motto. What do I care for the existence of the universal when individuality is suffering?"[48]

The belief in the value of the human personality is also the central tenet of Belinskii's literary criticism. In an essay "On the Russian Short Story and the Stories of Gogol (1835)," Belinskii called for a literature in which the plots were simple, and the author's creativity was expressed in characterization. Gogol's stories presented the "poetry of life" because the reader experienced empathy with characters: ". . . you sob with Filemon, experience with him the depths of bitterness and emotion. . ."[49] In his "Survey of Russian Literature in 1846" Belinskii criticized the Young Dostoevskii, warning him that "in art there should be nothing obscure or incomprehensible; its creations transcend the so-called 'real occurrences' in that the poet lights up with the torch of his imagination all the recesses of his heroes' inmost souls and all their secret motives. . . ."[50] Literature, by exploring the inner world of fictional characters (without passing judgment), pays respect to the individual personality in a way that Belinskii wished personality be respected in the real world. And Belinskii often used a consideration of a fictional character as a vehicle with which to move to a statement about real life, about the society in which he lived, to move, for example, from a consideration of Beltov, a character in Herzen's *Who Is to Blame*, to the question of parent-child relationships in Russia:

> How many mothers and fathers are there who really love their children in their own way, but consider it their sacred duty to drum in their ears that they are obliged to their parents for their lives and clothing and education! These wretched people do not even suspect that they are depriving themselves of their children and replacing them with foundlings and orphans whom they have adopted out of charity. They calmly doze on the moral rule that children must love their parents, and later, in their old age, they repeat with a sigh the well-worn truism that nothing but ingratitude can be expected from children. Even this fearful experience does not remove the thick crust of ice from their benumbed minds or make them realize at last that the human heart obeys its own laws, and will not and cannot accept any others, that love from a sense of duty or obligation is a feeling contrary to human nature, . . . that love cannot be demanded as though it were something we are entitled to, but must be won and deserved, no matter who the giver is, whether he be higher than us, or lower, whether it goes from father to son or from son to father. Now take

children; it often happens that a child regards its mother with indifference, although the mother suckles it, and this same child will set up a wail if, on awakening, it does not see its nurse nearby, whom it is accustomed to seeing at its side at all times. A child, you see, that complete and perfect expression of nature, gives its love to those that prove their love for it in actual deed, to those that for its sake deny themselves. . . .[51]

It is not the purpose of this article to assess the impact of Belinskii's writings on Russian social values and customs. I will cite only one example of that impact, a memoir of childhood in the late 1840's in which the author recalled that members of the circle of Belinskii (who was already dead) had a "fruitful influence" on his father's thinking.

. . . my father was an excellent teacher. In the evenings, in the course of joking and playing with me, he subtly taught me to read and write. More important, however, was something rarely found in ordinary families, that he and my mother raised me in such a way that I was always completely open with them and, needless to say, I loved them boundlessly. I never hid my misdeeds from them. On the other hand, I never experienced any type of physical punishment; this was replaced by calm explanations. . . . and this was not done in the doctoral tone of an instructor, which is always intolerable to children, but simply and naturally, as you would talk to a friend whom you love. I highly valued this manner of upbringing and all my life have preserved the warmest memories of my father and mother. This manner not only facilitates the development of children's powers of discrimination, but also implants in them a sense of their own personal value. How many good consequences would it have, if implemented in families and educational establishments.[52]

Had it been implemented, there might not have been a revolution in 1917.

Patrick P. Dunn teaches history at the University of Wisconsin–La Crosse. He is currently researching the childhood of members of the Russian intelligentsia under the hypothesis that their questioning of traditional Russian values was an extension of their untraditional upbringing.

REFERENCES

This article is a result of research done in part with the help of a Younger Humanist Fellowship from the National Endowment for the Humanities, to which I wish to express my gratitude.

1. In the Orthodox Church parish priests, or "black clergy," marry and raise families, while members of religious orders, or "white clergy," remain celi-

bate. In Russian masculine proper names are declined differently than feminine; hence the wife of Belynskii is Belynskaia, of Ivanov, Ivanova, etc. Belynskii's son Vissarion changed one letter of his family name so that it became Belinskii. Finally, different sources give different dates for Belinskii's birth, the earliest being 1810; Vissarion himself celebrated the date given in the text.

2. Letter to Botkin, April 16-21, 1840, in Belinskii's *Polnoe sobranie sochinenii,* edited and with notes by N. F. Bel'chikov (13 vols.; Moscow, 1953-56), XI, 512. This edition of Belinskii's complete collected works hereafter cited as Pss.

3. See " 'That Enemy is the Baby': Childhood in Imperial Russia," in Lloyd deMause, ed., *The History of Childhood* (New York: Basic Books, Inc., in press).

4. Sergei T. Aksakov, *Chronicles of a Russian Family,* trans. by M. C. Beverly (London and New York, [1924]), p. 205.

5. Based on material from her niece and nephew in D. P. Ivanov, "Neskol'ko melochnykh dannykh dlia biografii V. G. Belinskogo," and "Soobshcheniia pri chtenii biografii V. G. Belinskogo (A. N. Pypin)," both in *V. G. Belinskii v vospominaniiakh sovremennikov,* ed. by S. N. Golubov *et al.* (Moscow, 1962), pp. 30, 97-98.

6. The folk saying that "when the earth receives the parents, the children receive their freedom" has its literary counterpart in Ostrovsky's *The Storm,* where Kabanova tells her married son to "have patience and wait until I'm dead and then you will live your own lives."

7. Based on Ivanov, "Neskol'ko," pp. 27-28, and V. S. Nechaeva, *V. G. Belinskii: Nachalo zhiznennogo puti i literaturnoi deiatel'nosti, 1811-30* (Moscow, 1949), pp. 67-69. The concept of autonomy is based on my understanding of Erik H. Erikson, *Identity, Youth and Crisis* (New York, 1968), pp. 107-08.

8. Ivanov, "Neskol'ko," p. 30; the relative is identified as "Shch" and quoted in Alexander N. Pypin, *Belinskii: Ego zhizn' i perepiska* (2 vol. in 1; St. Petersburg, 1876), I, 13.

9. In a literary review some years later Belinskii believed he was fortunate to have been able to read Voltaire before he had learned to write (that is, gone to school); *Pss,* III, 206.

10. Ivanov, "Neskol'ko," pp. 29-32.

11. *Pss,* XI, 19.

12. Nikolai I. Novikov, "O vospitanii i nastavlenii detei," *Izbrannye pedagogicheskie sochineniia,* ed. by M. F. Shabaeva (Moscow, 1959), pp. 169-70.

13. "Vospominaniia Aleksandra Petrovich Beliaeva," *Russkaia starina,* XXIX (July-September, 1880), 6.

14. *My Past and Thoughts. The Memoirs of Alexander Herzen,* trans. by Constance Garnett, rev. by Humphrey Higgins (New York, 1968), I, 23.

15. "Vospominaniia N. Levakovskago," *Russkaia starina,* CXXXII (October-December, 1907), 130.

16. V. Lebedev, "Uchebnyia vospominaniia," *Russkaia starina,* CXXX (April-June, 1907), 626-27.

17. "Perepiska Belinskogo s rodnymi," ed. and notes by A. Askariants *et al., Literaturnoe nasledstvo,* vol. 57: *V. G. Belinskii,* III (Moscow, 1951), 30, 62, 66.

18. *Ibid.*, 58.
19. *Ibid.*, 60-62.
20. *Ibid.*, 169, 126, 146.
21. *Pss*, XI, 112.
22. *Ibid.*, 97-99.
23. "Perepiska," p. 90
24. P. P. Prozorov, "Belinskii i moskovskii universitet v ego vremia," in Golubov, p. 107. Belinskii also wrote his father that many of the characters in the play would be familiar to him.
25. Quotations are taken from the text of the play submitted to the censors, *Pss*, I, 425-26.
26. N. K. Mikhailovskii, "Belinskii dramaturg," *Russkoe bogatstvo*, 1898, #5(May), 160-62.
27. Both quotes from *Pss*, I, 425.
28. *Ibid.*, 429.
29. *Ibid.*, 435.
30. *Ibid.*, 498-99.
31. Mikhailovskii, p. 160.
32. *Pss*, I, 500.
33. I. I. Lazhechnikov, "Zametki dlia biografii Belinskogo," in *V. G. Belinskii v vospominaniiakh sovremennikov,"* ed. by A. A. Kozlovskii and K. I. Tiun'kina (Moscow, 1962), pp. 27-29, 33-34.
34. Just prior to his death G. N. Belynskii was granted nobility status earned through his long years of civil service; although noble status was of benefit to Vissarion in some ways, it did not raise his social standing in the eyes of the traditional nobility.
35. *Pss*, I, 223.
36. Ivanov, "Soobshcheniia," pp. 81-82; see also the letter of his old teacher at the gimnaziia, M. Popov, in Golubov, p. 36.
    On oral character formation and development I have consulted Karl Abraham, "The Influence of Oral Eroticism on Character Formation," *Selected Papers of Karl Abraham*, trans. by Douglas Bryan and Alix Strachey (London, 1965), pp. 393-406; Edward Glover, "Notes on Oral Character Formation," *Selected Papers on Psycho-Analysis*, Vol. I: *On the Early Development of the Mind* (London, 1956), 25-46; Humberto Nagero, "On Arrest, in Development, Fixation, and Regression," *Psychoanalytic Study of the Child*, XIX (1964), 222-39.
37. *Pss*, I, 431-32.
38. *Ibid.*, XI, 103-04.
39. *Selected Philosophical Works* (Moscow, 1956), p. 9. This is the only major collection of Belinskii's works in English, and I have used it where possible for the sake of those who do not read Russian. Hereafter references to this collection will be designated SPW.
40. *Pss*, XI, 512.
41. See note 7.
42. *Pss*, XI, 242-43.
43. *Ibid.*, 254.
44. *Ibid.*, 547.

45. *Ibid.*, 539.
46. SPW, p. 160.
47. *Ibid.*, p. 539.
48. *Ibid.*, pp. 170, 174.
49. *Pss*, I, 291.
50. SPW, p. 411.
51. *Ibid.*, pp. 475-76.
52. "R," "Byloe. Iz. vospominanii o piatidesiatykh i shestidesiatykh godakh," *Russkaia starina*, CVII (July-September, 1901), 560-61.

CHAPTER 6

The Popular Cinema as Reflection of the Group Process in France, 1919-1929

PAUL
MONACO

The concept of collective fantasy or mass psyche, however much used by psychohistorians in the past, was terribly unsatisfying as long as no specific empirical evidence could be pointed to which could be depended on to reflect the content of the fantasy at any particular time. Paul Monaco proposes we use persistent themes in popular cinema as a major index of mass fantasy, and demonstrates the significance of some central themes in French cinema during the 1920's to political conditions of the time.

The art historian Walter Abell has written: "Psycho-historically considered, art is one of the cultural symbols into which society projects its existent states of underlying psychic tension . . . Thus, we are led to conceive the higher forms of cultural expression in any society as manifestations of a 'collective dream'."[1] In support of his theory, Abell cites examples mainly from literature and architecture. The popular cinema, however, may offer a better reflection of the collective latent tensions in society than the works and artifacts of high culture. A movie is usually "essentially a group production".[2] And for that reason alone a popular film likely bears a closer relationship to the group processes within society than an individual artistic creation. The term 'mass culture' does have meaning, and that meaning is accented in the cinema. The high unit costs of feature films mean that they must appeal to a broad cross-section of society, rather than to an elite within society, in order to produce profits.[3] Films come and go quickly, being seen by millions. The 'timeliness' which a film must possess in order to strike the mass fancy should not be ignored. During the 1920's a feature film normally 'played itself out' within about six months after its première.[4]

Walter Abell speaks of all art works as manifestations of a collective dream. The nature of the cinema experience suggests that films have a unique kinship to dreams. Among Sigmund Freud's observations was that "our dreams think essentially in images."[5] All films—and most emphatically silent films—express themselves primarily through images. The rhythmic luminosity of the film projection itself produces an aura of hallucination.[6] The discoveries of REM-researchers during the 1950's and 1960's make the argument that the dream experience and the film experience are akin to each other particularly compelling:

> Approximately fifteen years ago, scientists discovered that dreaming occurs during sleep characterized by a particular patterning of electrical activity of the brain and by rapid movements of the eyeball, as if the eye were *watching* the pictorial content of a dream. When awakened from this stage of sleep, which occurs periodically through the night, subjects almost always are able to recall a vivid, perceptual hallucinatory (at the same time it seemed *real*), and somewhat distorted drama that would unhesitatingly be called a dream.[7]

The eye movements of the dreamer are not random, but are "associated with the visual characteristics of [his] dream."[8] The same is true of watching a movie: "The film spectator occupies a fixed seat, but only physically . . . Aesthetically he is in permanent motion as his eye identifies with the lens of the camera."[9] Any film projection "temporarily modifies" the psycho-motor comportment of any viewer,[10] in ways quite similar to the psycho-physiological 'third stage' which characterizes dream sleep.[11]

Several general elements reinforce the viewer's psychological absorption into the material presented on the screen. These include the dark magic cave environment of the movie theater, the continuous, uninterrupted nature of a film-showing, the rhythmic luminosity of the projection itself, and the social isolation of the spectator.[12] Specifically, the cinema has mastered techniques and devices that permit a film to cut from scene to scene ignoring limitations of time and space. "The primary structural . . . peculiarity of cinema is discontinuous presentation; the primary means of producing it is the cut."[13] By comparison, notable in dream recollections recorded by numerous REM-researchers, is the subject's use of the descriptive phrase: ". . . and then all of a sudden the scene changed."[14] Just that happens in films, with a frequency and abruptness duplicated in no other art form. Freud unintentionally points up this parallel between film and dream:

Sometimes, in a dream in which the same situation and setting have persisted for some time, an interruption will occur which is described in these words: 'But then it was as though at the same time it was another place, and such and such a thing happened.' After a while the main thread of the dream may be resumed, and what interrupted turns out to be a subordinate clause in the dream-material—an interpolated thought.[15]

Enrico Fulchignoni claims that "the movie screen compares to a doctor or a center for analysis to which crowds come to indulge in the rite of recognizing their most secret dreams."[16] Yet, the way in which a given film might reflect an individual's unconscious concerns is impossible to study and analyze. When particular films gain exceptional popularity with a defined group, however, those films become valid documents for analysis in terms of collective psychological categories. As Peter Bächlin, the author of *Film als Ware,* neatly puts it:

The popularity of a film, indeed the very reason for its existence, arises on the whole from the adaptation of its contents to the dominant thoughts, conceptions and basic wishes of contemporary society.[17]

The producers who make feature films do not worry about the medium and what can be done with it; they concentrate, instead, on keeping ahead of the tastes of the mass audience.[18] The popular cinema is a group phenomenon, and should be studied in that light. The 'basic wishes of contemporary society', of which Bächlin speaks, are likely latent. Very few popular films address themselves directly to manifest public concerns.

Historically the cinema is an industry and film is merchandise. An analysis of the latent meanings of the popular films of a given society must at least briefly inform itself of the rudimentary facts of how the film industry functioned in that society. During the 1920's some sixty to one-hundred feature-length films were produced annually in France.[19] Of those native productions, forty-eight can be documented as having achieved wide-spread national popularity in France from 1919 to 1929.[20] The mass audience in France during that decade was a 'national' audience. During those years movie-going could not be identified with any particular economic group, social class, age category, or sex.[21] Nor was the audience for films to be characterized as distinctly urban rather than rural. By the early 1920's there was a movie theater for every 9,000 inhabitants in France; the ratio of movie theaters to population was divided equally as between Paris, the other large cities, and smaller towns and villages.[22] A film which premièred in Paris was seen in Bordeaux and Marseilles, as well as in scores of provincial towns, within a time-span of a few weeks.[23]

During the 1920's the French film industry operated in a relatively free market. The two biggest film firms—Pathé and Gaumont—which had dominated pre-World War One movie-making, steered clear of film-production during the decade following the war.[24] Instead of making movies, both companies concentrated on safer commercial enterprises: the distribution and exploitation of them.[25] Film distribution in France was open and competitive, unlike the situation in the United States where the big producers used the 'block-booking' scheme to force their films on movie theater owners.[26] Pathé and Gaumont did own modest chains of movie theaters, but 97% of the cinemas in France were independently owned by individuals.[27] During the 1920's numerous foreign-made films were imported into France. Of these some (such as the Hollywood films of Charlie Chaplin and Jackie Coogan as well as a number of silent westerns) were popular with French audiences. The popularity of these films does not, however, invalidate the study of the most popular native-produced films as a dream-like reflection of the shared latent concerns of the mass audience in France.[28]

Latent collective meanings of films reveal themselves through analysis of manifest film contents. On the conscious level, movie-goers are, and have been since the advent of cinematography, primarily interested in the content of a movie—that is, the film story and its cinedramatic development.[29] Hence, attention to the cinematographic devices through which that content is portrayed is minimized. Still, the repetition of certain such devices in the popular films of a national cinema may reveal psychologically important tendencies. Moreover, the way in which technical means are used to intensify the impact of certain scenes cannot simply be ignored, and, in some cases, can be of great consequence.

For clarity it is best to begin the process of analysis with the thematic material which is easiest to recognize. Half of the most popular French films of the 1920's handle, in one way or another, an orphan story. The first popular orphan film of the Post-World War One era was Le petit Café which premièred in early 1919. In the film, the orphan Albert Loriflan is a waiter who has been tricked into a twenty-year contract by the café owner Philibert. Philibert had learned that Albert had inherited millions from a benefactor before poor Albert himself learned the good news. Albert cannot enjoy his money because he is bound by the contract to pay a high penalty if he quits his job. A happy ending "à la française" finds Albert out of the contract and in the loving arms of Philibert's daughter. During the 1919 cinema season the orphan theme caught on slowly. In La Nouvelle Aurore Giselle is an orphan who is eventually reunited to her long-lost father, who had been sent to prison unjustly. But Giselle reunited with her father stands dramatically peripheral to much of the action in the film's complicated plot. Equally peripheral to an intricate plot, albeit emotionally poignant, is the subtheme involving the little girl "Petite Ange" in *J'Accuse*. Little Angel is presented to the viewer as an orphan, but she turns out to be the daughter of a French woman who was raped by a German soldier during one of the attacks of 1914. In another popular production of the year 1919, *Travail*, the orphan story is more fully developed. Josine, a working girl, has been left an orphan and must care for her brother Nanet. She becomes the mistress of the brutal Ragu and her life is miserable. Eventually, however, she marries the idealist Luc, and little Nanet, who is raised in their loving home, grows and marries the daughter of a wealthy factory owner.

The story of Josine and little Nanet comes closest among the orphan themes of 1919 to paralleling what became an almost archetypal form of orphan story in French films of the twenties. The most intense portrayals of the orphan theme were exploited by French film-makers during the years 1921 to 1926 with repeated box-office success. Louis Feuillade's *Les deux Gamines*, for example, portrays the adventures of a double pair of orphans—Ginette and Gaby, Blanche and Renée. The viewer follows them down various rocky roads until all four attain adulthood and happiness. Two successful filmic adaptations from Lamartine by the director Léon Poirier—*Jocelyn*, made in 1922, and *Geneviève*, which appeared the following year—centered around orphan stories. The orphan story in each is different, but the emotional impact is similar. Jocelyn, a simple country curé, is entrusted with the care of an orphaned boy during the Terror of the French Revolution. The boy is, in fact, a girl; a girl with whom, in all due course, Jocelyn falls in love. In *Geneviève*, the good-hearted heroine from whose name the title comes, promises her dying mother to care for her younger sister Josette. Here the orphan theme is emphasized twice over. Josette comes of age, and becomes pregnant by a soldier who then falls in battle. Josette abandons her new-born baby. When the baby is found by the authorities, Geneviève says the baby is her own. She goes to jail and on her release learns that Josette has died and the baby has disappeared. A decade passes. One day Josette's son appears during a thunderstorm at Geneviève's humble door. When his true identity is by chance revealed, Geneviève becomes his protector and joins the household of his adoptive parents. In *La Mendiant de Saint-Sulpice* (1924), twin girls are born during a German bombardment of a French village in the year 1870. A cousin of the mother has one of them stolen during the confusion of the German attack, in which his own new-born child has perished. The rogue's aim is to raise the child as his own and someday cash in on an inheritance his own child was due to receive. Years later the twin girls are united not only with each other, but also with their true mother as well. *Enfant des Halles* (also 1924) is a typical film by the highly successful commercial director René Le Prince. A street urchin orphan of the Paris slums finds a baby girl abandoned in a pile of vegetables at the main market. The boy, named Berlingot, "adopts" the baby girl and takes her to live with the poor family which is keeping him. Later, Berlingot himself is adopted by a rich Canadian couple which has lost its two children in an auto accident. In truth, the little girl found in the vegetable pile was their daughter, who had been picked up and then abandoned by a vagabond who happened upon the scene of the auto accident. The wealthy Canadians die years later. Berlingot is left an orphan for a second time, but this time he is left a rich one. He happens to meet a young lady—the very girl he had found abandoned as a baby. They fall in love and marry.

The basic structure in such French orphan films can be stated simply. An orphan, abandoned and alone in the world, is taken in by a protector or reunited to its parents. In the denouement, the orphan is invariably rewarded with happiness and health, often with wealth, and sometimes with true love and marriage. In each case the story differs, but this variety reduces to uniformity at the psychic level. The popularity of the orphan theme was recognized already in the 1920's by one of France's keenest and most prolific writers on the cinema, Ricardo Canudo. In his *L'Usine aux images* (1927), to characterize the typical popular French cinema of the decade, he chose as representative *Taô*. He described this adventure serial which premièred in 1921: "It's about an orphan—naturally; beautiful, noble, and rich—naturally; exposed to interesting persecutions and saved, after many a hazardous adventure, by a young man who is poor, herculean, courageous, and generous—naturally; who turns out by accident to be her Uncle the Duke de Bellisle, with whom she—just as naturally as ever—falls in love."[30] Whether the film is set in the jungles of Cambodia as in *Taô* or in the Paris of Louis Napoleon as in Henry Roussel's *Violettes impériales* (1923), upon analysis the basic theme in both films is revealed as similar. *Violettes impériales* was one of the commercially most successful French films of the 1920's. Its story revolves around a poor orphan girl named Violetta who is taken under the protective wing of the Empress Eugénie. Violetta is appreciative, and demonstrates it when she saves the Empress from an assassin's bomb. Violetta takes Eugénie's place in the Imperial carriage for a visit to an orphans' home. Violetta knows the dangers; the carriage is bombed. But she survives, saved from the worst effects of the blast by a blanket of flowers presented to her by the little orphans. Eugénie rewards Violetta's loyalty by elevating her to the ranks of the nobility, whereupon Violetta can marry the nobleman she loves.

The plot of *Violettes impériales* is simple when compared to the intricate photoplay of *Joueur d'echecs* (1926). Nonetheless, the plot of *Joueur* evolves from an orphan story, indeed a double orphan story. The main characters are Boleslas, the orphaned son of a countess, and

Sophie, an orphan girl of unknown, but evidently impoverished, background. Both are taken in and raised by the Baron von Kempelen. Boleslas becomes a hero of the Polish nationalist movement. His life is endangered, and he is saved only by the unselfish sacrifice of the Baron. Not surprisingly, Boleslas and Sophie discover their true love for each other as they mourn the Baron's death. True love likewise awaits the orphan hero of *Paris* (1924). Jean Fleury, orphaned at an early age and hence forced to give up his studies and take a factory job, courageously catches a thief trying to steal Professor Roullet's design for a new locomotive. The new engine explodes—the thief is killed and Jean convalesces at the side of his one and only true love, Aimée, who will soon be Mme. Fleury. In *Les Misérables* (1925) Jean Valjean promises the dying young mother Fantine that he will care for her illegitimate daughter. This he does, and little orphan Cosette grows to find true love and happiness in her marriage to the lawyer Pontmercy. The orphan theme is developed in another adaptation from literature, *Les Mystères de Paris* (1922), in which a Duke becomes the protector of the orphaned bistro singer Fleur-de-Marie, and later discovers that she is his own daughter. Yet another variation on the motif of the orphan finding love and security is found in *Visage d'enfants* (1923). A little boy has been embittered by the death of his mother. When one day her vision no longer comes to him, he feels hopelessly abandoned. He is about to jump into the raging torrents of a river when his step-mother appears and saves him. In the arms of this woman, from whom he had felt himself estranged, he now discovers true love and happiness.

The frequency of repetition of the orphan story in the most popular films of the 1920's is in itself striking. No national cinema of any other land at any other time has been so singularly obsessed with this particular thematic material.[31] To interpret the meaning of the orphan films, caution demands consideration of other thematic material in the same set of films which seems to relate to the orphan motif.

Logic would first turn to the noteworthy presence of children in French films of this decade.[32] The association is clear: an orphan is a child bereaved of its parents. Among films which portray children which have nothing to do with the orphan theme proper, *Le Secret de Polichinelle* (1923), *La Terre promise* (1924), and *La Valse de l'adieu* (1928) merit mention.[33] *L'Homme du large* (1920) presents the coming of age of a fisherman's son. Abel Gance's serious-minded *J'Accuse* makes much of scenes of French children playing at war as the real war rages a few kilometers away. Gance employed the juxtaposition of children and soldiers again in his 1927 *Napoleon*. Jean Renoir's comedy *Tire au Flanc* (likewise 1927) reaches its most poignant satirical moment when a group of soldiers on manoeuvre run amuck amidst an outing of school children. In *Maldone* (1928) the restless "roulier" who has settled down temporarily to respectable family life finds his greatest joy in playing with his young son. In *Travail* the idealist Luc Froment becomes aware of the potential for reconciliation of social classes when he sees the children of workers playing happily with the children of a factory owner. When the sailor hero of *Le Baiser qui tue* (1928) fears that he has syphillis, his tortured mind conjures up the worst of all visions—he sees himself attacking his baby son. Finally, the hero of *Crainquebille* (1923) is the little newspaper hawker who befriends a lonely, abandoned, and distraught man. Tenderly and lovingly the boy takes Crainquebille home to live with him.

More examples of children in the most popular French films of the decade could be cited, but they need not be. The pattern is clear. The meaning of it, however, is complex. On the face of it, the portrayal of children in these popular films is not related to the orphan motif in an illuminating manner. What must be considered is not just what all orphans are—parentless children—but rather what orphans are specifically in the French films which depicted them. The thrust of these orphan stories is that an individual is abandoned, alone, lost in the world, and up against great odds. The resolution comes when the orphan is recognized for what he or she truly is. 'Recognition' is followed by reward: being reunited with parent or proper guardians, or else finding the security and happiness of true love.

What is elemental to the orphan movies—being abandoned and alone—is paralleled in another genre of the French popular cinema. Movies which portray the individual attaining his or her greatest achievements when alone and abandoned convey, in different form, the same message as the orphan films.

Abel Gance explained why he made *Napoléon* in a single line: "I did the film about Napoleon because he was a paradox in an epoch which itself was a paradox."[34] That may have been Gance's conscious intention and inspiration, but the emotional emphasis in the film is not on elements of paradox. The dramatic high points come in moments in which Napoleon is alone and abandoned and must master a situation through his force of character. Emphasis upon the lone individual abandoned is also exploited in the two Joan of Arc films which were popular with French audiences during the 1920's. This is particularly true of Theodore Dreyer's much acclaimed[35] *La Passion et la mort de Jeanne d'Arc*. The film's action is confined almost entirely to a courtroom where Joan faces her brutish interrogators. The composition is so dependent upon close-up and medium shots that Joan is seen almost exclusively isolated in the frame against a neutral background. There are few titles in the movie but one of those comes at a dramatic moment when Joan can mumble only: "Alone, alone, alone." Joan is taken to the stake alone, as she has suffered the abuses of her interrogators alone. Only in the very last scenes of the movie do the townsfolk recognize her true human worth and rise in protest against her persecutors. In *La merveilleuse Vie de Jeanne d'Arc* (produced in 1929, two years after the Dreyer film) the message is likewise clear that Joan must stand alone to realize her true heroism.

The dramatic high point in *Le Miracle des Loups* (1924) is when young Jeanne, the daughter of an advisor to the French King Louis XI, is surrounded by enemy Burgundians as she is on her way to deliver the King's message to his supporters. As the Burgundians close in upon her, the miracle from which the film draws its title occurs. Wolves appear from the surrounding forests, form a protective ring around Jeanne, and force the Burgundians to retreat in fear. She gets through to the besieged city of Perrone and delivers the message. In the meantime her father has been killed. "Alone and now orphaned," as a descriptive title informs the viewer, Jeanne rises to lead the defense of the town. When the battle is over, she is united with her long-lost true love, Robert Cottereau.

The hero of *Les Misérables,* Jean Valjean, is a loner when he first leaves prison. He assumes various disguises and performs a number of good works. At the end of the film he gains belated recognition for all that he has done. In *Travail* Luc Froment is abandoned and scorned by the very people he wished to help through a visionary reordering of society. Finally, however, he wins their approval and appreciation. The hero of the war film *Chignole* (1919) steals a plane against orders and shoots down an enemy German fighter single-handedly. Thus, does he win the approval of his officers and the hand of Sophie Bassinet. In another war film, *La grande Épreuve* (made nine years after *Chignole*), the soldier Paul undertakes alone the risky mission of blowing up a supply depot behind German lines. This he achieves, but he returns to the French trenches badly wounded. He recovers, however, in time to celebrate the armistice with his engagement to the lovely Claire.

Several films already mentioned as examples of the orphan film genre portray beside the orphan figure an abandonded, lonely character whose good works are recognized belatedly: *Jocelyn, Geneviève,* and *Les Mystères de Paris. L'Homme du large* is yet another movie which depicts the final triumph of an individual who has been left alone and abandoned. It tells of a fisherman's son who comes of age and falls in with a bad pack. As punishment, his father binds him in a fish-net and puts him into a little one-man boat which he sets adrift upon the sea. Alone, abandoned, and disowned, the young man is reborn through this experience. In the final scenes of the film he is seen, brave, courageous, and manly, captaining his own small craft at sea. A similar story of an individual who comes upon hardship, runs amuck, finds herself alone and abandoned, and wins redemption and recognition through her suffering is developed in Jacques Baroncelli's *La Légende de Soeur Béatrix* (1923). In an earlier film by the same director, *Le Secret du 'Lone Star'* (1920), the heroine is left alone after her father's suicide. In turn, her fiancé abandons her when she is accused of a felony. In the end she demonstrates her true human worth, whence her innocence is recognized, and she is reunited with her lover.

All of these popular French films which portray stories of orphans or other abandoned individuals are "hero" movies. Interestingly, the basic common elements in these films resemble elements discovered by Otto Rank some seventy years ago in his studies of myths from various cultures. Rank concluded that "the normal relations of the hero towards his father and his mother regularly appear impaired in all these myths."[35] In general, this is true of the French films under discussion here. Rank adds: "Summarizing the essentials of the hero myth we find the descent from noble parents, the exposure in a river and in a box, and the raising by lowly parents; followed in the future evolution of the story by the hero's return to his first parents."[36] The characteristic elements of the French films are close enough to those characteristics established by Rank for traditional myths to allow the generalization that in many instances the French popular cinema of the 1920's provides a throwback to the classical and primitive mode of telling a hero story.

In the French popular movies the 'exposure' of an orphan or of another hero figure who is abandoned is never literally in a river or in a box. But certain motifs in the French films do mesh with these elements, most dramatically the repetition of water imagery and seascapes on the one hand and the significance of landscape cinematography on the other.

Seascapes are important in such films as *La Bataille* (1923), *Le Baiser qui tue, Coeur fidèle* (1923), *J'Accuse,* and *La Nouvelle Aurore.* Water plays a dramatic-symbolic role as well in *Les Deux Gamines.* The orphans Ginette and Gaby go to the seashore to spread flowers on the water in memory of their mother who was lost in a shipwreck. They are offered a ride by a Monsieur Bersange and his sister; this incident marks the beginning of a development whereby the girls are united to their mother, who did not perish in the shipwreck after all. As has already been mentioned, the little boy in *Visages d'enfants* is saved from drowning himself in a raging river by his step-mother. In *Napoléon* the symbolic birth of the hero occurs when Bonaparte decides to leave behind the comfortable life which could be his on Corsica and sets forth in his little boat (using the French tri-color as a sail) upon the swelling seas in search of a greater destiny. Water imagery is, of course, important in *L'Homme du large,* as well as in *Maldone, Rose France* (1919), and *Le Secret du 'Lone Star'.*

This frequent repetition of water imagery is the unconscious representation of group psychic wishes dealing with birth. This interpretation follows the established analytical view that water dreams are most often birth-related in individual cases.[37] Other material, both manifest and latent, in French popular films of the 1920's reinforces the validity of this interpretation.

Landscape cinematography was prominent in the French cinema of the 1920's. On the surface, the landscape passages in popular French films often seem to be incidental and gratuitous—lingering visualizations of countryside with little apparent aesthetic or dramatic 'raison d'être' in themselves. In films as different in plot and technical development as *La Valse de l'adieu* (1928), *Le Femme nue* (1926), *La Dame de Monsereau* (1923), *Taô, Les deux Gamines,* and *Un Chapeau de paille d'Italie* (1927) landscape photography is significant. In the war films *J'Accuse, La Grande Épreuve,* and *Verdun, Visions d'histoire* (1927) landscape footage is essential. Likewise, landscape cinematography is dramatically and emotionally important in Marcel l'Herbier's *Rose France* and *L'Homme du large*. The same is true of the lone film by Jean Epstein which achieved broad popularity, *Coeur fidèle*. Jean Gremillion's *Maldone* has been repeatedly cited in histories of the cinema as a masterwork of landscape cinematography.[38] The earliest French films in which nature and landscape imagery were fully developed were directed by Jacques Baroncelli and Léon Poirier,[39] and between these two "cinéastes" five films were made during the 1920's which were among the most popular in France.

The most important French 'school' of cinematography during the 1920's was the impressionist movement in directing, which was inspired by the theoretical writings of Louis Delluc. It is not so important that a handful of directors tried to develop impressionism in the film by emphasizing a particular approach to landscape photography. More revealing for the purposes here is that many of the devices and techniques pioneered by the true cinematographic impressionists crept into the work of commercial film-makers. For this indicates that the French mass audience had a sharp and sympathetic eye for landscape photography, which was not true of other national audiences.[40]

Though production capital was often hard to come by in France during the twenties, French film-producers were notably willing to spend money for films shot on location.[41] This preference for shooting on location and filming outdoors (rather than in a studio) would not have been sustained were the results not appealing to French audiences. Moreover, investment capital in film research in France during the 1920's was directed almost entirely into the development of techniques for making color film—this while in all other lands research time and money were channelled into attempts to perfect a process for producing synchronized sound films.[42] Of the few studios built in France during the decade, most were built in the sunny south near Nice and were constructed as "glass cages" to create a filming atmosphere in which "natural, outdoor" lighting prevailed.[43] The cinema capitalists put their money where they think the mass audience's heart is. Thus, such investments (in filming on location, the development of color film, and building of glass-cage studios) are revealing as part of the psychohistory of a national cinema.

The common visual effect of landscape photography in the French films of the 1920's is a sense of affirmation, an impression of being at one with the world. There is no opposition between man and nature in the French movies of the 1920's, whereas just the opposite is true, for example, of the popular German films of the same decade.[44] Many of the French films allude directly to the life-giving and sustaining force of nature. As the director Marco de Gastyn accurately described his cinematographic characterization of Joan of Arc in *La merveilleuse Vie de Jeanne d'Arc:* "A peasant, she clings to the soil with all her atavism, as if she herself were a product of that soil."[45] In *La Force de sa vie* (1920) young Jean Paoli returns from Paris to his native Corsica, where he spends weeks communing with nature, thus regaining his spiritual as well as his physical energies. The hero of *Le Baiser qui tue* goes to his native Brittany, where his closeness to the soil speeds his recovery from wounds suffered when he saved his fellow sailors from a shipboard explosion. Napoleon too is portrayed as a son of the soil in the Abel Gance film of 1927; Bonaparte reaches his most profound thoughts while meditating in isolation in the Corsican countryside. Frédéric Chopin in *La Valse de l'adieu* returns to the peaceful Polish village of his birth from Paris when he reaches the limits of his emotional energies. The dramatic high point in the grandiose war film *Verdun, Visions d'histoire* comes when an elderly farmer shouts to weary French troops: "Don't let them pass, comrades." Those words keynote the Frenchmen's successful defense against the final German assault. As a title explains the farmer's words: "It was as if the land itself were speaking to them."

In general, landscape scenes in French films of the twenties are developed with a studied patience. The controlled slowness induces the feeling that the viewer is lingering in the spot being photographed. Landscape footage is often repeatedly edited into the filmic action. The final effect is that often the scenes of countryside and nature convey a sense of comfort and affirmation on the one hand, and a distinct feeling of "déjà vu" on the other. That editing in French films of the 1920's was slow-paced is an observation reinforced by various contemporary comments. Rex Ingram, an American film director who sometimes worked in France during the decade, characterized French productions by saying: "The immobility of the entire structural form combines with the amiable inaction of the performers."[46] Considering the most popular French films of the 1920's, this generalization holds for almost every case.[47] Elie Faure devoted much attention in his writing on cinema to criticism of the slow-paced editing and near total lack of visual movement in the typical French movies of the era.[48] The French style sometimes disturbed foreigners in particular. In an open letter published in the *Courrier cinématographique* in 1928 R. Waage, the director of the "Filmkuset" in Bergen, Norway, claimed that French-produced films were invariably received unfavorably by Norwegian audiences because they had "too slow movements".[49] In France itself, however, the general reaction to "la lenteur du développement" was most often favorable.[50]

It is in the landscape and seascape passages in French movies that the slowness and repetitiousness of the cinematographic development is most clear. These settings, and the manner in which they are presented on the screen, combine to create a feeling of affirmation, familiarity, and comfort. It is in just this way that the landscape cinematography in French films is akin to the water imagery in these same films. The landscape passages represent an unconscious birth motif. According to Freud, individual dreams of landscapes or other localities yield "a convinced feeling of having been there once before", whence landscapes symbolize the mother's womb. This meaning holds for female as well as male dreamers; Freud's original phrase "Das Genitale der Mutter" refers in this context to the genital rather than the sexual quality of the mother's equipment.[51] The landscapes in French films represent birth, as do the seascapes. For at the unconscious level what seem to be opposites (landscapes/seascapes) are interchangeable, an equivalence affirmed by the distinctive mode of cinematographic presentation in both cases: the camera lingering, familiarly and intimately.

The first collective obsession that can be established from the French popular cinema of the 1920's concerns children and birth. The obsession with children is reflected manifestly as well as latently. The meaning of this obsession with children and birth can be understood best in light of the demographic situation which existed in France after World War One. France was the single major European nation in which the birth rate had levelled off before the end of the nineteenth century. By the 1920's, France's population growth rate had already been at a near-standstill for almost five decades. In 1890 Arsène Dumont's *Dépopulation et civilisation* had appeared in France,[52] and on the eve of World War One Jacques Bertillon had published a work entitled *La Dépopulation de la France.*[53] Before World War One France was not yet losing population; compared to other European nations, however, she was no longer growing. Between 1871 and 1911 the total population growth rate was barely 9%.

In the same period population growth in European Russia stood at 78.2%, in Germany at 57.8% and in the United Kingdom at nearly 43%.[54] World War One brought France's relatively low population growth rate to a standstill. During the war France lost proportionately the most of any nation in human as well as in material terms.[55] 1,400,000 Frenchmen died, and twice that many were seriously wounded. In crude mathematical terms, the incorporation of Alsace and Lorraine into the French Republic after the war just about replaced the number of men that had fallen.[56] But, in fact, 30% of all French males between the ages of eighteen and twenty-seven had died in the war. This minimized the number of potential fathers in the demographic curve during the decade following the war. The war years themselves were marked by a startling decline in the rate of marriage, a trend that held throughout the 1920's.[57] The fertility rate had fallen during the war years too, and that decrease was not appreciably reversed in the post-war era.[58] In 1911 France had a population of 41,476,000. In 1921 the population was barely over 39 million. Only by 1936 did France again reach the forty-one million mark.[59]

In itself, a standstill in birth rate and even a slight loss in total population is no cause for undue national concern. Yet just such concern spread in France. At the end of the 1920's Ludovic Nadeau's popular *La France se regarde; Le problème de la natalité* appeared in print. Nadeau concluded that France's claim to be a major power was at stake in the population issue. He backed this argument with specific examples, citing as most important his claim that Germany would be forced to pay its reparation debts only when France took heed of the "répoulateurs" and began churning out progeny at record rates.[60] Another example of popular concern for the standstill in France's birth and population growth rate is found in a series of articles run by the Parisian daily *Bonsoir* during the year 1923. The items which appeared were demographic figures from a French and German town of equal size which were printed without further comment. The message was clear. For example:[61]

Montelimar (France)		*Limarteberg (Germany)*
pop. 13,150		*pop. 13,400*
1	marriages	30
0	births	40
4	deaths	4

The public concern over birth and population in France during the 1920's sprang from a fear of France's possible long-range loss of great power status, to be sure. More importantly, however, that fear was refined by the more immediate concern over a future challenge from the recently defeated but still larger and stronger neighbor on the other side of the Rhine. By the early 1920's Germany already counted over sixty million inhabitants; her rate of population growth was not retarded as was France's. The birth imagery and portrayal of children in the most popular French films represent the working off of this pressing group obsession. The wish-fulfillment which recurs time and again in these movies is one in which births abound and happy children romp and play with an unconscious eye on the national future. These popular films disguised what they were really about—the psycho-symbolic solution of one of the major problems to which post-war France was a sorry heir.

That very problem, however, would have been alleviated had developments in international relations gone as the French were led to believe they would go by the Versailles Conference. Those twenty million more Germans would have been a minor worry rather than a major threat had the two major co-designers of the Versailles settlement, the United States and Great Britain, shown themselves willing to live up to guarantees of France's security. This was not the case. Within a year of their formulation those guarantees were rendered worthless. The collective security provisions of the Versailles Treaty (Article 16 of the League of Nations charter associated with the Treaty, to be exact) were overshadowed by the refusal of the United States to join the League and by England's adoption of an increasingly more generous position towards Germany during the 1920's.[62] Wilson and Lloyd George had promised other separate protective treaties to France as well. But these treaties had to be ratified by both the United States and England before going into force. The British ratified theirs, which did not take effect, however, as the United States failed to follow suit. Increasingly France became alarmed for her security. She sought then to ensure it by forging a system of Eastern alliances, a project which she had begun during the first quarrels with Wilson and Lloyd George even before the Versailles Treaty had been finalized.[63]

The "entente cordiale" under whose aegis France and England entered the war as allies in 1914 became the "rupture cordiale" of the 1920's. France certainly wanted it to be otherwise. Her attempts to go it alone against Germany (notably the 1923 occupation of the Ruhr) as well as her searching out of substitute allies (Poland and the "Little Entente," and 'collective security' through the instrumentality of the League of Nations) were, in retrospect, but a sad charade. What France wanted was a return to the situation in which her security would be guaranteed by her old Allies, that is, her old protectors and guardians, primarily England and secondarily the United States.

France had been abandoned. She was a diplomatic orphan. This is the main group psychological meaning of the orphan theme in French movies of the decade following World War One. The orphan films present a recurrent, dream-like working off of the French national trauma

of having experienced in short order the disintegration of those very alliances which had meant victory instead of defeat in the First World War,
and which were assumed to be the necessary guarantee of French security for the future. Like the orphans and other heroes of her most popular movies, France found herself abandoned, for all practical purposes
alone in the world, and up against big odds.[64] The message in those films
is almost always the same—the orphan is recognized for what he or she
is, and is reunited to those who love him or her most, be it parents (i.e.,
the rightful guardians) or a true love (i.e., the proper partner). On the
group unconscious level the wish-fulfillment is that France should be
recognized for what she truly is, whereupon she would be reunited
(that is, re-allied) to her old protectors England and the United States.
There seems to have been two forms to that national wish: regain
protectors of 1917/1918, England and the United States; recover *alliance*, with England. The first is represented by the orphan regaining its
parents. The second, by the regaining of the old, true beloved.

The unconscious group wish in the orphan films finds a direct parallel
in the number of French films of the 1920's which end in marriage or at
least in a partnership which is presumed to be right and lasting. In the discussion of the orphan films, many titles have been cited which end in marriage or engagement. To be added to the list are *Les Exploits de Mandrin*
(1924), *La Dame de Monsereau, Le Miracle des Loups, La Force de sa
vie, Les Transatlantiques, Le Baiser qui tue,* and *Verdun, Visions
d'histoire.* This in itself is significant, for a word for marriage in French
is "alliance", the same word used for a formal diplomatic partnership,
an alliance between nations. The association here is clear; it makes the
argument all the more compelling that a persistent meaning of these
films refers to the group psychic wish to see the old protective partnership between France and England formally reestablished. The argument
is compelling twice over if a common dramatic situation in these most
popular French films is taken into account as well. Often the marriage or engagement that occurs signifies the reestablishment of a long-
standing true love that had in some way, often through a misunderstanding, been interrupted.

In *La Femme nue,* for example, the painter Rouchard falls in love
with and marries the model Lolette. Their life together is a joy on
earth until Rouchard makes the acquaintance of a seductive princess. A
misunderstanding occurs between him and Lolette over this. In the end,
however, the couple is reunited, and a mutual friend of theirs assures
Rouchard: "Imbécile . . . elle t'aime toujours." In *Violettes impériales*
Violetta cannot return the love of a dashing nobleman because of her
impoverished past. Her courageous deeds, however, merit her elevation
to the nobility, whence she can be united forever to her lover. In *La Rue
de la Paix* (1927) the lovely Manon and her true love, the designer
Laurent, have a misunderstanding over her relationship to the million-

aire Ally. In the last scenes Manon and Laurent are happily reunited, and Ally recognizes that these two people truly belong together. The heroine of *La Terre promise,* the Jewess Lia, loves the Christian André. She is urged to sacrifice for the good of all the Jews of her Bessarabian town, however, and marry her wealthy Uncle. She is about to do just that when Uncle Moïse himself recognizes that he was mistaken in asking for her hand. Lia and André wed, and the happy couple enters the "promised land" of marital bliss. In *La grande Épreuve* the brave French soldier hero Paul falls in love with a nurse named Claire. Because of a letter he finds in the pocket of his dying brother Max at the front he is misled into thinking that he and Max love the same girl. The misunderstanding is corrected. As bells toll the armistice of November 1918, Paul and Claire announce their engagement. The misunderstanding in *Le Secret de Polichinelle* is on the part of the parents of wealthy Henri de Jouvenal. They disapprove of his marrying the working-class Marie. Only when they come to know and love the illegitimate son of Henri and Marie do the elder Jouvenals recognize their error and bless the marriage. In *L'Homme du large* the sister of the young man who has gone bad gives up her lover and enters a nunnery to atone for the sins of her brother. As soon as she realizes that her brother has overcome his misspent past, the sister leaves the cloister and rushes to the passionate embrace of her true love. At the end of *Taô,* the Cambodian girl Soun retires to a Buddhist convent. This might seem to be a contradiction to what happens in *L'Homme du large,* but it is not. Soun has merely decided to devote the rest of her life to prayer and meditation, having realized that Jacques, whom she loves, rightfully belongs to his lover Raymonde, to whom he is now united until death do them part.

The common theme shared by all these films can be summarized succinctly. The original love relationship has been interrupted by a misunderstanding. That misunderstanding is recognized for what it really is, whence the correct, original relationship can be reestablished.[65] At the group psychic level this means that the original, informal partnership with Great Britain which had collapsed after 1919 because of a misunderstanding (or so the group mind wanted to interpret it) should be recognized as the right and natural partnership, whence would follow the fulfilled wish of the partnership being reestablished in a permanent, formal "alliance".

It is noteworthy that when popular French films of the 1920's deal with a 'triangle' love story, the second (or substitute) partner is neither undesirable nor an enemy. The substitute lover has come between two lovers only because an unfortunate misunderstanding has separated them temporarily. The substitute lover is not 'undesirable', but simply 'less desirable' than the proper partner. The portrayal of the substitute partner is furthermore usually sympathetic in that he or she in the long run recognizes the greater force of the true love relationship, and withdraws from the triangle. This elaboration of the triangle story points to the complex diplomatic relationship in which France found herself during the 1920's. When France's original protective alliances dissolved, she turned to a substitute partnership with several Eastern European nations. Based on the so-called "Little Entente" this arrangement was always considered, if not always openly recognized, as a substitute arrangement, a "pis aller", a "système hybride, force provisoire".[66] The French really wished that this substitute partnership would give way to the reestablishment of the original partnership. In these films there is, however, an unconscious refusal to offend the substitute partner; thus, the 'less desirable' rather than the 'undesirable' formulation in the triangle story.

It is common for feature films to portray violent deaths, accidents, murders, crimes, and so forth. Violence as a manifest element in a given cinema reveals little. Of greater importance are the differences between the ways in which filmic violence occurs and what it means. If there are crimes, who is the villain and who is the victim. If there are murders, what sort of murders and which weapons are used. These are the sort of subtle analytical considerations that reveal most about the real meaning of violence in the cinema of a particular nation in a particular era.

The source of danger in popular French films of the 1920's is always precisely defined. There is no question as to who is the culprit and scant development of suspense. The most popular French films of the decade included no detective movies, no whodunits. Danger is always recognizable and recognized—the hero (or heroes) must deal directly with it.

Often the villain in French popular films is portrayed as an outright brute, whether it be Ragu in *Travail,* Rollin in *La Mendiante de Saint-Sulpice,* Lau in *Le Miracle des loups,* Mlle. Benazer in *Les deux Gamines,* or Alerof in *Paris.* The same is true of the long-lost wretched father of Berlingot in *Enfant des Halles,* the mean Russian major in *Joueur d'échecs,* the abusive chief prosecutor in *La merveilleuse Vie de Jeanne d'Arc,* and the nameless archetypal brute in *Coeur fidèle.* The brute is big and aggressive; his choice victims are innocents, defenseless children, women, and, of course, orphans. In other French films of the decade in which the villain is not cut to the mold of the brute it is nonetheless always a single character who is up to no good. In *Violettes impériales* the evil-doer is Violetta's own brother gone bad, the wild-eyed anarchist bomber. The prime mover in all things bad in the film version of *Les Trois mousquetaires* (1921) is Cardinal Richelieu. In *Taô* it is the half-breed criminal of that same name.[67] In *L'Atlantide* (1921) it is the seductive temptress from whose name the film title comes. In *Napoléon* it is the rabble-rouser and English agent Paoli.

The portrayal of the single villain takes its meaning from the French situation of the 1920's. For all practical purposes France had only one enemy—a clear and recognizable source of potential danger, Germany. The characterization of the brute in these films reinforces this interpretation (France as orphan, France as abandoned and up against it; hence, Germany as brute).[68]

Another element typical to the handling of violence and danger in the popular French films is the blood the viewer sees. Its meaning is not to be disregarded. In films about World War One blood is a common and not unexpected visual motif: *J'Accuse, Chignole, La grande Épreuve.* The same is true of those other films which portray other wars and war scenes: *La Mendiante de Saint-Sulpice, La merveilleuse Vie de Jeanne d'Arc, Napoléon,* and *La Bataille.*

More precise and illuminating references to blood which is shown can be drawn from other films. In *Rose France* the young American Marshall Dudley Gold goes to a fortune teller to find out if the patriotic French girl Franciane really loves him. Not insignificantly, the woman draws a sample of Marshall's blood and reads from it of Franciane's passionate love for poor, suffering France. When Joan of Arc, in the Theodore Dreyer film about her trial and persecution, is finally forced into a confession by her interrogators, she must submit to a bleeding. In *Le Miracle des loups* the villain Lau tricks Robert Cottereau into firing upon his own true love Jeanne. In the last scenes of the film, however, Robert and a blood-covered Jeanne are reunited in a loving embrace. At the end of *Les deux Gamines,* the long-lost father of Ginette and Gaby is reunited with them. He had led a wretched criminal life. In the last reel he reforms. He offers blood to a dying hospital patient. It is a noble sacrifice, and as doctors finish bleeding him, a title tells the viewer that Manin had been morally regenerated. He dies peacefully, a hero born of this sacrifice. In *L'Homme du large,* when the young man who has gone bad robs the meagre savings of his own poor family, his sister attempts to stop him. In so doing, she is cut on the arm and bleeds copiously. A sequence of close-up and medium shots emphasizes her bleeding as she raises her hand to cross herself, symbolizing her decision to enter a nunnery to atone for the sins of her brother. In *Coeur fidéle,* when the crippled girl shoots the villain, he falls dead beside a baby's crib. A medium shot captures the joyous face of the baby and the blood-covered face of the slain brute in the same frame. In *Les Exploits de Mandrin* the evil Bournet d'Erpigny, who has nefariously seen to it that Mandrin be hanged in spite of the King's reprieve, is found stabbed to death, his shirt soaked in blood. In *Violettes impériales,* little Violetta emerges blood-splattered from the Empress's carriage after her own anarchist brother had planted a bomb. Blood flows too in *Jocelyn, Geneviève, Joueur d'éches, Taô, Travail,* and *Le Secret du 'Lone Star'.*

Violence can be dramatized in the cinema without a trace of blood being actually seen. This is emphatically the case in the films of other national cinemas of the 1920's, in which blood is never shown on the screen.[69] The blood that is repeatedly seen in French popular films is a minor detail; a minor detail, however, only on the surface level. On the unconscious level the blood seen represents the French blood lost between 1914 and 1918. Proportionately France had suffered the greatest human losses of the war. She had been bled, and she knew it. And during the 1920's the collective national psyche was obsessed with the memory of that bleeding. Commenting on the possibilities of Franco-German rapproachment towards the end of the decade, Georges Clemenceau wrote:

> And when Mr. Streseman [the German Foreign Minister] declares seriously that 'the path is now open for cooperation between Germany and her neighbors', he is acting as the spokesman for the most criminal people of all history who, *having been unable to take the very last drop of our blood*, now ironically offer us the privilege of reconstituting their strength at our costs.[70]

The blood which is seen in the popular French movies of the twenties relates to the theme of sacrifice in that same set of films. This theme reasserts itself repeatedly. In films such as *Genèvieve, Jocelyn, Violettes impériales, Joueur d'echecs*, and *Les Mystères de Paris* the theme of sacrifice is as strong as the orphan theme. In *L'Enfant des Halles* and *Les Misérables*, the sacrifice of the hero is undertoned, but its presence is still significant. The notion of sacrifice is blended into the hero stories in both Joan of Arc films, in *Napoléon*, and in *Chignole*. Ellen Frendy in *Le Secret du 'Lone Star'* is willing to sacrifice her own good name and even the true love of her fiancé in order to save the reputation of her deceased father. Lia in *La Terre promise* is ready to sacrifice and marry a man she does not love for the good of her people, as, indeed, is Prince Sasha in *L'Education de Prince*. In *Taô,* Soun leaps to shield Chauvy from Taô's bullets, which thus strike her instead. In *La Bataille,* in *Koenigsmark,* and in *L'Homme du large* the sacrifice occurs at the end of the film when in each case the heroine decides to forsake her own happiness for a loved one. In *J'Accuse* and *La grande Épreuve,* both heroes, Jean Diaz and the soldier Paul, respectively rise to the moment and sacrifice themselves against great odds. In *Les deux Gamines* Manin sacrifices himself to help another and earns his own redemption as a human being in so doing.

In the films cited, the sacrifice is always worth it—always, in some way, rewarded. What is repeatedly portrayed in all these instances of sacrifice is exemplified in the scenes of the 'raising of the dead' in Abel Gances *J'Accuse*.[71] French soldiers lying dead on the battlefield are resurrected. They march forward and confront their relatives and friends. Then they return to those various positions of death on the battlefield from which they miraculously rose. Each one of the soldiers now knows that his death "has served a grand sacrifice". The recurrence of the sacrifice theme in various popular French films of the 1920's reflects the on-going group obsession with the notion that France had made a noble sacrifice as a nation in World War One, and that the sacrifice had been worthwhile. Here the wish-fulfillment in the set of celluloid dreams comes closest to merging fully with the mythological. France's role in World War One was in no way 'sacrificial'; that it was, however, is precisely what the French group mind wanted to believe. France had entered the war in 1914 hoping for a swift victory and sweet rewards. Instead, the fighting bogged down within her own frontiers, and the war of attrition which followed cost her dearly. After 1918 in many quarters in France the view was held that France had won the war but not the victory—that Germany had come out better than she should have and France worse off.[72] Things turned sour. The promised German reparations went mostly unpaid. The alliances which were to assure France's future security disintegrated. The unconscious wish of the French group mind as revealed through the analysis of her most popular native-produced films was that she, the abandoned orphan, the old true lover, the good heroine, should be recognized for what she was, whence would follow the happiness and sense of security she deserved. The claim upon that recognition was embodied in the myth of France's sacrifice. The group mind wanted to believe in "France, yesterday the soldier of God, today the soldier of humanity, always the soldier of the ideal."[73] Thus, the group mind attempted to convince itself at the unconscious level by way of its film-dreams that France's role in World War One had been one of sacrifice rather than merely one of suffering. This was the group psychic way of working-off the collective trauma born of France's immediate post-war disappointments. For France had entered the war, then the peace, with naturally selfish aims and expectations which were quickly dashed by the evolution of the historical situation and the conflicting self-interests of other nations.

Only five French-produced films set in World War One attained broad popularity with the national audience during the 1920's. These movies were *Chignole, La grande Épreuve, J'Accuse, Rose France*, and *Verdun, Visions d'histoire*. Another half dozen films handle dramatic material dealing with some other war: *La Bataille, Joeuer d'échecs, La Mendiante de Saint-Sulpice, La merveilleuse Vie de Jeanne d'Arc, Le Miracles des loups*, and *Napoléon*. Three other films contain direct references to the First World War: *Les deux Gamines, Koenigsmark*, and *La Nouvelle Aurore*. In all these cases the references to World War One or some other war are conscious and undisguised. More revealing are the concealed references to France's wartime experience of 1914-1918. Shortly after the première of Theodore Dreyer's *La Passion et la mort de Jeanne d'Arc* in 1927, an English reviewer commented:

> To any who have an historical, political, sociological, or even a
> logical flair, Joan [the Dreyer film] will be a failure. We are tired
> of seeing the war anyhow, but how insufferable it would be if we
> saw it tricked out in a romanticism that made it just a sensation
> to wring our hearts. So with Joan.[74]

Intriguing it would have been had the author of those lines elaborated
upon that odd half-sentence—"We are tired of seeing the war anyhow . . ."
Elaborate he did not, but the meaning of those words can only be that
the Dreyer film, featuring hobgoblinish prosecutors who abuse and per-
secute the innocent, childlike, abandoned heroine Joan, is a parable of
World War One. The association between the Joan of Arc story and the
First World War is drawn directly in Marco de Gastyn's *La merveilleuse
Vie de Jeanne d'Arc*. Joan's childhood friend, Rémy Loiseau, who has
carried her standard, falls in battle. Later Joan goes to his grave to pray.
As she kneels, the tombstone inscription changes visually before the
movie viewer's eyes:

> Rémy Loiseau, Royale Lorraine, Rocroy, 1643
> Rémy Loiseau, Garde française, Fonteroy, 1745
> Rémy Loiseau, 3ème demi-brigade, Valmy, 1792
> Rémy Loiseau, 1ère Voltigeurs, Montmirail, 1814
> Rémy Loiseau, 156ème d'infanterie, Verdun, 1916

The reference here to an actual recent event in national history is blunt,
primitive, and rare. It is not the manner in which references to the shared
collective national experience normally occur in cinematographic
dreams. The manner in which national events and their consequences
are reflected in the popular cinema is oblique, disguised, and unconscious. The attempt here has been to try to unravel and decipher the
meaning of the repetitive themes and motifs of a particular cinema.
Psychological and historical categories of analysis have been interwoven
to get at the unconscious meaning of these popular movies for the group
mind of the audience to which they appealed. By these standards, the
interpretive analysis of the French popular cinema of the 1920's dis-
closes disguised patterns of reference to the shared trauma of World
War One and its immediate post-war consequences for France as a
whole.[75]

In the text the terms 'group mind' and 'collective unconscious' have
been used. They are catchphrases meant to describe a phenomenon
about which little is known. In this essay their meaning is figurative
rather than literal, and limited rather than all-encompassing. 'Group
mind' refers to concerns, some conscious, others unconscious, which
were evidently shared by large numbers of persons who composed the
mass movie audience in France during the 1920's. World War One was
an event which the nation shared as a nation, and every Frenchman's
consciousness of this personal sharing overlapping into the realm of col-

lective sharing was stimulated, heightened, and exploited in various ways during the war itself. The sense of nation and one's belonging to it was, of course, fostered in many ways, through many institutions, long before the cinema was discovered.

The 'group mind' refers to received ideas and notions which enjoyed broad conscious or unconscious currency. These were, at times, manipulated by governments or elements within society, but they were spawned in the first instance by shared experiences. The formation of the group mind is situational, hence historical. The intensification of the feeling of belonging to a group is precipitated by a rise in group consciousness (brought on by a shared experience, such as war) which, in turn, increases the level of participation in the shared feelings of the group unconscious. The 'group mind' has nothing to do with national character or race, and this is demonstrated in the analysis of the French popular cinema of the 1920's. Those films reflect a collective obsession with particular historical events and their aftermath; they reflect nothing of the 'Gallic spirit' or the 'French mentality'.

Not all individual members of a group, whether it be a nation or a social class within a nation, are fully aware of the group mentality and the extent of their absorption into it. Not all potential members of a group are individuals who actually do share in the group mentality. The integration of any given individual into the conscious or unconscious processes of the group mind, or alternatively an individual's remaining aloof or hostile to the group mind, is a variable which can swing either way in any individual case. In this regard material and situational conditions for integration into the processes of the group mind are as much modified by individual psychological factors as those factors are by material and situational causes of a determinant nature.

The analysis of films in this study derives its interpretations only through the shared, public, mass dimension. The notion that some may have that an individual's public concerns are relatively superficial in his individual psychology is irrelevant. The popular cinema is collectively produced, and the most interesting level of response to it is collective and unconscious.

Paul Monaco is a social and cultural historian who presently teaches at Brandeis University. The above article is a condensed and revised version of a chapter from his dissertation, Cinema and Society in France and Germany, 1919-1929, *which was accepted by the Faculty in the Program in Comparative History at Brandeis University in September, 1973. Mr. Monaco plans to extend and expand his researches into the economics and politics, as well as into the collective psychological aspects, of the popular cinema in other nations during the 1920's.*

REFERENCES

1. Walter Abell, *The Collective Dream in Art* (New York, 1966), p. 5.
2. Margaret Mead, "Why Do We Go To The Movies?", *Redbook Magazine,* March, 1971, p. 48. See also, Fritz Lang, "Arbeitsgemeinschaft im Film," *Der Kinematograph,* 18. Jahrg., 887, 17 February 1924, p. 7, and Eduard Jawitz, "Mein ideales Manuskript", *Der Film-Kurier,* 6. Jahrg., 77, 29 March 1924, p. 3.
3. Jean Galtier Bossiere, "Réflexions sur le cinéma 1920", Le Crapouillot, édition spéciale, "Histoire du cinéma", November, 1932, p. 6. And, Howard Lewis, *The Motion Picture Industry* (New York, 1933), p. 81; Jacques Durand, "Le film est-il une marchandise?", *Le Cinéma, fait social,* XXVIIème semaine sociale universitaire, 20-25 April, 1959, Brussels, p. 40; Peter Bächlin, *Der Film als Ware* (Basel, 1947), p. 38; Charles Ford, *Bréviaire du cinéma* (Paris, 1945), p. 88.
4. Henri Fescourt, *et al., Le Cinéma: des origines à nos jours* (Paris, 1932), p. 143; and *Die Lichtbildbühne,* 15. Jahrg., Heft 13, 25 March 1922, p. 17.
5. Sigmund Freud, *The Interpretation of Dreams,* trans. and ed. by James Strachey (New York, 1965), p. 82.
6. Jean Deprun, "Le cinéma et l'identification", *Revue Internationale de Filmologie,* no. 7, July/August, 1947, p. 38.
7. David Foulkes, *The Psychology of Sleep* (New York, 1966), p. 3. [Foulkes' italics.]
8. *Ibid.,* p. 47.
9. Edwin Panofsky, "Style and Medium in Motion Pictures", in Daniel Talbot, *Film: An Anthology* (Berkeley and Los Angeles, 1967), pp. 18, 19.
10. Gilbert Cohen-Seat, H. Gastaut, and J. Bert, "Modifications de l'E.E.G. pendant la projection cinématographique", *Revue Internationale de Filmologie,* Tome V, no. 16, January-March, 1954, p. 20. See also Y. Galfriet and J. Segal, "Cinema et physiologie des sensations", *Revue Internationale de Filmologie,* nos. 3, 4, October, 1948, pp. 292, 293 and Henri Gastaut and Annette Roger, "Effets psychologiques, somatiques, et électroencéphalographiques des stimulus lumineux intermittents rythmiques", *Revue Internationale de Filmologie,* Tome II, nos. 7, 8, pp. 215 ff.
11. Foulkes, *op. cit.,* pp. 21 and 23. Herman A. Witkins and Helen B. Lewis, *Experimental Studies of Dreaming* (New York, 1967), p. 9 and pp. 45-47.
12. Enrico Fulchignoni, *La Civilisation de l'image* (Paris, 1969), pp. 30, 31. Also, Agostiono Gemelli, "Le film, procédé d'analyse projective", *Revue Internationale de Filmologie,* Tome II, no. 6, no date, p. 136.
13. Raymond Spottiswoode, *A Grammar of the Film* (Berkeley and Los Angeles, 1965), p. 201.
14. Foulkes, *op. cit.,* p. 64.
15. Freud, *op. cit.,* p. 371.
16. Fulchignoni, *op. cit.* p. 72, 73.
17. Bächlin, *op. cit.,* pp. 12, 13.
18. Pauline Kael, "Movies: The Desparate Art", in Talbot, *op. cit.,* p. 54.
19. André Chevanne, *L'Industrie du cinéma* (Bordeaux, 1933), pp. 43-47.
20. The list of most popular French films for the years 1919-1929 was documented from the French film trade journals *Le Courrier cinématographique* and *La Cinematographie française.* See Paul Monaco, *Cinema and Society in France and Germany, 1919-1929,* unpublished dissertation, 1974, Brandeis University, pp. 300-368.
21. Durand, *op. cit.,* p. 34. Also, Georges Sadoul, *Le cinéma devient un art* (Paris, 1956), p. 442, and Claude Bonnefoy, *Le cinéma et ses mythes* (Paris, 1965), p. 63.

22. Chevanne, *op. cit.*, p. 77; Jacques Durand, *Le cinéma et son public* (Paris, 1958), p. 91. During 1919 the journal *La Cinématographie française* ran a series of articles and reports on film theaters in France under the title "Le tour de France projectioniste"—see, for example, *Le Cinématographie française,* 2ème année, numéro 4, 25 January 1919, pp. 79, 80; *ibid.,* numéro 6, no date, p. 76; *ibid.,* numéro 8, no date, p. 62; *ibid.,* numéro 24, 19 April 1919, p. 35. Also, *Le Courrier cinématographique,* 14ème année, 23 August 1924, pp. 17, 18, and *ibid.,* 30 August 1924, pp. 25, 26.

23. Paul Leglise, *Histoire de la politique du cinéma français:* "Le cinéma et la IIIème république" (Paris, 1970), p. 55. For a general comment on this aspect of the broad appeal of the silent cinema, see A. J. P. Taylor, *From Sarajevo to Potsdam* (London, 1966), p. 97.

24. Jacques Pietrini, "Le Défaitisme de Monsieur Pathé", *La Cinématographie française,* 3ème année, numéro 103, 23 October 1920, pp. 22, 23; Jean Mitry, *Index historique du cinéma* (Paris, 1967), p. 135; Alexander Jason, *Jahrbuch der Filmindustrie* (Berlin, 1923) I, 32; G.-Michel Coissac, *Histoire du cinématographe* (Paris, 1925), p. 481; Friedrich Zgliniki, *Der Weg des deutschen Films* (Frankfurt a.M., 1955), p. 412; Rene Jeanne and Charles Ford, *Histoire encyclopédique du cinéma* (Paris, 1947) I, 485.

25. Already in 1919 it was clear to Pathé and Gaumont that safer profits could be earned in the distribution and exploitation branches of the film industry. See, *Le Courrier cinématographique,* 9ème année, 12 July 1919, p. 2.

26. The practices of American firms are discussed thoroughly in Henri Mercilon, *Cinéma et monopoles* (Paris, 1953). See also Durand, *Le Cinéma et son public,* p. 1. The best discussion of American booking practices compared to those common in Europe is in Bächlin, *op. cit.,* pp. 39 ff.

27. Walter Dadek, *Die Filmwirtschaft* (Freiburg i. Br., 1957), p. 21.

28. Indeed, the types of foreign films which appealed to a national audience may well provide reinforcement of interpretive conclusions based on analysis of native-produced films.

29. See the discussion of film and film plots in: Bela Balazs, *Der sichtbare Mensch, eine Film-Dramaturgie* (Halle, no date), 2. Auflage, pp. 35-37; Robert Gessner, *The Moving Image* (New York, 1968), a monograph dedicated to studying 'what is fundamental in cinema as a story-telling art form'; Roy Huss and Norman Silverstein, *The Film Experience* (New York, Evanston, and London, 1968), pp. 127 ff.; Ernest Lindgren, *The Art of the Film* (London, 1948), pp. 35-37; Rod Whitaker, *The Language of Film* (Englewood Cliffs, 1970, pp. 139 ff.

30. Ricardo Canudo, *L'Usine aux images* (Geneva, 1927), p. 87.

31. Other national cinemas have, of course, produced orphan films. The American cinema of the 1920's was, in fact, fond of the genre. The important point is that these American orphan films differed in dramatic development and emotional impact from their French counterparts. Moreover, the popularity of the orphan film in the United States was neither so persistent nor nearly so intense as in France.

32. Since this essay concentrates on analyzing the unique mixture of themes and motifs in a particular popular cinema, it is always helpful to have comparative evidence at hand. The German popular cinema of the 1920's did not often show children. Sixty-three films could be documented as having been exceptionally popular with Weimar audiences. Of those, only *three* have any child actors, and in none of them are children central characters; see Monaco, *op. cit.,* pp. 369-462.

33. Little David, the adopted son of the Rabbi in *La Terre promise* is an orphan. But this fact is only once alluded to in the movie, whence the film has not

been counted among those of the orphan genre.

34. Carl Vincent, *Histoire de l'art cinématographique* (Brussels, no date), p. 21. Cited also in Jeanne and Ford, *op. cit.*, pp. 338, 339 and in Georges Sadoul, *Histoire du cinéma français* (Paris, 1962), p. 32.

35. Otto Rank, *The Myth of the Birth of the Hero* (New York, 1964), pp. 65, 66.

36. *Ibid.*, p. 72.

37. Freud, *op. cit.*, pp. 435 ff. See also, Rank, *op. cit.*, p. 73.

38. Henri Agel, *Miroir de l'insolite dans le cinéma français* (Paris, 1958), p. 99.

39. Sadoul, *Histoire du cinéma français*, pp. 24, 25.

40. The Germans, for example, produced very few films incorporating landscape passages during the 1920's. See, Ludwig Kapeller, "Die deutsche Landschaft als Filmbühne", *Die Lichtbildbühne*, Heft 13, 29 March 1919, pp. 30-32; Robert Spa, "Dans les studios de Berlin", *Ciné-Miroir*, 7ème année, numéro 147, 27 January 1928, no page number; Siegfried Kracauer, *From Caligari to Hitler* (Princeton, 1947), p. 75.

41. Émile Roux-Parassac, "Le Studio France", *Ciné-Miroir*, 7ème année, numéro 176, 17 August 1928, pp. 535 ff.; "Les Films tournés au Maroc", *Ciné-Miroir*, 4ème année, numéro 82, 1 September 1925, pp. 275, 276.

42. Kenneth Macpherson, "As Is", *Close-Up*, no. 1, July, 1927, p. 8.

43. Fescourt, *et al.*, *op. cit.*, pp. 154, 155.

44. The opposition of man and nature was particularly keen in the popular German 'mountaineering' films of Arnold Fanck and others. For general comments on the subject see Kracauer's *From Caligari to Hitler* and Lotte Eisner's *Die dämonische Leinwand* (Wiesbaden/Biberich, 1955). Specifically, see Léon Poirier, "Nature et cinéma", *La Cinématographie française*, 6éme année, numéro 270, 5 January 1924, pp. 23-25.

45. *Le Petite Illustration*, numéro 408, supplément cinématographique numéro 14, 24 November 1928, p. 10.

46. H. A. Potamkin, "Le Cinéma américain et l'opinion française", *La Revue du cinéma*, 1ère série, numéro 4, 15 October 1929, p. 56.

47. The single exception among the forty-eight most popular French films of the decade is *Un Chapeau de paille d'Italie*, which was directed by René Clair.

48. Elie Faure, *Fonction du cinéma* (Geneva, 1964), p. 29. The same idea is expressed in somewhat different form by Canudo, *op. cit.*, p. 37.

49. *Le Courrier cinématographique*, 19ème année, numéro 4, 29 January 1928, p. 9. That other foreign audiences reacted in much the same way as the unreceptive Norwegians to French-produced films is confirmed in O.B., "Vision d'histoire", *Close-Up*, Vol. II, no. 2, February, 1928, p. 20.

50. Agel, *op. cit.*, p. 99.

51. Freud, *op. cit.*, p. 435.

52. Ludovic Nadeau, *La France se regarde: Le Problème de la natalité* (Paris, 1931), p. 443.

53. Michel Huber, Henri Bunle, and Fernand Boverat, *La Population de La France: Son Évolution et ses perspectives* (Paris, 1950), p. x.

54. Nadeau, *op. cit.*, p. 10; Huber, Bunle, and Boverat, *op. cit.*, pp. 10, 11; André Armengaud, *La Population française au XXème siècle* (Paris, 1965), p. 8.

55. Jacques Chastenet, *Les Années d'illusions, 1918-1931* (Paris, 1960), pp. 15, 16.

56. *Ibid.*, pp. 14-16.

57. Armengaud, *op. cit.*, pp. 16, 17.

58. *Ibid.*, pp. 18, 19. A detailed discussion of the subject is found in Philippe Ariès, *Histoire des populations françaises et leurs attitudes devant la vie depuis le 18ème siècle* (Paris, 1948), pp. 386-427 and pp. 461-470.

59. Jacqueline Beaujeu-Garnier, *La Population française* (Paris, 1969), p. 9.

60. Nadeau, *op. cit.*, p. 5.

61. *Bonsoir* (Paris), 9 August 1923, p. 4.

62. Fernand L'Hullier, *De la Sainte-Alliance au pacte atlantique* (Neuchatel, 1955), II, 139 and 160 ff.; also, Chastenet, *op. cit.,* p. 79 ff. See also, Carl Bergmann, *The History of Reparations* (Boston and New York, 1927), for a discussion of England's attitude towards Germany and France's reaction to it.

63. Pierre Renouvin, *Histoire des relations internationales: "Les Crises du XXème siecle"* (Paris, 1957), I, 191 ff.; Frederick L. Schuman, *War and Diplomacy in the French Republic* (New York and London, 1931), pp. 253 ff.; Charles Petrie, *Diplomatic History* (London, 1948), pp. 332, 333. Also, Arno J. Mayer, *Politics and Diplomacy of Peacemaking: Containment and Counterrevolution at Versailles, 1918/1919* (New York, 1967) and Ivo J. Lederer, *The Versailles Settlement* (Boston, 1967). An interesting Marxist interpretation of France's falling out with England is to be found in W. J. Potjomkin, *Geschichte der Diplomatie* (Berlin, 1948), I, 114 ff.

64. Of particular interest are several French monographs written during the 1920's on this subject: Charles Gautier, *L'Angleterre et nous* (Paris, 1922); Alcide Ebray, *A Frenchman Looks at the Peace* (New York, 1927), trans. by E. W. Dickes; Henri Brenier, *French Points of View* (Marseilles, 1921), trans. by the author. See also, *Les Délibérations du Conseil de Quatre* (24 Mars-28 Juin 1919), notes de l'Officier Interprète Paul Mantoux (Paris, 1955), vol. II.

65. In a handful of French popular films the dream-wish is distorted with regard to the actual reuniting of the lovers. Instead, an emotional, psychological form of reuniting occurs, which serves to reinforce the group psychological wish-fulfillment motif of the most typical movies: *La Bataille, Koenigsmark, La Legénde de soeur Béatrix, Maldone, Les Trois mousquetaires,* and *La Valse de l'adieu.*

66. L'Hullier, *op. cit.,* p. 139.

67. The only exception to the rule might be found in *Taô.* But "L'Esprit du Mal" is revealed in quick fashion to be Taô, and the potential mystery is resolved before its cinedramatic development begins. The film story of *L'Atlantide* is curious, but it is no real mystery. The source of danger is clearly recognized, although it is peculiar.

68. During World War One popular propaganda in France had characterized the Germans as brutish—Huns who raped women and murdered babies. That the image of the "Boche" as brute carried over into the films of the 1920's on the subconscious level is not surprising.

69. The German popular films of the same decade scrupulously avoided showing blood on the screen. See, Monaco, *op. cit.,* pp. 253 ff.

70. Georges Clemenceau, *Grandeurs et misères d'une victoire* (Paris, 1930), pp. 329, 330. [My italics.]

71. The Gance film (which we re-made in a sound version in 1938) is often considered to be a pacifist film; see, René Jeanne, "Les Metteurs en scène français: Abel Gance", *Ciné-Miroir,* 2ème année, numéro 22, 15 March 1923, p. 86, and also Ford, *op. cit.,* p. 63 and Kevin Brownlow, *The Parade's Gone By* (London, 1969), pp. 533 ff. The film, however, has only some superficial and naive pacifist overtones, as a close viewing of it reveals. For a general discussion of war films and the reasons why none of them are truly pacifist, see Michael Radtke, "Irrwitzige Schlachten: Ein Film Anti-Krieg ist kein Film Anti-Krieg", *Film und Fernsehen,* 9. Jahrg., Heft 5, May, 1971, pp. 15-19.

72. Louis Forest, "Pourquoi les Allemands ne se semblent pas vaincus", *Le Matin* (Paris) 2 January 1919, p. 2. Articles of this sort and tone were to be found commonly in almost all popular French newspapers and magazines, particularly during the few years immediately following the war. Interesting are the

articles in this vein which appeared in the film trade journals, such as: P. Simonot, "Achevons la victoire", *La Cinématographie française,* 2ème année, numéro 13, 1 February 1919, pp. 3, 4, or *Le Courrier cinématographique,* 10éme année, numéro 39, 25 September 1920, which editorialized: "Don't do a thing my friends, just go on living. Germany will pay. You are the victors –dance! And you danced, and you're still dancing. But it's not Germany that is paying, it's us."

73. Chastenet, *op. cit.,* pp. 12, 13.
74. Kenneth Macpherson, "As Is", *Close-Up,* vol. III, no. 1, July, 1928, p. 9.
75. Two French film historians have written: "At the end of the war (World War One) one can say that France continued to exploit, though perhaps less forcefully, the themes that were popular before the war," Maurice Bardech and Robert Brasillach, *Histoire du cinéma* (Paris, 1966), 201. The statement is misleading. On the unconscious level the popular films of 1919-1929 were the reflection of group psychic tensions born of the post-war period. But even on the surface level, post-war French films differed from their pre-war predecessors. The pre-1914 favorites, the fantasy films and primitive science-fiction movies of Georges Melies, the comedies of Prince Rigadin and Max Linder, and the adventure serials of Louis Feuillade differ essentially in manifest content, and to some degree in technique, from the films which were popular in France after 1919. On the other hand, the persistence of the theme of the individual isolated and abandoned in French films right up to the eve of World War Two has been suggested in Raymond W. Whitaker, *The Content Analysis of Film: A Survey of the Field, An Exhaustive Study of 'Quai des Brumes', and a Functional Description of the Elements of the Film Language,* unpublished dissertation, 1966, Northwestern University, pp. 254 ff.

The popularity of each film was based on reports found in the two major French film trade journals for the period, *La Cinématographie française* and *Le Courrier cinématographique.* In a few cases monographs and other printed works on the French silent cinema were helpful in double-checking this documentation.

In so far as possible, the content analyses of the films were based upon the viewing of the films themselves. This work was greatly facilitated by the help of Madame Mary Meerson of the Cinémathèque française and the staff of the Cinematheque Royale de Belgique. Both archives permitted access to all pertinent film copies in their holdings. For those films for which no extant copy could be located, the content analyses were based on written summaries printed in the movie magazine *Ciné-Miroir,* or, in a few cases, on the original scenarios preserved in the Bibliothèque des hautes études cinématographiques.

French Popular Films (1919-1929)
In Alphabetical Order

Film Title	*Name of the Director*	*Year in Which the Film Premiered*
L'ATLANTIDE	Jacques Feyder	1921
LE BAISER QUI TUE	Jean Choux	1928
LA BATAILLE	E. E. Violet	1923
UN CHAPEAU DE PAILLE D'ITALIE	René Clair	1927
CHIGNOLE	René Plaisetty	1919
COEUR FIDÈLE	Jean Epstein	1923
CRAINQUEBILLE	Jacques Feyder	1923

Film Title	Name of the Director	Year in which the Film Premiered
LA DAME DE MONSEREAU	René Le Somptier	1923
LES DEUX GAMINES	Louis Feuillade	1920
L'EDUCATION DE PRINCE	Henri Diamant-Berger	1927
ENFANT DES HALLES	René Le Prince	1924
LES EXPLOITS DE MANDRIN	Henri Fescourt	1924
LA FEMME NUE	Léonce Perret	1926
LA FORÇE DE SA VIE	René Le Prince	1920
GENEVIÈVE	Léon Poirier	1923
LA GRANDE ÉPREUVE	A. Duges and A. Ryder	1928
L'HOMME DU LARGE	Marcel l'Herbier	1920
J'ACCUSE	Abel Gance	1919
JOCELYN	Léon Poirier	1922
JOUEUR D'ÉCHECS	Raymond Bernard	1926
KOENIGSMARK	Léonce Perret	1923
LA LÉGENDE DE SOEUR BÉATRIX	Jacques Baroncelli	1923
LA MADONE DES SLEEPINGS	Maurice Gleize	1928
MALDONE	Jean Gremillion	1928
LA MENDIANTE DE SAINT-SULPICE	Charles Burguet	1924
LA MERVEILLEUSE VIE DE JEANNE D'ARC	Marco de Gastyn	1929
LE MIRACLE DES LOUPS	Raymond Bernard	1924
LES MISÉRABLES	Henri Fescourt	1925
LES MYSTÈRES DE PARIS	Charles Burguet	1922
NAPOLÉON	Abel Gance	1927
LA NOUVELLE AURORE	Gaston Le Roux	1919
PARIS	René Hervil	1924
LA PASSION ET LA MORT DE JEANNE D'ARC	Theodore Dreyer	1927
LE PETIT CAFÉ	Raymond Bernard	1919
ROSE FRANCE	Marcel l'Herbier	1919
LA RUE DE LA PAIX	Henri Diamant-Berger	1927
LE SECRET DU 'LONE STAR'	Jacques Baroncelli	1920
LE SECRET DE POLICHINELLE	René Hervil	1923
TAÔ	Gaston Ravel	1921
LA TERRE PROMISE	Henry Roussel	1924
TIRE AU FLANC	Jean Renoir	1927
LES TRANSATLANTIQUES	Pierre Colombier	1927
TRAVAIL	Henri Pouctal	1919
LES TROIS MOUSQUETAIRES	Henri Diamant-Berger	1921
LA VALSE DE L'ADIEU	Henry Roussel	1928
VERDUN, VISIONS D'HISTOIRE	Léon Poirier	1927
VIOLETTES IMPÉRIALES	Henry Roussel	1923
VISAGES D'ENFANTS	Jacques Feyder	1923

CHAPTER 7

RUDOLPH
BINION

Hitler Looks East

The following lecture (in its German original, "Hitler blickt nach Osten") served to open an interdisciplinary colloquium on Hitler held at Heidelberg University on April 5 and 6, 1975.

It is well known that Hitler called for Germany to conquer more land. How did he justify this aim? His basic supportive argument in *Mein Kampf* is headed: "The Four Ways of German Politics."[1] These were four ways out of an alleged disproportion between population and soil. Hitler rejected three of these ways—emigration, birth control, and intensified industrialization—in favor of the fourth: the conquest of new land in eastern Europe. After *Mein Kampf* he recurred ever and again to this argument of the "four ways" as long as he openly advocated eastward expansion (until 1930).

Hitler had already used this argument of the "four ways" some three years before he began writing *Mein Kampf,* in which he made his first public pitch for eastward expansion. At a Nazi Party meeting of May 31, 1921, in a speech called "Versailles and the German Worker," Hitler declared (according to a résumé in the Party newspaper):

> ... There are only three ways for a dynamic people to preserve itself insofar as it does not want to become more of a plaything than ever of the other rising nations by deliberately restricting

births. Colonization. Germany came too late and found no room
left in the world to discharge its excess vitality. Emigration. What
people wants to give away its children as cultural fertilizer for
other countries? As these first two possibilities were taken from
the German people, it set about creating a means of survival by
developing industry and exporting goods. The Socialists deliberately opposed all national power politics—today German labor is
internationalized by finance capital, by the Versailles document.
Hitler contrasted the Brest-Litovsk peace treaty with this dictated
peace of enslavement. Point by point he went through the treaty.
No German knows its 14 points, whereas every child knows Wilson's 14 points—the Jewish press has done a good job. And what
do the 14 Brest points provide? Start of immediate peace without
reparation payments, without the surrender of a single gun, of a
warship, immediate free trade, compensation for the German as-
sets worth 6 billions confiscated in Russia.

Then Hitler added:

Through the peace with Russia, Germany's nourishment as well as
the existence of work were to be supplied through the acquisition
of land and soil, through raw materials imports and friendly relations between the two countries. Versailles: the opposite. Rape of
the territories that assured Germany's nourishment . . .

and so forth.[2] The corresponding passage of Hitler's outline for a speech
called "Workers and Peace Treaties," which overlaps this one on "Versailles and the German Worker," reads: "Brest-Litovsk was to assure
German people's nourishment through I. soil II. securing of raw materials for industry and trade."[3]

The acquisition of land and soil in eastern Europe for the German
people's nourishment and increase: this demand is reminiscent of the
third point of the Nazi Party Program, issued on February 24, 1920:
"We demand land and soil for our people's nourishment." But there, in
the Party Program, Germany's lost overseas colonies had been meant.
Conceivably Hitler transferred the demand to eastern Europe already in
the ninth month of the Party Program, when he declared in the course
of a speech of November 19, 1920, on "The Worker in the Germany of
the Future" (according to a Munich police report): "And then, when we
are inwardly strengthened, we can turn to the east as well."[4] In any
event, Hitler's formulation of May 31, 1921, would seem to derive from
Ludendorff. At the close of 1915 Ludendorff wrote to Hans Delbrück
concerning Poland: "Here we shall win breeding ground for the men
needed for further battles to the east."[5] And Ludendorff's instructions
of December 1917 for the Brest-Litovsk peace negotiations specified:
"Annexation of Lithuania and the Courland, including Riga and the
islands, as we need more land for the people's nourishment."[6]

The notion of more land to feed an increasing population remained constant with Hitler after May 1921. On the other hand, he dropped that "existence of work" from his later representations (it was just a courtesy to his title "Versailles and the German Worker") along with those "raw materials imports and friendly relations" (which he nonetheless actualized for a brief spell under the Germano-Soviet Pact of 1939-1941). His later conclusion was all but reached in his outline for that similar speech with a similar title, "Workers and Peace Treaties": "German colonization: 8th-13th century. First the eastern march, then the northeastern march. Is our people fit for that? Prerequisite: power."[7] It was reached by late December 1922, when he revealed his program for a future German dictatorship to Eduard Scharrer, a confidant of Chancellor Cuno. As Scharrer reported Hitler's view to Cuno:

> . . . Abroad, Germany would have to go over to a purely continental policy, avoiding any damage to English interests. The breakup of Russia with England's help should be attempted. Russia would provide enough land for German settlers and a broad field of activity for German industry. Then England would not butt in when we settle with France.[8]

Thus by the time Hitler's eastern policy emerged, its clear derivation from Ludendorff's eastern imperium of 1917-1918 was no longer in evidence. Yet not just the concepts and terms, but the very argumentation (the "four ways") that Hitler had used to deplore the loss of the eastern conquest of 1917-1918 reappeared intact in his later call for an eastern conquest. Hence at bottom the eastern conquest he urged in private as of December 1922 and in public beginning with *Mein Kampf* was for him Ludendorff's eastern conquest over again. But instead of "at bottom" we are justified in saying: "unconsciously." In urging the conquest of Soviet Russia, Hitler was unconsciously urging a repetition of Ludendorff's failed conquest of Soviet Russia. Consciously Hitler denied any and every connection between Ludendorff's eastern operation and his own eastern aims. In *Mein Kampf* he asserted as he set forth the need to expand the "motherland" to the east so that the "Germanic mother" could nourish her offspring sufficiently: "In this we National Socialists consciously put an end to the course of Germany's prewar foreign policy. We pick up where Germany left off six centuries ago."[9] Unconsciously it was more like six years.

What was the source of Hitler's latent purpose of repeating the lost victory of 1917-1918? Brest-Litovsk was a stock subject of his speeches from the very first. Of his early oratory he wrote in *Mein Kampf:*

> At the very first sentence containing a criticism of Versailles you had the stereotyped cry flung at you: "And Brest-Litovsk?" "Brest-Litovsk?" . . . I set the two treaties side by side, compared

them point by point, showed the truly boundless humanity of the one as against the inhuman cruelty of the other. . . .

He added that he "repeated and repeated" this demonstration "dozens of times in ever varied form. . . ."[10] He went on to affirm that "the orator receives a continual correction of his speech from the crowd he is addressing, inasmuch as he can see from the faces of his listeners how far they are able to follow and comprehend his presentation and whether by the impact and effect of his words he is attaining the desired end. . . . A popular orator of genius," he concluded,

> . . . will always let himself be carried along by the great masses so that instinctively the very words flow from him which he needs to speak to the hearts of his listeners of the moment. But should he err ever so slightly, he has the living correction before him all the time. As stated above, he is able to read from his listeners' facial expressions whether, first, they comprehend what he is saying, second, whether they can follow it as a whole, and third, to what extent his presentation has carried conviction.[11]

These assertions of Hitler's are all borne out by numberless reports of early Nazi meetings from army, police, newspaper, and Party sources. Hitler did indeed adapt his set piece on Brest-Litovsk to his audiences while striving to put its basic point across. The intense interchange between orator and listeners suggests the possibility of unconscious counterinfluence, the more since the basic point he was striving to put across was mere polemical sham (he had no use otherwise for "boundless humanity"). Anomalously, it was in the midst of a rehash of his set piece contrasting Brest-Litovsk with Versailles that on May 31, 1921, he came out with that grievance about Germany's loss of the land and soil taken from Russia. He never recurred to that set piece again.

The suspicion that the idea latent in Hitler's policy of land and soil— to repeat Ludendorff's failed eastern conquest—came from his public is supported by the fact that its specifics can be traced to no personal determinants such as underlay his other, older, anti-Jewish policy in its entirety. But we need not rest content with a mere suspicion. By April 1920 for certain, and in all likelihood from the start of his political career in September 1919, Hitler saw the supposed Jewish menace as international. Also, Bolshevism was for him Jewry triumphant. Accordingly, Bolshevik Russia was in his view the power center of the international Jewish menace. Russia was in addition the chief breeding ground of the Jewish race. Consequently, when he proceeded to turn that regret over the loss of the land conquered from Soviet Russia in 1917-1918 into an argument for a new conquest of land from Soviet Russia, obvious premises lay ready to hand. At the same time, those ready premises necessitated that foregone conclusion. If the Jews were a deadly international danger with their power center and their biological center both in Russia, then that danger would have to be met not just within Germany's borders, but in Russia as well. By destroying Jewish power only in Germany, Germany would only incite world Jewry to revenge. "To grasp the evil by the root and destroy it root and branch," as Hitler proposed to do with the Jewish menace, necessarily meant to conquer Soviet Russia.

Hitler came close to forcing this conclusion over the seventeen months in which he turned his look back at Brest-Litovsk into a look forward. On April 12, 1922, he declared after over an hour's raging against the Jewish-democratic-plutocratic-Bolshevistic world peril: "There are only two possibilities in Germany! . . . Either victory of the Aryan side, or its destruction and victory of the Jews."[13] On October 22, 1922, he developed the ideological aspect of this theme in the course of a memorandum on building up the Party:

> . . . What is involved here is not winning a majority or even so-
> called political power. What is involved is a life-and-death strug-
> gle between two world views that cannot coexist. Their clash will
> leave only victors and victims. This conception has become second
> nature to Marxism (witness Russia). A victory of the Marxist idea
> means the total extermination of its opponents.[14]

Therewith Hitler implicitly grounded his scheme to destroy Soviet Russia with England's help. Conversely, logic pushed for carrying the domestic life-and-death struggle between two world views into Russia itself. The anti-Bolshevik grounding lay the closer at hand when, to go by Scharrer's report to Cuno, Hitler prefaced his maiden mention of the scheme in December 1922 with the words: "With the suppression of Bolshevism in Germany, iron-fisted dictatorship must rule."[15] Instead he then reverted to his problematical premises of a year-and-a-half previous—to the Germans' right to grow at others' expense and to secure their food and raw materials on the European continent, meaning through its subjugation. Beginning with *Mein Kampf*, he then routinely promoted the eastern conquest on this basis—loudly until the Nazis' great leap forward in the national elections of September 1930.

At the same time Hitler synthesized his expansionist and his anti-Semitic policies on the theoretical plane, though only indirectly, by way of the historic law that peoples all struggle among themselves for living space—all except the Jews, who live off other peoples as parasites and thus jeopardize humankind, themselves included, by their growing ascendancy. This intellectual development of Hitler's has been retraced by Eberhard Jäckel with great skill.[16] Concerning its outcome, Hitler's final synthesis, we need note here only that the one world-historical imperative, killing Jews, was not the logical ground for the other, conquering land. Besides, Hitler kept the completed theoretical integration of these two intellectually and psychologically distinct political aims to himself, for he had the 1928 manuscript containing his perfected thesis locked up in a safe.[17]

He also kept to himself, or almost, the racial-ideological premises worked out between May 1921 and December 1922 for the eastern conquest even as he employed instead the Ludendorffian language of soil and nourishment and raw materials supplies and blockade-proof continental sphere. He talked this way only somewhat cautiously in public after late 1930—I shall return to this point—yet quite starkly again in his political and military councils after his accession. To Reichswehr commanders on February 3, 1933, after four days in office, he foretold "the conquest of new living space in the east and its ruthless Germanization."[18] Before roughly the same group enlarged by SA and SS leaders on February 28, 1934, he again pointed ahead to "creating living space" for Germany in the east.[19] On November 5, 1937, he briefed his five top political and military assistants on his contingency planning "to solve the German space question."[20] In a military conference of May 23, 1939, he held forth about "expanding our living space in the east and securing our nourishment."[21] Meanwhile in *Mein Kampf* he cited Judeo-Bolshevism's mortal designs on Germany only as the last of many reasons for Germany not to ally with Soviet Russia.[22] In his secret book of 1928 he merely observed in an improbable context that, populous as it was, the Soviet Union was no military, but only an ideological, menace.[23] In his memorandum of August 1936 on the Four Year Plan initiating economic mobilization he cited the threat from international Jewry based in Russia, but altogether separately from Germany's need for more living space as a "definitive solution" to German economic problems.[24] The Anti-Comintern Pact that Germany concluded with Japan in November 1936, and Italy a year later, carried a hint of secret aggressive designs. Actually the Pact was spineless: its sham defensiveness was a propaganda ploy to justify German rearmament.[25] But the preliminaries did prompt Hitler to remark to the Japanese negotiators in June 1936 that he had "always seen Europe's sole salvation in the uncompromising fight against Communism" and in July 1936 that the Bolshevik threat could be met only by a dismemberment of the Soviet Union.[26] Here, in talks with Japanese negotiators behind closed doors, Hitler for the first time (to the best of my knowledge) derived his eastern aim explicitly from his anti-Semitism or anti-Bolshevism. Then in 1938 Heydrich told a confidant: "It is the Führer's will to liberate Russia from the Communist yoke. The war with Soviet Russia is a settled matter."[27] On June 2, 1940, with France falling, Hitler told an army headquarters group in Belgium that he expected a "reasonable peace settlement" with Great Britain that would free him "at last" for his "great and proper task: the showdown with Bolshevism."[28] But only when the invasion was mounted did he reopen in full that parenthesis of October 22, 1922—"(witness Russia)"—which had followed his assertion that the fight against Bolshevism was a "life-and-death struggle between two world views." On March 30, 1941, in handing down the operational plan ("Barbarossa") to 200-250 assembled army commanders, he announced an impending "struggle of two world views against each other," adding: "What is involved is a struggle of annihilation."[29] Then, while he ordered the army to kill captured Communist officials (the "Commissar Order"), Heydrich instructed his SS henchmen that "eastern Jewry is the reservoir of Bolshevism and therefore, in the Führer's view, is to be annihilated."[30] With the start of the attack, secret instructions went out to the press to switch its tack to "the annihilation of Bolshevism" and some days later to the link between Bolshevism and Jewry.[31] Living space had taken second place.

Now to recapitulate. Hitler promoted his policy of eastward expansion among the Germans on grounds that had originated as grounds for deploring the loss of Ludendorff's eastern imperium. Between times he had worked out other grounds for his eastern policy, ones drawn from his anti-Semitism, but these he then kept to himself, or almost, until at long last the attack on Soviet Russia was mounted. At that point he brought out the anti-Semitic grounds and put them before the other, power-political ones. It follows that the anti-Semitic grounds for the policy were *his own* grounds for it. They were also the more simple and logical grounds for it. If Hitler nonetheless kept them to himself and argued from the other, power-political grounds exclusively as he solicited and achieved dictatorial power for the express purpose of waging that eastern war, the clear reason is that these were *the Germans'* grounds for the war. Indeed, Hitler worked up the underlying tendency to relaunch Ludendorff's lost eastern conquest into an expansionist program derived in its entirety from the German experience of the First World War and aimed at an unconscious repetition of that experience. Unfortunately, time does not permit my developing this point here.

How did Hitler of all people come to sense, and supply, the traumatic need of a nation overwhelmed by fate in 1918? Elsewhere I have attempted to show how, through his relationship to the German nation, Hitler recreated his primal relationship to his mother.[32] When she conceived Adolf, Klara Hitler was—like Germany following World War One—suffering from the aftereffect of a traumatic blow of fate, in her case the loss of her three previous children at a few weeks' interval. Adolf was born to the task of making up for that loss. The traumatized mother, while nursing and tending her new child at exceeding length, suspended her fertility for the exact duration of her earlier experience of motherhood (from first conception to third death) and therewith lived through that experience unconsciously a second time. Hitler's nursing was his constitutive experience, to which he harked back in working out his doctrine of feeding ground. The nursling's oral aggression underlying this doctrine surfaced unmistakably when he declared on March 23, 1927:

> How can we feed the nation? Either we export people or goods, or we strive to adjust land and soil to population. Nature lays this possibility at every living creature's cradle. That is the self-preservative instinct. The child does not ask, when it drinks, whether the mother's breast is being tortured. Hunger and love are healthy instincts.[33]

This infantile fixation point of Hitler's beneath his politics of land and soil must not, though, be mistaken for their point of departure. Their point of departure was Germany's traumatic need, which Hitler sensed unconsciously. The basic formative experience that fitted him to sense that need unconsciously then fed into his articulation of it. (So did, from the Germans' side, the starvation that had accompanied their experience of the war and defeat.) The mere oral-aggressive fixation would not of itself have brought Hitler to replace a revisionistic demand for the return of Germany's colonies with a continental expansionist aim going back to 1917-1918. And this eastward expansionism is my subject.

But how did Hitler the orator integrate that eastern aim, which he brought out only gradually following his Putsch fiasco, with his anti-Jewish aim, which remained his controlling political purpose? The integrating formula, which he elaborated in his innumerable speeches of the late 1920s even as he built up his mass following, ran: removing the Jews ensures national unity, which ensures the conquest of feeding ground. At times it came out only: the removal of the Jews is the precondition for national unity, itself the precondition for the conquest of feeding ground. But even then the context ordinarily admitted of no possible doubt that the preconditions were considered sufficient of themselves to generate the necessary means. So: Jews alone sow disunity among Germans; through unity alone will Germans be victorious—the rest will take care of itself. The formula can best be grasped schematically:

Such was Hitler's message already in his political beginnings, when its end term was still only the repudiation of the Versailles treaty. Some

pointed excerpts from Hitler's early speeches follow. Please keep your
eyes on the diagram as I read them rapidly in chronological order.

> What can help us now? Only the greatest unity of all breeds of
> Germans. . . . The Treaty of Versailles must go![34]

> Merciless war on those drones who brought us to misery! We
> want a single German people back however much the whole Jew
> pack kicks.[35]

> It's Judah that incites the various classes and even the workers
> themselves against one another. . . . The Jewish motto is: Divide
> and rule! . . . Our byword must be: Unity, not division![36]

> Against all divisions, for a single Germany! Out with the Jew
> band![37]

> Everywhere you hear the cry: "Bourgeoisie here, proletariat
> there!" But never the cry: "Germans, join together to fight for
> your freedom!" . . . Germanic will shall yet smash the Jew's skull!
> Salvation comes from the innermost depths of the German people.[38]

> Our motto must be: How do we create the basis for a united
> Germany? Out with the Jews, who are poisoning our people.[39]

> Germany has never yet been conquered from without, always
> from within.[40]

> We are fighting the Jew primarily . . . because of his action as dis-
> integrative force in our entire national life.[41]

> We knew and know that the German nation can only help itself
> and that it will do so if the national will is joined to that end.[42]

> We want to shake off the oppressive yoke imposed on us, but first
> we must have the will to do so. . . . After the will, [the] deed.[43]

> Workers of the head and hand must realize that they belong to-
> gether and can only raise our nation back up in unison or else go
> to ruin separately. . . . Once the national will is strengthened we
> shall regain political power. . . . Blind, solid, unshakable faith in
> the irresistible power of the German people . . . must be reawak-
> ened, it will then clearly point the way we must go.[44]

> Unity! If we stop fighting among ourselves, then . . . we shall
> achieve the position that is rightly ours.[45]

> Nations are fit to rise high only when they have undergone in-
> ternal reforms making it possible to direct the entire race in closed
> ranks to foreign policy goals. . . . The cleavage: proletariat and
> bourgeoisie . . . comes of the inner Judaization of the people, of
> all peoples![46]

Away with the splintering among Germans of all parties! . . . Iron bonding of all compatriots, away with the alien rabble![47]

The division of Germans into two classes, confronting each other by now in downright deadly antagonism thanks to the tireless agitation of the Jews, must be surmounted. . . . We are convinced that a peaceful solution of class conflicts is possible only if we remove the poisoner. That is why the Jewish question is the core question for us National Socialists. This question cannot be solved with tenderness, but . . . only by brute force.[48]

We do not fear weaponry; given the will, the deed will succeed.[49]

There can be . . . no salvation before the agent of discord, the Jew, has been put out of commission.[50]

In the beginning was the will.[51]

Do we want to restore Germany's freedom and power? If so, then let us first rescue it from its spoiler![52]

You must come to will a change. And when you do, then things will in fact change for Germany. . . .[53]

Cowards cry: But we have no weapons!—Weapons here, weapons there! If the whole German nation has but the will to fight for its freedom, then the instruments we need will come to hand! . . . The inner struggle must precede the outer![54]

Our aspirations abroad can be imposed only through a prior inner cleansing![55]

If 60 million people had only the one will to be fanatically national, the weapons would spring from their fists![56]

That takes us to the Putsch of November 1923. On refounding the Party after his incarceration, Hitler declared in Nuremberg: "From this day forth we shall again work together to steel the German people's will to freedom until someday no power will be able to bend that will any longer, but instead it will quell Germany's need."[57] As here already, so afterwards in calling for the eastern war Hitler stressed the second term of his formula:

Does a people have the strength for the fateful struggle for the land and soil it needs to nourish its children? That is the only standard and the only issue here. What do we mean by the strength of a people? We mean that tight unity and that compact will to fight for its earthly existence. . . . We can attain no strength, since the prerequisite for strength, the unity of these 60 millions, is lacking. . . . We must recognize that, so long as the fragmentation lasts, the whole people is headed for decline—unless and until the German people comes to its senses and declares that the whole people is a community that has to fight for its existence.[58]

A people has freedom only when it closes ranks. . . . We must all grow into the great community of fate.[59]

To conquer land and soil, strength is needed. That lies in unity. . . . And the people may not be diverted by other problems. It must have a single goal.[60]

The German people is rent asunder. . . . The result is that . . . when the time comes for ensuring the nourishment of the German people . . . our German people's strength does not suffice. . . . On this earth, not weapons in themselves signify strength, . . . but the first requirement for any and all strength is will, the people's attitude of will. . . . Help does not come along one day and say: Tattered and torn nation, here is your unity. But this nation will one day have to reach out for its freedom, and if it lacks the requisite strength and unity of will, then freedom is denied to it.[61]

One thing stands above economic disputes and professional conflicts, above all the divisions in daily life, and that is the community of a people that numbers over 60 millions and has too little land to live, and for whose existence no one provides unless it does so itself.[62]

There is a single goal: honor, freedom, and bread for the German people, and the way to it is called struggle. That is why the German people should close ranks to become a power factor in world history capable of obtaining the feeding ground corresponding to its natural increase.[63]

Above all we need not weapons, but a people that recognizes, beyond its day-by-day problems, its great existential need and is determined to stand up for that need. . . . If you ask whether one can lead a people to power without its possessing weapons, I shall briefly indicate how . . .[64]

So spoke Hitler—on and on. None of these quotations from his speeches of the 1920s is the least bit exceptional; any one of them can be matched a hundred times over. For eleven years he reworded the same message continually without ever changing it. Undoubtedly none of his listeners was ever quite conscious of this primitive, hocus-pocus-like formula for his political discourse. It was no less bound to register with Germans as the basic sense of his politics.

The first thing to be said about this basic sense of Hitler's politics is that it was nonsense. Such disunity as existed among Germans was not the Jews' doing; closed ranks will not ensure victory if the material means are simply unobtainable. Inherent in Hitler's victory formula, then, was a double assurance that it would yield no victory in the end: the extermination of the Jews together with their influence would hardly produce national unity, which would not suffice anyway for victory. To be sure, no reasonable person would have expected Hitler to rely on his magic formula alone to conquer Europe however insistently and fanatically he recited it—but reasonable expectations play no role unconsciously. A second point to note about Hitler's magic formula is that it was derived from Germany's supposed war experience of 1914-1918. At the outset of that war the Germans had been united and victorious; then the Jew had sown disunity among them until they snatched defeat from victory. Such was the legend to which Hitler subscribed. Here, for instance, is how he put it in 1921:

> As long as the people, in inner awareness of the national imperative, still stood squarely behind the German armies, these remained victorious. The progressive stifling of this elemental involvement of the entire people in its history led to a debilitation of the front. . . . The condition for a rebirth consists, therefore, first and foremost in the removal of whatever can affect our people divisively in any way

—namely, of the Jews.[65] This legend remained constant through all Hitler's variations on it and was cited by him ever and again to validate his magic formula.[66] What matters here is not how widespread it was or wasn't at the time, but that it was a legend and so took in no one unconsciously. Even the paranoiac does not fool himself unconsciously with his delusions. A third point about the formula is that it provided no cause, on the contrary, to go after Jews outside Germany. Hence it was for Hitler a mere device for use with his public. Finally, national unity was, by the terms of the formula, no aim in its own right, but only a means to the conquest of land. Nor did the "national community" he invoked interest Hitler in its own right, outside the formula, even as a euphemism for dictatorship. Incidentally, his conception of the Jews' work of decomposition was not restricted to the class struggle; he could also cite other divisions wrought by Jews among Germans, such as "the division into parties promoted by Jewish influence and pushed to a drastic extreme."[67]

This last observation—that the "national community" was, by the terms of the formula, a mere means to the end of conquering land—leads me to the main point of my presentation. This point is that systematically beginning in late 1930, but quite frequently already in the latter 1920s, Hitler toned down or even muted the first and the third terms of his magic formula (removal of the Jews, conquest of feeding ground), and that the second term (national unity) then served to recall the first and the third through the old-established associative channels. Doubtless he muted the first and third terms of the formula out of prudence toward the foreign world, yet also because his message was pitched below the level of clear consciousness within Germany itself. In addition, he often expressed the ticklish concepts "removal of the Jews" and "conquest of land" through mild substitutes equivalent in his usage, such as "Marxism" for Jewry, or "freedom" for the course of conquest. Already before 1930 he accustomed his public to an increasing use of such soft synonyms along with, and then gradually in place of, the two ticklish concepts. Let me illustrate this. Once in November 1928, even as he was calling outright for a racial purge and a land grab, Hitler stated the treble aim of his movement in passing as "to steel the body politic, to give it faith again, and one day to stand up for freedom."[68] In context, this was transparently his old, fixed formula without seeming euphemistic. Two years later he took to expressing himself in this way only. Thus on November 7, 1930:

> The key to foreign markets and supplies is named not diligence, but concerted force. . . . If a great people is determined to sacrifice everything in the service of the nation, then a power so compelling emerges that it can transform the image of the world and the age. . . . If the entire nation had the spirit of the SA and SS, then we would today already be out of our servitude.[69]

And the next day:

> We . . . are convinced that the time will pass away again when the German people dissipated its strength internally. Then the hour will strike for which millions are longing. And so let us fight for our children's bread.[70]

Then a few days later:

> I have the firm conviction that the moment the German people . . . turns its whole strength outwardly again, the yoke of servitude will be broken.[71]

From then on out he also strongly accentuated the middle, or connective, term of his magic formula. His modified oratorical pattern is best visualized schematically somewhat like this:

In his famous speech of January 27, 1932, to industrialists in Düsseldorf, the stress fell heavily on national unity, though the two associated concepts did find some muffled expression. "Forming the will of the nation as a whole is essential," he declared;

it is the point of departure for political operations [abroad]. . . .
If we want to develop a new domestic market, or to solve the
problem of [living] space: ever and again we shall need the con-
certed political strength of the nation. . . . But that is never to be
attained by a Reichstag bill for negotiating a few heavy batteries,
eight or ten tanks, twelve airplanes, or for that matter even a few
squadrons: that is all beside the point! In the life of nations, technical weapons have continually changed. What needed to remain
unchanged was the national will. . . . With today's body politic,
no active foreign policy can be conducted any longer. . . . If from
the tiniest cell [the Party in 1919] a new body politic does not
form to vanquish the "ferments of decomposition," then the nation as a whole will be unable ever to rise again. . . . We are inexorably resolved to exterminate Marxism in Germany down to
the last root.[72]

From just about any of his further utterances of 1932 can be seen how
skillfully Hitler intimated the first and the third terms of his magic formula while outwardly putting the whole stress on the second. Here is a
random illustration from the electoral campaign of July 1932:

Is that German if our people is torn up into thirty parties? . . .
Our aim is to do away with those thirty parties and restore unity
and order in Germany in the awareness that national greatness depends . . . before all else on the strength of a united people.[73]

"Is that German . . . " was necessarily answered "No, Jewish" in the back
of every listener's mind, where similarly "national greatness" could not
fail to assume spatial contours bulging eastwards.

For the most part, Hitler's cover terms did not merely convey the
real terms of his formula, but they also denoted the first practical measures to be taken toward either extreme—toward the removal of the
Jews or the conquest of living space. Statements from around the time
he took power are particularly instructive. On December 4, 1932, he
spelled out those first practical measures to a Reichswehr colonel:

1. Repression of Marxism and its effects to complete extinction.
   Preparation for a new national unity of mind and will.
2. General spiritual and ethical rearmament of the nation on the
   basis of this new unity.
3. Technical rearmament.
4. Organization of national strength for national defense.
5. Attainment of formal recognition from the rest of the world
   for the new situation already brought about.[74]

Four days after taking office he extended this short list in a talk to
Germany's top brass (as noted by one of the generals present):

Overall political goal solely the recovery of political power. Here
the entire state apparatus (every agency!) must be brought to bear.

1. Internally. Complete reversal of present domestic situation
in Germany. No tolerance for manifestation of any sentiments
(pacifism!) opposed to the goal. He who won't bow must be bent.
Extermination of Marxism root and branch. Youth and entire nation must be attuned to the idea that only struggle can save us
and everything must yield to this idea. . . . Toughening of youth
and strengthening of will to defense by any and all means. Strictest
authoritarian rule. Removal of the cancer of democracy!
. . .

4. Buildup of the armed forces most important requirement for
reaching goal: winning back of political power. . . .[75]

Here the emphasis on national defense over the expansionist war meant
only that the expansionist war was for later.[76] Likewise, the displacement from the Jews themselves to their institutional and intellectual
mischief meant only that their turn would come later. And now Hitler's
cover theme of ending divisions among Germans—that intoned hyphen
between the muted terms of his politics—sounded shriller behind the
scenes of the incipient dictatorship.

The middle term of Hitler's formula, while linking his two policies logically, separated them psychologically. It also subordinated the
anti-Jewish to the expansionist policy by making them means and end
respectively. This too is a sign that Hitler was addressing his expansionist policy to the Germans—that through it he was acting out a national
determination. All indications are, moreover, that this was the source
of his political appeal. His anti-Semitic track did not run beyond fringe
agitation in and around Munich—not even to a proper Putsch there, but
only as far as the Odeonsplatz and the Landsberg jail. But then in the
late 1920s, as soon as the prohibitions against his speaking in public
were lifted, he preached the eastern land grab high and low. With that
he rapidly built up a mass following on the national level. That following simply took his anti-Jewish aim into the bargain. Germans were
hardly surprised when in due course the Jews disappeared from Germany and German-controlled Europe. They rather looked the other
way if they could—but those involved made little fuss as a rule, and
some could not even remember afterwards. The bond between Hitler
and the Germans was his war policy—that is, the unconscious repetition
of Germany's catastrophic war of 1914-1918. To live through a catastrophe anew is routine in the emotional life of individuals. It could also
be so in the emotional life of peoples. That the war Hitler promised and
delivered is a case in point requires a full-scale demonstration. For this
I hope I have here provided some points of reference that can hardly be
interpreted otherwise.

Rudolph Binion teaches in the Comparative History and the History of Ideas programs at Brandeis University. He is presently preparing a book on Hitler and Germany.

REFERENCES

1. Adolf Hitler, *Mein Kampf* (Munich, 1935), pp. 144-54.
2. Bundesarchiv Koblenz NS26/51/208-9.
3. Werner Maser, *Hitlers Briefe und Notizen. Sein Weltbild in handschriftlichen Dokumenten* (Düsseldorf, 1973), p. 276.
4. Reginald H. Phelps, "Hitler als Parteiredner im Jahr 1920," *Vierteljahrshefte für Zeitgeschichte,* Vol. 11 (1963), p. 327. In all likelihood "to the east" (*"nach Osten"*) is a mistake for "to the outside" (*"nach aussen"*). The somewhat fuller report in the *Völkischer Beobachter* of November 25, 1920, on the same Party meeting contains no such indication: see Bundesarchiv Koblenz NS26/51/18-20.
5. Egmont Zechlin, "Ludendorff im Jahr 1915. Unveröffentlichte Briefe," *Historische Zeitschrift,* Vol. 211 (1970), p. 352.
6. Werner Hahlweg, *Der Friede von Brest-Litowsk. Ein unveröffentlichter Band aus dem Werk des Untersuchungsausschusses der Deutschen Verfassunggebenden Nationalversammlung und des Deutschen Reichstages* (Düsseldorf, 1971), p. 118. Hitler first met Ludendorff in April or May 1921.
7. Maser, p. 268.
8. Eduard August Scharrer to Wilhelm Cuno, December 30, 1922: Bundesarchiv Koblenz R431/2681/88.
9. Hitler, pp. 741-42.
10. *Ibid.,* pp. 519, 523-24, 524. Hitler's last-quoted statement also applied to his speech on "the true causes of the World War." He treated this subject too on May 31, 1921—early along.
11. *Ibid.,* pp. 525-26, 527.
12. Bayerisches Hauptstaatsarchiv, Allgemeines Staatsarchiv, Sonderabgabe I 1478/76 (speech of April 6, 1920). Cf. Phelps, p. 302 (speech of May 11, 1920): "The evil must be grasped by the root."
13. *Adolf Hitler. Sein Leben und seine Reden,* ed. Adolf-Viktor von Koerber (Munich, [1923]), p. 29.
14. Albrecht Tyrell, *Führer befiehl. . . Selbstzeugnisse aus der "Kampfzeit" der NSDAP* (Düsseldorf, 1969), pp. 49-50.
15. Scharrer to Cuno, fol. 88.
16. Eberhard Jäckel, *Hitlers Weltanschauung. Entwurf einer Herrschaft* (Tübingen, 1969).
17. *Hitlers zweites Buch. Ein Dokument aus dem Jahr 1928,* ed. Gerhard L. Weinberg (Stuttgart, 1961), p. 225.
18. *Ausgewählte Dokumente zur Geschichte des Nationalsozialismus 1933-1945,* ed. Hans-Adolf Jacobsen and Werner Jochmann (Bielefeld, 1966), unpaginated.
19. Wolfgang Sauer, "Die Mobilmachung der Gewalt," in Karl Dietrich Bracher, Wolfgang Sauer, and Gerhard Schulz, *Die nationalsozialistische Machtergreifung. Studien zur Errichtung des totalitären Herrschaftssystems in Deutschland 1933/34* (Cologne, 1962), pp. 749-50. At greater length in Robert J. O'Neill, *The German Army and the Nazi Party 1933/39* (New York, 1966), pp. 40-41.
20. Jacobsen and Jochmann. Further: Gören Henrikson, "Das Nürnberger Dokument 386-PS (das "Hossbach-Protokoll"). Eine Untersuchung seines Wertes als Quelle," in *Probleme deutscher Zeitgeschichte,* Lund Studies in International History 2 (Stockholm, 1971), p. 175.
21. Jacobsen and Jochmann.
22. Hitler, pp. 750-52.
23. Weinberg, p. 128.
24. Wilhelm Treue, "Hitlers Denkschrift zum Vierjahresplan 1936," *Vierteljahrshefte für Zeitgeschichte,* Vol. 3 (1955), pp. 204, 206.

25. Hans-Adolf Jacobsen, *Nationalsozialistische Aussenpolitik 1933-1938* (Frankfurt/Main, 1968), p. 427; Walter Laqueur, *Russia and Germany* (Boston, 1965), pp. 170, 176-95, 196-98; Josef Henke, *England in Hitlers politischem Kalkül 1935-1939* (Boppard am Rhein, 1973), pp. 95-96; Axel Kuhn, *Hitlers aussenpolitisches Programm. Entstehung und Entwicklung 1919-1939* (Stuttgart, 1970), pp. 196-98.
26. Theo Sommer, *Deutschland und Japan zwischen den Mächten 1935-1940* (Tübingen, 1962), pp. 31, 34 (June 9 and July 22, 1936).
27. Gert Buchheit, *Hitler, der Feldherr* (Rastatt, 1958), p. 167.
28. Andreas Hillgruber, *Hitlers Strategie: Politik und Kriegführung, 1940-1941* (Frankfurt/Main, 1965), p. 145, and *Deutschlands Rolle in der Vorgeschichte der beiden Weltkriege* (Göttingen, 1967), p. 105.
29. Franz Halder, *Kriegstagebuch,* Vol. II, ed. Hans-Adolf Jacobsen (Stuttgart, 1963), pp. 336-37.
30. Helmut Krausnick, "Judenverfolgung," in Martin Broszat, Hans-Adolf Jacobsen, and Helmut Krausnick, *Konzentrationslager, Kommissarbefehl, Judenverfolgung* (Olten, 1965), p. 365.
31. Jacobsen, *Aussenpolitik,* p. 459, n. 21.
32. Rudolph Binion, "Hitler's Concept of *'Lebensraum':* The Psychological Basis," *History of Childhood Quarterly,* Vol. 1 (1973), pp. 187-215.
33. *Adolf Hitler in Franken. Reden aus der Kampfzeit,* ed. Heinz Preiss (Nuremberg, 1939), p. 40.
34. Bayerisches Hauptstaatsarchiv, Allgemeines Staatsarchiv, Sonderabgabe I 1478/68-69 (speech of March 4, 1920).
35. *Ibid.,* 94 (speech of April 9, 1920).
36. Phelps, p. 300 (speech of April 27, 1920).
37. Bayerisches Hauptstaatsarchiv, Allgemeines Staatsarchiv, Sonderabgabe I 1478/104 (speech of May 19, 1920).
38. Phelps, pp. 303-4 (speech of June 11, 1920).
39. Bayerisches Hauptstaatsarchiv, Allgemeines Staatsarchiv, Sonderabgabe I 1478/119 (speech of June 24, 1920).
40. Phelps, p. 311 (speech of August 25, 1920).
41. Bundesarchiv Koblenz NS26/51/14 (speech of August 31, 1920).
42. Phelps, p. 316 (speech of September 5, 1920).
43. *Ibid.,* p. 318 (speech of September 20, 1920).
44. Bundesarchiv Koblenz NS26/51/16-17 (speech of October 26, 1920).
45. Bayerisches Hauptstaatsarchiv, Allgemeines Staatsarchiv, Sonderabgabe I 1478/248 (speech of November 5, 1920).
46. Bundesarchiv Koblenz NS26/51/18-19 (speech of November 19, 1920).
47. *Ibid.,* fol. 106 (speech of March 21, 1921).
48. *Ibid.,* fol. 112 (speech of April 17, 1921).
49. Bayerisches Hauptstaatsarchiv, Allgemeines Staatsarchiv, Sonderabgabe I 1480/40 (speech of April 21, 1922).
50. *Adolf Hitlers Reden,* ed. Otto von Kursell (Munich, 1925), p. 47 (speech of September 18, 1922).
51. Preiss, p. 15 (speech of January 3, 1923).
52. Kursell, p. 67 (speech of April 20, 1923).
53. *Ibid.,* p. 74 (speech of April 24, 1923).
54. Koerber, p. 73 (speech of August 1, 1923).
55. *Ibid.,* p. 84 (speech of August 21, 1923).
56. Kursell, p. 157 ("Aussprüche Adolf Hitlers").
57. Preiss, p. 30 (speech of March 2, 1925).
58. Bundesarchiv Koblenz NS26/54/118, 123, 124 (speech of March 6, 1927).
59. Preiss, pp. 38, 40 (speech of March 23, 1927).
60. Bundesarchiv Koblenz NS26/54/145 (speech of March 26, 1927).
61. *Ibid.,* NS26/52/18, 20, 21, 22 (speech of August 8, 1927).
62. *Ibid.,* NS26/54/203 (speech of November 11, 1927).
63. *Ibid.,* NS26/55/3 (newspaper résumé of speech of September 30, 1928).
64. Preiss, p. 139 (speech of November 30, 1929).
65. *Völkischer Beobachter,* January 27, 1921: Bundesarchiv Koblenz NS26/51/34-35.

66. A few examples out of hundreds: *Völkischer Boebachter,* April 28, 1921: Bundesarchiv Koblenz NS26/51/114; *Im Kampf um die Macht. Hitlers Rede vor dem Hamburger Nationalklub von 1919,* ed. Werner Jochmann (Frankfurt/ Main, 1960), pp. 70-78 (speech of February 28, 1926); Bundesarchiv Koblenz NS26/55/123-34 (speech of November 9, 1928); Preiss, pp. 90-91, 100 (speech of December 8, 1928), and 160-61 (speech of November 13, 1930); Bundesarchiv Koblenz NS26/52/76 (speech of November 7, 1930) and 90-92 (speech of November 8, 1930).

67. *Völkischer Beobachter,* January 27, 1921: Bundesarchiv Koblenz NS26/51/36.

68. Bundesarchiv Koblenz NS26/55/140 (speech of November 9, 1928). Hitler drew the cover term "freedom" from his earlier, revisionist vocabulary: "For freedom we need in the first instance solidarity in our own land," he typically declared on August 1, 1923 (Preiss, p. 11). A rich early source for the use of cover terms is Hitler's speech of February 28, 1926, to Hamburg's "National Club": Jochmann, *op. cit.*

69. Bundesarchiv Koblenz NS26/52/76, 79, 82. "Foreign markets" and "foreign supplies" were transparent cover terms for "land and soil": compare the wording in the speech of January 27, 1932 (below): "If we want to develop a new domestic market, or to solve the problem of [living] space . . ."

70. *Ibid.,* p. 103.

71. Preiss, p. 177.

72. Max Domarus, *Hitler. Reden und Proklamationen 1932-1945* (Munich, 1965), pp. 84-88. "Ferment of decomposition" was a familiar epithet for the Jews (attributed to Theodor Mommsen); Hitler here pluralized it ("ferments") by way of ostensibly disguising the reference.

73. Preiss, p. 186 (speech of July 30, 1932).

74. Thilo Vogelsang, "Hitlers Brief an Reichenau vom 4. Dezember 1932," *Vierteljahrshefte für Zeitgeschichte,* Vol. 7 (1959), p. 437.

75. Thilo Vogelsang, "Neue Dokumente zur Geschichte der Reichswehr 1930-1933," *Vierteljahrshefte für Zeitgeschichte,* Vol. 2 (1954), pp. 434-35.

76. This holds even if Hitler did conclude that, once "political power" were regained, expansionism would be pursued either economically or ("and probably better") militarily: *ibid.;* cf. above, n. 18.

CHAPTER 8

Childhood History and Decisions of State: The Case of Louis XIII

ELIZABETH
W. MARVICK

Historians have labeled "early modern" the first half of the seventeenth century in France. In this period between the reigns of Henry IV and Louis XIV political scientists have reason to see a transition from renaissance to modern politics. In the reign of Louis XIII, patterns of bureaucratic, centralized control were established. There was a distinct break with the model of personal rule through traditional institutions that had characterized the reigning style of Henry IV. After Henry's death in 1610 a governmental revolution took place—a monarchical challenge to medieval judicial and aristocratic institutions. This marked a decisive turn toward the absolutism for which the French monarchy was later to be noted.

Louis XIII's son and successor, Louis XIV, would find that he was in large part the creature of a state machine not of his making and not always susceptible to his lead. It was an engine fashioned by the efforts of his father and of his father's prime minister, Richelieu. This paper explores the personality of Louis XIII who was largely responsible for transforming French politics.

CHILDHOOD HISTORY AND POLITICAL HISTORY

The momentous consequences of decisions made by the regime of Louis XIII give it prime significance for political history. Moreover, its special *tandem* character makes it a period exceptionally well suited for study of the role of personality in political decision making. It provides striking examples of conflicting tendencies in policy formation which do not lend themselves to explanation by looking only at the conscious intentions of the king and those who helped him direct French state machinery.

Recent studies of the regime's administrative history have emphasized its paradoxical nature. New trends were set in motion which threatened destruction of the independent powers of courts and bureaucracy. These, it is argued, were unintended consequences of the policy of Richelieu. Ranum has noted the cardinal's apparent deep respect for the traditional rights of the great nobility.[1] Yet the regime inaugurated the last phase of the *grands'* capacity to muster resistance to an increasingly powerful monarchy. Moote comments on a related point, the centrally-appointed *intendants* who were to replace the older, local, semi-hereditary *officiers:* "It is certain that neither Louis XIII nor Richelieu . . . expected the intendants to become permanent replacements for officiers, but that was what happened." Again, he writes, "By background, temperament and the influence of those around him, Louis XIII had as many reasons to temporize with his officiers as to run roughshod over their privileges and powers. What then explains the attacks which that monarch unleashed against his judicial and financial officials?" As an explanation, Moote proposes that special "conditions of early seventeenth-century France and Europe" forced Louis unwillingly to attack these privileges: "In spite of his desire to reign as Louis *le Juste,* Louis XIII constantly clashed with law courts and taxing bureaus."[2]

Moote interprets the "governmental revolution" as a product of inadvertence. The king's temperament was unsympathetic to it. It was forced upon him by financial necessity. Richelieu was its involuntary instrument because of loyalty to his master's interests.

A difficulty arises. This notion that the governmental revolution was not a product of the personality of its architect is incompatible with other descriptions of the temperament of the king. Strongwilled and proud, Louis had an intense desire to exercise power and a fierce jealousy of his prerogatives. The impression he made upon the course of public policy was achieved by continual calculation of strategy, consultation, and application of relentless pressure to implement decisions.

Unlike Richelieu, who preferred to manipulate, Louis did not hesitate to use domination for his power objectives. Long before the cardinal entered the scene, the king's "taste for command" had been amply demonstrated. Typical was his tongue-lashing of the Parlement of Paris: a royal historian noted that the king who had "an impetuous spirit" told this judicial body that "there was no use talking about obedience where the Parlement was concerned and that if he had people to whom he wished to teach that virtue it wouldn't be there he would send them . . . but into his companies of guards where there was an entirely different kind of obedience and that if they gave him a half dozen of these young counselors . . . and mixed them among his musketeers, he'd soon bring them around to that virtue."[3] Moote cites another cutting remonstrance of the king to these lawyers who were growing restive under increasing monarchical pressure: appearing suddenly before them the king announced, "You are here solely to judge between Master Peter and Master John and I intend to put you in your place, and if you continue your undertakings I will cut your nails to the quick."

Moote recognizes that such frank exclamations of an intention to dominate are inconsistent with a picture of a responsive, equitable ruler. The "other side of his character" he writes, showed "on many occasions . . . a monarch who considered himself the father of his people and whom it was appropriate to call 'just'."[4] An earlier historian of the reign went so far as to claim that Louis was "by nature tender and good."[5]

Apologists would apparently contend that a rather kindly, well-intentioned leader was required by circumstances beyond his control to set France on a course toward one of the most feared and efficient despotisms since ancient times. The giant steps toward absolutism were taken independently of the personal dispositions of the one who directed them.

The apparent paradox between character and policy may be resolved by understanding the psychic constitution of the policy maker. The aim here is to help resolve that paradox by the use of information on the childhood of Louis XIII.

A combination of two circumstances makes the rule of Louis XIII particularly suitable for trying to understand the role of personality in political decision making. First is the advantage deriving from the nearly complete documentation on policy formation under the political system. What was known to the political actors is almost fully known to us: few dispatches have been lost; by now most have been decoded when necessary and their authenticity established. Confidential communications recorded in diaries, correspondence and memoirs are confidential no longer. Their abundance makes evaluation for accuracy rather easily possible by cross reference. Thus two major problems in the study of contemporary political decision making are avoided. These are the difficulty in assessing reality as it presented itself *to the actors themselves* and the uncertainty in determining *decision content* due to the undocumented or confidential character of directives.

French seventeenth-century documentation also supplies another kind of information which is particularly scarce in modern contexts where decision makers are not recruited from a hereditary elite: detailed observations on the early history of political figures.

A common and reasonable complaint about contemporary psychobiography is that it is based on meager information about the childhood history of its subjects. Psychoanalytic theory is genetic theory; its insights are linked to the stages in an individual's maturation from child to adult. The analysis of political behavior in terms of such theory requires systematic knowledge of the dynamics of a personality system—knowledge which can only be validated by details of developmental history. Such details are rarely available. However, much information on the earliest history of heirs to kingly thrones is available and often it is abundantly validated by multiple independent sources. But, as often, those "born to rule" do not take office; when they do they may have neither the opportunity nor the will to wield power in fact.

It is a happy accident that the regime of Louis XIII meets conditions both for analysis in terms of childhood history and in terms of political importance. On the one hand there is a detailed record of Louis' infancy and early development. On the other there is plentiful evidence of his close supervision of significant political events throughout his realm from the time he seized power in 1617 until his death in 1643.

The diary of Louis' first physician, a 9,000-entry record kept over a period of twenty-six years, is the basis of most of the statements concerning the king's development in the pages that follow. In this unique journal we find unfolding the clinical history of the future Louis XIII registered day by day with unequalled thoroughness and attention to detail.[6]

But the availability of this diary poses a perhaps unprecedented problem—what to do with overabundant information. For, customarily, sequential data on the childhood experience of important political figures is not only scarce but also gathered with a polemical purpose. These drawbacks usually make it suspect by virtue of its selectivity. The mass of data on Louis XIII, however, is almost overwhelming in quantity and comprehensiveness.

In analyzing the information in Héroard's journal the first task is to sort the data. The sheer volume of the reports requires that they be organized according to some rule that makes them meaningful.

It was such a contingency, among others, that Lasswell helped to meet in adapting Freud's developmental theory of personality to the demands of decision making analysis. Using information from psychoanalytical interviews of political actors he proposed a *classifying* operation. He sought to identify objects of drives (*id* objects toward which were directed aggressive or libidinal impulses), forces modifying these drives to make them compatible with reality (adaptations of the *ego*), and inhibitions imposed on egoistic striving toward drive satisfaction by the *superego*. In distinguishing these mental functions behind the overt responses of individuals, meaningful interpretation of political behavior is promised.

Thus, when information on childhood history is plentiful, a new approach to political biography is offered by Lasswell's scheme. If the contacts of the individual with the outside world can be scrutinized from infancy onward, each of the various behavior patterns of the adult can be traced back to the point at which it assumed its characteristic psychic functions. The relationship of an actor to persons, institutions, policies, and practices in the political arena "may be examined for the purpose of discerning their appeals to impulse, conscience and reason."[7]

A few examples of apparently paradoxical adult behavior by Louis may serve here as illustrative cases. If the psychic meaning of seeming inconsistencies in this king's mode of relating to persons, practices and policies can be identified, some of the puzzles which his regime has presented to historians may be resolved.

Among these puzzles, most perplexing perhaps is the wide range of personality types in Louis' chosen entourage through the years of his reign. For example, we need to explain the continued presence of such contrasting aides as Richelieu—proud, ascetic, hardworking, passionately orderly and deferential to the king—and Cinq-Mars, the "favorite" of Louis' last years—extravagant, petty, vain, lazy and ungrateful. Concerning Cinq-Mars' "bad temper" the king complained to Richelieu:

> I told him, "A man in your position must think of becoming worthy of an army command . . . but laziness is entirely contrary to this occupation." He responded brusquely that he had no such intention . . . and that as for changing his style of life he could live in no other way. And then we came into the courtyard, he picking on me all the while and I on him.[8]

Of the relationship between institutions and personality Lasswell asked, "Do we find that though a given enterprise required great ruthlessness to succeed, the moral scruples of the original founders led to the choice of men incapable of the acts of illegality and brutality necessary to success?"[9] What personality factors are operative when leaders choose agents to carry out institutional change?

Louis XIII did indeed use illegality and brutality to effect the "governmental revolution" of his reign. But until Richelieu he did not find the suitable mixture of ruthlessness and compliancy that made possible the changes in internal and external policy. His first "right hand man" was the Duke of Luynes who was timid and had a short memory; though submissive he was also disorderly. He was thought to be not merely indecisive, but somewhat cowardly as well.[10]

In applying the triple-appeal principle to person-occasion relationships, Lasswell cited instances in which "popular justice involves the direct gratification of very deep destructive tendencies." One instance he noted was "the ritualistic semi-formal modes of action" of a lynching party.[11] The reign of Louis XIII, illustratively, was a time of many executions. The king had frequent opportunities to garner the psychological "gratification" of such occasions. When the Duke of Montmorency was sentenced to death for treason, a delegation of his relatives and partisans, seeking a pardon for him, found Louis at a favorite diversion— chess playing. The whole group threw themselves at the king's feet. Calmly he replied:

> No, there will be no clemency; he must die. No one should be disturbed to see someone die who has so richly deserved it. One ought only to pity him because he has been led by his own fault into so great a misfortune.

> Go tell him that all the clemency I can allow him is that the executioner will not touch him, that he will not put the rope over his shoulder [to bind him to the scaffold] and that he will do nothing except to chop his head off [lui couper le cou].[12]

The triple-appeal principle is also a useful guide to understanding the ways in which political actors respond to social doctrines, myths and legends, Lasswell argues. In seventeenth-century France these exemplifications of national culture were mingled with the beliefs and revered objects of the Roman Catholic church. For example, a basis for the charismatic power of kings was the belief that they possessed the power to heal scrofula by touching the afflicted. Of interest here is the perspective from which the royal thaumaturgic power was exercised— the viewpoint of the king himself.

The duty to perform mass ceremonies wherein hundreds of poor and scabrous subjects received the healing touch of the king was not an inviting one to the fastidious young Louis XIII. Nor was it one which his father took very seriously. As soon as the dauphin was able, these duties were assigned to him while Henry pleaded indisposition. Nevertheless, there is good reason to believe that Louis took the reality of this healing power, residing in himself, quite literally. In his mind it was linked to an idealized conception of himself as a candidate for sainthood, as the true descendant of Saint Louis. Indeed, he allowed his official historian to enlarge his legendary healing power to include a therapeutic influence on kidney trouble—much to the disgust of the more tradition-minded.[13]

In Louis' mind, religious ritual and doctrine played a practical, egoistic role as well as one sometimes contributing to his ideal view of himself. Nowhere was the combination of these two functions of magical practice more evident than on the king's deathbed. His hopes for achievement of sainthood were clear. He was told that the longer his final illness lasted, the closer he would come to the perfection of a martyr-saint. His last malady was prolonged for three months. During his suffering Louis arranged for the minutest details of his death, including the gift of his heart after the event. It was to become a relic in the church of St. Louis, founded by Louis XIII himself. The ritual preliminaries to his death conformed to methodical plans he had laid out over a period of years. Some were matter-of-fact precautions to insure salvation. He counted on getting to heaven

> to reign there with my God. . . . Not that I am assured of going
> there directly after I leave my body. . . . But at least, God willing,
> I will always have the certain expectation of it.

Although similar to those taken by many contemporary believers, Louis' plans were so exceptionally thorough and extensive that they excited remark from many witnesses. For example, he had made a special breviary for his final hours in which he had marked in advance the passages to be recited at various stages of his agony.[14]

Louis' fondness for certain kinds of administrative practices was connected with his passionate desire for order and his concern with the details of rituals. This entailed attention to the "letter" of the law. Ranum points out the influence of this preoccupation, given the anachronistic state of administrative management under the *ancien régime:*

> In theory administrative practices were formal and fixed . . . but
> in reality they were loose and easily adaptable for personal ends
> by strong officers. . . . Richelieu . . sometimes took advantage
> of it.

For Louis, however, codes of rules had a great attraction; in his mind "such documents assumed an importance quite unusual for the time."[15]

Historians have been struck by incongruities in the policies and practices of the regime. To resolve apparent paradoxes they have sometimes sought to distinguish policy consequences which were *intended* from those which seemed merely *incidental.* In particular, two issues have been preoccupying concerning Louis' policies. Did he intend a policy of aggrandizement aimed at making France politically hegemonous over territory extending to her "natural" frontiers? Second, was it his intention to combat the power of Empire, Pope and Spanish monarchy to the advantage of a Gallicist French royal policy?

On both these questions evidence is ambiguous. But intentions are not necessarily univalent. In the light of the triple-appeal principle it is not in point to ask which was the intended aim but rather to explain the psychic function performed by *all* significant behavior.

Again, one of the most puzzling aspects of the reign has been how Louis XIII, fervently pious, mistrustful of Protestants, fiercely jealous of his authority, attentive to and respectful of traditional forms, nevertheless followed, over a period of eighteen years, a policy of alliance with Protestant against Catholic powers, of reconciliation with domestic Huguenots, of denigration of the independent powers of nobility and traditional courts and, above all, of effective collaboration with Richelieu, one of the most ambitious and manipulative figures in political history.

Psychoanalytic theory offers a useful approach to puzzles of this kind. It promises answers to such questions as, which practices served Louis' ego needs? Which policies gratified libidinal or aggressive drives with little regard for the reality principle? Which other and possibly incompatible policies served to emulate his ego ideal or satisfy his conscience demands? More complicated questions which the triple-appeal principle helps answer are: Under *what conditions* did the key decision makers gratify id impulses? *When* was Louis' egoistic adaptation (to internal psychic reality and to external social facts) paramount and possible? The documentary resources available concerning Louis XIII permit tentative applications of the Freudian schema.

THE CHILDHOOD HISTORY OF LOUIS XIII

1. Earliest Vicissitudes of the Id: Impairment and Gratification of Drives

Optimism about life—or pesimism—is a posture established at an early age, Ferenczi claimed. The first months of life determine whether children "preserve the feelings of omnipotence . . . and become Optimists, or whether they go to augment the number of Pessimists who never get reconciled to the renunciation of their unconscious irrational wishes."[16]

Insofar as this dichotomization of humanity is valid, it is clear enough that Louis XIII's first weeks of life—frustrating as they were—help to account for the fact that, as an adult, he was certainly numbered among the world's pessimists.

This first dauphin born to France in eighty years was the son of Henry IV, first king of the Bourbon dynasty, and of Marie de Medicis, descendant both of Habsburgs and of Florentine merchant princes. Louis' delivery on September 27, 1601, was normal and quite swift; he was a robust neonate with vigorous reflexes, good size and color. His superior natural endowments were to be of great value to him through infancy and childhood. Almost from the beginning, his environment put obstacles in the way of normal development.

A few hours after Louis' birth it was decided that he was having difficulty sucking the breast of the wet nurse assigned to him. A surgeon was called in who cut the membrane under his tongue in three places. This was a common practice of the time. But in his case it may have been applied with more thoroughgoing zeal because of the concentration upon the boy of so much attention from many appointed servants. Spitz's research has suggested the possible effects of comparable surgical measures at such an early age. To flood a neonate's sensory system with so massive a stimulus before any part of his body is libidinized enough to isolate and localize sensation may well have a fundamentally traumatic effect on psychic development.[17]

The first three months of the baby's life—that critical time for adjustment of the nursing couple—was a history of cross-purposes and failures for Louis.

A good part of Louis' infantile problems can be traced to the characters and aims of his appointive household. Foremost among these in his earliest weeks was his doctor, Jean Héroard, whose diary is the source of most of the clinical information available to us on his early development. Héroard's supervision of his infant patient's care was minute and total.

From the context, it would seem that Héroard had had little experience with infants. He attributed a strong sucking drive to the persistence of hunger in the baby: from the first he pictured Louis as unsatisfied by the quantity of his nurse's milk. Supervising the suckling process with intense attention he immediately concluded that the wet nurse chosen by the queen was unsuited to his precious charge. He judged that Louis was not sucking properly. The nurse responded nervously, possibly to Héroard watching over her as well as to the baby. On one occasion she nearly allowed Louis to fall to the floor from a velvet cushion on which she held him as the king awkwardly tried to pick him up.

Héroard promptly decided that nurse's insufficiency of milk required auxiliary feedings from supplementary wet nurses and the administration of boiled pap. That she actually lacked milk seems doubtful; in the well-founded fear of losing her job she overate so much one night that she vomited. During the night, after she had fed him, Louis himself "vomited great quantities of milk".

The baby's doctor also deprecated the quality of the nurse's milk: "He has never suckled Hotman without its disagreeing with him," he said later. Possibly responding to overfeeding, or uncertain handling, or both, the baby was "racked by cramps" after feedings and broke out in a rash soon after birth. In his third week Héroard noted "angry hives between his legs, fomented by his nurse's milk." Again, "suckled avidly and for a long while; manifest inadequacy of milk in his nurse who has small breasts and hot, light-colored milk."

Héroard had his own candidate for the post of wet nurse to the dauphin, but the queen, from a distance, overrode his suggestions. Eventually, however, he was successful in getting Hotman replaced, for, not surprisingly, the baby failed to thrive. At the age of three months "his body was getting thinner" and a week later the doctor observed that the deep folds at the back of his neck and the base of his fingers had disappeared. His stomach was like a "skinned rabbit" and his body was red all over.[18] The new nurse sent by the queen was Antoinette Joron and she was to remain in Louis' service from the end of December, 1601 into his adulthood.

From the journal it would seem that Héroard's ambition was to control completely the physical inputs and outputs of his infant charge. Before Louis was two weeks old the physician had started to regulate the baby's stools by the use of suppositories. We are not told how much evacuation was "enough" but the standard was clear to Héroard himself. Clinical observations have prompted the generalization that premature stimulation of the anal region in this way may importantly alter the normal course of the phase of oral primacy.[19] It seems likely that the fact that the nursing relationship was inevitably *not* completely controllable by Héroard intensified his focus on this zone. In any case Louis' excretory processes were a lifelong preoccupation for the doctor, whose attention to them evoked corresponding responses from the child over the years.

Although the nurse the queen approved to be Hotman's successor was not of Héroard's choosing, a short trial of her convinced him she would do. The difference seems to have been one of rapport between the physician and nurse since her supposed supply of milk was not different from her predecessor's:

> He nursed with such big gulps, as he had always done, that he swallowed more in one than another might have done in three, and with just a few mouthsful he got a breast completely flat. This nurse [Joron] was astounded by it and said she didn't know how she'd be able to feed him, but since she was docile and timid we figured that the lack of milk would turn out all right, seeing that she had had enough of it before.

No small part of the credit for Louis' successful adaptation to this new nurse may have been due to the fact that, soon after her arrival, Héroard absented himself from his little patient for the first time since the dauphin's birth. The doctor was gone for several weeks and when

he returned Louis' and Antoinette's mutual adjustment was well established. Héroard delightedly reported that Louis had fixed him with his
gaze and "smiled at me for a quarter of an hour without being dis-
tracted."[20]

By May of 1602 the dauphin had regained his reputation for precocity, even if it was a bit exaggerated in this report from his mother,
the queen, an infrequent visitor:

> As for my son, it's hardly credible how big and fat and strong he
> is. . . . Already he recognizes the king and me very well. . . . and
> understands what is said to him and makes his desires understood
> by all around him. . . . Already one can see that he has excep-
> tional judgment for his age.[21]

During the first two years of his life, Louis' doctor and nurse were
unquestionably his primary, symbiotic family. Héroard was omnipresent and his physical contact with the baby was extensive and intimate.
He felt his pulse every morning ("found the little bird" as the child was
later to say), handled his head and body for temperature and other signs
of health or illness, administered the suppositories and the lotions, po-
tions, unguents and compresses which he continually prescribed. When
the baby had a night of teething difficulties it was the first physician
who stood, with elbow on his cradle, throughout the ordeal "holding
his right hand in mine".[22]

Louis' relationship with Doundoun, as he was to call his nurse,
seems to have given scope for complete gratification of oral drives—so
far as this was still possible—and for satisfying tactile experience. "Within a period of seven or eight hours she changed the breast she offered
him fifteen or twenty times" an account of the time related, "suckling
him the better part of each day."[23] The nurse had no duties but this
and was therefore available on demand.

In other ways too, the dauphin's privileged status meant that his opportunities for exploration of self and environment were probably
greater than those of less important babies. For example, constant
access to sources of warmth and a "dresser" assigned to him alone
meant that he was left free of swaddling clothes at least a good part of
the day, even in his earliest months. At five months Héroard reported
he put his hands in his mouth "all the time", indicating arms free of
restraint.[24]

While Doundoun was a source of drive satisfaction, Héroard's function was more complex. Before Louis was eight months old he could
direct oral aggression toward the doctor: "I put my little finger in his
mouth," Héroard noted, in order to take "out of him" a piece of bread
he was chewing that stayed underneath his palate. "He bit me, clench-
ing his teeth firmly on my finger twice."[25]

Louis' stutter, first noted by the doctor when the child was fifteen months old, could be interpreted as a symptomatic response to Héroard's handling. Growing resistance by the child to Héroard's constant intrusion with suppositories is suggested by the fact that, at fifteen months, the physician reported the use of the "first laxative medicine."[26] This seems to have been one of the first silent demonstrations of the dauphin's stubbornness which was to become such a notable personality trait.

Unfortunately, the contemporary abridgment of Héroard's diary does not permit us to follow what was apparently a prolonged struggle with Louis over toilet habits. The child insisted on using a shallow potty for defecating until he was six years old, refusing to perform on the "pierced chair" which was available to him and obliging his entourage to produce the *"bassin"* at a moment's notice at all times. During his first year he had apparently been kept seated on the chair for prolonged periods without result. In his fifth year he "promised to go caca on his chair" if his nurse would give him some chestnuts and "laughingly asked for it in order to get them." Nevertheless, the hoped for performance was postponed. In fact, it was three years before Héroard emphasized in a marginal note, "makes caca seated on his chair for the first time."[27]

This tenacious anal mode of responding was to be reflected again and again in his unwillingness to surrender his belongings (*"les siens"*)— people as well as things—and an exceptional lack of pliability. The interplay between doctor and child reveals how Héroard reinforced the tendency to anal regression by interpreting Louis' childish resistances to "bad humors" inside him and redoubling his efforts to extract them. For example, the three-year-old had been peevish and surly (*"hargneux"*), talking back to his governess, denying his "fault": "It's not I who's stubborn—it's the *'borgne'* [the one-eyed mason who was brought in to frighten the child into compliance.]" Then, Héroard reported, "makes caca—tannish, light-colored, much. Peevish, short-tempered as he always was when he retains such 'humors'."[28]

2. Early Ego Development: Hatching from the Symbiotic Shell[29]

Louis' weaning at the age of two took place long after he had learned to walk and had acquired other motor skills facilitating his development of the capacity for autonomous reality testing. In today's clinical literature, successful weaning from the breast or bottle is seen as stimulating the differentiation of the self from the nursing figure. The nurse begins to be perceived as a separate object. But in Louis this discrimination was slow to develop and in some respects remained more than usually incomplete through his childhood and into his early youth. For his nurse continued to be his private possession in a physical sense—a "transitional" or *part* object—which impeded her becoming a "true" object separate from himself. Both before and after weaning he habitually fell asleep in her arms; in cases of stress during the day he cried, "Take me, take me, Doundoun!" and as she held him in her lap he was instantly calmed, in the same way that a child is soothed as he pops his thumb in his mouth or goes into a trance with a "security blanket". On awakening he often had himself put in his nurse's bed where he merged himself with her in a trouble-free state equivalent to remaining asleep. As he began to "open doors by himself" and run more freely about in the garden at the age of three, he flew into a rage if he discovered his nurse had not followed him closely. Héroard thought it noteworthy that on one occasion he was so eager that "he even left his nurse behind— that being one of his greatest passions, to have her with him."[30]

To be further understood, Louis' ego development in the first two years must be put in a wider family context. After the early months, other figures in his surround besides the primary symbiotic ones of doctor and nurse began to be important for the dauphin. In his immediate environment were a number of siblings who bore an interesting relationship to him—both as childhood intimates and as possible political threats in later life. There were two older half-brothers and two half-sisters attached to the royal nursery. There was an almost exact age-mate—a half-brother who was the son of Henry's ambitious mistress, the Marquise de Verneuil. Before Louis was three, two full sisters were added to his household.

The "maternal" role was played chiefly by Héroard and the wet nurse. The earliest significance of Louis' generative mother, Marie de Medicis, in the psychic life of her first-born was not as a nurturing, intimate figure—she was never to be this nor indeed to give any sign of a physical attachment to her son. As Louis grew able to understand the meaning of the word "mother" he showed his grasp of the usual connection between the biological and the emotional ties. At three and a half he remarked, "It's not in Mother's stomach that I used to be, it's in the stomach of Maman Doundoun—*she's* my mother." Then he said to a half-brother, "Get away from there! I don't want you to be next to my mother." Héroard added, "It was of his nurse that he was speaking."[31]

Although their relationship was not intimate, Louis' and Marie's contacts were mostly good-humored and informal. This may have been due to the fact that, politically, interests of mother and son were inseparable. She was the basis of his claims to succeed to the throne. Those who joined their fates to those of the dauphin—and Héroard was prominent among them—were politically allied with the queen, whatever their awe and fear of the king may have been. Henry had already divorced one wife who had failed to produce an heir and his illegitimate male offspring gave at least two living mistresses hopes of usurping Marie de Medicis' place should her procreative powers fail.

Louis had been made very early to understand by servants that his claims to precedence were based on the status of his mother. At the age of two he was shown his parents' marriage bed and told, "That's where you were made." He understood enough of the meaning of this fact to respond, "with Mother." As a three-year-old he was explicit about "his team" and the "opposition": "I love my little sister more than my [half-] brother because he has not been in Mama's stomach with me as she was." Of a mistress whom he was told his father loved, "But if I don't love her she's only a whore."[32]

More than siblings and mother, the outstanding figure in this "extended" family circle was the great Henry IV himself. Freud wrote, "The child's first years are governed by grandiose overestimation of his father. Kings and queens in dreams and fairy tales always represent, accordingly, the parents."[33] But Henry *was* a hero king. The adulation shown him by personal servants and public alike must have increased the awe in which paternal figures in any case are likely to be held by their little sons.

The charismatic qualities of Henry IV's leadership were owed to the circumstance that he had, by brave deeds and personal renunciation of his Protestant faith, brought peace to his subjects after half a century of civil war. This basis of his authority in popular gratitude was enhanced by an earthy charm and informal manner characteristic of modern democratic leaders. In his intimate life, too, Henry showed the diffuse but strong demands for affection and admiration which often typify self-recruited democratic politicians with a populistic appeal. His heterosexual libidinal drives were entirely uninhibited and his appetite was omniverous. His wish for reconciliation among those who supplied affection to him included his various mistresses, wives and children. The king insisted that the proud Marie welcome his mistresses to the royal court. He frequently insisted also that Louis' prerogatives be laid aside so that the king's bastards might be on a footing of equality with the dauphin in the nursery. To Louis himself he was by turns affectionately demonstrative and brusquely imperious, awesomely dignified and childishly spiteful.

This brief account does not include the entire cast of characters important in Louis' early ego development. It includes enough of the critical cast, however, to continue with the dauphin's history.

As a one-year-old, Louis had already been subjected to the oral trauma of the first week and had suffered a crisis of nurture in his third month. During his first year he had been subjected to continual anal stimulation and intrusive controls by Héroard. He was also gratified by the total indulgence of his nurse. His progress in hatching from the symbiotic shell may have been progressing exceptionally slowly; nevertheless he had regained his physical sturdiness and showed better than average motor development. However, in addition to the continued manipulative policies and intrusions of Héroard, another special feature of his affective environment created unusual problems for the little boy's strivings towards psychic and physical autonomy. An outstanding feature of what may be called his political position in the royal household contributed to these problems: this was the exaggerated importance given by those in his entourage to his phallic development.

The survival of the new Bourbon dynasty and those whose fortunes were linked to it depended on Louis' future generative capacity. This was largely responsible for the fact that from infancy Louis' genital interests were prematurely stimulated.

Héroard's journal records courtiers' efforts to prepare the dauphin for the performance of future marital duties. The Spanish infanta, whom Louis was actually to marry at the age of fourteen, was the fantasized partner. Before he was a year old, Héroard reported, he was "listening to stories that a lady-in-waiting told him about the infanta, that he will sleep with her. He laughs at that." A few months later he was more knowledgeable: "Where is the infanta's darling?" Héroard asked the fourteen-month-old. "He puts his hand on his cock."[34]

Around this time, near his first birthday, there was a sudden upsurge of genital exhibitionism and excitement:

> September 15: A page has arrived with a message; "as he was turning around the dauphin calls, 'Hey!' and pulls up his skirt, showing him his cock."
> September 16: "He shows his cock to M. d'Elbenne; carried to the queen he sees an Italian lady-in-waiting; is afraid of her because of her coiffure."
> September 30: A gentleman arrives with his young daughter to see the dauphin who is in his cradle. "He laughed hard at her, pulled up his dress, showed him his cock but especially to his daughter, while holding it and laughing . . . he shook his whole body. People said he understood the suggestiveness of this. . . . He showed her his cock with such ardor that he was altogether beside himself. He lay on his back in order to show it to her."[35]

The encouragement by all around him of genital interests resulted in a ritual in which obeisance was actually paid to the one-year-old's phallus as a joke. Courtiers must have shown him how to convert a hand-kissing ceremony into one in which "he has everyone kiss his cock." Héroard himself participated in this little ritual. He reported, "He has us kiss his cock."[36]

During this period of pre-oedipal genital excitation, around Louis' year-old mark, he was increasingly exposed to intensely stimulating sexual experiences. Henry began to be with him for considerable periods and to show much interest in and affection for the child. This was the beginning of Louis' passionate attachment that would link his genital strivings and anxieties to passive desires with respect to that dangerous object, his father.

Henry's approach to the child was openly sensual; the baby responded ardently. The ten-month-old Louis was taken to look for the king in the queen's bed. "Not finding him there," Héroard writes, "he gets very angry. He goes in the king's bedroom, who puts him to bed with him with untold caresses." Arriving after an absence the king "kisses him, kisses his breast." During the same winter he was put in bed to play with the king and queen. The abridgment does not tell us of what this play consisted, but it was typical of Henry that a little later "he threatens him with the whip." In the following summer the king goes to bed, has Louis' clothes taken off and "has him put in bed next to him. He gambols freely."[37]

As a visitor to the royal household, the king's mistress engaged in seductive behavior that Héroard described more explicitly: "The marquise often put her hand up under his dress; he had himself put on his nurse's bed where she played with him often, putting her hand under his dress."[38]

The age and stage of development at which Louis experienced these exciting advances insured that several erotic zones at once would be involved in his response. First, of course, he was still at the breast. Héroard noted:

> While nursing he scratches his 'merchandise', erect and hard as wood. He often took great pleasure in handling it and in playing with the tip of it with his fingers.[39]

Then, apparently, he was in the early stages of a long struggle over toilet habits. One of the rare instances in which the abridgment relays the information which we know to have been so important to Héroard is the entry on September 8, 1602: "Does his business squatting on the rug." The genital and anal enjoyments are mixed in the same month when Héroard observed, "Plays with his cock and at hitting with his hand on the buttock of his [three-year-old] brother. Grinds his teeth." We are told the meaning of the teeth-gnashing on an occasion later when the dauphin's powers of speech were more advanced:

> He was gnashing his teeth and grimacing. I scold him for it. He says, "It's because I want to make caca."[40]

The multiplicity of stimuli is illustrated in a scene which shows the transports of infantile sexuality. Louis was sixteen months old and beginning to run about freely:

The dauphin chases [a Mlle. Mercier] who was yelping because M. de Montglat had put his hand on her buttocks. . . . Montglat chases her into the corner and wants to smack her rump; she cries out very loud. The dauphin hears it, starts to yelp too, delighted, and jumping up and down with his feet and whole body with joy . . . pointing them out to everyone with his finger.

Later, the baby was playing with a little girl. He

kisses her, puts his arms around her, drags her down, throwing himself on her, jumping with his whole body and gnashing his teeth.

Still later,

He tries to whip Mlle. Mercier on the buttocks with a bundle of switches. A courtier asks him, 'Monsieur, what did M. de Montglat do to Mercier?' He starts to clap his hands . . . and got warmed up to such an extent that he was transported with delight having been a good quarter of an hour laughing and clapping his hands and flinging himself on her like a person who understood the joke.[41]

Recent psychoanalytical research has shown that the kind of early genital arousal which Louis experienced is quite common. However, one clinician has concluded, strong castration anxieties are not likely at this age unless two additional conditions are present. The first is earlier subjection of the child to experiences which produced an instability in self and object representations. We have seen how Louis' experience with Héroard might have sufficed to impede such conceptualization of himself, even if the oral trauma and other nurturing impediments had not occurred. There is also the likelihood that the prolonged, total availability and indulgence of the nurse further served to imperil normal development of this critical aspect of ego capacity.

The second condition likely to arouse intense castration fears at this early genital phase is the observation of the anatomical difference between the sexes.[42] And it was perhaps fateful that Louis' excitement as a one-year-old coincided with the arrival of a newborn baby sister. Ceremonial treatment of children as well as adults meant that he was regularly taken to "Madame's" bedroom to see her dressed. The anatomical difference between him and his sister was certainly emphasized by many in the entourage at the time, but since Louis lacked the power of speech Héroard can give only ancillary information on the dauphin's response. By the time he possessed this power, at the age of three, he responded to quizzing on the subject by denial: "He says his cock is not like Madame's: 'Mine is pointed,' he says," Héroard recorded in March of 1605. The courtiers did not accept this defense against the dangerous truth and continued to press the boy to articulate the observation he must have made as a one-year-old. Thus, two months later he admitted, Héroard wrote, " 'that the infanta has a little vagina like Madame's,' said in a whisper . . . ashamed to say it out loud."[43]

Without either of these aggravating conditions it is likely that Louis' oedipal anxieties and conflicts would have been exceptionally severe. As it was, however, he left earliest babyhood with impaired capacity to cope with the demands his environment was to make on him in his remaining years of childhood.

3. Oedipal Crises and the Superego

The dauphin's weaning coincided approximately with his first whipping at the age of twenty-three months. Psychoanalytic research suggests that this form of discipline may strengthen the anal component of the libidinal life of the victim and intensify castration fears. This was certainly the case with Louis. Sadistic and masochistic fantasies associated with whippings were to have an unusually large place in his mental life. Anally fixated aggression explains, as will be seen, what seems to have been the motive power in the many cruel acts and petty rituals in which the adult king persevered.

But the *actual* whippings to which the dauphin was subjected were not the only source of, nor were they the principal material of his habitual regression to the anal mode of coping with reality. For, as has been seen here, this was a tendency long before whippings began to be applied.

Whatever the weight that should be given to the various impediments to Louis' normal development, together they would seem to have over-determined the events of the oedipal phase "proper". To bracket this period loosely, we will include developments from the end of his second year to the end of his fifth. It is important to notice that the scenes cited are not so much *critical* as they are *typical.* They are selected because they show *patterns* of Louis' responses to stimuli. If they, or something like them, had each happened only once, we should have little confidence in their determining power. The fact that a child with normal natural endowment and minimum conditions for development (and Louis' were far above minimal) is resilient and adaptable means that for a pathological outcome to result, similar encounters with similar outcomes had to occur again and again.

About the time of the dauphin's second birthday his anxieties took a quantum jump. Certainly the whippings activated anal fantasies and intense castration fears. A few nights after the first one he was awakened by a nightmare, "dreaming that a beast was biting him on the right buttock." During the winter he developed a pattern of avoidance of his little sister and his sleep began to be disturbed. "He didn't sleep at all during the night having drummed continually on his breast and called out the French and Swiss rolls. . . . On awakening [sic], asked for his tambourine."[44]

During the winter and spring of Louis' third year the recalcitrance and rages for which he was beginning to be noted were followed by whippings, usually with a bundle of switches—the *verges*—applied to bare or covered buttocks. Although these were usually administered at the insistence of the king, the child's passion for his father was unabated. "The king comes to see him and plays with him gaily," Héroard recorded. But a little later, "He almost burst from screaming so loudly and all was so confused all afternoon that I didn't have the courage to note what he did, except that he wanted to beat up the whole world, screaming beyond belief, afterwards whipped a long time." The dauphin was beginning to talk and Héroard increasingly noticed his stutter. Interestingly, he attributed its onset (forgetting he had made a note of it several months before) to an exciting episode of play "when the king, in bed, took pleasure in having him banter with little Frontenac, who stuttered. He gets irritated when he can't pronounce readily."[45] The dauphin was to feel very irritated very often in the months to come.

In February, 1604 Héroard first noticed the fatigue which was frequently to be the aftermath of contests of will between the boy and the king:

> He wanted to leave the room against the king's wishes. The king threatens him with the whip but he is stubborn. . . . Continues. The king commands that he be whipped.

In a rage, "having wanted to hit and scratch," he was led back by the king who again "handled him roughly." Afterwards, he "falls asleep in the arms of his nurse" although his supper was untouched on the table. This lassitude was apparently associated with passive fantasies. For example, the two-and-a-half-year-old Louis "gets into a bad humor" soon after waking, "screams, is whipped, puts his hand on his back end, saying, 'Tickle me, Tickle me!' "[46]

By the time the dauphin was about six the pattern of inviting whippings was set. At chapel he "is peevish" to Mme. de Montglat, who prevented his leaving to go watch the changing of the guard. "He thumbs his nose at her, [*lui fait les cornes*] and says, 'Fie, how ugly you are!' He gets on her back, tries to make her fall, throws his book at her head." The next day he was whipped for these and a whole list of other offenses but he "doesn't weep at all, only screams, 'That's enough, that's enough.' "[47]

However, from the first Louis had also taken the active, sadistic side of the whipping experience. As a five-year-old the pattern was clear. Playing war games with his age mates, "He plays at whipping Roger de

Frontenac on the hand. Warming up to the game, asks for the switches, they don't bring them. . . . He throws himself on his valet to beat him up, in a rage, chewing his tongue in the usual way."[48]

In fact, however, whippings were infrequently applied during most of Louis' early childhood. When they occurred it was usually at the explicit direction of his father, whose "whipping orders" countermanded the clemency instructions of the queen. She believed, apparently at the suggestion of Héroard, that the rages and depressions brought on by corporal punishment were dangerous to her son's health.[49] The servants who had to administer them, especially Mme. de Montglat, the governess, and the chambermaids, no doubt thought the dauphin's response was dangerous to themselves. Often more striking than the whipping occasions were those on which the child, though ungovernable, was *not* whipped:

> Made caca next to Mme. de Montglat's chair. . . . Won't allow her
> to clean his behind with her handkerchief. . . . On his way to his
> room he meets her coming out of the dressing room, gets into a
> peevish humor. "Go through by the other door!" Mme. de M. is
> reluctant and goes as far as the table with him pulling her by the
> dress, crying and screaming, bursting with rage. She is obliged to
> give in and does so. He conducts her as far as the door. She scolds
> him and leads him into the room, screaming all the while and be-
> side himself. Does his best to bite her finger with extreme fury.
> Approaches the table, threatening her, "I'll kill you if you go
> through by way of the dressing room again. . . . Get to your knees,
> Mamanga!" Then, when she's done this, "Put your face down on
> the ground!" She rises angrily not having done that.

Instead of whipping him, they brought in Bongars, the great mason, with his dangerous-looking tools, of whom Louis was afraid. "He is calmed down, with difficulty," Héroard concluded.

This reluctance to whip meant that other methods were systematically and continually used to attempt to control the little prince. His fears were exploited in order to manipulate him into tractability. These fears were myriad: he was afraid of the rain and the thunder, of the sound of gunfire, of the evening dew, the masons, wood carrier, locksmith, etc. etc. and of course, of losing his penis. Héroard, who never administered corporal punishment, was most adept at manipulating the boy by such fears: "Monsieur," he told him, "your cock is gone." "What? Isn't it there?" Louis answered anxiously, "showing me the place for it. He was leaning against the croquet stick," Héroard continued, and "I wanted to scare him about it."[50]

It is little wonder that the four-year-old boy needed to ward off a host of dangers at bedtime. Saying his prayers he pleaded, "and guard me from all my enemies, visible and invisible," and added, "on his own,"

Illustration 1. A drawing by the dauphin when he was nearly six. Héroard wrote "starts to make the bird, marked "A". Afterwards to make Doundoun, his nurse. Finishing the navel he sketches what is lower down and having made it says, "And there's what I don't want to say," [and starts to laugh]. Started his faces with the two eyes, then nose, mouth, and afterwards the outline of the head, and follows sketching below." (Ms. Fr. 4022, fols. 462, 463.) Photo of the Bibiothèque Nationale, Paris.

Héroard said admiringly, "and from Bongars and Thomas [the masons]
... from the one-eyed one, from the hunchback, from the *charbonnier*.
...."—all servants around the château who were called in to threaten
the child when he was stubborn.[51]

In the course of 1604, crises between father and son increased in intensity. A long visit to Fontainebleau began in September, as the dauphin drew near his third birthday. A memorable scene took place in that autumn. Booted "like the king" and with his little drum, ("it was one of his greatest delights,") he went to see the king:

> The king says, "Take off your hat." He has trouble getting it off,
> the king takes it off him. He gets mad at that; then the king takes
> away his drum and his sticks; that was still worse. "My hat, my
> drum, my sticks!" To spite him the king puts the hat on his own
> head. "I want my hat!" The king whacks him on the head with it.
> That makes him furious and the king with him. The king takes
> him by the wrists and raises him in the air, arms extended as on a
> cross. "Hey! You're hurting me! Hey, my drum, my hat!"....
> Carried off ... bursting with anger.... Cried a long time without
> subsiding... finally whipped, crying, "Hey! Whip me up higher!"[52]

After this, the dauphin directed his aggression towards Mme. de Montglat: "Kill Mamanga, she's naughty; I'll kill the whole world, I'll kill God!" But the manifest outcome of the conflict was evident as far as the king was concerned. Louis' attempt to test his own strength against his father's was, for the time being, almost completely ended. Thenceforward he was to make a deliberate effort—without the earlier gaiety which had characterized him—to comply with the wishes of the king. Héroard reported a new pained docility in the performance by Louis of the role of his father's servant. "At the sight of his father," the doctor wrote, "he no longer wears that bold, gay expression he used to have."[53]

Ritual responses became frequent: "Who is the dauphin?" he would be asked, "Papa's little valet," he replied. To his father's commands he would say, "At your service," as he served him with determined submissiveness. The traumatic "hat" scene was actually reenacted in a morning ritual Louis himself developed on the return to St. Germain:

> He goes to bid good morning to the portraits of the king and
> queen that hung in his bedroom. Holds in his hands his white
> velvet cushion; puts it on his head, using it as a hat. Takes it off,
> saying, "*Bonjou'* papa, *Bonjou'* mama!" and all of a sudden
> throws the cushion to the floor.[54]

Again and again we see the emotional cost of Louis' submission to his father, the king. "Very compliant with the king," Héroard noted in the margin. The child relayed the king's order that his own dinner be brought into the room with the king. "Papa said so," he said:

asked for nothing at the king's table . . . at dinner's conclusion the king gave him a quarter of a candied dried pear. Very nice, obedient, timid and respectful. Immediately after the king left, asked, "Make caca."

At supper he lacked appetite:

During the supper he told me, "My cock hurts me." Pissed. . . . pulse a little fast. . . . didn't want to say his prayers. "I want to say the '*Sancta*'; I don't want to say, 'Our father'."[55]

A more passive response to such encounters with his father was shown on an occasion in 1606. Arriving, the king asked, "Well, son, have you been well whipped?" "No, not every day," responded the little boy. Actually, he had not been whipped since the king's last visit, more than three months before. This was remedied: a week later he was whipped for "being naughty" in chapel. His passive response to the experience was demonstrated: "Afterwards, he wanted to keep the verges, saying to them, 'You're my darling.' "[56]

Interpretation of the outcome of Louis' oedipal struggles seems relatively straightforward. His earliest experiences had made probable a regression to anal modes of coping with the dangers of the phallic phase. Louis' relations to himself and capacity for forming object relations had been seriously impaired. His stutter showed that some of his energies were diverted from maturational tasks to coping with inward stress. The effects of Héroard's intrusions, of massive genital arousal and of the discovery of the anatomical sex difference were visible in the little boy of twelve to eighteen months in a violent castration anxiety. His early, passionate libidinization of his father linked his genital strivings to the king—a dangerous object. Courtiers asked the toddler of fourteen months, "Where is papa's darling?" Héroard reported, "He slapped himself on the stomach." "Where is the infanta's darling?" "He slapped his cock." A child who had had particular difficulty in relinquishing his bowel contents without anxiety had been plunged, without resolving this earlier struggle, into an exceptionally threatening genital stage.[57]

When crises came, Louis was unable to cope with aggressive impulses so dangerous and the frustration of love so passionate. Both love and aggression were turned inward. The beloved little boy of his father, "papa's darling" whom he had longed to be, and the naughty stubborn boy who deserved and received chastisement from an all-powerful and terrifying king were erected intra-psychically as objects, respectively, for libido and reprisals. The struggle for self-mastery continued within Louis' personality. His object relationships were always to bear the mark of their narcissistic function. In the chastened boy of five were discernible the basic patterns of behavior of the adult king.

A fantasy about the dauphin and his father that Héroard and Louis shared illustrates the little boy's yearning and ambition:

D.: I'll go hunting, I'll kill a wild boar with my sword . . . then I'll chop its head off.

H.: You'll catch a deer, have its foot cut off. You'll bring it to papa, who'll caress you, call you his darling, take you into his beautiful hall at the Louvre.

D.: M. de Verneuil [his half-brother] won't get in—*He's* stubborn. . . . Then papa will give me a little pistol. What will he tell me?

H.: He'll tell you, Monsieur, "My son, I give you this pistol. Go out to war against my enemies. . . ."

D.: (Getting animated.) I'll kill them all, ratatatat. (He was getting warmed up as though he were in the thick of battle.)

H.: When you return, papa will kiss you, call you his darling.

Even in fantasy the dauphin needed external support:

D.: Salignac [his favorite soldier] will be with me. . . . When papa goes away, Salignac will stay with me.

Doctor and child told each other this story again and again.[58]

Both the narcissistic regression and its anal mode seemed forseeable from the time of the little boy's desperate struggle for self-mastery. With that struggle still raging the child had found his ego too weak to conquer the dangerous aggression stimulated by the new relations with the king. The king offered little ego support to his child; on the contrary, Henry rarely lost an opportunity to impress on Louis the helplessness of the son's condition in comparison with himself. "Returning from the hunt," Héroard related, the king "kisses him, embraces him." At the same time Henry compounded the effects of his seductiveness with the following threat:

While they were eating the king asked if he didn't want to have him sleep with him and told him, "If you won't have me sleep with you, I'll go sleep with Mama Doundoun."[59]

To the little boy who sought to emulate his great father:

The king said . . . "My son, you're a little calf."

D.: "And you too, papa," because he thought he was the same as the king.

K.: *I'm a bull!*[60]

Normally, resolution of oedipal conflicts is achieved through identification with the father. His chastening aspect is established within the psyche as a superego where it directs libidinal and aggressive impulses, harnessed by the ego, onto acceptable objects in the outside world.

But Louis' ego was not equal to these tasks. His attacks of rage continued to be murderous and beyond his control. He needed Héroard, his *alter ego,* to disguise their destructiveness and prevent his being carried away.

The doctor tried to present Louis' punitiveness in a form which rationalized it in public terms. In a fury, the five-year-old boy threatened, as he often did, to put someone in "p'ison". Héroard makes a marginal note: "Administrator of justice [*justicier*] ; hates to see wrong done."[61]

By the time Louis reached adolescence, he himself had learned to provide the "marginal notes" rationalizing his actions. Héroard was at his side to record them. One time Louis was playing a war game and one of the dogs he was having pull cannons up a plank balked:

> He beats it roughly, in a rage. Then he tries it again. The dog goes over without trouble, whereupon he says, sternly and coldly, "That's how stubborn, bad people have to be treated," and, giving it a biscuit, "and recompense the good . . . men as well as dogs."

"And thus," Héroard concluded, "the excess to which his anger had brought him in front of everyone present was concealed."[62]

If the history which has here brought Louis to the age of about five seems one of pathology, this should not imply that a pathological outcome was inevitable. Many, though fewer, examples of "normal" oedipal trends were visible in the same five-year-old. In particular, rapport between father and son was real, despite its complications. If Henry had lived into Louis' young adulthood those conflicts we have followed through the oral, anal and oedipal phases might have been resolved in the prince's adolescence. This possibility was obviated by Henry's murder when Louis was eight. However, it is neither justified nor necessary to make a judgment here on the degree to which the dauphin's development was irremediably perverted during his childhood. Psychohistory does not aim at diagnoses of its subjects but at understanding their social and political behavior. In Louis' case it is possible to observe that behavior and trace it back to his childhood experience. In this way can be understood what were his resources for adapting to external reality and what were his models for moral conduct.

POLITICAL CONSEQUENCES

1. Id Appeals: Narcissistic Objects for Love and Hate

Along Louis XIII's path toward maturation the struggle in the anal phase had permanently captured a good part of the energy which might otherwise have flowed towards real persons in the outer world. The mode which drives assume at that early stage of development—the sado-masochistic mode—permanently colored Louis' style of relating to per-

sons around him. The adult king was to earn the title of Louis the Just.
An apter designation might have been Louis the Merciless.

In Henry IV's reign, forgiveness of evil designs against the state had
been the rule. In the reign of Louis XIV, too, executions of political
enemies were to be exceptions, acts of mercy the dominant pattern. A
courtier's paean to the young king Louis XIII, however, had to admit
that clemency was no virtue of his monarch:

> One sees his edicts more religiously observed than those of his
> father in whom softness was a safeguard against . . . severity.

Louis, on the contrary,

> leaves ordinary justice to run its course, having learned that the
> best cement of the laws is the blood of those who flout them.[63]

Long before Richelieu's reputation was joined to the king's, Louis'
harshness revealed his lack of capacity to regard others as true objects.
Instead, his tendency was to treat them as expendable, inanimate objects to be discarded and abused without pity once they had been
cast out.

As a four-year-old he could "joke" with a lackey by remarking "I'll
chop off your head with a larding fork and lard your ass and your nose
with it." But at twenty-one he was in command of his armies besieging
a town held by Protestants. Editors of Héroard's diary remarked on the
"painful impression" created by his account:

> He goes to camp at ten in the morning, up above a battery where
> there were two cannon. He aims one of them twice, fires on the
> peasants who were barricading themselves. The second time he
> kills two of them.[64]

This was a casual gratification of aggressive impulses; more often the
victims were selected with care. The little boy who frequently threatened and fantasized chopping off the head or other member of those
around him had, as an adult, numerous opportunities to gratify his
sadistic aims.

Not only the objects of Louis' aggression but also of his libido had
the character of part objects rather than true ones. They represented
narcissistic relationships whose meaning can be understood with the
help of the information available on his childhood development.

Each crisis with his father had been a further turning point in the
capacity of the little boy to direct his affect onto realistically individu-
ated persons. Evidence that this affect was withdrawn from the outside
world and redirected inward was manifested by his silent reveries and
evident, melancholy lassitude. Libido was directed toward the little
boy his father had loved and to figures in the outer world who represented this lovable boy—"papa's little valet"—as he felt himself to be.
In loving himself in these narcissistic objects he assumed the role of his

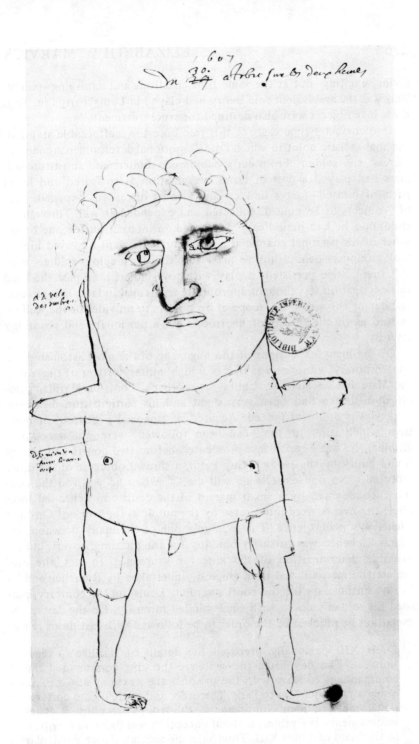

Illustration 2. A year later, Louis' skill and objectivity have increased in this sketch of his governor, Giles de Souvré. The dauphin is now six years old and has left the nursery. (Ms. Fr. 4022, fol. 495 *Vo.*) Photo of the Bibliothèque Nationale, Paris.

loving, exciting—but at the same time chastising and damaging—parent. This was the ambivalent role Henry had played in Louis' early life. Thus these love objects were also destined for cruel treatment.

One character-type cast for this role bore the ineffaceable stamp of the anal-sadistic point to which Louis' emotional development tended to regress: the soldier. From early babyhood, soldiers and substitute soldiers had played a part in Louis' imagination as treasured and loved parts of himself—faeces in fact—and also as discarded, expelled, "cut off" objects to be ranged, collected and expended at will. Throughout childhood he had periodically developed an infatuation for one or another of his personal guards; as a pre-toddler Héroard observed him to look anxiously behind him to make sure that his precious soldiers were still there.[65] He persisted in play with toy soldiers long past the time this occupation was thought appropriate to his age. In later life, as commander of the army, the scope of his powers to provide for the welfare as well as of the deaths of his troops was a passionate and absorbing interest.

Of the many executions of the reign one of the most astonishing to contemporary witnesses was that of a high military officer of the realm, the Maréchal de Marillac. Unlike his brother's, Louis de Marillac's political influence had been very slight and his participation in a conspiracy was doubtful indeed. Accused of financial procurement practices which, even if they had been followed, were not necessarily criminal, he was nevertheless prosecuted before two courts and finally found guilty by the second. Guy Patin, a shrewd observer of the time, reported, "No one expects he will die."[66] When he was, on the contrary, condemned by a small margin of the court and beheaded soon after, the events were interpreted by the public as the work of Cardinal Richelieu's malevolence. This was only one of the many occasions on which Richelieu was to suffer obloquy for the puzzling, covert, but inexorable determination of the king for vengeance. In fact, the case against the marshall had been gingerly undertaken by Richelieu and he had no enthusiasm for the court's verdict. Louis, on the contrary, pursued his soldier's doom with singleminded intensity. On the day of the execution he proclaimed the order to be followed with fastidious relish:

Louis XIII personally prepared the details of Marillac's execution. . . . The day after the sentence the king commanded the commandant to leave with the prisoner the next day at 6 a.m. in order to conduct him to Paris. The order and route of the cortége, the number of men comprising it, the troups preceding it as reinforcement—everything without exception was fixed and written in the hand of Louis XIII. Thus he alone regulated with particular care—one might almost say with loving care—this execution which he had desired with all his strength.[67]

Soldiers and military figures were not the only objects of Louis' narcissistic love-hate impulses. These were also directed at other figures, both male and female, who showed no martial tendencies whatever. Of the young men to whom Louis became attached, one of the earliest had great political importance. This was Charles Albert, created Duke of Luynes by the king's favor. As a soldier-hero, Luynes would have been miscast; he was far different from the stalwart soldiers so proudly displayed, arranged, and sent to their deaths. Luynes was sweet, indecisive, adulatory, and weak. Louis treated him indulgently, occasionally propitiated him, sometimes contemptuously. The woman whom he selected for the duke's wife was one of the very few with whom the king himself had been able to engage in lighthearted flirtation with erotic overtones.

Louis felt the need to explain his attachment to one who patently lacked those qualities he himself most admired: boldness, physical courage, tireless energy, orderliness, self-discipline. "I love him because he loves me," he suggested once. Clearly, Luynes represented tendencies repressed by Louis in himself: laziness, fear of battle, failure of discipline, genital gratification.

Needless to say, the young king's indulgence of Luynes had a reverse side—sadistic gratification. The side of himself which he had repressed was rediscovered in the former falconer. Louis' ambivalence towards Luynes was soon evident. He continued to lavish gifts of power, goods and prestige on his favorite, yet he whispered in contemptuous asides to others his distaste for Luynes' consequent delusions of grandeur, overweening bearing and pretensions to wield royal authority. In conversations with intimates,

> The king began to tear down the constable and to utter everything that he had been imagining against him. . . . Every time that the king could speak in private it was to make incessant complaints of the constable.

It seems clear that Louis wished to chastise Luynes as the naughty young boy he once had been had been chastised by a powerful father. The ultimate renunciation of Luynes impended when, as Bassompierre reported, Louis could no longer get vicarious pleasure from the marriage of Luynes to Marie de Montbazon, so that

> suddenly the extreme devotion he had had for *Mme. la Connétable* changed into such a hatred that he warned her husband that the Duke of Chevreuse was in love with her. . . . He told me, "May God forgive me, but I had such great pleasure in revenging myself on him and in giving him this pain."[68]

Luynes' premature death from natural causes prevented him from meeting the fate that seemed to be in store for him: ruthless rejection by his monarch.

After Luynes, Louis did not again load his narcissistic love-hate objects with political authority. Peter Paul Rubens, then an observer in the court of Louis and his mother, wrote of a new favorite, François Barradas,

> This man enjoys such preference that the entire Court is astonished and even the Cardinal has become . . . jealous. . . . With all that, the King has told Barradas that he is not . . . to think of taking part in matters of state.[69]

Richelieu had made it possible for the king to separate his need for ego support from his attachments to objects representing in fantasy his father's darling little boy. But Luynes' death did not end Louis' periodic infatuations with favorites who played this role.

Towards the end of the king's life Richelieu, with his uncanny intuition, selected Cinq-Mars, Marquis of Effiat, as a likely figure to win the king's affection. Beautiful, self-indulgent, extravagant and lazy, the young marquis was the woman-chasing lascivious son Henry IV might well have wished Louis to be. With one hand, Louis fed Cinq-Mars' decadent impulses and appeared utterly enslaved to his whims. With the other, he complained of him and railed against his extravagances, his heedlessness, his lack of gratitude towards his benefactor. And finally, on discovery of his favorite's complicity in a plot against Richelieu, Louis sent his *mignon* to his death. Richelieu was apprehensive of the aftermath of such a sacrifice by the king of one of his few apparent libidinal attachments. He need not have been. A royal counselor observed Louis carefully the day after Effiat had been executed. He reported to the cardinal:

> His majesty did not seem to me at all afflicted when I told him the news of the deaths. . . . He merely indicated impatience to learn if they had died in a Christian way.[70]

Louis had unhesitatingly sacrificed his libidinal object to his egoistic need for the cardinal's support—with all the more satisfaction, we may suppose, because his sadistic aims toward Cinq-Mars could simultaneously be gratified.

Louis XIII died in May of 1643 when his elder son was four-and-a-half. This premature demise was perhaps a fortunate event for the mental health of the future Louis XIV, for in his last years "Louis the Just" had begun to show signs that his son might be the next person cast in the role he himself had once played vis-à-vis his own father. Returning to St. Germain in 1640, the king wrote to Richelieu concerning the two-year old boy:

> I found my son much handsomer than before but very stubborn. I am by no means prepared to suffer these bad traits [humeurs] in him.[71]

Fate prevented the recapitulation of Louis XIII's poignant history. Louis XIV was to grow up without any of the blows to his childish narcissism that his father had suffered. The "Sun King" was the apple of an indulgent mother's eye.

2. Ego Appeals: Resources and Handicaps in Meeting Reality

We have indicated in tracing Louis' childhood history that his ego development was impeded by assaults on his bodily integrity through the persistent intrusive control imposed by Héroard, the unnaturally prolonged "total immersion" in his nurse's protective arms, and the massive and premature genital stimulation to which he was subjected. All these patterns seem to have insured impaired representation of the body image and overintensification of castration anxieties, making regression to the anal phase very likely. Louis was never to lose his fear of being robbed of his precious possessions, deprived of external support. Without Héroard or some substitute for him the king was capable of acting sporadically, occasionally mercilessly, but he was incapable of sustaining a sense of mastery for any length of time. Fatigues, depression or somatic disturbances overcame him when external ego support failed.

The stable *alter ego* he needed for the conduct of state affairs he finally found in Richelieu. It is clear that the cardinal's performance made him a psychological substitute for the first physician who had been a necessary ego support for the young king. The symbiotic nature of their collaboration is illustrated by Richelieu's intuitive understanding of the king's psychosomatic suffering:

> Your majesty's mind so completely dominates your body that the slightest emotional upset affects your whole being. Many occurrences of this have made me so certain of the truth of my diagnosis that I am convinced that I have never seen you ill in any other way.

On many occasions, Richelieu played "doctor" to Louis as Héroard had done before him. Richelieu saw his duties to the king to include taking his "temperature" and "feeling his pulse." For example, war had to be avoided because Louis

> being by nature delicate, with a weak constitution and a restless impatient disposition ... cannot, without endangering your health, commit yourself to a program of long duration ....[72]

For Richelieu's "medicine" to be acceptable for Louis, two conditions had to be met. First, the cardinal had to respect the king's autonomy, keep his distance, and defer to the royal position of mastery. For, while an *alter ego* was necessary in order for the king to sustain political control, any person who filled this role was likely also to be the object of hostility and fear. Louis had resisted Heroard's efforts to control and extract his body's precious contents. Despite everything, he had achieved partial physical integrity and a rudimentary concept of himself as separate from others. To this extent it was necessary to prevent the reabsorption of the self by the other—always an impending, dangerous possibility.

Louis' long association with Héroard had been one in which the two came to learn to keep a bearable distance between them. When Louis was a child, experiments took place: the doctor would threaten to withdraw his support; the four-year-old would respond anxiously, "But who will cure me?"[73] Similar patterns for establishing satisfaction of needs were worked out between Louis and his minister. At various times Richelieu offered (or threatened) to withdraw as the king's councillor. On the Day of Dupes—that occasion on which Louis renounced his mother and her party in favor of the cardinal—he was actually packed and ready to leave when he was called to the king's lodge at Versailles and admitted to a fuller trust than he had until then enjoyed.

Not surprisingly, Richelieu's correspondence with his aides shows he was not overly confident of the stability of the delicate balance. Continued assurances of the king's affection were necessary because, side by side with Louis' need for his *alter ego* was his hostility to and mistrust of the person who filled this role. On occasion Louis would lash out with suspicious criticism of the cardinal. Then those "creatures" of Richelieu whose task it was to keep the minister informed on the king's state of mind would report Louis' anxiety that the cardinal had taken offense. "What keeps his majesty downcast," wrote Bouthillier, "is that he now fears that your eminence may be angry about what he wrote you yesterday." So great was the king's worry on this point that Bouthillier wrote, "In the name of God, sir, if you have already made some response which might give him such an impression, let me keep it from him when it arrives here."[74]

At the same time Armand needed to avoid all evidence of sycophancy, maintain the impression of independence of judgment and represent himself as an objective critic of the king's intentions. For Louis' real dependence on his minister by no means meant that he abdicated independent reality testing. His profound pessimism made him impervious to flattery and suspicious of rosy predictions. His deep mistrust of anyone on whom he was dependent meant that he was always open to advice contrary to the minister's judgment. This agonizing fact was known to Richelieu who also knew that it was useless to attempt to prevent advice from other sources from reaching the king's policy-making councils, since Louis deliberately encouraged "multiple advocacy." The king became enraged when "matters affecting the good of my service" were not reported to him.[75] Louis' official historian was well aware of the kinds of judgment on which his master prided himself. He wrote, "This was one of the qualities of this great prince, that he always chose the best opinion from among those which were diverse."[76]

Like his fundamental mistrust, other pathological components of Louis' personality had consequences both functional and dysfunctional for decisive, realistic leadership. He was obsessively attentive to detail. This contributed, of course, to careful organization and analysis of problems and a strong sense of responsibility: "The king declared that he would not leave the scene of an impending battle until he saw that everything was entirely perfect. He assembled his council to deliberate on what had to be done before he went away."[77]

But such attention to minutiae meant that he was often seduced by petty concerns, especially those to do with military preparations and the security of positions and prisoners. Richelieu tactfully warned his master against this preoccupation:

> God has seen fit to give your majesty the force of character necessary to act with firmness when confronted with business of the greatest importance. But as a balance to this noble quality he has often allowed you to be sensitive to matters so small that no one in advance would suspect they might trouble you. . . .[78]

The king's tenacity, another manifestation of his anal fixation, was demonstrated in excessive secrecy and periodic bouts of obstinacy which showed inflexibility in adjusting to reality. From the first, Héroard had noted the little boy's retentive memory and capacity for silence. Louis was not yet five when the doctor recorded that he had memorized the proverb, "He who holds his tongue is wise," and added "of his own accord, 'Therefore, he who lets it go is mad.' "[79] Bellemaure observed that it was owing to the king's "wise holding of his silence" that he had been able to seize the reins of power from his mother's minister.[80] On the other hand, Richelieu admonished the king that in some matters he must learn to "let go":

> . . . I have reminded you many times that there is no prince in a worse position than he who, not always able to do those things by himself which it is nevertheless his duty to perform finds it even harder to let others do them for him.[81]

As for stubbornness, Bellemaure wrote, "He undertakes nothing . . . which he does not pursue to the very end."[82] It is noteworthy that despite Louis' ambivalence towards Richelieu, as towards everyone else, he remained "stubbornly" supportive of the cardinal to the very end.

Of all the issues during the reign in which Louis was able to mobilize his ego resources for decisive and realistic action, certainly one of the most important was his commitment to Richelieu. Special qualities possessed by the cardinal seem to have made his offered support at once useful and tolerable.

It was as a preacher that Richelieu first entered the young king's purview in 1612. The future cardinal's power over words, both written and spoken, was the most manifest of his skills. His eloquence had become evident to Louis with a spectacular oratorical display before the king at the meeting of the Estates General in 1614. Again in 1625 he gave a dazzling exhibition of oratory before the king and the Assembly of Notables at Fontainebleau. A few months later he was admitted to a greater degree of the king's confidence.

Louis' handicap with words was two-faceted: on one side was his stutter—an impediment apparent even in his use of the written word. Letters in his own rather gross and childish hand show occasional repetitions of words and a marked lack of fluency. In his oral delivery "he was so extreme a stutterer that he would sometimes hold his tongue out of his mouth a good while, before he could speak so much as one word."[83] The other side of the king's handicap also reflected the function his oral inhibition had served in his development. This was his tendency to use words recklessly, as "cutting weapons." The cardinal warned him against this danger:

> The blows from a sword are easily healed. But it is not the same with blows of the tongue, especially if they be from the tongue of a king.[84]

For both these tendencies to undermine his own political needs, Richelieu's supple tongue and pen supplied an antidote and a substitute.

Another consideration recommending Richelieu as an ego support was his position as Marie de Medicis' minister. Since childhood, Louis' political interests vis à vis his half-sibling rivals were identified with those of the queen. Héroard, his indispensable *alter ego,* had likewise been her ally. When Henry was murdered in 1610 the queen became sole guardian of the eight-year-old king's political interests. In the years that followed she proved a weak reed to lean on. Her bad judgment led her more and more to turn over affairs to Concino Concini, husband of her intimate childhood friend, Leonora Galigai. Increasingly, Concini's disastrous policies seemed inimical to the interests of the young king himself.

In spite of Marie's failure as an ego supplement, Louis found it very difficult to renounce her collaboration. Richelieu had been *her* councillor, however, and in increasingly accepting the counsel of his mother's minister he was able to reject the woman who had commissioned him. In the years of Marie's forced exile which continued to her death, the presence and support of Richelieu strengthened Louis in his refusal to permit his mother's return. With Marie's creature at his side he had no further need for the queen herself.

3. Superego Appeals: Conscience and Models

Normal resolution of the oedipal crisis in little boys results in establishment of an unconscious internal monitor within the ego—a conscience—which censors the dangerous aggressive and libidinal drives formerly directed towards real father and mother figures. The result is to allow the ego to channel drives onto acceptable objects and bring its energies to the tasks of latency—acquiring the skills to cope with the outside world. We have seen that Louis' oedipal conflicts were not fully resolved in this way. He had entered the genital phase of development already handicapped in achieving ego maturity. He found himself unable successfully to cope with the threatening and capricious behavior of an exceptionally dangerous and seductive father. Instead of introjecting a representation of the paternal figure as an unconscious moral guide and censor, he continued unconsciously to reenact the struggle between boy and parent, discharging drives first towards one, then towards the other, narcissistically in a form characteristic of that earlier stage of development at which his emotional energies had been diverted and captured.

Thus the grown king's "conscience" was always rudimentary and archaic. There is little to show that he suffered from conscious guilt. Sometimes his outbursts of aggression and cruelty were followed by somatic symptoms which showed their narcissistic meaning in his unconscious. Like a pre-oedipal child he feared retaliation rather than loss of self-esteem. He feared Richelieu's retributive anger at his disloyalty and occasional hostility. He reenacted scenes in which he competed with hated siblings for his father's capricious favor. On one occasion he went so far as to represent to Richelieu that a military leader who had had great successes had had far more men than was actually the case. This he did, he admitted, for fear that Richelieu would compare the king unfavorably with this commander.[85] His conscience was *externalized:* on his deathbed, his confessor testified, he had a real encounter with the devil.[86]

While Louis had a reputation for extreme piety, his devotional practices were ritualistic and lacked moral content. One of those who had both the opportunity and the detachment to consider Louis over a prolonged period was a former tutor, Nicolas de Vauquelin. Long after Louis' death he was asked to write a memorandum advising the queen on the upbringing of Louis XIV. He advised her to choose a preceptor

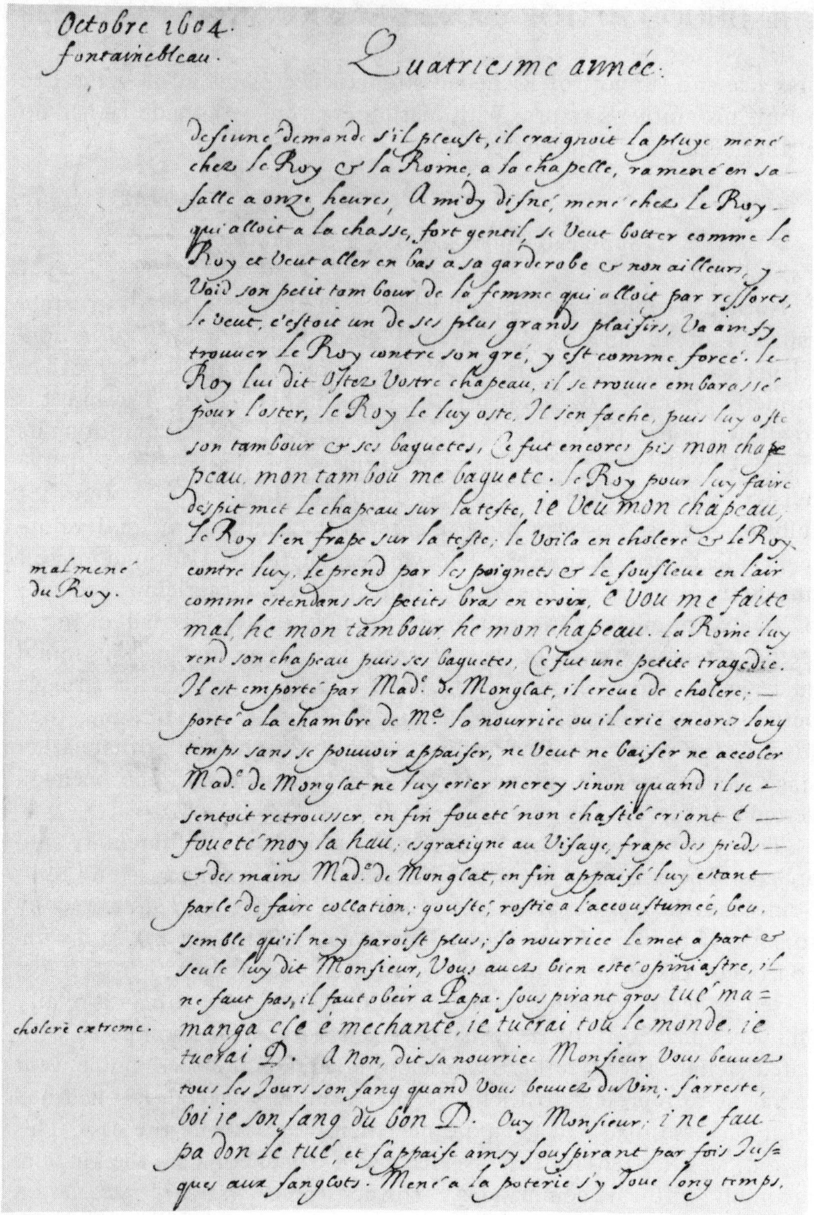

Octobre 1604.
fontainebleau.

Quatriesme année.

desjeuné, demande s'il pleust, il craignoit la pluye. mené chez le Roy & la Royne, a la chapelle, ramené en sa salle a onze heures, A midy disné, mené chez le Roy qui alloit a la chasse, fort gentil, se veut botter comme le Roy et veut aller en bas a sa garderobe & non ailleurs, y void son petit tambour de la femme qui alloit par ressorts, le veut, c'estoit un de ses plus grands plaisirs, va ainsy trouver le Roy contre son gré, y est comme forcé. le Roy lui dit Ostez vostre chapeau, il se trouve embarassé pour l'oster, le Roy le luy oste. Il s'en fache, puis luy oste son tambour & ses baguetes, Ce fut encores pis mon chapeau, mon tambou me baguete. le Roy pour luy faire despit met le chapeau sur sa teste, ie veu mon chapeau, le Roy l'en frape sur la teste; le voila en cholere & le Roy

mal mené du Roy. contre luy, le prend par ses poignets & le souleve en l'air comme estendans ses petits bras en croix, e vou me faite mal, he mon tambour, he mon chapeau. la Royne luy rend son chapeau puis ses baguetes, Ce fut une petite tragedie. Il est emporté par Mad.e de Monglat, il creve de cholere; porté a la chambre de Me sa nourrice ou il crie encores long temps sans se pouvoir appaiser, ne veut ne baiser ne accoler Mad.e de Monglat ne luy crier mercy sinon quand il se sentoit retrousser, en fin foueté non chastié criant e fouetté moy la hau; esgratigne au visage, frape des pieds & des mains Mad.e de Monglat, en fin appaisé luy estant parlé de faire collation; gousté, rostie a l'accoustumée, beu, semble qu'il n'y paroist plus; sa nourrice le met a part & seule luy dit Monsieur, Vous avez bien esté opiniastre, il ne faut pas, il faut obeir a Papa. sous pirant gros tué ma=

cholere extreme. manga ele é mechante, ie tuerai tou le monde, ie tuerai D. A non, dit sa nourrice Monsieur vous beuvez tous les jours son sang quand vous beuvez du vin. s'arreste, boi ie son sang du bon D. Ouy Monsieur; i ne fau pa don le tué, et s'appaise ainsy souspirant par fois jus=ques aux sanglots. Mené a la poterie s'y joue long temps,

Illustration 3. A comparison of Courtaud's version of Héroard's diary for Louis' first three and one-third years (above, Ms. N. A. Fr., 13008, fol. 142) with original entries for February 2 and 3, 1605 (opposite, Ms. Fr. 4022, fol. 30 *Vo*). Courtaud's abridgment is of the "hat" scene in which Louis was "roughly handled" by the king. "It was a little tragedy", the text concluded. The greater complexity of the original text is exemplified by the marginal entries: "loves dogs", "Nota: Discretion for [showing] his nature towards the king". The third note describes Louis' little sister's reaction to her weaning. The body of the text concerns the dauphin's own part in that dramatic event. Photo of the Bibliothèque Nationale, Paris.

il auoit grand peur de se nourir et faire mal en quelque sorte qu'on fust à la
S. nom... luy dict d'Oostland sakopide, tete, tetete le manie, le patrouille.
l'eust volontiers sabatté. Il aime fort les chiens, menè a sept heures en la chambre
de la R.ne M. S. amusé a voir des personnages à la tapisserie où il y auoit des petits enfants
la Q. oy luy dict mon fils ie veux que vous fassiez vng petit enfant à l'enfant de
hoc non papa, remercie. L. R. ie veux que vous luy fassiez vng petit dauphin
comme vous. D. non pa si vou plai papa mettant sa main au chapeau et
faisant la reuerence. M. D. Monglat luy dict M. dites a papa qu'il fasse
des hoquetons ... aux archers que vous ... D. heo non dictes
si vou meme ... mesme et luy fait faire plusieurs fois la pareille reuerence. Sans le
pouuoir persuader de le faire. remene a huit heures et demie en sa chambre ...
de mesche. ... mis au lac au lit, où il se fait mettre de la bougie et a ...
dormi s'endort iusques a sept heures trois quarts apres minuit.

Le m... Al Jeudy. Esueillé a sept heures trois quarts apres minuit. Doula...
se iour de mesure, faict parler son petit doigt. demande, fait demander et res...
luy mesme a huit heures. bon bon visage, guay, VESTU, coiffé, mene ...
heures et demie desiuné bouillon, humé peu, pain trempé dedans, allé
fus guay. l'on parloit de la guerre, sa nourice va dire, mon dieu que ie crain...
la guerre. D. heo moi ie ne la crain pa. hochant la teste, mene chez la
R.ne qui commande que Madame fust sevrée par les mains de M. D. M. n'est
pas en estat de l'estre, dict qu'il ne vault plus tetter que Pasque est venu. M.
D. veult la nouristande dans une Jauciere, s'en va dire tout bas. Madame
madame vela de la mostade peu metter, mettre a vote teton, mene ...
mene en sa chambre. a midy disné. hachis et panade en peu ...
moelle de veau sur du pain. beu. chapon bouilly peu poulet
rosty, pelé d'une aesle. poire au fiel, une auer... ... beu deux fois
... nettie gache a dieu amen. massepain une trosche. l'a dormi à ba...
s'va ... soubz sa table, et s'amuse s'eal sans dire mot aux deux petits pieu
d'argent que luy auoit donné M. de Guadalor... ... iusques a trois heure et dem...
une retenue bastien a se plaisses prendre par m. Jehan Martin. troubl...
poire au fiel auec pain esmié. beu. massepain une trosche. mene ... iusqu...
a cinq heures. mene au Roy au cabinet de la R.ne. s'amuse a troupes cheva...
auec du nul d'Austriche qui vel de luer... a de la meme droguée a six heures ...
en sa chambre. Soupe. panade et hachis de chapon bouilly si toute ...
moelle de veau et chapon bouilly, des poux, la croupion, vng peu du Blan...
beu. poulet rosty vng peu d'une aisle. poire au fiel. une auer pain esmié
beu. vaf... vng peu de bon bonnage... poirause dit ... che qu'il y en auo...
gar grotte... beaucoup. au mis nettie gache a dieu amen. massepa...
vne...

who would lead the king to a religious feeling different from Louis'
XIII's piety:

> It is to be wished that this could be achieved by a devotion other
> than that of his father who adopted it more through convention—
> as he did everything else—than by express intention and without
> the practice of good deeds which true devotion has the effect of
> inspiring. For his piety was really great . . . in appearance but . . .
> very sterile in its effects.[87]

Nevertheless, even if the king's moral sense lacked the automatic,
unconscious and regulatory character of a fully developed conscience,
moral standards or guides were perceptible in his behavior which derived from a model of conduct with consistent referents in the outside
world. To the extent that his drives were regulated by this model and
his ego guided by it, it is appropriate to consider superego appeals in his
decision making patterns. These are best discussed under the term "ego
ideal", as Jones has used it, to describe "our conscious ideals in a positive sense; the superego, or at least its unconscious part, being more
concerned with . . . condemning."[88] In this positive sense of the term it
is possible to trace the formation and characteristics of Louis' ego
ideals and the significance they had for his later policy objectives.

From infancy, the image of Louis' father, the great king, savior of
the nation and founder of the dynasty, was clearly a powerful model
for Louis. Henry was the object of emulation; his enemies were the
little boy's enemies. From a very early age, Héroard's diary shows
"papa's enemies" meant the Habsburg Spanish power. In a diary entry
Héroard attributed hostility to the Escurial menace to his three-year-old
patient. Henry went off to war in February, 1605, and the doctor asked
the child: "To whom will he give battle?" "To his enemies," Louis replied. "Who are these enemies?" Héroard pursued, and relates

> He was in the act of naming the Spaniards and had pronounced
> the first syllable of the word—"Against the Span..." then, catch-
> himself, he said coolly, "Turks."[89]

As heretics, the Turks were acceptable to "cover" for the Spanish threat.

In one other respect Henry's model was a decisive one for his heir.
The father's procreative capacity was a power held up to the little boy
as an obligatory standard for performance. We have seen the consequences of premature genital stimulation for the personality formation
of the child. But he clearly incorporated among his more urgent duties
the example set by Henry to become a "Sire" in the familial as well as
the political sense.

There was an aspect of Henry's behavior which was a negative model
for Louis' own: his promiscuity. Louis' egoistic interests were, as we
have seen, intimately bound up with his position as the first legitimate

heir to the throne and with the solidity of his mother's position as the legal consort. The king's mistresses and their many offspring were menaces to the position of Louis and Marie. Before the dauphin was three Héroard reported that he responded "coolly, having thought about it," to the court fool's inquiry as to whether he would follow the sexual morals of his father when he grew up. "Will you be as bawdy as your father?" was the daring question, *"No!"* was Louis' emphatic reply.[90]

The salience of a model is noticeably affirmed in choosing the name of the emulated one for one's own. When Louis was to be baptized, just before his fifth birthday, he was desolated to learn that he was not to be given his father's name. Insult was heaped on injury: his envied half-brother had received the magic name of their great sire. Héroard pointed out to the little boy the virtues of his own namesake, Saint Louis. One objective in this seemed to be to offer an alternative model of sexual conduct. Marital fidelity had been a conspicuous attribute of that hallowed king. As a four-year-old Louis was reciting the proverb "which I love so much: 'Happy is the man who finds a virtuous woman.' "[91] The incompatibility between the two models was obvious to many observers.

PERSONALITY AND DECISION MAKING:
THREE IMPLEMENTATIONS OF POLICY OBJECTIVES

We have seen how the triple-appeal principle helps to explain the long range objectives of Louis XIII's policies: to strengthen his ego sufficiently to gratify his aggressive aims on objects compatible with his ego ideals. During his long reign three projects were successfully executed which stand out as critical implementations of this design. One was the result of a decision made at the beginning of the reign—to assume power personally by seizing it from his mother's minister, Concini, Maréchal of Ancre. The second was formalized in the middle of the reign: this was to make a permanent commitment to Richelieu, implemented explicitly on the Day of Dupes. The third was a program adopted soon after the beginning of active rule and pursued until its successful result near the end of the reign—the siring of sons to carry on the legitimate line. The accomplishment of each project may be considered in the light of the tri-partite principle.

Soon after Henry IV's murder, Marie de Medicis began to devolve more and more authority on Concini until he became the arrogant wielder of all royal power. As such he became vainglorious and heedless of the legitimate source of his authority, the adolescent boy king. Louis' official coronation had taken place soon after his majority was proclaimed in 1614. By 1616 he seems to have conceived the plan of killing Ancre in order to seize power in fact.

No task could have had a more powerful *triple* appeal to the young king than one putting this obstacle to his control of the throne out of the way. The gratification promised the id must have been a powerful temptation: Ancre was vulgar, lewd, self-indulgent and extravagant—a very naughty boy indeed—in many respects the prototype of all the *mignons* whom Louis was alternately to indulge and to chastise.

Moreover, Louis' ego and superego interests were in harmony with the objective chosen by the impulses: to free himself from internal threats and external control he had to act against the marshall. Ancre's insidious domination at once tempted Louis to relapse into passivity and deprived him of his most precious possessions—his royal prerogatives. Further, what could be more syntonic with the ego ideal so powerfully modelled by his father than to assassinate the foreign interloper who had usurped Henry's place at the side of his wife and at the head of the realm?

The king's capacity for secrecy and biding his time never showed to better advantage. The marshall, taken unaware, was shot dead by the captain of Louis' guard outside the Louvre on April 24, 1617. Luynes had rather reluctantly given his support to the plot. Héroard, still very much an influence in 1617, may have given more active encouragement than his journal reveals. He gave no hint of it beforehand but, after recording the deed blandly, left two pages of his diary blank to celebrate the triumph of his protégé. Louis' euphoria at coming into his rightful legacy was greater than any he was to have again.[92]

The second landmark of the reign was the confirmation of Richelieu as the king's chief councillor and minister. The decision to make it was forced upon Louis by the queen mother. As we have seen, Marie was in part an ego extension for her son. Her growing hostility to Richelieu came to a climax in 1630 when she finally refused to be part of the royal council unless Richelieu was dismissed from it. Until then, Louis had used both his mother's and his minister's support. His mistrustful nature had allowed him to use one against the other. Now forced to choose between them, he found Richelieu not only more necessary to his ego but also more attuned to his ego ideals. Since Richelieu's return to the court with Marie he had gradually drawn away from the ultramontanist zealots of the queen's party and adapted to policies more in keeping with the "great designs of Henry IV".

By 1625, Richelieu's enemies had become the powers Louis long ago had identified as "Papa's enemies". In that year the cardinal addressed to the king a memoir which commenced with the gratifying news: "All things are now combining to strike down the pride of Spain."[93] In sustaining the cardinal's influence against Marie's, Louis obtained not only a powerful ego supplement but one which could be used to implement those aggressive drives which were morally validated by the example of his great father. This time therefore, with characteristic secrecy, the king concealed his intention to "cut off" Marie completely until he could identify her co-conspirators at court—a strategem which allowed him to engage in the "great purge" which followed her departure. From the day that Marie was repudiated Louis kept his promise to Richelieu to use him as his instrument. In fact, his stalwart defense of Richelieu against virulent enemies over the years can be attributed to the fact that he explicitly identified Richelieu as one of *"les siens"*—a precious belonging that was in some respects a part of himself.

Third of Louis' triumphs was the procreation, twenty years after the consummation of his marriage, of two sons to inherit the throne and secure the future of the line. Of the three successes this one may have cost the greatest effort.

As an object of Louis' drives Anne of Austria, the Spanish infanta, had handicaps and advantages. For a few months in 1620 the court witnessed a romantic infatuation of the king with the queen. She had become a narcissistic object. This role, more usually assumed by males in Louis' entourage, was no doubt partly advanced by a comparable earlier role performed by his sister Elisabeth. This sister had literally changed placed with Anne when their two marriages were formalized in 1615. Moreover, for years Louis had "rehearsed" his relations with Anne using Elisabeth as partner in childhood play. Louis' official historian remarked on the resemblance between Louis himself and the new queen of France at the time of their marriage: "so much alike that one would have taken them for brother and sister."[94]

The king's letters to Anne during their brief romance bear the peculiarly narcissistic stamp of those to Elisabeth: to his wife he followed professions of devotion by solicitude for the "distress you certainly have at my absence". "If the trip tires you it will only be on account of your impatience to see me—which is always a pleasure to me." To Elisabeth: "the affection I bear you will never change because I know that you will always love me." To another sister, bidding her come for a visit, "the inconvenience to you will actually be a pleasure since it will bring you close to him you love best in the world [himself]."[95]

Based on such unstable foundations, the romance was shortlived. After a miscarriage which was blamed on the queen's imprudence, there was ill-feeling between them. Although Louis continued to perform his marital duties without impairment though with little enjoyment for the rest of their married life, the partners were otherwise to be "at arm's length".

Anne had always been suspect by Louis on account of her Spanish origin. In 1632 the king discovered a possibly innocent correspondence between her and her brother, the king of Spain. One of Louis' tests of Richelieu was to use him as his own ally against the queen's suspected subversion. Richelieu was equal to this demand, although it seems that he was sympathetic with the hapless Anne, whose almoner he had officially been. After the queen had been exposed and denounced, a formal document of forgiveness was presented by Richelieu on behalf of the king and negotiated in exchange was a promise from the queen for future good behavior.[96]

In view of the coolness between man and wife and Louis' lack of enthusiasm for using his conjugal rights, the birth of two sons after twenty-three years was regarded as near-miraculous. As the achievement of a political objective it had great significance: its effect was to stabilize royal policy. By producing male progeny the king had vitiated the aspirations of his brother, the Duke of Orleans, to succeed him. These hopes had been at the root of the conspiracies of past years. In 1640 a second son was born to solidify still further the Bourbon hold on the throne.

Soon after these triumphs of policy the cardinal fell ill. He died in 1642. With Louis' chief support gone, and, one may speculate, his chief objectives accomplished, his energies seemed to fail and his chronic ailments gained the upper hand. Long a sufferer from what was apparently ulcerative colitis, he took to his bed in February, 1643 and died on May fourteenth, the anniversary of his father's assassination thirty-two years before.

* * *

By reviewing details of Louis XIII's childhood history we are able to explain some of the apparent paradoxes in the political behavior of the adult king. As for the chief objective of state policy, little had changed for Louis since Héroard had said of him as a baby, "He has a strong taste for everything which has to do with war—as much men as instruments."[97] In the prosecution of the most destructive war in the history of Europe to that time, Richelieu supplied his intellect as a support for the king's insufficient ego so that Louis was able to gratify his aggressive drives by manipulating populations and resources as though they were of no more importance or value than the chessmen which had so absorbed his attention as a child.

The characterization of Louis' personality system that has been made here is necessarily sterotypic, and it is well to emphasize in concluding the complexity of real psychic life in comparison with all attempts to understand it. Héroard has presented us with more information on the early history of an individual child than has perhaps ever been made available in written form. Confrontation with so much data is sobering.

In dealing with it, the limitations of psychoanalytic theory—as of any disciplined method of organizing data—should be borne in mind.

It seems undeniable that Richelieu was Louis' Héroard, but he was also sometimes, and in some respects, his father and/or mother, nurse ... and so forth. Yet above all he was a supremely efficient, obedient and loyal prime minister—and an agent the most rational and democratically oriented modern chief of state might wish to have as his chief executive. And Louis himself, despite his character defects, his physical symptoms, his cruelty deeply rooted in his childhood experience, his projective mistrust, was also a witty, gifted, and shrewdly realistic monarch. He was a slave to defensive strategies and in some important respects conscienceless; at the same time he could be called a moral man, in the sense that he strove to do "right" and the justice thus commanded was consonant with some of the highest morality of his day. Freud wrote, "A hero is a man who stands up manfully against his father and in the end victoriously overcomes him."[98] By this standard it is not certain that Louis was no hero.

In the final analysis we are reduced to "mere" probabilities: it seems probable that Louis' interaction with Richelieu at a given time reflected the partial symbiosis with Héroard from which the king was never freed; it was likely that his relations with "loved" ones would show the ambivalence which arose from his competition for the love of a father who was at once endearing and fearsome, manly and infantile. But even with all the information on Louis' childhood, our ability to predict his behavior in specific situations is less than complete. In acknowledging that his complexity of character prevents putting full confidence in our ability to anticipate the political choices he made, we are reminded of the limitations of psychohistory, as of any theoretical apparatus, in predicting human behavior. Louis XIII may have been no more complex than other important men of his time; we simply know more about him. Is there good reason to suppose that, as far as the complexity of political actors goes, the situation is different today?

Elizabeth Marvick is Adjunct Professor of Government at the Claremont Graduate School. She holds a Fellowship for 1974-75 from the American Council of Learned Societies to prepare a psychoanalytical study of the regime of Louis XIII and Richelieu.

REFERENCES

Some of this article is adapted from a paper presented at the Annual Meeting of the American Political Science Association in September, 1973. Thanks are due the American Council of Learned Societies for a grant aiding preparation of the study.

1. Orest Ranum, "Richelieu and the Great Nobility: Some Aspects of Early Modern Political Motives." *French Historical Studies,* III (1963), 184-204.
2. A. Lloyd Moote, *The Revolt of the Judges: the Parlement of Paris and the Fronde, 1643-1652* (Princeton: 1971), 46; 43.
3. Charles Bernard, *L'Histoire de Louis XIII,* XV(Paris: 1646), 261-262.
4. Moote, *Revolt,* 42.
5. Marius Topin, *Louis XIII et Richelieu* (Paris: 1876), 40.
6. The original manuscript and a contemporary abridgment are, *Bibliothèque Nationale,* Mss. (BN), Fr., 4022-4027 and N. A., 13008-13011. Reference to the latter is made necessary for the dauphin's first three and one-third years for which the original is missing. A published abridgment is Jean Héroard, *Journal de l'Enfance de Louis XIII,* ed. by E. Soulié and E. de Barthélemy, cited here (as *S.&B.*) in preference to mss. where possible. For a discussion of these sources see Elizabeth W. Marvick, "The Character of Louis XIII: the Role of his Physician," *Journal of Interdisciplinary History,* IV (Winter, 1974), 347-374.
7. Harold D. Lasswell, "The Triple-Appeal Principle: A Dynamic Key," in *The Analysis of Political Behaviour: an Empirical Approach* (New York: 1949), 181. (Reprinted from the *American Journal of Sociology,* 37 (1932), 523-528.
8. "Lettres du Roi Louis XIII au Cardinal de Richelieu et à M. de Bullion," *Mélanges* (Société des Bibliophiles François: 1903), 23-24.
9. Lasswell, "Triple-Appeal," 185.
10. Louis Batiffol, *Le Roi Louis XIII à Vingt Ans* (Paris: 1910), 483.
11. Lasswell, "Triple-Appeal," 191.
12. Georges Mongrédien, *La Journée des Dupes* (Paris: 1961), 144.
13. Charles Bernard, *Histoire des Guerres de Louis le Juste* (Paris: 1638), 93-94; on Bassompierre's outrage at this extension of the king's imputed magical powers see Beauvais-Nangis, *Mémoires,* II (Paris: 1665), 494.
14. Jacques Dinet, *L'Idée d'une Belle Mort* (Paris: 1656), 28; Dubois, *Mémoires* in F. Danjou, ed., *Archives Curieuses de l'Histoire de France,* 2e Série (Paris: 1838) 423-424.
15. Orest Ranum, *Richelieu and the Councillors of Louis XIII* (Oxford: 1963), 154.
16. Sandor Ferenczi, *Sex in Psychoanalysis* (New York: 1956), 197.
17. René Spitz, *The First Year of Life* (New York: 1967), 64-7.
18. BN, N. A. 13008, fols. 1-23. Hereafter cited as *Courtaud*. On the relationship of cutaneous symptoms to rapport between nurse and nursling, see Spitz, *First Year,* 224-234.
19. James C. Moloney, "Some Simple Cultural Factors in the Etiology of Schizophrenia," *Child Development,* XXII (1951), 163-183. See also D. W. Winnicott, *The Child, the Family and the Outside World* (Harmondsworth, England: 1964), 43, and Andrew Peto, "Body Image and Archaic Thinking," *International Journal of Psychoanalysis,* 40 (1959), 223-237.
20. *Courtaud,* fols. 22; 23 *Vo.*
21. BN, *Cinq-cents Colbert,* 86, fol. 52.
22. *S.&B.,* I, 22-23.
23. BN, Fr., 10321, fol. 2.
24. *Courtaud,* fol. 22
25. *Ibid.,* 93 *Vo.*
26. *Ibid.,* fol. 79.

27. BN, 4022, fols. 3 *Vo;* 410.
28. *Ibid.,* fol. 40.
29. These terms derive from Margaret Mahler, *On Human Symbiosis and the Vicissitudes of Individuation,* I (New York: 1968), 133.
30. BN, 4022, 50; 48. On the relationship of time of weaning to transitional objects, see Benjamin Spock, "The Striving for Autonomy and Regressive Object Relationships," *Psychoanalytic Study of the Child,* XVIII (1963), 361-364.
31. BN. 4022, fol. 40.
32. *S.&B.,* I, 308.
33. Sigmund Freud, *Moses and Monotheism* (New York: 1939), 11.
34. *S.&B.,* I, 34.
35. *Courtaud,* fols. 43-45.
36. *S.&B.,* I, 34; *Courtaud,* fol. 47.
37. *S.&B.,* I, 32; 44; 51.
38. *Ibid.,* 45.
39. *Ibid.,* 50.
40. *Courtaud,* fol. 130.
41. *S.&B.,* I, 42-43.
42. Herman Roiphe, "On an Early Genital Phase, with an Addendum on Genesis," *Psychoanalytic Study of the Child,* XXIII (1968), 357-358.
43. BN, 4022, fols. 14, 35 *Vo.; S.&B.,* I, 120, 135.
44. *Courtaud,* fols. 85, *Vo;* 69.
45. *S.&B.,* 60-61.
46. *Ibid.,* 65.
47. BN, 4022, 415 *Vo.*
48. *Ibid.,* fol. 245.
49. BN, *Cinq-cents Colbert,* 86, fol. 277.
50. BN, 4022, fol. 60 *Vo.*
51. *Ibid.,* fol. 87 *Vo.*
52. *S.&B.,* I, 95-96. [See illustration 3, p. 170, for Courtaud's version of this scene.]
53. *S.&B.,* 98.
54. *Courtaud,* fol. 165; 4022, fol. 11 *Vo.*
55. *Ibid.,* 199 *Vo.*
56. *Ibid.,* 226 *Vo.*
57. *S.&B.,* I, 38. The dynamics of regression of this kind are discussed in Humberto Nagera, *Early Childhood Disturbances, the Infantile Neuroses and the Adulthood Disturbances* (New York: 1966), esp. 66.
58. BN, 4022, fol. 54.
59. *S.&B.,* I, 206.
60. BN, 4022, fol. 115 *Vo.*
61. *Ibid.,* fol. 329 *Vo.*
62. BN, 4025, fol. 262
63. Bellemaure, *Le Pourtraict du Roi* (Paris: 1618), 36-38.
64. BN, 4022, fol. 83; *S.&B.,* I, *xxv.*
65. *Courtaud,* fol. 17.
66. Gui Patin, *Lettres, 1630-1672,* I (Paris: 1907), 42.
67. Louis Vaunois, *Vie de Louis XIII* (Paris: 1943), 403-4.
68. Bassompierre, *Mémoires,* Michaud et Poujoulat, eds., (Paris: 1854), 20, 26.
69. Peter Paul Rubens, *Letters* (Cambridge, Mass.: 1966), 105.
70. *Archives des Affaires Etrangères* (AAE), *Mémoires et Documents,* France, 844, fol. 35.
71. AAE, *Mémoires et Docs.,* 244, fol. 317.

72. Richelieu, *Political Testament*, H. B. Hill, trs. (Madison, Wisc.: 1961), 36; 38-39.
73. BN, 4022, fol. 242 *Vo*.
74. AAE, *Mémoires et Docs.*, 815, fol. 157.
75. Orest A. Ranum, *Richelieu and the Councillors of Louis XIII*, 17.
76. Bernard, *L'Histoire de Louis XIII*, XVII, 355.
77. *Ibid.*
78. Richelieu, *Testament*, 36.
79. *S.&B.*, I, 205. This had a literal significance for Louis, who often *held* his tongue.
80. Bellemaure, *Pourtraict*, 37.
81. Richelieu, *Testament*, 40.
82. Bellemaure, *Pourtraict*, 41.
83. Edward, Lord Herbert of Cherbury, *Autobiography* (London: 1888), 136.
84. Richelieu, *Testament*, 41.
85. AAE, *Mémoires et Docs.*, 815, fol. 275.
86. Dinet, *Belle Mort*, 59.
87. BN, *Cinq-cents Colbert* 98, fols. 177-213.
88. Ernest Jones, *The Life and Work of Sigmund Freud* (New York: 1957), III, 283.
89. BN, 4022, fol. 26.
90. *S.&B.*, I, 69.
91. *Ibid.*, 173.
92. *Récit Véritable de la Mort du Maréchal d'Ancre (Histoire Universelle de M. de Thou* (Basle: 1742), XI), 18-20.
93. D.-L.-M. Avenel, ed., *Lettres, instructions et papiers d'Etat du Cardinal de Richelieu*, II (Paris: 1856), 78.
94. Bernard, *L'Histoire de Louis XIII*, I, 60.
95. Eugène Griselle, ed., *Lettres de la main de Louis XIII* (Paris: 1914), 9-11.
96. AAE, *Mémoires et Documents*, 827, fol. 307.
97. *Courtaud*, 145 *Vo*.
98. *Moses and Monotheism*, 10.

CHAPTER 9

Theodore Roosevelt and the Progressive Era: A Study in Individual and Group Psychohistory

GLENN
DAVIS

Historians are primarily concerned with the causes of events, yet one vital aspect of the historical record, the causes associated with the formation of important personalities of history, has only recently begun to be investigated. This has been a loss both for a fuller knowledge of the past and as a source for psychoanalytic interpretation. The following article contains a reconstruction of the vital events surrounding the personality formation of Theodore Roosevelt and an analysis of the effects of some of these early events.

Before Theodore Roosevelt, Sr. married Martha Bulloch of Georgia, he led the life of the youngest of five brothers. Years later, his youngest daughter Corinne would write that her father told her how he deplored "being the fifth wheel of the coach."[1] The Roosevelt boys were known for their energy. Corinne writes that her paternal grandmother was known as "the lovely Mrs. Roosevelt with those five horrid boys."[2] Holding his own in this lot helped the father of the president to develop into an athletic individual who liked adventure and had a sense of daring. His habit of driving carriages fast and even wrecklessly belies a certain insecurity and intensity. At one point, he spoke of his father's fear when he once took him for a ride, but added, "fortunately, nothing broke."[3]

Theodore developed a strong sense of morality and responsibility. He was most concerned with the right thing to do in various situations and was appalled when he felt an individual was committing an unchari- table act. It was a natural thing for him to stop to give a boy a ride, or ask a strange child why he was crying. Yet, he was not humorless, had a real zest for life, and was apparently popular with the young ladies.[4]

Forcefulness was clearly a family trait. If a young man looks up to his oldest brother, Silas Weir Roosevelt was an aggressive and egotistical model. The young Roosevelts tended to go into businesses related to the foundation laid by their father Cornelius, and Silas threw himself into the tasks with the greatest zeal. When the physician Hilbourne West had thought Silas' plans for innovations of a mill a bit impractical, Silas burned back with the following message:

> You began to snear at my pictures which you attempted to scratch out and left unfinished, probably being frightened when you real- ized what you were doing. And it is very well for you that you did not frighten in good time. Beethoven used to play sundry dis- chords, and when his friends complained it was . . . against the rules of music, he answered, "I make the rules." All I have to say is that, if there should be no mechanism in a mill fit for my pur- pose, I make the machinery; and if you have entirely overlooked the arts of designs in constructing the factory, it is not my fault. Make a cigarette of that and smoke it.[5]

Martha Bulloch's life, before she met Theodore at age fifteen, was a very different experience. Her father traveled to the Georgia piedmont from Savannah during 1840, ostensibly for health reasons, but really because of an affair of the heart.[6] Their home on the piedmont was of the grand southern mansion tradition. Doric columns in front of a Greek revival structure gave classic elegance to a home which overlooked a prosperous plantation well staffed by many slaves. Mr. Bulloch experi- enced this existence for a mere nine years before dying of a stroke of apoplexy while teaching the Sunday school of which he was a superin- tendent. His wife was left with a large plantation and family for which to care.

Mrs. Bulloch's daughter Mittie, mother of the president, was the darling of the family and soon after adolescence considered a rare beauty. The stereotype of the southern belle is not descriptive of the range of types of women who lived on the plantations, but nevertheless Mittie does fit this image. She was a delicate and beautiful ornament who was pampered and upon whom few demands were made. Her main function in life was to be beautiful and charming. One prominent mem- ber of Savannah said, "She was a remarkably beautiful woman in those days, and as full of spirit and courage as she was beautiful. . . ."[7] She enjoyed a close relationship with her siblings, especially her sister Anna who, a bit sturdier than delicate Mittie, was forever watching over Mittie's well being and nursing her in sickness. Educated by tutors and finishing school and knowledgeable of the southern romantic tradition, she filled the role beautifully, a maiden secure in her feudal castle.

After Theodore Roosevelt met Mittie Bulloch, he would not see her again for another three years. Yet, in that fleeting visit, he obtained a gold thimble she had worn as a keepsake.[8] One can imagine the intensity of the young Northerner traveling several hundred miles to visit a fifteen-year-old of whom he had heard tales of charms. After the three years passed, they met again in Philadelphia during May of 1853. Mittie spent some time in New York and their relationship began.

Theodore would later express his romantic idealization of Mittie when he wrote, "Those sofas at Mary's became almost sacred."[9] Mittie agreed on engagement and her mother gave sanction to the choice. The correspondence that summer gives an intimate glimpse of romantic courtship. Emotions are intense and written in full detail. On May 31, Thee wrote, "A week will have passed tomorrow since I last wrote or spoke to you; one third of the time to be passed by me in purgatory is concluded and I am beginning to calculate how many hours will be required after leaving here to reach Roswell. . . ."[10] Mittie's devotion is likewise growing, yet she retains that certain coquettish humor which had charmed countless suitors. She once ended a letter, "I am always yours (unless something else comes up),"[11] but was careful to keep the humor low-keyed and close to expressions of the deepest devotion.

A central theme to the courtship of the young couple is their health. In almost every letter, Theodore inquires as to the physical state of his betrothed. Both are consciously aware that their health is intimately associated to their emotional states of mind. Thee writes Mittie, ". . . felt vividly in my mind the last morning of our parting the blood rush to my temples, and I had as it was in the store, to lay against the bathroom door for a few minutes to regain command over myself."[12] On another occasion he writes, ". . . yesterday in the afternoon I took a glass of water and found to my astonishment that I had in a measure lost control over my hands . . . before reaching home, I felt as though some malicious individual had placed two coals behind my eyes."[13] The biographer Carleton Putnam notes, "She [Mittie] also had periodic 'palpitations.' Although at first the latter led her to a 'candid opinion' she had 'some disease of the heart,' she finally decided they were 'entirely nervous' which seems plausible in view of the excitement of her impending marriage."[14] Theodore's concern for Mittie's health is ceaseless: "Remember your promise to tell me exactly all about your health and I will rely fully upon what you say."[15] Somatic states were means of communication between them.

As the wedding date approaches, the language of the letters intensifies. Love is almost more than human and Mittie attaches spiritual significance to their meeting: "Does it not seem strange to think we should have met and became engaged, after only knowing each other time to create passing interest, and then to be separated for almost three years. Sometimes when I think of it all I feel as if it were ordered by some higher power."[16] Theodore is engulfed in a similar spirit. "There seems to be a dreamy shadow of you hovering round and softening my whole existence; it weaves itself, without interfering with any of my pursuits."[17]

Besides the themes of concern for Mittie's health and spiritual love, Roosevelt is clearly a man of charity. He frequently identifies himself with others' misfortunes and when possible, gives a helping hand. On one occasion he saw a boy who needed a ride and helped him reach his mother although it took three hours of driving through a blinding rain storm and almost impassible mud.[18] The same month he spent a good deal of time helping his mother recover from a fall from a horse.[19]

The successful Georgia wedding took place December of 1853 and Theodore brought his young bride to her New York home. The house was a new brownstone, not one of New York's magnificent homes nor as large or luxurious as Roosevelt's father's, but elegant and comfortable. Roosevelt was now a manager for his father's hardware store interests and his young bride would be well provided for.

By June of 1854, Mittie was pregnant. Unfortunately, few records survive surrounding the birth of Anna, known to the family as Bamie. One occurrence is known: there was some sort of accident in which her back was severely impaired. The cause is mysterious. Putnam believed that she was probably "the victim of an undiagnosed, or at least unacknowledged, attack of poliomyelitis which she was able in time to overcome sufficiently to live an exceptionally active life."[20] But the family occasionally referred to the fact that she had been dropped by a nurse while bathing and would probably never be able to walk.[21]

Theodore verbalized his grief. He observed a little child who lost an eye and remarked: "A little child sat in our pew this morning that had lost one of its eyes. A person evidently the father was with it and it was almost painful to see the way in which he took care of it. I could not help thinking all the time that might be in store for us—poor little thing. I never think of Bamie without pain. It seems such a dreary dreary life that is in store for her. We must try to teach her as soon as we can to fix her hopes of happiness far above this little world of ours."[22]

But Bamie was not the only member of the family in need: there was Mittie. With the help of nurses, she tried to do her duty towards her daughter but not much time passed before she felt more insecurities. It was a difficult goal to achieve success both as a beautiful ornament and mother, and as her maternal duties increased, she worried more about the former. That May, when Theodore's business required a trip from New York, Mittie felt utterly desolate and abandoned. There was some trouble with the nurse and Mittie had to cope with the household for a while on her own:

> I am in a great deal of trouble at present. I dismissed Bridgett this morning to leave on the first of June and I suppose I shall have to advertise for a nurse and *that immediately*. I am going to try to get Mary Roosevelt to help me. . . . I dreamed again that you were attached and loved someone else.[23]

There is a fear that she is losing her husband and she reaches out for closeness, "Without you Thee I feel as though life would lose its charm." They must draw closer: "Thee, I wonder if you feel as I do but I want our interests to become more and more the same. I do not want the least shadow of reserve to be between us."[24] Theodore, as usual, is careful to reassure her of his love: "You know darling you ought not to blame me for trying to enjoy myself to the utmost" and in reference to his time alone while Mittie visited her family he continues, ". . . while it is a pleasure trip to you it is by no means a pleasant stay-at-home to me even with every amusement I can find."[25]

Evidently Mittie's trip back to the womb of the South was a much needed respite from the pressures of modern family life. There she regained her chivalrous confidence and joked to her friends how Thee carried her up stairs but was afraid of straining his back. She was again cared for by her sister Anna who "has rubbed me with camphor every night since I have been unwell . . . my hair has not stopped dropping in the least and is painfully thin but Anna thinks she sees some fine hair coming."[26]

Two years before the birth of the Roosevelt's second child, Mittie's mother came to live with her daughter and son-in-law. It is through her eyes, preserved in a series of detailed letters to her daughter, Susan, that it is possible to reconstruct the crucial first few months of the life of Theodore Roosevelt, Jr. During 1858, Mittie had to cancel her carriage drive because of pains although she did not believe birth was imminent. Martha Stewart Bulloch was by her side and related to Susan:

> . . . when the different servants were flying about for doctors and for Susan Newberry, the nurse, I was almost the whole time alone with Mittie—Anna had taken Bamie over to Lizzy Ellis'—I sent over for her, but she was too unwell to come—I could not bear the idea of having no female friend with me, so sent for Mrs. Roosevelt and she came over. Mittie continued to get worse and worse until quarter to eight in the evening when the birth took place. She had a safe but severe time. She is this morning as well as one could wish to see her. It is as sweet and pretty a young

baby as I have ever seen; weighed eight pounds and a half before it was dressed. No chloroform or any such thing was used, no instruments were necessary, consequently the dear little thing has no cuts or bruises on it . . Mittie says I must tell you she thinks the baby hideous. She says it is a cross between a terrapin and Dr. Young.[27]

During the crucial first month of life, the baby "Teedie" had the advantages of a secure beginning. By November second, when he was a week old, Grandma Bulloch would observe, "Mittie's doing remarkably well, the baby's sleeping better at night and is of presently in just fine health." Mittie was able to nurse her own child, which indicates she must have been fairly comfortable in her maternal role. ". . . Mittie suffers less from her new vocation of 'nursing mother' than any person I have ever known. I am convinced there is more in skillful nursing in respect to the flow of milk than persons generally imagine."[28]

During Teedie's first month, Mittie nursed her baby herself. Grandma Bulloch wrote to Susan: "Mittie continues as well as could be . . . as for the baby, like other babies, he makes a little fuss at night, is a fine little fellow and appears in perfect health. Mittie has a great overflow of milk, has a plenty for him and it gives her, as you, little or no trouble."[29] There was little or no overt problem with sibling rivalry: "Bamie is delighted with the baby . . . she says she has two babies now . . . her little dog . . . she says he is a cunning little fellow . . . I think they will name him Theodore."[30] But the nursing paradise would not last long. When he was not yet a month old, Mittie would name Teedie the "little berserker"[31] and the household would soon have a difficult time meeting his expanding needs. His mother began to withdraw, and the custom of nurse care invaded his little world.

The Roosevelts' first dry nurse, Susan Newberry, was well recommended. Martha Stewart Bulloch describes a woman of magnanimous nature: "Mary, . . . in one of her charitable rounds found a woman who tho' poor herself, had taken charge of one or two children who had actually been deserted by their parents . . . and the poor children but for this woman would have perished. This is the woman Mittie has engaged for a nurse. She has other recommendations, also."[32]

Yet by December household tensions began to rise. Grandma Bulloch had been living in the house since Teedie's birth and wanted now to go to her own home. But Mittie would not have it. Apparently, the grandmother had been the organizing force who kept the children and their affairs in order. Martha commented that Mittie, "thinks with a young baby, and Bamie suffers so . . . , that she ought not to be left alone."[33] The fact that she would live nearby was not enough, for she was needed to help in the day-to-day chores.

Mittie had an attack of influenza in addition to her headaches in December and soon had an argument with one of the nurses. Dr. Davis would come in to adjust the braces and there was a regiment of baths and exercises. One morning, Mittie asked a nurse to wipe more softly. In a rare moment of rebellion, the nurse flung a towel at Bamie and told Mittie to wipe herself for she had not been rough. Mittie accepted her apologies the next day but only agreed to keep her until she could find a new nurse.[34]

Teedie's days in intimate contact with his mother were over by one month. For some mysterious reason, he now found himself in the hands of his grandmother and a succession of nurses, a bottle was replacing the breast, and he was soon to be required to train his excretory functions as the laws of society began to descend. Even when he was ill, either the nurse or the grandmother attended to his needs; Martha Bulloch wrote when he was four months old: "He is a fine little fellow and has become quite fat and larger. He cries a good deal. She [Mittie] has a very nice nurse for the boy . . . the boy could be placed entirely under her care now, only that his measles are not quite well—and Mittie prefers my attending to it."[35]

During February of 1860, when Teedie was 15 months old, a third child was born to the Roosevelt home. Ellie's start in life was not as easy as his older brother's. Although Mittie tried, she was not able to nurse him at her breast. Though the family thought it best for Mittie to nurse him with a bottle, the doctor insisted on a wetnurse. Unfortunately, according to Martha Bulloch, the wetnurse was a real "bog-bottom." Martha was put off by the circumstances surrounding the birth of the girl's own child, Patrick. Martha related, "She said that her husband's name is Smelley but her name is Connie Sheron—that she does not go by her husband's name at all. But I suppose Patrick will rejoice in the name of Smelley, a name very suggestive of the want of soap and water and plenty of clothes to change."[36]

Martha continued the narrative of Ellie's first few months of life, "Little Ellie is not so well—his vaccination is at its height." By October 9, 1861, Ellie would see the last of his formula; weaning was difficult and painful and he lost some weight. She observed of Ellie that, "He is not satisfied at present with any person to take care of him but myself. A wonder he has permitted me to come upstairs to write this note."

Things developed to the point at which Martha observed, "I am obliged to keep out of his sight, when it does not suit me to hold him." Mittie was not one to hesitate at delegating duties: "If sister only lived next door, how often I would turn them over to her for a few hours each day."[37] Ellie eventually stopped rebelling against his nurse Delia, but to his grandmother's eyes, seemed reconciled but not happy. He grew to be the prettiest in the family and liked to play with his older brother Teedie. But there was a real sensitivity. Martha wrote, "Ellie asked me this morning if I was sometimes lonesome without him. I told him yes."[38]

Mittie continued to have difficulty with life's stresses. Before her mother made a trip to the south to visit her son who had been wounded fighting for the Confederacy, Mittie was stricken with many intense chest pains. She felt similar pains when her husband left for his wartime administrative job in Washington. She wrote to Theodore, "I wish you were not so good. It makes me feel so sad. I am not so strong-minded as you know, and feel so dependent."[39] G. Wallace Chessman summarized Mittie's intensified anxieties as follows:

> . . . as the family's activities broadened and intensified, Mittie re-
> treated more often to her room. It was said that her health was
> delicate, and likely she welcomed an excuse to get away. Some-
> how she had kept up before, but the case was getting too much
> for one accustomed to more leisurely Southern ways. Increasingly
> she showed a passion for cleanliness, an incompetence at money
> matters and housekeeping, a disposition to be late for appoint-
> ments. When she appeared at parties, so immaculately groomed in
> her beautiful gown, she impressed all with her charm, but she just
> couldn't manage life efficiently. . . .[40]

The biographer of Mittie's eldest daughter, Lilian Rixey, described how Mittie's headaches allowed her to find retreat in her room for several hours until excitement calmed down. Some time later, somatic symptoms took a compulsive turn, and she found she was not able to leave the house until taking two baths, one for washing and one for rinsing. Another writer related that, "she had a sheet spread on the floor each night next to her bed so that she might say her prayers in comfort and not be conscious of the possibility of dirt when addressing the Lord. When ill and the doctor came, a sheet would be spread over the chair where he was to sit."[41]

The Civil War must have been a confusing event for the Roosevelt children. Teedie was a military child from the very start. As he was active, he was difficult to hold still for fitting of clothes. "Are me a soldier laddie?" the child asked his mother. She answered in the affirmative so that he could be fitted. Teedie knew his father was gone and that his mother behaved strangely when he voiced sympathy for the Union soldiers.[42] Teedie was a bit young to understand why he antagonized his mother when he marched up and down the living room floor in triumph to the sound of every Union victory, but he could not help notice her reaction.

Age four was really Teedie's watershed time. Before then, he developed a sense of trust in the world, an ability to absorb his surroundings and a profound interest in exploration. Although his health was never robust, his list of ailments was not far worse than the average childhood diseases of the time. If Ellie reacted to an inconsistent mother and father taken away by circumstances of war by extreme sensitivity and attachment to his grandmother, and Bamie by a need to emulate her parents, Teedie remained active and searching; his solution was yet to be attempted, but he was quite willing to try a variety of life strategies and weigh their effect. There was certainly mischief and vitality; at the same time there was sickness and nonactivity. Mittie was aware of the active side from an early date: "Teedie is the most affectionate and endearing creature in his ways, but begins to require Papa's discipline rather sadly. He is brimming full of mischief and has to be watched all the time. . . ."[43]

He showed a precocious intelligence and could often delight an adult audience with his humor. Once, during his fourth birthday party, he remarked that he "loved chicken, roast beef, and everything that was good better than salt water."[44] On another occasion he was left in a room alone with the dignified Dr. William Adams and said while pointing to a painting of the Transfiguration, "There, Dr. Adams, see Jesus a-flootin' up to Heaven wiv his coat-tails behind!"[45]

Yet on the other hand, from the fall of 1861, when Teedie was just three, accounts of stomach problems and colds in addition to the typical childhood illnesses were all too frequent. His father wrote with utmost concern that "Teedie is too much sick. It worries me, and while I hope a great deal for next summer, I cannot help feeling that there must be something about the furnace or something that prevents them all from being healthy."[46]

Central to the childhood and character of Theodore Roosevelt is the problem of his asthma. A strong case can be made that Roosevelt's asthma was psychosomatic, caused by personality factors which can in turn be related to his great quantity of personal aggression, his idolization of his father, attitudes towards women, need to bring himself to the point of possible death countless times, and bizarre episodes played out in the American West.

The starting point lies in something very basic to Roosevelt's personality, the concept of oral rage. This will be seen to be the pressure cooker, a source of the aggression observers found of almost unbelievable intensity. Although our documentation of his earliest years is limited, the assumption of oral deprivation sufficient to provide a permanent source of oral rage is confirmed by all that we do have in our evidence. The fragile personality of his mother, her withdrawal from his intimate care when he was only one month old, her somatization of feelings, her compulsive fear of dirt, her dependency on her mother, her fear of abandonment by her husband, and the confusing shifts of caretaking between grandmother and the different nurses all contributed to the establishment of oral rage in his first year. Besides this there is only the information that when he was ten months old he had a lot of trouble with his teeth,[47] but beyond this we have no further evidence from his first year, and must reach forward to his adult personality for further indications of oral rage.

Soon after Roosevelt's death, an article appeared which was entitled, "The Man Built Around a Set of Teeth."[48] Its author was amazed at the frequency and intensity Roosevelt used his teeth to show his aggressivity. To many, the fierce shining molars became a symbol for Roosevelt's very being. During 1898 he received a letter in New York mailed from Arizona with nothing on the envelope but a drawing of a set of teeth and a pair of spectacles.[49]

Jacob Arlow speaks of oral symbols and relates teeth to tools: "Because the teeth are so intimately related to the discharge of oral drives, especially aggression, symbols for the teeth seem to be chosen primarily according to their functional significance .. certain tools, therefore, are especially suited to represent the extension of the functions of the teeth in discharging of oral drives."[50] The "big stick" now takes on added significance. In each of the cartoonists' pictures, Roosevelt's mouth is open. The entire body is poised as an instrument of aggression; there is often a weapon in hand, and the stance leans forward, ready to pounce. His arm is raised and the hand most often clenched.

Oral images from Roosevelt's life are prominent in all accounts of him. Reformer Jacob Riis related how TR "snapped his teeth together and defied the party leaders."[51] One poet composed the following couplet:

So Teddy came runnin' with his glasses on his nose
And when the Spaniards saw his teeth, you may well believe they
        froze.[52]

Another observed that when TR was on the way to the rostrum to make a speech and the way was blocked, "The candidate flashed his favorite grin and bit his way to the stage."[53] On another occasion he was heard to say, "I have a horror of people who bark but don't bite!"[54] He often used phrases as, "in the teeth of opposition," or else, "If the fathers cause others to eat bitter bread, the teeth of their own sons shall be out on edge."[55]

This material concerning oral rage may shed light on the question of why Teedie, about the time of age four, began to wheeze. Asthma may be caused by a variety of conditions, but most psychiatrists and psychologists isolate the following categories: there is genetic or inherited cause. This would be analogous to say the disease leukemia in which certain factors are missing in the individual's genetic structure for production of chemical equipment needed to ward off the disease. Asthma may be caused by allergic reaction to vegetation or infection by bacteria or a virus. Finally, there is the case, often interrelated with one or more of the above, of psychosomatic induction.

Psychosomatic induction is defined in simplest terms are a real physiological disorder whose roots lie in psychic function. Mittie Bulloch's headaches and chest constrictions have already been mentioned, as has the tendency of both parents to communicate via somatic language. The two most common psychosomatic illnesses are the peptic ulcer and asthma, two illnesses which troubled Roosevelt's youth.

The following research in the area of asthma will be brought to bear on the scanty factual knowledge concerning the time of first onset of Teedie's wheezing. Franz Alexander and Thomas M. French found a preponderance of the oral personality in young children whose asthma came soon after a separation from the mother. The asthma was a turning inward of the frustration and began as a suppressed cry for the mother so that eventually the child cannot breathe.

Strongly correlated with this type of asthma is the "urge to prove fearlessness." In group studies, these authors also found that the mother was the rejecting type and many of her functions had been taken over by the father. Also, oddly enough, almost all of the cases evidenced the birth of a sister before age four. The greatest disposing factor is the loss of a secure situation such as from regular breast to the bottle in early infancy. The mechanism is basically oral aggressive response to oral longings, guilt and anxiety, overcompensation for oral aggression by successful accomplishments in responsible activities, increased unconscious oral-dependent cravings as reaction to excessive effort, and hyperactivity.[56]

Goldberg's study of psychosomatic disease led him to conclude that in many cases of ulcers in young children, the mother had been prudish and had compulsive tendencies. Cleanliness was overdone and she would illustrate psychosomatic illness herself, the most frequent being headache.[57] Lindy Burton's study of asthma yielded similar results. Most often there was a faulty mother-child relationship. The mother is unable to accept her maternal role and the child reacts by defiance. The triad is orality—dependency—masochism. Oral fixations are followed by a real need for the mother which is frustrated and follows by an inward-turning of sadistic impulse which results in body disorder.[58]

Laparello's work found exaggerated dependence on the mother, frustration and aggression as central motives, Sachar related oral strivings and Knapp found that when there are psychic gains for assuming the asthmatic role, asthma is increased. McDermott and Cobb's study of fifty cases of asthmatic children displayed a pattern of consistently improved physical condition when taken out of their troubled homes. Adler found a statistical vulnerability to the second-born of the family

(Roosevelt's position) to asthma. Mutter and Schliefer studied a group of forty-two families whose children were hospitalized for asthma with a control group of families of similar socio-economic position and found a startling consistency of emotive problems within the families whose children had asthma: "We see that families with ill children were more poorly organized in their psychological and social functioning, they exposed their children to a wider range of threatening social changes, producing a greater stress for which the children were less prepared." In another of his studies Franz Alexander stressed the maternal component. In case "Q" a young doctor related his feelings of sexual attraction to his stepmother at approximately the same time that his asthma attacks began. Alexander postulated from this and many similar cases: "From our studies of bronchial asthma we have found that throughout the life of patients subject to psychogenic asthma attacks, there seems to run as a continuous undercurrent, sometimes deeply suppressed, a fear of estrangement from the mother or mother substitute." This adds empirical support to Freud's classic approach to asthma which emphasizes if it occurs during the oedipal stage it can be thought of in terms of rage against the father who has a more complete access to the mother; the rage is manifested in what David Bakan terms bodily processes which do not heal but can appear in self-destructive forms as asthma.[59]

The time of the onset of Teedie's asthma is important to the role it played and what it can say of his personality development. There has been disagreement as to the date of the onset, but evidence had been vague. Carleton Putnam wrote that the asthma occurred while Teedie was still in infancy although there is no documentation of this fact.[60] Norman Kiell dated the asthma as occurring at age two, but again gives no proof.[61]

Fortunately, though, the abundance of correspondence by Martha Bulloch, Mittie Roosevelt and Theodore Roosevelt, Sr. makes it possible to state with reasonable assurance that the asthma began about when Teedie was in the middle of his fourth year. All of these individuals included a great amount of detail concerning the health of the children in their letters. There was chicken pox, colds, fevers and other childhood problems, but the first mention of the word asthma came June 22, 1863. As far back as January of that year Teedie's health had degenerated; he had more fevers, colds, and poor appetite for certain periods. In May of 1863, Martha Bulloch wrote: "Teedie was very much benefited by his trip to the country." But from Long Beach the next month comes, "They had sent Teedie back on the previous Thursday as the physicians thought his attack of asthma was over. The doctors were mistaken . . . he had the same symptoms of difficulty breathing as soon almost as he returned to Long Beach."[62] It is difficult to believe that a woman as Martha who wrote in the greatest detail to her daughter

Susan concerning the colds and aches of her grandson would not have mentioned the asthma if it had occurred at an earlier time. Whether the mother accompanied the boy as he was shifted out to the country and back is not certain, but if she did not, the "cure" of fresh country air probably intensified rather than relieving his asthma. A further factor was the father's growing absence for war duties during the year prior to the outbreak of the asthma.

Of the few records remaining concerning the fourth year of Teedie's life, it is possible to examine one incident of significance. The importance of the event in Roosevelt's own eyes is illustrated by the fact that he chose to describe the event in his own autobiography. Roosevelt relates the incident in some detail:

> I bit my elder sister's arm. I do not remember biting her arm, but I do remember running down to the yard, perfectly conscious that I had committed a crime. From the yard I went into the kitchen, got some dough from the cook and crawled under the kitchen table. In a minute or two my father entered from the yard and asked where I was. The warm-hearted Irish cook had a characteristic contempt for "informers," but although she said nothing she compromised between informing and her conscience by casting a look under the table. My father immediately dropped on all fours and, having the advantage of him because I could stand up under the table, got a fair start for the stairs, but was caught halfway up them.[63]

The wrath of Theodore Roosevelt, Sr. must have been great, indeed. His son Teedie had touched a soft spot which caused the eruption. Roosevelt had a protectionist feeling towards women in general and had based much of his existence around helping little children in need. The man who helped set up the Children's Aid Society and Orthopedic Hospital, who sat with his ailing daughter for hours on end and was brought almost to tears by the sight of a handicapped child would not sit still as his boisterous son attacked Bamie. From Teedie's eyes, it must have seemed that he unleashed a fearful monster.

It is now possible to propose a mechanism for the asthma which followed soon after. Roosevelt, Sr. played, under these circumstances, both maternal-paternal functions. There was no way to get closer to his mother and Teedie was not satisfied to take Ellie's strategy of extreme attachment to the surrogate of his grandmother. Teedie felt the intense devotion and increased affection his father felt towards children in need. His aggressive orality had been under severe control and he was taught not to harm others, especially girls. As a result, the aggression went inward. The difficulty breathing was an extremely successful stifled cry for closeness and care, and during his attacks he found his father's love intensified.

The asthma created attention. He wrote in his autobiography how "I was a sickly, delicate boy, suffered much from asthma, and frequently had to be taken away on trips to find a place where I could breathe. One of my memories is of my father walking up and down the room with me in his arms at night when I was a very small person, and of sitting up in bed gasping, with my mother and father trying to help me."[64] He did not go to school, but was instead privately instructed at home. His father wrote Mittie, "Omit no effort to relieve him."[65] Lincoln Steffens would later be told by TR, "I remember, I think I remember—him carrying me in my distress, in my battle for breath, up and down the room all night. Handsome dandy that he was, the thought of him now and always has been a sense of comfort. My father—he got me lungs, strength—life."[66] Grandma Bulloch told of how Mittie and Thee would take Teedie on special trips to help relieve him. It was consistent that Teedie's asthma was worse when separated from his father and the instructions Mittie requested were rarely as effective as his presence for quieting the ailment.

By the time he was ten years of age, his parents' attitudes towards him changed. As Teedie became Theodore, his father viewed his oldest son less as a suffering child and more as a youth whose convalescence was very much in his own power. Roosevelt, Sr. kept training the boy and pushing his vital force outwards. Theodore must get into shape. His diaries are filled with descriptions of hunting with his father in which twenty-mile hikes were common. It was clear Theodore felt he had to keep up. On one excursion during his trip to Europe in 1868, the young asthmatic hiked thirteen miles and climbed a mountain which was eight thousand feet above sea level. Keeping up with his father was no easy task, for Roosevelt, Sr. was a man who said of himself, "I never seem to get tired."[67] Just as asthma was once the means of asking for love, physical perseverance was now necessary.

During the trip of 1869, an incident occurred which is reflective of the psychodynamics. This incident is similar to another person who felt intense ambivalencies towards his father—Woodrow Wilson. Wilson's father insisted on his son showing guests signs of his manhood by displaying to them new hairs on his mustache. On September 26, 1869, when the ten-year-old boy had an attack of asthma, his father made him smoke a cigar while in bed.[68]

It is evident that Roosevelt's time had come. His father was asking him to become a man, as was his mother who looked forward to a second male protector in the family. The day after Theodore's first smoke he was left behind when the family went on a sightseeing tour. It is not surprising that one of the only dreams Theodore recorded—as an exception to Hofstadter's observation that he "fled from repose and introspection was a desperate urgency that is sometimes pitiable"[69]—was a nightmare that evening. He wrote, "The Devil was carrying me away and I have cholera morbus [gastro-intestinal disorder]."[70] The young man was being punished for his physical condition. Yet the diaries indicate no feeling of conscious hostility towards his mother and father.

Roosevelt, Sr. kept his boy training to turn the aggression outwards, and it was now Theodore and not Elliott who dominated and directed play with his siblings. The climbing continued through his European trip. He explored, climbed an 8,000-foot mountain during his stay in Germany and fought off his asthma and intestinal disorders. The more he did outwardly, the less he suffered inwardly. One day he walked twenty miles though his father tired after twenty-two.[71]

Theodore was beginning to direct his intensity outward. He was victorious in combative play with his brother, chased and cornered dogs, and was active in mock battles. Below is a facsimile of a drawing Theodore made during 1869. The omnipresent teeth are drawn as instruments of aggression. One is further inclined to see it as a self-view because of the small size of the eyes.

After the European tour, another incident bears examination. Theodore's father came to him and said, "Theodore you have the mind but you have not the body, and without the help of the body the mind cannot go as far as it should. You must make your body. It is hard drudgery to make one's body, but I know you will do it." According to later memories of his sister Corinne, "The boy looked up, throwing back his head in characteristic fashion, then with a flash of those white teeth which later in life became so well known . . . said, 'I'll make my body!' "[72] The only vestige of rage was shown in the fact that Theodore

Figure 1 [73]

replied to his father's challenge through the defiant gestures of throwing back his head and flashing his teeth.

For physical development, Theodore worked furiously at Wood's gymnasium. His schooling was provided by private tutors. Of all the books he was exposed to, Roosevelt had keenest interest in *The Last of the Mohegans,* the tale of a race dying out under the onslaught of a fitter civilization.[74]

The family planned a second European trip for the fall of 1872. For this trip, Theodore had two new possessions which would prove vital for his functioning. When he received a gun from his father he discovered he was severely myopic. The problem was detected and a pair of glasses prescribed.

By late November, the Roosevelts' ship had reached the Mediterranean. After a brief reunion with Mittie's expatriated Confederate brothers in Liverpool, and some travel on the continent, they headed for a new area, Egypt of the Ottoman Empire. Theodore recorded his first reactions to Alexandria in his diary:

> Alexandria. How I gazed on it! It was Egypt, the land of my dreams; Egypt, the most ancient of all countries! A land that was old when Rome was bright, was old when Babylon was in its glory, was old when Troy was taken! It was a sight to awaken a thousand thoughts, and it did.[75]

Theodore could be proud of the fruits of his physical training. Now it was his father who wrote: "I feel as if I must keep up with Teedie."[76] When they climbed a pyramid, "Father was so exhausted that we were almost afraid he would faint."[77] It was not long before Theodore and his father began hunting birds together. On the 583-mile journey to the First Cataract they devoted a few hours almost every day to the sport. This consistency illustrates a sort of initiation, almost a puberty rite. It is not known where Elliott was during this time, for only the father and eldest son went out each day with guns in hand.

Theodore recorded the first bird he killed, "One of these was the first bird I had ever shot and I was proportionably delighted."[78] Corinne observed, "The boy of fourteen was already leading his equally indomitable father into different fields of action."[79] Although Roosevelt later wrote, "This bird collecting gave me what was really the chief zest of my Nile journey. . . . The birds I obtained up the Nile and in Palestine represented merely the usual boy's collection,"[80] this was simply not the case. In a remarkably short time, he killed hundreds of birds.[81]

Although the environment was barren, Theodore was filled with life. His physical growth continued at an astonishing rate. Pringle writes, "He seemed miraculously to add an inch or two during the brief journey up the Nile, and when the expedition returned to Cairo a complete set of new clothing had to be obtained."[82] Now Elliott was becoming delicate. He did not have his brother's Spartan attitude and longed for the time he could "sit down to breakfast, dinner, and lunch in our own house."[83] Though Theodore had three asthma attacks, none had stopped his vigorous activity, while Elliott had been incapacitated three times.

The Egyptian portion of the trip had been completed, the Roosevelt family was given a view at the cradle of civilization and their elder son had looked with open eyes. He came out with hundreds of birds, many of which were skinned and dissected. He had learned not to be intimidated and was at home in a variety of cultures; he could deal with an Arab merchant using only the language of his hands or play games with a Syrian sailor.

His pubertal rite accomplished, Theodore could now be asked to live away from his parents. The children were taken to Dresden, where they lived with German families for five months. Roosevelt, Sr. was able, through connections with American council, to contact Dr. Minkwitz, City Counselor and member of the Reichstag. He agreed to take the children into his home.

There were also plans for Mittie. Her health had deteriorated as family responsibilities became more complex. Her chest pains and headaches had grown more intense in addition to bouts of consumption. During this period she would look in on her children in Dresden while living in England with her brother. The family reunion would take place in New York after a five-month period.

For a family man like Roosevelt, Sr., who would be in New York alone, such a change meant adjustment. But health came first. If, in the recesses of his mind there was some wish to spend time alone, there was no overt indication of it. As many men of his period and class, he perceived his wife as one of the children:

> I felt dreadfully to think that I was leaving you yesterday to try to take care of yourself for the first time in your life. I have no doubt you are just as well able to do it as I am to take care of you, but I have always been accustomed to think of you as one of my little babies.[84]

He reminds her to write twice a week and to seek help from Bamie if it is necessary. There is almost a fear that Mittie had reached a maturity which would render her an adult:

> I am afraid to call you my dear little baby; now after three weeks of independence I may be addressing a strong-minded woman. I do not believe it, however, and after writing three letters to each of the exiles in Dresden, I write this to the little girl who seems most to need my care, and whose place should be on my knee even if it turned Connie off.[85]

A letter of Mittie's soon before reunion with her husband illustrates some of the complexities of their relationship:

> I love you and wish to please you more than anyone else in the whole world and will do everything I can to please you that is not

> unreasonable. I think that you have been perfectly lovely to me
> in your care of me always and so good and indulgent and thought-
> ful and I am so proud of you and honor and respect you so *don't
> be too hard upon me.* I have decided that your dear letters are
> just a little plaintive and it rather comforts me to receive the
> "private" letter to see that you have one little scrap of the devil
> in you yet, but I wish my darling husband that you understand
> that I am open to reason and if he can really point out the bad in-
> fluence I will try to do all I can to please him. I perfectly well
> understand who influenced you to write me but I am going to *try*
> to love you just the same whether you do as I desire or not.[86]

Mittie reaffirms her childish position after what must have been a more
than usually forward move by her husband to request her to take responsibilities. The indirect reference to the "devil in you" might have
been a reply to the only indirect note by Thee that he missed his wife's
pleasures.

The younger Theodore prospered in the German atmosphere:

> They were the very kindest family imaginable. I shall never forget
> the unwearied patience of the two daughters. The father and
> mother, and a shy, thin student cousin who was living in the flat,
> were no less kind. Whenever I could get into the country I col-
> lected specimens industriously and enlivened the household with
> hedgehogs and other small beasts and reptiles which persisted in
> escaping from partially closed bureau draws.[87]

Discipline and hard work characterized his stay. He rose at six-thirty
and studied until nine after breakfast. Then came a short break until
more study which lasted until twelve. After lunch, more study until
three followed by exercise or visits about the city for the remainder of
the afternoon. Study was continued after supper until bed at ten.[88] His
health, rather than being the fearful subject it had been, while still
plagued by asthma, could now be joked about:

> Dearest Motherling:
> Your unhappy son had his third attack of asthma, accompanied
> by a violent headache, the day before yesterday. He has given that
> up and has gone into another disease now. Picture to yourself an
> antiquated woodchuck, his voice hoarse from gargling and a cloth
> resembling in texture and cleanliness a secondhand dust man's
> cast-off stocking around his head; picture yourself that, I say, and
> you will have a good likeness to your hopeful offspring while suf-
> fering from an attack of the mumps.[89]

Theodore continued to develop in spite of some sickness. When his
mother came to visit, he walked on the outside "in a protective manner" and told her of his delight with his new boxing gloves. As his
aggressive nature found expression in hunting birds while the family

was in Egypt, he now turned to boxing. Mittie remarked during her
visit, "Teedie has a bloody nose, and Ellie a knock on the head of which
they were proud," or else, "The children have just left another boxing
match in which bleeding noses and swelled lips were common."[90] A
little later she added, "Teedie's eye is perfectly black this morning."[91]
By the time the stay at Dresden was finished, Theodore would return
more toughened by both the German stoicism and his own continuing
fight to turn his aggression outward.

Elliott, however, did not absorb the Spartan aspects of German culture. The "Dresden Literary Club" described by Mittie illustrates Ellie's
position in the family. She remarked on the story Theodore wrote:
" 'A Jackal Hunt' . . . , a thrilling, highly sarcastic account of his shooting a cat on the plain of Sharen between Gaffa and Ramelegh, which he
mistook for a jackal."[92] Yet Ellie's story was entitled "The Bloody
Hand."[93] In it, a woman observed that her husband was behaving
strangely, and when she went in to check on her children she saw him
cut their throats, but he then knocked her out and the woman was subsequently put in jail for the crime.[94] It is a story filled with anxiety,
ambivalence and feelings of abandonment.

As Elliott's anxiety continued to be focussed inward and his physical
health declined, Theodore continued to focus energy outwards, and the
brothers' roles reversed. Much can be said about this from a series of
drawings completed during the stay at Dresden. Theodore had decided
to picture his interpretation of the Darwinian theory of evolution, and
in so doing presented a symbolic representation of his self-concept as
well as that of his younger brother Elliott. Theodore dominates. In all
pictures, Theodore's back is to Elliott. Though in one, Elliott was
transformed into a bull, he is staring up at Theodore (turned stork)
searching to follow his lead. Theodore's evolution is purposeful, assertive, and has objective (see Figure 2).

In Figure 3, Theodore is confronted with a problem. There is a tree.
He is transformed into an upreaching giraffe whose development allows him to obtain the goal. Theodore's favorite song while in Dresden
became, "My love, She is a Giraffe."[95]

In Figure 4 he is looking at a fish but the growth of a beak allows
him to devour it. Also evident is the fact that the instrument that gives
Theodore newly developed power is the growth of a long protruding
shape on the anterior side of his body. The phallic meaning of this will
be clearer in the context of drawings which follow.

The separation from his parents had strengthened his phallic defenses. He was even able to express a note of criticism of his father.
One of the few comments not filled with unconditional adulation
towards his father came May 29th in a letter to his mother: "Father
was considered very pretty and his German exceedingly beautiful,

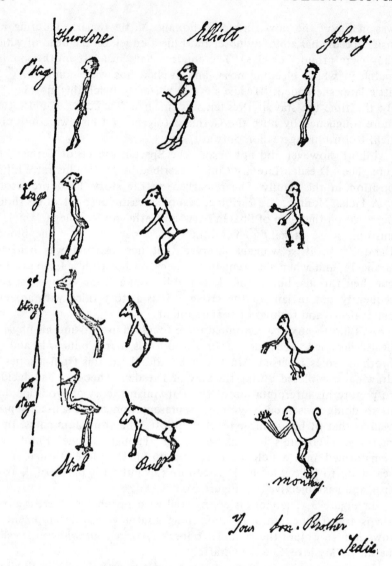

Figure 2[96]

neither of which statement I quite agree with."[99] He began to show a capacity to laugh at himself and could even joke about his own illness. For the first time in his life he stayed in a regular school for a while.

It is in this atmosphere of growth that Figures 5, 6 and 7 were created. The purpose of the drawings was described by Theodore in a letter to an aunt in which they appeared. He had been angered that the

Figure 3[97]

Figure 4[98]

women of the house in Dresden were dismayed by his habit of bringing dead animals into the house. He writes:

> My arsenic was confiscated and my mice thrown (with the tong) out of the window. In cases like this I would approach a refractory female, move in hard, corner her, and hang the mouse very near her face until she was thoroughly convinced of the wickedness of her actions.[100]

There are several layers of meaning to this. For one, it is clear that Theodore gains great delight in proving his bravery, showing the courage to go near what frightens others. Also clear is forward, assertive and combative behavior. The enemies come, but Theodore is ready for them with a mocking grin. On a deeper level, there is something else in action here. Just as the development of the beaks attract attention in the evolu-

Figure 5[101]

Figure 6[102]

Figure 7[103]

tion pictures, the objects of defense in Figures 5, 6 and 7 are also significant. The developing adolescent is being attacked for his mischiev-
ousness. The phallus is being attacked by women yielding sharp instruments (especially Figure 6). The reaction is important. Theodore
proudly presents his object of virility and struts forward: the women
are turned back in fear and their sharp instruments are dropped. In
other words, Theodore's activities are preserved and generated by assertive and forward action rather than shame or fear.

By the time of the family reunion of November 5, 1872, many
psychic patterns and resolutions were formulated. Ellie's resolution involved coping with rage and anxiety inwardly. The psychic costs were
sometimes steep. Soon after his return from Europe, Roosevelt, Sr.
wrote of his son's strange illness, "Its foothold conquers the brain with
all its attendant horrors of delirium etc. The doctor says that there is no

cause for anxiety as it is only necessary to avoid all excitements for two or three years and he will entirely outgrow it." A week later he added, "He evidently has a fear of being left alone at night (i.e. he is nervous) although he stoutly denies it, he sleeps in my bed. I think it would be very wise for Theodore and himself to occupy the large bed in the room for a while together; I should be afraid to leave him alone." Three days later he added, "Ellie is looking and feeling better again and of course hope springs forth as he improves. It certainly seems to show that there is nothing organic at present which the doctor can be positive of. This last attack seemed to him to be hysteria. . . . There is one fortunate feature connected with Ellie's sickness. Anything like a dispute seems worse for him than any other excitement. . . , to grumble reduces his spirits to zero at once."[104]

The evolution and tragedy of Elliott's inward and self-destructive strategy can be briefly traced, for in many ways it is the antithesis of his brother Theodore's. As Theodore defied his asthma, repressed the rage towards his parents, and paid the price of intensive externalized aggression throughout his years, Elliott remained closer to his feelings of abandonment, yet further from a workable resolution.

Later when Elliott was sent West, his health improved. He rode, hunted, and gained respect among the cowboys of the dude ranch at which he was staying. Soon before reaching this oasis, he included the following in a letter:

> Oh, Father, will you ever think *me* a "noble boy," you are right about Tede he is one and no mistake a boy I would give a good deal to be like in many respects. If you ever see me not stand by Thee you may know I am entirely changed, no Father I am not likely to desert a fellow I love as I do my Brother even you don't know what a good noble boy he is and what a splendid man he is going to be as I do. No, I love him. Love him very *very* dearly and will never desert him and if I know him he will *never* desert me.
>
> Father my own dear Father God bless you and help me to be a good boy and worthy of you, goodby.
>
> Your Son
>
> P.S. This sounds foolish on looking over it but you touched me when you said always to stand by Thee in your letter.[105]

Elliott began this letter by acknowledging his father as the ultimate authority, and poured forth his unqualified praise at the same time he hid his frustrations for not living up to the standards of his idol. The game of competition was not for Elliott and he claimed he could not study with his brother simply because they were not at the same level. The tone of the letter grew increasingly heavier as Ellie's repressions wore thinner. Freud called the process of converting a feeling to its opposite reaction formation and it is this dynamic which fills the letter. Although he was soon to leave school because of a nervous breakdown, he said his life was "free of care."

The material concerning Theodore is the heart of the letter. Ted is a "noble boy" and he refuses to admit there are feelings of hostility or jealousy concerning his brother. "No, I love him," are the words he insists on convincing himself with as he converts the unacceptable emotion into its opposite. He was determined to consistently love his brother, even at the cost of internal dischord, and he believed he meant his words.

By the next decade, Elliott continued to make stringent emotional demands on himself. His personal diary of 1883 includes the following:

> When my worship for women began I cannot tell . . . or perhaps when the poor little mother turned to Connie on that night and called me her loving son and only comfort—maybe when as the years have gone by and I have seen the two sisters unselfishly and with only thought for us boys . . . [following phrase illegible] My darling Anna [his wife]—a child in years, a woman in experience and knowledge—a Christian in deed and fact . . . in beauty and grace of figure is only a shadowing of the perfect lovliness of . . . God's great goodness growing with the love of this dear woman . . . She seems so pure and high and ideal that in my roughness and unworthiness I do not know how I can be happy. . . . How can I who have been but a wanderer and self-amusing dilettante ever command the love from ever of so earnest and true a woman. . . . Dear old Brother Thee I envy and *love* you . . . [the following pages are ripped from the diary][106]

The next ten years held intense disillusionment for Elliott. Anna held high standards for the behavior of her husband, both socially and vocationally, and Elliott could not measure up. Hunting accidents increased in number, his life as a business man became inconsistent, and drinking became a problem. During 1889 he panicked and ran away to the South without contacting his family. Perhaps he remembered the comfort he derived when his father sent him to Texas, away from his achieving brother. Anna threatened divorce but agreed to stay married if Elliott would go to France for cure of his alcoholism. A court order turned the $175,000 estate to her. Anna's health declined and she refused until death to see her husband. Elliott soon disappeared and during 1893 died anonymously, living in drunken squalor with a mistress on West 102nd Street. His brother Theodore had long since given up on him and had continually urged Corinne to leave him be. He communicated to his sister Bamie, "But I do wish Corinne could get a little of my hard heart about Elliott; she can do, and ought to, nothing for him. He can't be helped and he must simply be let go on his own gait. He is now laid up from a serious fall; while drunk he drove into a lamp post and went out on his head. Poor fellow! If only he could have died instead of Anna!"[107]

Theodore's course continued to take an almost antithetical nature to Elliott's after the family's return from Europe during 1872. He scheduled intense activity with almost a compulsion and began a pattern of avoidance of introspection about which John Chamberlain has called philosophical irresponsibility. His revolt against his own bodily weaknesses had created an action which served as a drug; the result was a fear of reflection, the negative of spiritual courage.[108]

The young man's conscience was becoming as disciplined as his body. He lived the stringent Victorian morality of the times with greater consistency than most. For example, he read avidly the magazine *Our Young Folks* which was mainly composed of transparent moralistic stories supporting the view that women should be good and innocent, and moral virtues are always clear and simple. As late as 1913, Roosevelt would believe this "the very best magazine in the world."[109] His friend of pre-Harvard days, Frances Theodora Parsons, remarked that to some he was known as a prig because he violently disapproved of boys and girls who did not absolutely behave "under the moon" when not being watched.[110] His diaries would later be filled with incidents in which he was proud he had preserved his moral integrity. His view that sexual relations should be severely limited and mostly associated with procreation was later reflected by a disdain for bachelors, disapproval of families without many children if the finances and health of the parents were sufficient, and hatred of any sort of loose living, whether from diplomat or Bowery bum.

Theodore continued building his body with the fervor that he displayed in hunting, dissecting and stuffing. At sixteen, he recorded in his diary that he was five feet and eight inches in height with a thirty-four inch chest and twenty-six and one half inch waist. Putnam describes, "He gave the impression of a taut vitality and a will which had begun to transcend the slightness of his physique."[111] The diaries from this period are also filled with exact records of his defeats and victories in competitive sports.

Several years later, when Theodore left for Harvard, he was encouraged by his father to live up to all his potential. He was advised to take care of his morals, health and studies in that order and requested to send a copy of his schedule. His father gave him the following quotation, "... prepare the boy to take the father's place in the great battle of life."[112]

As the second half of his sophomore year came to pass, Roosevelt had good reason for confidence. He could look towards a family whose standards he was successfully meeting. Yet he was not made aware that his father was dying. A malignant fibrous tumor of the bowel had been growing rapidly and was located in such a way that the doctors could not operate. It was Bamie who did her best to protect her oldest brother. She had increasingly taken Mittie's place in doing household chores. It had been Bamie who had gone with Theodore to Harvard to establish a room. She made sure he received a second floor apartment to protect his considerably improved asthma from ground floor dampness. Theodore had been home Christmas of 1877, and knew his father's health was not good. He merely assumed he was overworked, and as befitting a man who "never does think of himself," in need of a rest.

Two months later, when his father finally died, Theodore, as the rest of the family, went into an initial period of numb shock. He could not get himself to write entries in his diary. Finally on February 12 he managed to say:

> He has just been buried. I shall never forget these terrible three days; the hideous suspense of the ride; the dull, inert sorrow, during which I felt as I had been stunned, or part of my life taken away; and the two moments of sharp, bitter agony when I kissed the dear, dead face and realized that he would never again on this earth speak to me or greet me with his loving smile, and when I heard the sound of the first clod dropping on the coffin holding the one I loved dearest on earth. He looked so calm and sweet. I feel that if it were not for the certainty, that as he himself has so often said, 'he is not dead but gone before,' I should almost perish. With the help of God I will try to lead the life as he would have wished.[113]

On one level, Theodore had already been meeting parental demands. As Putnam put it "During the Christmas vacation of 1877, the elder Theodore had told him that he never caused him a moment's pain, and that he was 'the dearest of children to him.' Theodore had returned affection with, 'I do not think there is a fellow in college who has a family that loves him as much as you do me, and I am *sure* that there is no one who has a father who is also his best and most intimate friend, as you are mine. I have kept the first letter you wrote me and shall do my best to deserve your trust.' "[114]

The shock of mourning was followed by an aching sorrow:

> Sometimes when I fully realize my loss I feel as though I should go wild—my joys he shared and in sharing them doubled them and soothed all the sorrows I ever had; every event in my life is bound up with him; he was as pure and unselfish as he was wise and good.[115]

Yet, accompanying this were intense feelings of inferiority by comparison:

> I often feel badly that such a wonderful man as Father should have a son of so little worth as I am . . . during services today I could not help recollecting sadly of how little use I am, or shall ever be in this world, not through lack of perseverance and good intentions but through sheer inability. I realize more and more every day that I am as much inferior to Father morally and mentally as physically.[116]

Theodore Roosevelt entered the stage of manhood with a stable constellation of psychic defenses against his oral rage. Unlike his brother Elliott, Theodore was able to construct a personality which integrated his father's demands to be "hard" and phallic with his own biting rage resulting from his mother's personality.

The death of Theodore Roosevelt, Sr. was concurrent with the entrance of his children into adulthood. The behavior of each during and after the traumatic event is emblematic of their means of coping: Corinne, his youngest daughter ,wrote her friend Edith Carow (later Theodore's second wife): "Oh Edith, it is the most frightful thing to see the person you love best in the world in terrible pain and not able to do a thing to alleviate it. . . . And Edie, this fearful suffering is really turning his hair gray and he had not a white hair before."[117] Besides close empathetic response to her father's suffering, there was concern with how her brothers and sister would respond to the disaster.

There was reason for worry about Elliott. Lash concludes that "the death of his father was not only a terrible sorrow but a disaster."[118] Elliott described how on February 9 he had brought his father ether and held him. Roosevelt, Sr. never said anything but "oh my" and repeatedly vomited. The suffering man grabbed his son in painful delirium and was only able to sleep after the doctor gave him chloroform. Elliott recounted the horror: "I felt so sick I stayed to smoke a cigar and after felt well and became myself." In his last moments, Roosevelt, Sr. gave the weaker of his sons a feminine name, the nickname Elliott would later give to his own daughter Eleanor: "As I lifted him once the dear feeble hands crept over the side of my face and I think he called me Nellie. . . . During his illness, he said, 'Nellie, when I am gone you must take my place in tenderness and care of your mother.' "[119]

Elliott spent the days after the funeral collecting a scrapbook as a final tribute to his father. The *Tribune* commented, "There is given to some men such a rare combination of thought and action that the two processes become almost identical; and when these are associated with high moral purpose, the results are a character which exceeds estimation." *Harper's Weekly* included, "The death of such a man is a great public loss, and the universal sincerity of sorrow among those who knew him shows that in the crucial hour the true test of manhood is felt to be that helpful, hopeful, bold and efficient service to his fellowmen which is the glory of Theodore Roosevelt's memory."[120]

In contrast, a short time after the funeral, Theodore was back at Harvard actively pursuing the course his father had directed for him. He continued a rigorous academic schedule of French, German, Rhetoric, Anglo-American Constitutional History, Themes, Comparative Anatomy, Physiology and Botany. "He asked questions, and uttered protests, his eyes gleaming from behind his spectacles. He said that the matter at issue had not been clearly presented."[121] Roosevelt later remarked on his beloved magazine *Our Young Folks* which "taught me more than any of my textbooks . . . the necessity of character as the chief factor in any man's success . . . for all the laws that the wit can devise will never make a man a worthy citizen unless he has self-reliance, energy, courage, and the power of insisting on his own rights and the sympathy that makes him regardful of the rights of others."[122]

The intensity of his expression of aggressiveness lay in other areas. Rough sports, hunting and physical exercise had great importance in his daily routine. He spent no less than three hours daily in the gym.[123] Anyone who keeps such unrelenting schedule does not feel right—emotionally and physically—when the exercise is reduced. Harvard would be no different from his earlier days in Dresden when his father sent him two presents of boxing gloves and a shotgun, and his son replied with letters gloating over the injuries he inflicted on opponents.[124] Thayer described his Harvard boxing: "When time was called after the first round his face was dashed with blood and he was much winded, but his spirit did not flag, and if there had been another round, he would have gone into it with undiminished determination."[125]

Freshman year set the precedent for his active schedule:

Rose at 7:15, went to Chapel at 7:45, breakfasted at 8:00, studied from 8:30-9:00, attended recitations from 9:00 to 12:00, studied from 1:30 to 2:30, attended another class 2:30-3:30, exercised from 3:30-6:00, had dinner at 6:00, studied from 7:00 to 8:30, visited and received the visits of friends, from 8:30 to 10:30 and at 11:00 went to bed.[126]

Within the year of 1876, it is estimated that he traveled over a thousand miles in the Maine wilderness—330 by wagon, 210 by canoe, and 540 by foot.[127]

Roosevelt was not a youth with whom to trifle. On one occasion he was bothered by an annoying dog. He warned its owner that if it approached him again, he would kill it. Later, the dog approached and Roosevelt took out his revolver and shot it dead.[128]

During October of 1878, Roosevelt first saw the woman he would take as his wife. In his memorial after her premature death, he would write, "I loved her as soon as I saw her sweet, fair young face."[129] It is impossible to avoid comparison to Roosevelt's mother. Roosevelt nicknamed her "Sunshine" which precisely described her "sweet, pure and innocent character."[130] Just like his mother, Alice was shy but warm-hearted, overly protected, dependent on males and gay in spirit. Roosevelt's attitude towards her was similar to his attitude towards his mother. She was a "child-wife." In the first three months after he met Alice he applied the word "sweet" to her thirty-one times and "pretty" thirty times in his diary.[131] All description is related to sunlight, bright-ness, and purity. Roosevelt must have consciously recognized the simi-larities of his love for Alice with his love for his mother when he wrote, "Motherling, you mustn't feel melancholy, sweet motherling: I shall only love you all the more."[132] He also reflected the view of the ma-ternal wife in the comment, "She is so pure and holy that it seems al-most a profanation to touch her."[133] He was reassured that his own stringent "purity" was of such consistency that he could tell her every-thing he had ever done, which was very important to him.[134]

Roosevelt illustrated his sensitivity to feminine rejection. During the initial stages of their relationship he told a friend, "See that girl? I am going to marry her. She won't have me but I am going to have her."[135] When he was not immediately given a guarantee of engagement, he plunged into the depths of despair. One evening he simply disappeared in the woods in a deep gloom. Friends telegraphed his home so that Theodore might be persuaded to return; a cousin succeeded in getting him back.

He had constant fear that some one would run off with Alice and even ordered a pair of French dueling pistols with which to meet the occasion. He wrote in his diary after her acceptance of marriage October 27, 1880: "I am so happy that I dare not trust my happiness. How she, so pure and sweet and beautiful can think of marrying me I cannot un-derstand, but I praise God it is so."[136]

Another major decision concerning his future relates to early experi-ences. His academic interests had changed soon after his father's death; he moved away from the natural sciences and towards politics and law. He stopped taking field notes and severed connections with the Harvard Natural History Society. His two interests were in the very areas from which Theodore Roosevelt, Sr. had been blocked. First, because of his Southern wife, the elder Roosevelt did not fight in the Civil War. His son's aggressive and martial interests were manifested in the choice of a research project on the War of 1812. Secondly, young Roosevelt turned to law. With his older sister's encouragement, he spoke with Joseph Choate, a lawyer and member of the group that, years earlier, had de-termined to break the Tweed Ring's hold over New York. The Ring was responsible for the blocking of Roosevelt, Sr. from a political post he desired.

Roosevelt graduated Harvard with a distinguished record which was marked by his personality. Exercise was integrated with aggressive intellectuality. Forward-reaching ambition was guarded in the recesses of his mind, manifested only by an occasional slip as when he went to see the President of the University and said, "Mr. Eliot, I am President Roosevelt."[137]

Soon after graduation, Roosevelt determined to go on a hunting trip in the West with his brother Elliott. One Dr. Dudley Sargeant falsely diagnosed a weak heart during this period and with no knowledge of the mistake, Roosevelt decided he would rather die than lead a sedentary life. Just as the infant ceaselessly explored the world of the playpen, just as the adolescent took gun and knife in hand to find game in Egypt, the existence of an American wilderness was an overwhelming temptation as a means of expressing aggressive feelings. The brothers' differences were most evident during this trip: disciplined Spartan versus poetic Epicurean. Theodore wrote Corinne:

> As soon as we got here he took some ale to get the dust out of his throat; then a milkpunch because he was thirsty, a mint julep because it was hot; a brandy smash to leap the cold out of his stomach, and then sherry and bitters to give him an appetite. He took a very simple dinner—soup, fish, salmi de grouse, sweetbread, mutton, venison, corn, macaroni, various vegetables, some puddings and pies, together with beer, later claret and in the evening shanigaff. I confined myself to roast beef and potatoes; when I took a second help he marveled at my appetite—and at bed he wondered why in thunders he felt 'stuffy' and I didn't. . . . The good living also reached his brain, and he tried to lure me into a discussion about the intellectual development of the Hindoos, coupled with some rather discursive, logical digressions about the Infinity and the Infinite, the Sunday school system and the planet Mars—together with some irrelevant remarks about Texan 'Jack Rabbits' which are apparently about as large as good sized cows...[138]

Roosevelt returned to law studies and work on publishing his study of the naval war of 1812. The chief incompetent of his *Naval War of 1812* was Thomas Jefferson.[139] Here was an individual in many ways the opposite of the twenty-two year old historian and the virtues he expounded. Jefferson lacked preparedness, a subject which would obsess Roosevelt's political ideology. He only sponsored the construction of small boats which held few guns. Jefferson was primarily a doctrinaire philosopher while Roosevelt was a man for whom action took priority over theory. Jefferson belonged to the Enlightenment while Roosevelt's psychology was of the Industrial Revolution. Things must work and herald progress. Also important, Jefferson lacked in the martial qualities.

After a delayed honeymoon during which Roosevelt climbed a mountain to a height of 14,000 feet, Roosevelt was approached by Joseph

Murray who was anxious to infuse the State Legislature with names of families held in high public esteem. Roosevelt won his first election but encountered some condescension from seasoned politicians. John McManus planned a practical joke for the young upstart. He claimed he would toss him up in a blanket. Roosevelt heard of the plan and approached him, "By God, McManus, I understand that you are going to toss me in a blanket. If you try anything like that, I'll kick you, I'll bite you, I'll do anything to you . . . you better let me alone."[140] The strength of the reply was enough to stave off the attack. He soon drew respect for his aggressive measures to stop corruption and end domination by vested financial interests.

The ideology and issue of Roosevelt's initiation into politics is not as important for understanding his character as a key series of incidents which occurred during this period. During the fall of 1883, Roosevelt came upon the notion that nothing would be better than killing a large bison buffalo. His desire soon grew to obsessional proportions and he organized an expedition to the Dakotas. Joe Ferris, the man he chose to be his guide, originally hailed from New Brunswick and came to the Dakotas with his brother. He brought a puritanical sense of morality, frugality, and the ability to work with sustained effort.[141] Gregor and Lincoln Lang, whom Roosevelt later employed, were rugged Scotch immigrants.

As Roosevelt and his guide Ferris began the hunt, a heavy rain began. Putnam suggests, "One would have thought that after a forty-five mile ride the previous day and a talk past midnight, superimposed upon his earlier indisposition, his long rail trip West, and the late arrival at the Pyramid Hotel, Roosevelt would have welcomed an excuse for a day's rest. Ferris advised it. . . ."[142] This was not in the man's psychology. The rain had given the rock a greasy, slithering and highly dangerous quality. The conditions meant poor visibility and for Roosevelt, steamy glasses. Hunts under such conditions were generally considered impossible. But Roosevelt was determined to have a buffalo, and, with the aid of a generous salary, convinced Ferris.

When Ferris and Roosevelt returned that evening, they were splattered with mud and without buffalo. The pattern continued for five days. On September 14, Roosevelt stated he would not return empty handed. The men were out three days when tracks were sighted. Roosevelt and Ferris held their horses and approached on hands and feet. Unfortunately, Roosevelt stumbled on a cactus bed and filled his hands with the needles. He took a shot, missed and was forced to pursue. The sun was setting but Roosevelt insisted on charging on horseback. Roosevelt's horse bucked and the stock of his firing rifle gashed his forehead open; then the bison charged. Roosevelt was badly shaken and the bison escaped. Putnam relates the events of that evening:

No sooner had they fallen asleep again than it began to rain, and they were obliged to spend the rest of the night cowering and shivering under wet blankets. Roosevelt, lying in bed with a cut over his eye and his hands sore from the cactus spines, with nothing in his stomach but a hard biscuit, exhausted yet unable to sleep for the cold and rain, now made a remark . . . Ferris heard Roosevelt mutter into his blankets, "By Godfrey but this is fun!"[143]

The next raining day, Roosevelt insisted on continuing despite numb fingers and a close call with quicksand. He was also thrown ten feet from his horse and hurt his head. After a rest at the Lang Ranch, Roose-

amazed to watch the hunter go into an orgy of incomprehensible chants as he danced about the carcass. Ferris' dismay was soon assuaged by the presentation of a hundred dollar bill. Roosevelt later wrote, "The flesh of the bull tasted uncommonly good. . . ."[144]

It is difficult to ascribe a motive for the above without reference to the family constellation in which Roosevelt was formed. Roosevelt had consistently repressed all possible expression of hostility towards his mother and father, who had made such conflicting demands on him. He thought most often at the conscious level of his father, who had so frequently performed maternal-paternal functions.

The following is characteristic of Roosevelt's statements concerning his father: "I often feel badly that such a wonderful man as Father should have a son of so little worth as I am," or "Oh, how unworthy I am of such a father. . . ." He paid special attention to the verse of the Bible, "But that the world may know that I love the Father: and as the Father gave commandment, even so I do." Roosevelt's political imagery was fraught with such phrases as, "We must not prove false to the fathers from whose loins we sprang, and to their fathers, the stern men who dared greatly and risked all things that freedom should hold aloft an undimmed torch in this wide land. . . . Let us show ourselves to be worthy to be their sons." Examples are frequent. "My father combined strength and courage, with tenderness and unselfishness," "I was fortunate in having a father whom I have always been able to regard as an ideal man . . . he really did combine strength, courage, will and energy of the strongest man with *the tenderness, cleanliness, and purity of a woman.*" (Italics added) "He was one of the most valiant people I have ever met." "My father was the best man I ever knew." Roosevelt also stated that his father was the only man of whom he was ever afraid.[145]

Such attitudes bear examination for several reasons. A man's love for his father is more complex than mere adoration. Along with admiration and love goes the aspect of questioning certain aspects of the paternal model, and periods of rage at his power to restrict freedom. Development of personal autonomy involves conflict with the wielder of power. The counterpart of any love is therefore ambivalence.[146] Yet these feelings never appear to have been brought to consciousness in the case of Roosevelt. Instead, they were repressed. The inevitable guilt over these feelings was also unresolved. When aggression is not released, it often takes bizarre and symbolic forms.[147] Norman O. Brown's words have relevance:

> Killing is always the father (oedipal). In the wisdom of primitive war, the enemy blood is kindred blood . . . head hunting. An enemy must be killed for a boy to grow up; a head must fall. The boy kills the father in the person of an enemy. And the slain enemy becomes his guardian spirit; the enemy head (superego) presides over the house .. the brothers overcame the father and all partook of his body.[148]

One walks into the Roosevelt home at Sagamore Hill and is presented with a display of big game heads decorating the walls of his house, so vibrant with the forces of nature. Aggression and rage towards parents in the integrative form of the father were never recognized, but remained at this primitive level. He used his phallic aggressiveness to overcome and murder the father, but only at the symbolic level. Even at that level the severed head continued to stare from the walls of his house.[149]

Theodore Roosevelt returned from the primitive West to a second term in the New York State Legislature. A colleague observed that he was "full of life and happiness."[150] Roosevelt planned to go home shortly after he completed work on a bill concerning New York aldermen, but a telegram came telling him his wife was ill. He returned immediately. The trip must have been agonizing as Roosevelt's coach proceeded through thick fog at a snail's pace. It seemed that the very atmosphere was responding to Roosevelt's impending misfortune. His biographer Carleton Putnam observed the cruel irony of a *New York Times* editorial of the day which included, "It is suicidal weather. Life does not seem worth living to a sensitive person easily influenced by atmospheric conditions. There is something comfortless and unhappy in the raw and chilly air, something suggestive of death and decay in the dampness that fills the mind."[151]

Elliott met him at the door and said, "There is a curse on this house! Mother is dying and Alice is dying, too."[152] His wife Alice had an advanced case of Bright's disease and was barely able to recognize him. Just before three o'clock, his mother succumbed to typhoid fever. Roosevelt returned to his dying wife and she passed away in his arms two o'clock the next day. Roosevelt's diaries contained the comment that "the light had gone from his life forever," and except for a memorial, he would never speak of his first wife again.[153]

Roosevelt held true to pattern. Hyperaggressiveness, which had been the primal means of coping with maternal abandonment, was once again his solution to emotional crises. He returned to Albany three days after the funeral and was in his seat in the Assembly the following morning. His activity was determined and frenetic. He was soon out West again and engaged in a series of adventures which included a near duel with a French nobleman, catching thieves with a rifle, knocking a bully unconscious in a barroom brawl as well as intense literary activity, including work on a biography of Thomas Hart Benton. He admired Benton's virile expansionism and self-discipline.[154] He responded to criticism of Benton's imperialistic sympathies with, "It was not written to please those political and literary hermaphrodites, the Mugwumps."[155]

Roosevelt's make-up was too active to allow mourning. Within two years, he had remarried to his childhood friend, Edith Carow. His pre-presidential career included posts as United States Civil Service Commissioner (1889-95), President of the Police Commission of the City of New York (1895-97), Assistant Secretary of the Navy (1897-98), and a brief period as Governor of New York (1899). His books included *The Wilderness Hunter, The Winning of the West* (the story of the conquering of a primitive land and people by a superior and more powerful civilization), and *Governor Morris of New York*.[156] He wrote, "The most ultimately righteous of all wars is a war with savages."[157] The settlers knew the Indian for what he was, "Filthy, cruel, lecherous, and faithless."[158]

Before he achieved the Presidency, Theodore had five children by Edith. Although he loved children and could be a joyous playmate, he was a stern father. He stated, "I would rather one of them should die than to have to grow up weaklings."[159] On one occasion his two young sons appeared before him and said, "Father, we have consulted together as to which one of us must die, and we have decided that it shall be the baby."[160]

Ted, his oldest boy, suffered the most. One day his wife would reminisce how Ted was taught to swim by being dunked in water over his head by an overzealous father who did not heed his wife's warnings. "They were taught that sickness is always a shame and is often a crime.[161] Hermann Hagedorn wrote, "But Theodore, remembering his own struggle for health and vigor, and grateful to his own father for resisting temptation to coddle him under the affliction of his own boyhood asthma, brushed aside her warning convinced that he knew best what a boy needed to become a man."[162] Some of the Spartan rubbed off on Edith, and when Ted was injured on one occasion, she bravely remarked, "Theodore, I wish you'd do your bleeding in the bathroom, you're spoiling every rug in the house."[163]

But Ted's infirmities soon became a real problem. Edith wrote Anna Roosevelt, "Ted is such a piece of quicksilver that I am in constant anxiety about his life and limb. Theodore thought his leg was broken the other day and declares he will never live to grow up."[164] He had mysterious headaches, as his uncle Elliott had experienced fainting spells. Specialists at Johns Hopkins University could find nothing organically wrong and concluded the trouble was emotional.[165] When the elder Roosevelt went off to war for an extended period, his health greatly improved.

One doctor had bluntly written to Roosevelt that his son had experienced a nervous breakdown, and that the father was the cause. With surprising insight, Roosevelt responded to the doctor, "I shall give plain proof of great weakness of character by reading your letter to Mrs. Roosevelt who is now well enough to feel the emotions of triumph. Hereafter I shall never press Ted either in body or mind. The fact is that the fellow, who is particularly dear to me, had bidden fair to be all the things I would like to have been but wasn't, and it has been a great temptation to push him."[166]

His eldest daughter Alice had her own emotional conflicts. During an interview with the *New York Times* on her ninetieth birthday, she gazed at an old picture of herself and brother and in almost a girlish tone said she liked everything but physical contact with people: "No one must ever touch me. I don't want to be touched. That's probably some psycho thing that I don't understand."[167]

Roosevelt continued to be an aggressive politician in his various roles. The *Philadelphia Record* recognized him as a central force on the Civil Service Commission:

> His colleagues were quiet men, who supported him to a considerable extent, but he did the fighting in the newspapers, before Congress and everywhere else, and of course bore the brunt of the subsequent attack which by and by came largely to be personal to himself, as he became recognized as the leading spirit on the Commission.[168]

As Police Commissioner of New York, Roosevelt was similarly active. He wrote his sister Anna, "Twice I have spent the night in patrolling New York on my own account, to see exactly what the men are doing."[169] It was not unusual for him to dine at someone's home, pull his coat over his person and then go prowling for policemen who might not be doing their duty. He was known to chase a lazy patrolman, bring him to the station, eat a hearty breakfast, catch a little sleep and be ready for work the next day. Roosevelt was not amused when a reporter disguised himself with glasses and chattering false teeth and went about scaring policemen with great success. Corinne later observed, "Any recreant policeman would faint if he suddenly came face to face with a set of false teeth in a shop window."[170] His bark was not without bite.

Roosevelt's friend, Henry Cabot Lodge, was instrumental in gaining
Roosevelt the Assistant Secretaryship of the Navy. McKinley's one fear
was that Roosevelt would have preconceived ideas about the international situation which might hamper his own pacific inclinations. At the
time that Lodge reassured the President with respect to Roosevelt's
militarism, Roosevelt was speaking of conquering Canada as retribution
for England's financial role in Venezuela: "Personally, I hope the fight
will come soon."[171]

Preparedness became Roosevelt's political ideology as it had been
his personal one. He built his own body to meet the pressures of the
surrounding world. He applied discipline to the arduous task of muscu-
lar development in the gym, boxing ring, and the West. Roosevelt's attitude supports the historians who question the motives behind the
Spanish-American War.[172] Sympathy for the Cubans was less important
than Roosevelt's private emotions. As he himself stated, "I do feel that
it would be everything for us to take firm action on behalf of the
wretched Cubans. It would be a splendid thing for the Navy, too."[173]

The emphasis was on national strength produced by conscious effort. "If . . . we fail to provide plenty of ships of the very best type . . .
we run the risk of causing the nation to suffer some disaster which
would warp and stunt our whole national life. . ."[174] He couched virtues
of martial spirit in terms of character, "for from the standpoint of the
nation as of the individual, it is character that is the one vital possession."[175] A country had to train itself to expand its power and prestige
in the world. If it failed to do this, then, as Roosevelt's biographer
Harbaugh observed, "At the least it would fail to fulfill its potential, of
which there was no greater failing for the individual or nation in Roosevelt's value system."[176]

By November of 1897, months before the Maine was destroyed,
Roosevelt's mind was made up:

> In the next place to speak with a frankness which our timid
> friends would call brutal, I would regard a war with Spain from
> two standpoints: first, the advisability on the grounds both of
> humanity and self-interest of interfering on behalf of the Cubans,
> and of taking one more step toward the complete freeing of
> America from European domination; second, the benefit done
> our people by giving something which isn't material gain, and es-
> pecially the benefit done our military forces by trying both the
> Navy and Army in actual practice. I should be very sorry not to
> see us make the experiment of trying to land, and therefore feed
> and clothe, an expeditionary force, if only for the sake of learn-
> ing from our own blunders. I should hope that the force would
> have some fighting to do; it would be a great lesson, and we would
> profit much by it.[177]

The war would be America's puberty rite, its maiden big game expedition, an initiation into the community of nations with Roosevelt at the helm. As Roosevelt had once told himself, the time had come for America to turn her energies outwards.

Roosevelt later declared he would have left his wife's deathbed to answer the call of war.[178] He wrote, "It is my chance to cut my little notch in the stick that stands as a measuring rod in every family."[179]

Roosevelt's heroics in Cuba illustrate a belief in his own invincibility. One man was killed as he "stood beside a tree with me." During one battle he yelled at his men who knelt behind trees, "Are you afraid to rise when I am on horseback!"[180] On his most famous charge, he proceeded up a hill with only four men behind him before the others could join in; a bright polka dot handkerchief attached to his hat dared the bullets to strike. His horse was shot and a bullet knicked his elbow, but he was one of the first to the top of the hill and leveled a Spaniard with his revolver.[181] During that one battle alone, 86 of the 490 Rough Riders were killed or wounded. Although by the end of the War over half his men had been killed, wounded or sick, Roosevelt was never incapacitated. He once told a friend he determined that if shot but not killed he would proceed with a charge regardless.[182] He calmly declared that the odds were three to one against a wound being fatal[183] and added, "I am quite content to go now and to leave to my children at least an honorable name."[184] Harbaugh stated, "In a desecration of the human spirit that will forever bar him from the immortality of Jefferson, Lincoln, and Wilson, he invited post-battle visitors to 'look at those damned Spanish dead.' "[185]

Roosevelt returned a hero. His exploits as well as favorable political maneuver allowed him to gain the Governorship of New York. A short time later, his friends gained him the Vice-Presidential nomination in spite of his lack of enthusiasm for the passive post.

The Presidency was important to Theodore Roosevelt and in this position he thrived. In a sense, it represented the ultimate accomplishment. Its importance to him was betrayed earlier when Lincoln Steffens and Jacob Riis asked if he aspired to the position. Stefens related:

> . . . entering in, Riis did ask him to settle our dispute. Was he working towards the presidency? The effect was frightening. TR leaped to his feet, ran around his desk, and fists clenched, teeth bared, he seemed about to strike or throttle Riis, who cowered away, amazed. "Don't you dare ask me that," TR yelled at Riis. "Don't you dare put such ideas into my head. No friend of mine would ever say a thing like that, you, you.". . . he backed away, came up again to Riis, and put his arm on his shoulder. Then he beckoned me close and in an awed tone of voice explained: "Never, never must you ever either of you remind a man at work

in a political job that he may be President. He loses his nerve, he
can't do his work; he gives up the very traits that are making him
a possibility. . . . But if I ever get to thinking of what it might
lead to," he stopped, held us off, looked into our faces with his
face screwed up into a knot and with lowered voice he said
slowly: "I must be wanting to be President. . . . But I won't let
myself think of it. . . . Go away now, and don't you ever mention
the—don't you ever mention that to me again.[186]

Roosevelt brought to America a true era of phallic politics. During
one Army-Navy football game Roosevelt led his cabinet as he jogged
across the field. Bigness characterized Roosevelt's definition of government. Large organizational structures were acceptable as long as they
were controlled. When Justice Holmes voted against one of Roosevelt's
views of the extension of the power of government, he said, "I could
carve out of a banana a judge with more backbone than that."[187] Virility
was a prime virtue. He was disturbed by the effeminacy of men such as
Henry Adams and Henry James. During 1905, he wrote Lodge of
Adams' *Democracy* (published anonymously in 1880) "The other day
I was reading *Democracy,* that novel which made great furor about
twenty-five years ago. It was written by Godken, perhaps with assistance
from Mrs. Henry Adams. It has a superficial rotten cleverness, but it
was essentially false, essentially mean and base, and it is amusing to
read. . ."[188]

Roosevelt determined to set the virile example. His hunting did not
diminish in intensity. He wrote from Texas during 1901:

Soon we saw the lion in a tree top, with two of the dogs so high
up among the branches that he was striking at them. He was more
afraid of us than of the dogs, and as soon as he saw us he took a
great flying leap and was off, the pack close behind. In a few
hundred yards they had him up another tree. Here I could have
shot him (Tony climbed almost up to him and then fell twenty
feet out of the tree), but waited for Stearst to get a photo, and he
jumped again. This time, after a couple of hundred yards the dogs
caught him, and a great fight followed. They could have killed
him by themselves, but he clawed four of them, and for fear he
might kill one I ran in and stabbed him behind the shoulder,
thrusting the knife you loaned me right into his heart. I have always wished to kill a cougar as I did this one, with dogs and
a knife.[189]

In a letter to his son Kermit, sent from the White House in 1905, he
wrote the following:

I still box with Grant who became champion middle weight
wrestler of the United States. . . . So far it is evident that the jiu

jitsu man could handle the ordinary wrestler. . . . With a little practice in the art I am sure one of our big wrestlers or boxers would be able to kill any of those Japanese, who though very good men for their inches and pounds, are altogether too small to hold their own against big, powerful, quick men who are well trained.[190]

Roosevelt issued a directive that each officer in the service should be able to ride one hundred miles in three days. To answer the grumbling the edict evoked, he rode the full one hundred miles, in the middle of winter, in one day.[191]

It is likely Roosevelt was sincere when he wrote in his autobiography, "In my judgement the most important service that I rendered to peace was the voyage of the battle fleet around the world."[192] Just as he wanted to show people he could ride fifty miles in less than a day or was tough enough to hunt in the wilds, his fleet would display to the world that America could do something the European powers doubted possible. It was strictly a Roosevelt affair. He wrote, "I determined on the move without consulting the cabinet, precisely as I took Panama without consulting the cabinet. A council of war never fights, and in a crisis the duty of a leader is to lead and not take refuge behind the generally timid wisdom of a multitude of counselors."[193] This is not to deny what are thought by many to be Roosevelt's accomplishments, the Peace of Portsmouth, conservation, food and drug laws and anti-trust legislation, but only to illustrate areas in which interaction of personality and policy is especially evident.

After he had left the Presidency, having no release for his aggressiveness in political action and the extension of American government and military power, Roosevelt decided to organize a major expedition in Africa. John Morton Blum remarked, "It seemed as if Roosevelt actively sought relief through his own death by a charging lion."[194] Obserivng Roosevelt's reaction to killing game, Edward Wagenknecht questioned Roosevelt's expressed motive that he was pursuing only scientific information. Roosevelt himself reminisced, "When I killed a white goat with Jack Willis, the yell of delight I let loose could be heard for two miles in any country." He had rubbed his hands together and danced with joy.[195] During 1909, Roosevelt observed, "Two days ago I saw one of the finest sights anyone can see: the Manchi warriers killed a lion with their spears, two of them being mauled." Wagenknecht remarked, "I confess [being] unable to explain how a man who loved animals as Roosevelt did could still enjoy killing them."[196]

Roosevelt admitted his fascination with the process of death. He remembered in his autobiography that his first interest in naturalism was associated with a dead animal:

I remember dramatically the first day that I started upon my career as a zoologist. I was walking up Broadway and as I passed the market to which I was sometimes sent to get strawberries, I suddenly saw a dead seal laid out on a slab of wood. That seal filled me with every possible feeling of romance and adventure. I asked where it was killed, and was informed in the harbor.[197]

Even in childhood, the line between curiosity and the venting of personal aggression had been thin. In his diary at age nine, Theodore wrote of taking down bird nests with sticks.[198]

According to Gardner, Roosevelt can be credited with a total of 216 big game animals killed during the African expedition among which were nine lions and thirteen rhinos. In a scene reminiscent of his desire to get a buffalo during the 1880's, he now wanted a lion, the king of the jungle. He told a friend, "If only I can get my lion, I shall be happy, even if he is small—but I hope he will have a mane!"[199]

Reading the personal pocket diary which Roosevelt kept while on his African trip is somewhat like reading a score card. The important aspect to the keeper of the diary is the number of animals killed. Roosevelt describes with perfect neutrality an instance of how he watched a friend take pictures of a panting animal until Roosevelt took out a revolver and killed it.[200] Many entries in the diary of 1909 include detailed information on the victims of the hunt—height, weight, distance shot from, type of animal, etc. Also included are sketches of the animals, complete with pencil marks indicating where the animals had been hit. During one period, Roosevelt alone averaged four big game animals a day for many weeks. On November 17, he personally killed seven giraffes.[201]

The timing of the killing is suggestive that it was primarily the expression of aggressive drives. There were several hiatuses in killing due to weather or travel. After the rest, Roosevelt used more bullets to kill each animal. On May 16, after such a rest, he killed a rhino with six shots, yet had used at most three to kill the same type of animal during more active periods.[202] Decreased accuracy of shooting due to lack of practice during inactive periods may partially explain the phenomenon, yet the fact remains, Roosevelt chose the hunt as his principal activity after the Presidency. The big stick had turned into a big gun.

The last major events in Roosevelt's life were associated with war. He predictably became the major American spokesman for early entry into the World War. The article, "Two Sides of Americanism" was written in an emotional single draft with few pencilled corrections. He wrote, "There is no place for fifty-fifty Americanism in the United States. He who is not with us, absolutely and without reserve of any kind is against us, and should be treated as an alien enemy."[203]

Roosevelt took the loss of his youngest boy in the war with intense melancholic grief. For the first time in his life, the glint went from his eyes, and the years of abuse of his body began to take their toll. He was found crying bitterly in the corner of his home in Sagamore Hill. He wrote, again with unusual self-knowledge, "It is a very sad thing to see the young die when the old who are doing nothing as I am doing nothing are left alive. . . . To feel that one has inspired a boy to conduct that has resulted in his death has a pretty serious side for a father—."[204] Only during the final hours did he know his battle had been fought and the world must be left to younger men. What remained was the calm after a great storm. The body was beyond pain and had reached tranquility. The Colonel turned to Edith and said, "I wonder if you will ever know how I love Sagamore Hill." For one of the rare times of his life, he gave in and let his kindly valet, James Amos, lift him into bed. He then requested that the light be turned out and died in his sleep a little after four that morning.

Personal tragedy looms as the product of the realities of his mind and the fateful circumstances he encountered. For Roosevelt's resolution of his primal conflicts was embodied in political roles of limited duration or personal aggressiveness which was ultimately destructive. What was left was a despair as profound and as penetrating as the wail of a newborn babe denied the comforts of sustenance and love.

It is difficult to recapture the intensity of the relationship between Theodore Roosevelt and his contemporaries. As early as 1898, *McClures Magazine* ran a piece which emphasized that ". . . Mr. Roosevelt was the most hated as well as most loved man in New York."[205] Another said, "Few presidents produced more contradictory attitudes and conflicting judgements among his fellows than Theodore Roosevelt. The man simply inspired strong words."[206]

A man who reached so deeply into the interior of his epoch touched the complexities and diversities of the people while at the same time personifying their basic cultural unity. What was consistent to all who wrote of him was intensity and the feeling that TR was deep inside of everyone.

A starting point for recapturing the timbre of the relationship is Roosevelt's death, which catalyzed reflection. People were startled. He was not an old man, and many felt that "Great Heart died in the midst of his pilgrimage." America felt a void. Robert Gordon Anderson composed the following:

Roosevelt is dead. Why should that line
Strike at my ear, as if told
The death of some close kin of mine,
Father or brother, friend of old?

Robert Jay Chapman added:

> Life seems belittled when a great man dies;
> The age is cheapened and time's furnishings
> Stare like the trappings of an empty stage.
> Ring down the curtain! We must pause, go home
> And let the plot of the world reshape itself
> To comprehensive form. Roosevelt is dead![207]

So burst forth the flood of emotions. It was as if a close relative of the nation's had died. His friend, Henry Cabot Lodge, attempted to address the Senate, but his voice quavered and his body began to shake. He was forced to sit down without speaking his piece.[208] Harry Simpson said, "It comes too close to my heart to make a statement. It is the most irreparable loss that could have come to the country.[209] William White added, "Not since the death of my father has death stabbed me so poignantly ... I have never known another person so great nor another man so dear."[210]

People generally expressed his impact in terms of energy. An English doctor related that ordinarily he felt some of his vital force go out of him each time he treated a patient. After treating Roosevelt, however, for the first time in his life he was invigorated: it seemed as if "some kind of vital energy had passed from him into me instead of me into him!"[211] A naturalist who was with him during one of the big game hunts was surprised that "the fact that the Colonel was with us gave us energy to do things we couldn't possibly have done otherwise."[212]

Roosevelt's presence was not noticed or merely felt, it was experienced. One comment of a visitor to the White House during Roosevelt's presidency is typical: "His personality so crowds the room that the walls are thin and threaten to burst outward. . . . you go to the White House—you shake hands with Roosevelt and hear him talk—and then go home to wring the personality out of your clothes."[213] William Allen White felt an inspiring force:

> I went home from our first casual meeting. . . . I was afire with the splendor of the personality I had met and walked up and down our little bedroom at the Normandy trying to impart to her [his wife] some of the marvel that I saw in that young man. . . . I have never known a man as he, and shall never again. He overcame me. And in the hour or two we spent together, he poured into my heart such visions, such ideals, such hopes, such a new attitude towards life and patriotism and meaning of things, as I had never dreamed men had.[214]

Even Woodrow Wilson, political foe and personally repulsed by his character, found that "I couldn't resist the man"[215] when Roosevelt visited him at the White House. One reporter from an anti-Roosevelt newspaper complained that he couldn't keep hating him if he got within twenty feet of the man, which was very upsetting since his stories were being ruined.[216] Another said, "You had to hate the Colonel a great deal to keep from loving him."[217]

The concept of transference of energy is vital. One remarked:

> . . . one never gets away from Mr. Roosevelt's personality. It sticks by me, so when he comes into a room and stands as he always does for one second before doing something characteristic, he electrifies the company and gives one just the sensations which a pointer does when he first quivers and takes a stand on quail. No matter how worn out and tired out might be, suddenly to see a pointer whirl and come to stand, electrifies me instantly so nothing will do unless it be to see the President enter a room.[218]

Woodbury Kane was a polished Harvard man, the pinnacle of Eastern polish and conformity to his elitist class. He knew Roosevelt when they were both students. Kane was known as independent, felt admiration or closeness to few, and had a distinct distaste for Roosevelt. Roosevelt was upper crust but he somehow went beyond the confines of his own class and this put Kane off; a young Harvard man and member of the Porcellian Club should be well mannered and refined, and should arrange his day with the expected proportion of work, fashionable leisure, and sport. Roosevelt was out of line and even had the audacity to run through Harvard yard instead of proceeding at the expected steady walk.

Yet even Kane came under Roosevelt's spell over ten years later when he became a member of the Rough Riders. He had come face to face with Roosevelt's full force of power. The following transpired a few years after the War when Roosevelt received an honorary degree at Harvard. Owen Wister confronted Kane, "When we were in college, you didn't seem to like him much. How do you feel now?" Kane immediately countered, "If I were crossing the Brooklyn Bridge and he ordered me to jump over, I'd do it without asking why." The President, who was walking just in front of the two men said, "What are you fellows dangling behind for? Come alongside." Wister had time to ask Kane before they reached the President, "Complete surrender?" "Absolutely, old man."[219]

At the opposite end of the social spectrum, Roosevelt's servants felt similarly. James E. Amos, who wrote *TR: Hero to his Valet*, confessed there was nothing about the man to which he did not feel drawn.[220] A White House servant testified, "There he is . . . I don't know what there is about that man which makes me feel so. I have seen a good many presidents come and go in this old house, and I like them all . . . but I declare I feel as if I could go twice as far and twice as quick whenever he asks me to, and do it twice as gladly."[221]

Americans were never a people to fall under the spell of mass hypnotism. The society is too pluralistic and its leaders too accessible. But Roosevelt came very close.

"Why I was on my feet before I knew it," was a common reaction when Roosevelt was getting on the Platform to speak. "There's just a kind of magnetism you cannot resist when you are in his presence."[222] One observer was puzzled and perhaps a little irritated by the intensity of Roosevelt's impact when speaking. He realized TR had not made a good speech, but to the crowd, it did not matter.[223] One afternoon, there seemed a competition between Roosevelt's howling voice and a booming and drenching thunderstorm in Oyster Bay. He was the victor; although everyone was drenched the storm stopped before TR was finished, and no one had left.[224]

Lincoln Steffens made an observation about Roosevelt. He told him directly:

"I—I don't know, but I have known you for a long time, and my impression is that you don't think things out in your mind but in somewhere else in your nervous systen—and form your conclusions, say, in your hips."

"Do you know that is true," Roosevelt responded. "I do think down—down there somewhere."[225]

One man summarized that his force was "an inexhaustible ardor that expressed itself in the love of life. . . . Men felt it in him as they felt in their first love, or the birth of a first child, or the first challenge of death, and went from his presence with a sense that their lips had been touched with burning coal and they had been capable of doing what they had not dreamed they could."[226] One man just said, "I have seen Niagara and I have seen Roosevelt.[227]

Such was the chemistry between the man and the times; a storehouse of potential energy released in full force upon contact of the two elements. But such force of interaction does not appear out of a vacuum and is dependent on both the man and the age for its power. Its creation was a process which can only be approached by confronting didirectly the most basic forces which molded each.

Washington McCarthy composed a eulogy of Andrew Jackson which described a great man in history, "He, who embodies in its greatest fulness, the spirit of such an age . . . received the admiration of his contemporaries . . . And why? Because they see in him their own image. Because, in him is concentrated the spirit that has burned in their own bosoms. Because in him exists in bodily form . . . the spirit that gives them life and motion. . . ."[228] Another has said, "Successful public men are not merely themselves. They are records and graphs of the activities and aspirations of their own day."[229]

In a sense, such a man is as "inside" a period as it is possible to go.

Sidney Hook wrote he is an "expressive symbol and instrument of social and historical forces."[230] Erik Erikson uses the term historical actuality.[231] In this case, an individual's development coincides with the
development of the community so that there is a resonance between
them. Erikson continues, "A true leader . . . is obviously defined by his
intuitive grasp of the actualities of the led, that is, of their readiness to
act resourcefully in certain directions. . . ."[232] The reason he may do so
is because his personal conflicts and resolutions are a microcosm of a
workable resolution for society. Some individuals' experience comes
closer to the centrality of the mass. Erikson adds, "The main objects
of psychohistorical investigations is to try to relate the particular identity needs of a given leader to the 'typical identity needs' of his historical times."[233]

A contemporary of Roosevelt's conceptualized this in a similar
manner:

> The process of evolution has established a probability that a man
> will find himself at home in the world he comes, and prepared to
> share in its activities. . . .
> At any particular stage of individual existence, these elements,
> together with the suggestions from the world without, are found
> more or less perfectly organized into a living, growing whole, a
> person, a man. Obscurely locked within him, inscrutable to him-
> self or to others, is the soul of the whole past, his portion of the
> energy, the passion, the tendency to human life. . . . There is ex-
> plosive material stored up in him, but it cannot go off unless the
> right spark reaches it ... . they partake in the nature of gods, in
> that the thoughts entertained of them is a constructive effort of
> idealizing the imagination, seeking to create a personal symbol of
> its own tendency. . . .[234]

Journalist Bainton Chandler wrote, "He embraces more sides of American character than any other statesman who has arisen since Abraham
Lincoln. . ."[235] A merchant friend wrote, "Roosevelt can best be understood by saying that he was a symbol of America; he had all of the
qualities developed to almost ideal form. . . ."[236] Another said, "He
was America."[237]

As the most basic forces of Roosevelt's character lie in his childhood
years, so do the roots of American culture during the Progressive Era.
Lloyd deMause's psychogenic theory provides a theoretical framework
for tracing the dynamics of the process. Modes of childrearing, like
other parameters of culture, are unique to particular periods. Parents of
each generation treat their children in altered ways. This in turn forms
a new generation with different psychic structure who in turn mature
into different parents.

A survey by deMause of the history of childhood illustrates continuous evolution of child-rearing modes analogous to man's physical evolution in relation to the sweep of geological time. The nineteenth century introduces a new level deMause terms the "socializing mode" in which beating is less important and the "raising of a child became less a process of conquering its will than of training it, guiding it into proper paths, teaching it to conform, socializing it. . . . Also, in the nineteenth century, the father for the first time begins to take more than an occasional interest in the child, training it, and sometimes relieving the mother of child-care chores."[238]

This structure provides the crucial nexus between the individual development of Theodore Roosevelt and the group psychohistory of "affective leadership," the intense and deeply-rooted emotive relationship between the leader and the led. The initial maternal deprivation, primal rage, ambivalencies towards the father and later intense demands to train and guide energies into constructive patterns are areas in which the Roosevelt family was representative of the social mores of dominant American middle-class culture.

The early portion of the nineteenth century has often been called the time of anti-institutionalism in America: older orthodoxies had been fragmented by the changes in Jacksonian America and not replaced by new ones necessary for America to make the transition from rural-agrarian to urban-industrial culture.[239] As society became more atomized, the institution of the home became more important as the agent of cohesion. The importance of motherhood and the child likewise grew in status. Although it is not possible here to trace in depth the changes in homelife, representative sources can suggest the social alterations.

Childhood during the 1830's and 1840's attained a higher status and was considered a distinct stage of life.[240] After 1800, the chapters on childhood increasingly replaced the family tree as the introduction to the subject's life . . . after 1830, more biographers and autobiographers emphasized that the early years of life provided a positive thrust for, rather than merely an indication of, later development.[241] Anne Louise Kuhn summarized the child's importance:

> To the religious group, the young child was exceedingly important as a potential member of the Church body and the inheritor of the kingdom. To those of an economic or political turn, the young child was the future businessman or citizen, equally capable of earning a million dollars or aspiring to the presidency. To the socially minded, improvement of society was dependent upon the equal rights of every child in the new republic to our admiration and legal protection. To those interested in the sciences, the child was significant as a growing being and participant in progress.[242]

The mother's role grew in importance. One writer stated, "Perhaps there is no proposition so hackneyed, and at the same time little understood, as that women are the prime cause of all good and evil in human action. . . . Yes, mothers, in a certain sense, the destiny of a redeemed world is in your hands."[243]

The belief of the efficacy of the mother culminated in the theory of maternal impressions. The greatest of all determinants was a mother's mind during pregnancy. If a child is born with a clubfoot, for example, the probability is great the mother dwelled too greatly upon the thought of a clubfoot. The respected Dr. John Eberle related how a black child was born to a white woman who contemplated too intensely the picture of an Ethiopian.[244]

Sexuality largely revolved around what Ben Barker-Benfield calls the "Spermatic Economy." Economic terms were applied to sex, mainly because of the desire to economize the energies involved. The body was seen as a closed system of energy and the woman was warned to direct her drives entirely into motherhood.[245] There was control of sexuality. Onanism was a sin. Dr. R. L. Trall, in writing *Sexual Diseases,* included a long list of diseases caused by masturbation. Dr. Smith's *Handbook of the Diseases of Women* traced every one of them to masturbation. Doctors believed masturbation was a major cause of insanity.[246]

Of crucial importance are the implications of such demands upon mothers. Stress was placed on diminishing physical means of discipline at the same time every aspect of a child's behavior was expected to be controlled and trained. Distancing devices such as wet-nurses and swaddling were less popular and corporal punishment de-emphasized.[247] The mother had to therefore resort to psychic rather than physical means of control.

Because of these circumstances, the psychic rather than more physical means of control of earlier periods was bound to be more drastic, with graver implications for the mother. The control was more subtle, persistent, guilt-bound and personalized. It was the basis for the particular kind of discipline and aggression common to Roosevelt's generation.

Only in this light can the specific dynamics of the Roosevelt household have more meaning. Martha Bulloch Roosevelt's failure and retreat came only after attempting to fulfill the demands of a closer maternal role. Strong psychic ties were established with her children which made the eventual abandonment more painful to parent and child. In many ways, approach and retreat was a form of control in which she manipulated her children so that they would care and protect her. Roosevelt, Sr. attempted to gain close proximity to the lives of his children. His closeness, though, only came with control. He comforted Teedie during asthmatic attacks, but later planned his physical regimen.

Historians have unknowingly captured the primary theses of closeness yet greater control in their analyses of social structures created by Roosevelt's generation during their adult years.

Wiebe's *Search for Order* is most reflective. Antebellum America, he says, was a society with a discipline vacuum. Arguing that the United States of the Reconstruction period was "a society without a core," afflicted by "a general splintering process," Wiebe shows how the nation was incapable of facing the challenges of urbanization, industrialism and immigration.

Wiebe finds the lack of social planning and cooperation of mid-century dangerous. America was little more than "island communities" without the institutions and attitudes to cope with change. Imperative new virtues as "regularity, system, continuity—clashed increasingly with the old."[248] Wiebe summarizes his thesis:

> By contrast to the personal, informal ways of the community, the new scheme derived from the regulative, hierarchical needs of urban-industrial life. Through rules with impersonal sanctions, it sought continuity and predictability in a world of endless change. It assigned far greater power to government—in particular to a variety of flexible administrative devices—and it encouraged the centralization of authority. Men were now separated more by skill and occupation than by community.[249]

Samual Hays' work, *Response to Industrialism, 1885-1914,* sketches the evolving discipline of industrial methods in relation to specialization:

> To the uncritical observer, the record of industrialism has been written in the production statistics, the accomplishments of investor-heroes, and the rising standard of living of the American people. Even more significant, however, were the less obvious and less concrete changes: the expansion of economic relationships from personal contacts within a village community to impersonal forces in the nation and the entire world; the standardization of life accompanying the standardization of goods and of production; increasing specialization in occupation with the resulting dependence of people upon each other to satisfy their wants.[250]

John Garraty touches upon the issue of the urge for discipline in his widely read *The New Commonwealth, 1877-1890*. He believes the title *New Commonwealth* is justified because of a basic change America underwent between the years 1877 and 1890: "This change took the form of a greatly expanded reliance by individuals upon group activities. Industrialization with its accompanying effects—speedy transportation and communication, specialization, urbanization—compelled men to depend far more than in earlier times on organizations in managing their affairs, to deal with problems collectively rather than as individuals."[251]

George F. Fredrickson, a leader in the discipline of intellectual history, in which ideas in themselves, outside of the people who create them, change society, sees a search for discipline in *The Inner Civil War: Northern Intellectuals and the Crises of the Union*. In counter-distinction to ante-bellum humanitarian appeals, the United States Sanitary Commission was a group of the new disciplined intellectuals. The Commission was concerned with "a matter of teaching order and discipline and in its operation the Commission showed an almost excessive concern for the preservation of discipline in all its forms." Fredrickson continues, "A less tangible influence of the Sanitary philosophy came from its encouragement of a new attitude towards suffering. The Commission's concept of 'scientific' philanthropy with its tough-minded 'realism' and emphasis on discipline and efficiency could lead to a genuinely hardhearted approach to the problems of the unfortunate—an approach which could readily be justified in terms of 'scientific' social theories."[252]

Samuel Haber's treatment of the evolution of the professions in America is an additional example of increased organizational impetus and consolidational discipline. Although he observes a nadir in professional consciousness from 1830-1880, new forces were emerging during the later portion of that period: "Not only did new professions seem to appear more rapidly, but the old and new professions took on a fresh spirit and moved effectively towards legislation enactments that restricted entry into their calling and placed control into the hands of the professionals themselves." Haber continues, "A contrast between the 1830's and the 1880's is revealing. By almost any standard both were decades of turbulent expansion. Yet while in the 1830's this growth was wide open and uncontrolled, in the 1880's it was tempered by new and distinctive restrictions."[253]

The hallmark of the progressive impulse was the rise of a new class of professionals, experts in specialized fields of government, science, and management, men first relied on in Washington by the expert commissions of Roosevelt's administration. They worked with fervor and dedication to better society through their own training, science in combination with zealous moral purpose.

In addition to the search for order and discipline, historians apply to the Progressive Period what James R. McGovern calls the "virility impulse." He writes:

> This may be described as an exaggerated concern with manliness and conventional concomitants—power and activity. Social Darwinism is usually called upon to explain the phenomenon without inquiring why, in personal terms, it was so attractive to its supporters. Symbolically, the period begins with Roosevelt's charge up San Juan Hill and ends with his loathing of cowardly officials for refusing his offer to lead a cavalry charge across No Man's

Land. . . . It was a time when the Big Stick and the Bull Moose captured the public favor. Above all, however, the period was marked by activity—strenuous and dedicated effort to alter America and the world.[254]

McGovern observed that even those who did not live up to the heroic image idealized those who did.[255]

Those who saw Roosevelt observed strength defending against weakness and rage. They knew of his sickly asthmatic origins and were aware his bull neck was the product of training rather than genetic endowment. His men in Cuba knew he carried extra pairs of glasses with which to compensate for natural deficiency. His appeal lay in his ability to overcome inability through determination. Strong and weak alike idenfieid with the phenomenon.

The study of the psychic origins of the Progressive Period and its representation in the psychology of Theodore Roosevelt is a study of both the period's weaknesses and strengths. The realities of "socialization," a closer yet more controlling parenthood, held important implications for the years to come.

America was in need of planning and organization. Martha Bulloch Roosevelt's attempts for closeness, Theodore Roosevelt, Sr.'s holding of his son during asthma attacks and concern with development, multiplied by millions on the social level, created individuals of determined nature. America could move into the industrial age, solve problems of science, industry and technology, and begin to get a hold upon commercial competition and the quality of consumer goods. She would enter the world of nations and learn the necessity of abandoning the isolation of earlier years in favor of vigorous involvements.

Yet, along with the closeness came control. Herein lies much of America's aggression, jingoistic nationalism, wars, and bureaucratic overcontrol. America's entry into the twentieth century was colored by both accomplishment and alienation of many of its citizens and relationships abroad. Both the greatness and the tragedy of the twentieth century lies in one of mankind's greatest dilemmas, the means of achieving close relations between individuals and nations without the need to dominate. We are only beginning to see how much of the answer lies in the psychohistorical study of individual and group development.

Glenn Davis received his training in history at Oberlin College and Columbia University, and has completed a book entitled Theodore Roosevelt and an Epoch: A Study in Psychology and History.

REFERENCES

I would like to thank Lloyd deMause for his help during the research and writing stages of this paper.

1. Corinne (Roosevelt) Robinson, "My Brother Theodore Roosevelt: The Nursery and its Duties," Unsigned typed manuscript, Harvard University, Haughton Library, bMS Am1785.3 #11.
2. *Ibid.*
3. Letter, Theodore Roosevelt to Martha Bulloch, Sept. 16, 1853, 65M-11 bMS Am1785.7 #38.
4. Corinne Roosevelt Robinson, *My Brother Theodore Roosevelt* (New York: Charles Scribner's Sons, 1921).
5. Letter, Silas Weir Roosevelt to Hilbourne West, Sept. 16, 1847, 65M-65.1 #98.
6. Carleton Putnam, *Theodore Roosevelt: The Formative Years, 1858-1886* (New York: Charles Scribner's Sons, 1958), p. 1.
7. *Ibid.*, 7.
8. *Ibid.*, 3.
9. *Ibid.*, 3.
10. Letter, Theodore Roosevelt to Martha Bulloch, May 31, 1853, bMS Am1785.2 #100.
11. Carleton Putnam, *Theodore Roosevelt*, 3.
12. *Ibid.*, 12.
13. *Ibid.*, 13.
14. *Ibid.*, 13.
15. Letter, Theodore Roosevelt to Martha Bulloch, May 31, 1853, bMS Am1785.2 #100.
16. Carleton Putnam, *Theodore Roosevelt*, 2.
17. *Ibid.*, 13.
18. Letter, Theodore Roosevelt to Martha Bulloch, Aug. 4, 1853, 65-11 bMS Am1785.7 #38.
19. Letter, Theodore Roosevelt to Martha Bulloch, Aug. 18, 1853. 65M-11 bMS Am1785.7 #38.
20. Carleton Putnam, *Theodore Roosevelt*, 20.
21. Lilian Rixie, *Bamie: Theodore Roosevelt's Remarkable Sister* (New York: David McKay Co., 1963) p. 4.
22. Letter, Theodore Roosevelt to Martha (Bulloch) Roosevelt, May 31, 1857, 65M-11 bMS Am1785.7 #38.
23. Letter, Martha (Bulloch) Roosevelt to Theodore Roosevelt, May 11, n.d. 65M-65.2 #97.
24. Letter, Martha (Bulloch) Roosevelt to Theodore Roosevelt, May 23, n.d., 65M-65.2 #97.
25. Letter, Theodore Roosevelt to Martha (Bulloch) Roosevelt, May 16, 1855, bMS Am1785.7 #38.
26. Letter, Martha (Bulloch) Roosevelt to Theodore Roosevelt, May 15, 1855, 65M-111 bMS Am1785.7 #34.
27. Carleton Putnam, *Theodore Roosevelt*, 23.
28. Letter, Martha (Stewart) Bulloch to Susan (Elliott) West, Nov. 2, 1858, 65M-11 bMS Am1785.7 #3.
29. Letter, Martha (Stewart) Bulloch to Susan (Elliott) West, Nov. 1, 1858, 65M-11 bMS Am1785.7 #3.
30. *Ibid.*
31. Letter, Martha (Stewart) Bulloch to Susan (Elliott) West, Nov. 2, 1858, Houghton, 65M-11 bMS Am1785.7 #3.
32. *Ibid.*
33. Letter, Martha (Stewart) Bulloch to Susan (Elliott) West, Dec. 1858, 65M-11 bMS Am1785.7 #3.
34. *Ibid.*
35. Letter, Martha (Stewart) Bulloch to Susan (Elliott) West, March 12, 1862, 65M-11 bMS Am1785.7 #3.
36. Letter, Martha (Stewart) Bulloch to Susan (Elliott) West, May 7, 1860, 65-11 bMS Am1785.7 #3.

37. Letter, Martha (Stewart) Bulloch to Susan (Elliott) West, Sept., 1861, 65-11 bMS Am1785.7 #3.
38. Letter, Martha (Stewart) Bulloch to Susan (Elliott) West, Nov. 29, 1862, 65M-bMS Am1785.7 #3.
39. Letter, Martha (Bulloch) Roosevelt to Theodore Roosevelt, June 2, 1873, 65M-111 bMS Am1785.7 #34.
40. G. Wallace Chessman, *Theodore Roosevelt and the Politics of Power* (Boston: Little, Brown and Co.) p. 14.
41. Carleton Putnam, *Theodore Roosevelt*, 53.
42. Lilian Rixey, *Bamie*, 10.
43. Carleton Putnam, *Theodore Roosevelt*, 24.
44. *Ibid.*, 24.
45. *Ibid.*, 25.
46. Letter, Theodore Roosevelt to Martha (Bulloch) Roosevelt, Jan. 8, 1862, 65-11 bMS Am1785.7 #38.
47. Letter, Martha (Stewart) Bulloch to Susan (Elliott) West, Aug. 22, 1859, 65M-bMS Am1785.7 #3.
48. Max Trell, "The Man Built Around a Set of Teeth," *Gateway to Health* (Nov., 1925).
49. Noel F. Busch, *TR: The Story of Theodore Roosevelt and his Influence on Our Times* (New York: Reynal and Co., 1963) p. 144.
50. Jacob A. Arlow, "Notes on Oral Symbolism," *Psychoanalytic Quarterly*, XXLV, No. 1 (1955), p. 71.
51. Jacob A. Riis, *Theodore Roosevelt the Citizen* (New York: Grosset and Dunlap, 1903), p. 56.
52. Charles Hanson Toune, ed., *Roosevelt as the Poets Saw Him* (New York: Charles Scribner's Sons, 1923) p. 24.
53. Joseph Gardner, *Departing Glory: Theodore Roosevelt as Ex-President* (New York: Charles Scribner's Sons, 1973) p. 22.
54. Corinne Roosevelt Robinson, *My Brother Theodore Roosevelt*, 163.
55. Theodore Roosevelt, *American Ideals*, Vol. XIII of *The Works of Theodore Roosevelt*, ed. by Hermann Hagedorn (20 Vols; New York: Scribner's Sons, 1926) p. 122.
56. Thomas M. French and Franz Alexander, *Psychogenic Factors of Bronchial Asthma* (Menashe: George Banta, 1941).
57. E. M. Goldberg, *Family Influence and Psychosomatic Illness* (London: Lavistock, 1958).
58. Lindy Burton, *Vulnerable Children* (New York: Schocken, 1968), 180.
59. Thomas J. Luparello et al., "Psychogenic Factors and Bronchial Asthma," *New York State Medical Journal*, LXXI, No. 18 (Sept. 15, 1971), pp. 2161-2165; Edward J. Sachar, "Some Current Issues on Psychosomatic Research," *Psychiatric Annals*, VIII, No. 2 (1972), pp. 22-35; Peter H. Knapp, "Psychosomatic Medicine: an Interpretation," *Psychiatric Annals*, II, No. 8 (1972), pp. 22-36; Neil McDermott and Stanley Cobb, "A Psychiatric Survey of Fifty Cases of Bronchial Asthma," *Psychosomatic Medicine*, I, No. 2 (1939); A Adler, *The Practice and Theory of Individual Psychology* (New York: Harcourt, Brace and World, 1927); Arthur Z. Mutter and Maxwell J. Schleifer, "The Role of Psychological and Social Factors in the Onset of Somatic Illness in Children," *Psychosomatic Medicine*, XXVIII, No. 4 (1966), pp. 333-343; Franz Alexander, *Psychoanalytic Therapy: Principles and Application* (New York: Ronald Press Co., 1946), p. 135; David Bakan, *Disease, Pain and Sacrifice: Towards a Psychology of Suffering* (Chicago: Beacon Press, 1968).
60. Carleton Putnam, *Theodore Roosevelt*, 26.
61. Norman Kiell, "Effects of Asthma on the Character of Theodore Roosevelt," paper made available by Lloyd deMause.
62. Letter, Martha (Stewart) Bulloch to Susan (Elliott) West, June 22, 1863, 65M-bMS Am1785.7 #3.
63. Theodore Roosevelt, *Autobiography* (New York: Macmillan, 1913) pp. 8-9.
64. Theodore Roosevelt, *Autobiography*, 12.
65. Letter, Theodore Roosevelt to Martha (Bulloch) Roosevelt, Aug. 14, 1873, bMS Am1785.2 #100.

66. Lincoln Steffins, *The Autobiography of Lincoln Steffins,* Vol. I (New York: Harcourt, Brace and World, 1931) pp. 350.
67. C. Wallace Chessman, *Theodore Roosevelt and the Politics of Power,* 15.
68. *Theodore Roosevelt's Diaries of Boyhood and Youth* (New York: Charles Scribner's Sons, 1928) p. 74.
69. Richard Hofstadter, "Theodore Roosevelt: The Conservative as Progressive."
70. *Theodore Roosevelt's Diaries of Boyhood and Youth,* 74
71. Carleton Putnam, *Theodore Roosevelt,* 66.
72. Corinne Roosevelt Robinson, *My Brother Theodore Roosevelt,* 50.
73. Theodore Roosevelt's diary, 1869, bMS Am1541.
74. Carleton Putnam, *Theodore Roosevelt,* 87.
75. *Theodore Roosevelt's Diaries of Boyhood and Youth,* 276.
76. Henry F. Pringle, *Theodore Roosevelt* (New York: Harcourt, Brace and World, 1956) p. 14.
77. Carleton Putnam, *Theodore Roosevelt,* 86.
78. *Theodore Roosevelt's Diaries of Boyhood and Youth,* 291.
79. Corine Roosevelt Robinson, *My Brother Theodore Roosevelt,* 57.
80. Theodore Roosevelt, *Autobiography,* 19.
81. *Theodore Roosevelt's Diaries of Boyhood and Youth,* 275-320.
82. Henry F. Pringle, *Theodore Roosevelt,* 15.
83. Carleton Putnam, *Theodore Roosevelt,* 27.
84. Letter, Theodore Roosevelt to Martha (Bulloch) Roosevelt, May 3, 1873, bMS Am1785.2 #100.
85. Letter, Theodore Roosevelt to Martha (Bulloch) Roosevelt, June 22, 1873, bMS Am 1785.2 #100.
86. Letter, Martha (Bulloch) Roosevelt to Theodore Roosevelt, Oct. 15, 1873, 65M-111 bMS Am1785.7 #32.
87. Theodore Roosevelt, *Autobiography,* 21
88. Elting E. Morison, ed., *The Letters of Theodore Roosevelt* (8 Vols.; Cambridge: Harvard University Press, 1954) Vol. I, 10.
89. Carleton Putnam, *Theodore Roosevelt,* 107.
90. Letter, Martha (Bulloch) Roosevelt to Theodore Roosevelt, n.d. 65M-111 bMS Am1785.7 #34.
91. Letter, Martha (Bulloch) Roosevelt to Theodore Roosevelt, June 18, 1873, 65M-111 bMS Am1785.7 #34.
92. Letter, Martha (Bulloch) Roosevelt to Theodore Roosevelt, June 8, 1873, 65M-111 bMS Am1785.7 #34.
93. *Ibid.*
94. "The Dresden Literary Club," 1873, bMS Am1541 #288.
95. Corinne Roosevelt Robinson, *My Brother Theodore Roosevelt,* 59.
96-98. Included in Fifteen Diaries, 1869-1910, bMS Am1541 and Letters from Dresden, 1873, bMS Am1540 #516. Sketches also published in Corinne Roosevelt Robinson's *My Brother Theodore Roosevelt.*
99. Corinne Roosevelt Robinson, *My Brother Theodore Roosevelt,* 76.
100. *Ibid.,* 77-78.
101-103. Letters from Dresden, 1873, bMS Am1540 #516.
104. Letter, Theodore Roosevelt to Martha (Bulloch) Roosevelt, Nov. 27, 1873, bMS Am1785.2 #100
105. Joseph P. Lash, *Eleanor and Franklin,* 32.
106. Diary, Elliott Roosevelt, Feb., 1883, bMS Am1785.7 #47.
107. Elting E. Morison, ed., *The Letters of Theodore Roosevelt,* Vol. I, 392.
108. John Chamberlain, "The Progressive Mind in Action."
109. Henry F. Pringle, *Theodore Roosevelt,* 17.
110. Francis Theodora Parsons, *Purchance Some Day* (Limited private printing, 1951).
111. Carleton Putnam, *Theodore Roosevelt,* 126.
112. C. Wallace Chessman, *Theodore Roosevelt and the Politics of Power,* 22.
113. Carleton Putnam, *Theodore Roosevelt,* 148.
114. Elting E. Morison, ed., *The Letters of Theodore Roosevelt,* Vol. I, 18.
115. Carleton Putnam, *Theodore Roosevelt,* 149.
116. *Ibid.,* 151.

117. Carleton Putnam, *Theodore Roosevelt: The Formative Years, 1858-1889* (New York: Charles Scribner's Sons, 1958), p. 148.
118. Joseph P. Lash, *Eleanor and Franklin* (New York: Norton, 1971), p. 10.
119. Diary, Elliott Roosevelt, February 9, 1878, Harvard University, Houghton Library, bMS 1785.7 #47.
120. Diary, Elliott Roosevelt, March 2, 1878, Houghton, bMS 1785.7 #47.
121. Henry F. Pringle, *Theodore Roosevelt* (New York: Harcourt, Brace and World, 1956), pp. 23-24.
122. *The Autobiography of Theodore Roosevelt* (New York: Macmillan, 1913), p. 25.
123. Elting E. Morison, ed., *The Letters of Theodore Roosevelt* (8 vols; Cambridge: Harvard University Press, 1954), I, p. 24.
124. Letter, Theodore Roosevelt to parents, June 15, 1873, Houghton, bMS Am154 #1.
125. William Roscoe Thayer, *Theodore Roosevelt: An Intimate Biography* (New York: Houghton Mifflin, 1919).
126. *Letters,* I, 24.
127. Carleton Putnam, *Theodore Roosevelt,* 163
128. *Ibid.,* 179.
129. Theodore Roosevelt, *In Memory of My Darling Wife Alice H. Roosevelt and My Beloved Mother Martha Bulloch Roosevelt* (New York: by the author, 1884).
130. Carleton Putnam, *Theodore Roosevelt,* 68.
131. Diary, Theodore Roosevelt, Nov., Dec., 1878, Jan., 1879.
132. Carleton Putnam, *Theodore Roosevelt,* 191.
133. *Ibid.,* 209
134. Nicholas Roosevelt, *Theodore Roosevelt: The Man as I Knew Him* (New York: Dodd, Mead, and Co., 1967), p. 61.
135. William Henry Harbaugh, *The Life and Times of Theodore Roosevelt* (New York: Collier Books, 1961), p. 24.
136. Nicholas Roosevelt, *Theodore Roosevelt,* 61.
137. Frederick S. Wood, *Roosevelt as we Knew Him* (Philadelphia: John C. Winston, 1927), p. 3.
138. *Letters,* I, 46.
139. Theodore Roosevelt, *The Naval War of 1812,* Vol. VI of *The Works of Theodore Roosevelt* ed. by Hermann Hagedorn (20 vols.; New York: Charles Scribner's Sons, 1926), p. 275.
140. Carleton Putnam, *Theodore Roosevelt,* 252.
141. Lincoln Lang, *Ranching with Roosevelt* (Philadelphia: Lippincott, 1926), p. 45.
142. Carleton Putnam, *Theodore Roosevelt,* 330.
143. *Ibid.,* 340. Ferris' testimony is probably very accurate. He remained a life-long friend to Roosevelt and had no motive to malign his reputation. Putnam relied on careful primary researches of Hermann Hagedorn who interviewed Ferris, Hermann Hagedorn, *Roosevelt in the Badlands* (New York: Houghton Mifflin, 1921).
144. *Ibid.,* 345.
145. *Ibid.,* 151; Theodore Roosevelt, *Fear God and Take Your Own Part,* Vol. XVIII of *Works,* 226; *The Autobiography of Theodore Roosevelt,* 8; Carleton Putnam, *Theodore Roosevelt,* 56; *Ibid.,* 46; *The Autobiography of Theodore Roosevelt,* 7.
146. Wolfgang Lederer, "Historical Consequences of Father-Son Hostility," *Psychoanalytic Review* LIV, No. 2 (1967), 52-79; Less Forrest, "The Paternal Roots of Male Character Development," *Psychoanalytic Review,* LIV, No. 2 (1967), 81-89.
147. Albert Bandura, *Adolescent Aggression* (New York: Ronald Press, 1959); Charles Brenner's work on the psychoanalytic theory of aggression deals with the concept of displacement; the phenomenon during infancy is discussed by C. C. Alber, "The Presuperego 'Turning Inward' of Aggression," *Psychoanalytic Quarterly,* XXX (1961), 171-208; John Dollard et al., *Frus-*

tration and Aggression (New Haven: Yale University Press, 1939), this combines psychoanalytic and behavioristic orientations; Ruth-Jean Eisenbud, "Masochism Revisited," *Psychoanalytic Review,* LIV, No. 4 (1967), 5-27; The subject of masochism as aggression turned inwards is treated frequently in *The Psychoanalytic Study of the Child* and *The Collected Works of Sigmund Freud;* George Gero, "Sadism, Masochism, and Aggression: Their Role in Symptom Formation," *Psychoanalytic Quarterly,* XXXI (1962), 31-41.

148. Norman O. Brown, *Love's Body* (New York: Random House, 1966), pp. 164-65.

149. Roosevelt's home is open to the public as an historic area at Sagamore Hill, Oyster Bay, New York.

150. William Henry Harbaugh, *Theodore Roosevelt,* 51

151. Carleton Putnam, *Theodore Roosevelt,* 384.

152. Henry F. Pringle, *Theodore Roosevelt,* 36.

153. Carleton Putnam, *Theodore Roosevelt,* 390-91.

154. Theodore Roosevelt, *Thomas Hart Benton,* Vol. VII of *Works,* 172.

155. *Letters,* I, 122.

156. Theodore Roosevelt, *The Wilderness Hunter* (1893), *The Winning of the West* (1889), *Governour Morris of New York* (1888), Vols. II; VIII, IX, and VII of *Works.*

157. Theodore Roosevelt, *The Winning of the West,* Vol. VII of *Works,* 57.

158. *Ibid.,* 390.

159. *Theodore Roosevelt the Child* (W. Stracker, privately printed: copy #32 of 100).

160. *Ibid.*

161. Eleanor B. Roosevelt, *Day Before Yesterday: Reminiscences of Mrs. Theodore Roosevelt, Jr.* (New York: Doubleday, 1959), p. 41.

162. Hermann Hagedorn, *The Roosevelt Family of Sagamore Hill* (New York: Macmillan, 1954), pp. 37-38.

163. *Ibid.,* 38.

164. *Ibid.,* 21.

165. Lilian Rixey, *Bamie: Theodore Roosevelt's Remarkable Sister* (New York: David McKay Co., 1963), p. 114.

166. *Ibid.,* 116.

167. *New York Times,* Feb. 12, 1974, p. 1.

168. William Henry Harbaugh, *Theodore Roosevelt,* 80.

169. *Letters,* I, 462.

170. Corinne Roosevelt Robinson, *My Brother Theodore Roosevelt* (New York: Charles Scribner's Sons, 1921), p. 50.

171. *Letters,* I, 504.

172. See Howard K. Beale, *Theodore Roosevelt and the Rise of America to World Power* (New York: Macmillan, 1956): John Morton Blum, *The Republican Roosevelt* (Cambridge: Harvard University Press, 1954); Edward Burns, *The American Idea of Mission: Concepts of National Purpose and Destiny* (New Brunswick: Rutgers University Press, 1957); David Burton, *Theodore Roosevelt: Confident Imperialist* (Philadelphia: University of Pennsylvania Press, 1968); G. Wallace Chessman, *Theodore Roosevelt and the Politics of Power* (Boston: Little, Brown and Co.); William Henry Harbaugh, *Power and Responsibility: The Life of Theodore Roosevelt;* George E. Mowry, *The Era of Theodore Roosevelt and the Birth of Modern America* (New York: Hill and Wang, 1948).

173. *Letters,* I, 638.

174. *Ibid.,* 696.

175. Theodore Roosevelt, *Literary Essays,* Vol. XII of *Works,* 84.

176. William Henry Harbaugh, *Theodore Roosevelt,* 101.

177. *Letters,* I, 717.

178. William Henry Harbaugh, *Theodore Roosevelt,* 105.

179. *Ibid.,* 105.

180. Henry Pringle, *Theodore Roosevelt,* 184.

181. Col. A. Z. M. Azory, *Charge! The Battle of San Juan Hill* (New York: Long-

man, Green, and Co., 1961).
182. *The Autobiography of Theodore Roosevelt.*
183. *Ibid.*
184. *Letters,* II, 862.
185. William Henry Harbaugh, *Theodore Roosevelt,* 107.
186. *The Autobiography of Lincoln Steffens* (New York: Harcourt, Brace and Co., 1931), pp. 259-60.
187. William Henry Harbaugh, *Theodore Roosevelt,* 161.
188. *Letters,* V. 10.
189. Joseph Bishop, ed., *Theodore Roosevelt's Letters to his Children* (New York: Scribner's, 1919), p. 94.
190. *Ibid.,* 78.
191. Corinne Roosevelt Robinson, *My Brother,* 278.
192. *Letters,* V, 721.
193. *The Autobiography of Theodore Roosevelt,* 548.
194. John Morton Blum, *The Republican Roosevelt,* 157.
195. Edward Wagenknecht, *The Seven Worlds of Theodore Roosevelt* (New York: Longmans, Green, and Co., 1958), p. 19.
196. *Ibid.,* 20.
197. *The Autobiography of Theodore Roosevelt,* 17.
198. Diary, 1867, in *Theodore Roosevelt's Diaries of Boyhood and Youth* (New York: Charles Scribner's Sons, 1928).
199. Joseph Gardner, *Departing Glory: Theodore Roosevelt as Ex-President* (New York: Charles Scribner's Sons,(1973), p. 131.
200. Joseph Bishop, ed., *Theodore Roosevelt's Letters to His Children,* 81.
201. Pocket diary, Theodore Roosevelt, April-Nov. 1909, Houghton, bMS Am1541.
202. *Ibid.*
203. Theodore Roosevelt, original draft of "Two Sides of Americanism," 1917. Houghton.
204. *Letters,* VIII, 1355.
205. Ray S. Baker, "TR: A Character Sketch," *McClure's Magazine,* XII, No. 1 (1898), p. 30.
206. George E. Mowry, *The Era of Theodore Roosevelt and the Birth of Modern America,* 109.
207. Charles Hanson Toune, ed., *Roosevelt as the Poets Saw Him* (New York: Charles Scribner's Sons, 1923), p. 151.
208. William Manners, *TR and Will,* 310.
209. *Ibid.,* 310.
210. *Ibid.,* 309.
211. Lawrence A. Abbott, *Impressions of TR* (New York: Doubleday, Page and Co., 1924), p. 259.
212. Hermann Hagedorn, ed., *Works,* Vol. V. xvii-xviii.
213. Edward Wagenknecht, *The Seven Worlds,* 107-08.
214. *Ibid.,* 108.
215. *Ibid.,* 110.
216. Charles Willis Thompson, *Presidents I've Known* (Indianapolis: Bobbs-Merrill Co., 1929), p. 112.
217. William Manners, *TR and Will,* 27.
218. Lawrence F. Abbott, ed., *The Letters of Archie Butt* (New York: Doubleday, Page, and Co., 1924), p. 233.
219. Owen Wister, *Roosevelt: The Story of a Friendship, 1880-1919* (New York: Macmillan, 1930), p. 8.
220. James E. Amos, *TR: Hero to his Valet* (New York: John Day, 1927).
221. Jacob Riis, *Theodore Roosevelt the Citizen* (New York: Grosset and Dunlap, 1903), pp. 337-38.
222. Joseph Gardner, *Departing Glory,* 225.
223. *Ibid.,* 279.
224. Rev. Ferdinand Cowles Iglehart, *Theodore Roosevelt: The Man as I Knew Him* (New York: Christian Herald, 1919), p. 283.
225. *The Autobiography of Lincoln Steffens,* 580.
226. Hermann Hagedorn, *The Roosevelt Family,* 246.

227. Frederick S. Wood, *Roosevelt as we Knew Him* (Philadelphia: John C. Winston, 1927), p. 302.
228. John William Ward, *Andrew Jackson, Symbol for an Age* (New York: Oxford University Press, 1955), p. 1.
229. John Dewey, "Theodore Roosevelt," *The Dial*, Feb. 8, 1919, LXVI, No. 783, p. 105.
230. Sidney Hook, *The Hero in History* (Boston: Beakon, 1943), p. 154.
231. Erik Erikson, *Insight and Responsibility* (New York: Norton, 1964), p. 208.
232. *Ibid.*, 208.
233. Richard I. Evans, *Dialogue with Erik Erikson* (New York: Harper and Row, 1967), p. 66.
234. Charles Horton Cooley, *Human Nature and the Social Order* (New York: Schrocken Books, 1902), pp. 318-19.
235. George B. Chandler, "Roosevelt, the Representative American," *Anglo-American Magazine*, IV (December, 1900), pp. 293-94.
236. Rev. Ferdinand Cowles Iglehart, *Theodore Roosevelt*, 413.
237. Noel F. Busch, *TR:The Story of Theodore Roosevelt and his Influence on Out Times* (New York: Reynal and Co., 1963). A more complete view of the relation of TR to his contemporaries includes the following sources (those cited are characteristic): George Sylvester Vierck, *Roosevelt: A Study in Ambivalence* (New York: Jackson Press, 1920); Bernard deVoto, ed., *Mark Twain in Eruption* (New York: Harper and Bros., 1922); John Allan O'Laughlin, *From the Jungle Through Europe with Roosevelt* (Boston: Chapple, 1910); Willard Gatewood, Jr., *Theodore Roosevelt and the Art of Controversy;* Lewis Einstein, *Roosevelt: His Mind in Action* (Cambridge: Houghton Mifflin Co., 1930); Charles Eugene Banks and Leroy Armstrong, *Theodore Roosevelt: A Typical American* (Chicago: S. Stone, 1901); Donald Wilhelm, *Theodore Roosevelt as an Undergraduate* (Boston: J. W. Luce and Co., 1910); William Draper Lewis, *The Life of Theodore Roosevelt* (United Publishers, 1919); John Burroughs, *Camping and Tramping with Roosevelt* (New York: Houghton Mifflin, 1907); Thomas C. Addison, *Roosevelt Among the People* (Chicago: T. W. Walter, 1910); the following journalism pieces present the same intensity: "Character and Success," *Outlook*, March 31, 1900, pp. 725-27; character sketches: *Review of Reviews*, August, 1900, pp. 181-86; *Contemporary Review*, October, 1900, pp. 763-78; *McClure's*, November, 1901, pp. 40-47; "The Energy of Roosevelt," *Current Literature*, September, 1900; "The Man," *Nation*, March 3, 1900; "Personal Sketch," *Outlook*, October 29, 1903; Personal qualities: *Collier's*, March 6, 1909, *Outlook*, September 22, 1906; May 25, 1907; November 27, 1909. Also, "David Graham Phillips and the Virility Impulse of Progressives," *New England Quarterly* 39 (Sept., 1966).
238. Lloyd deMause, ed., *The History of Childhood* (New York: Psychohistory Press, 1974), p. 52.
239. See Stanley Elkins, "Institutional Breakdown in an Age of Expansion," in *Slavery* (Chicago: University of Chicago Press, 1959).
240. Harvey J. Graff, "Patterns of Dependency and Child Development in the Mid-Nineteenth Century: A Sample from Boston, 1860," *History of Education Quarterly*, XIII, No. 2 (Summer, 1973), 138.
241. Joseph Kett, "Adolescence and Youth in Nineteenth-Century America," *Journal of Interdisciplinary History*, II, No. 2 (1971), 28.
242. Louise Anne Kuhn, *The Mother's Role in Childhood Education: New England Concepts, 1830-1860* (New Haven: Yale University Press, 1947), p. 28.
243. Unsigned article, "The Good Wife," *The Mother's Assistant and Young Lady's Friend*, XIV (Jan., 1849), p. 13.
244. John Eberle, *Treatise on the Diseases and Physical Education of Children* (Philadelphia: Grigg and Elliott, 1844), p. 12.
245. Rev. E. P. Dyer, "Maternal Love," *The Mother's Assistant*, XV, No. 1 (Jan., 1850), p. 6; Ben Barker-Benfield, "The Spermatic Economy: A Nineteenth-Century View of Sexuality," in *The American Family in Social-Historical Perspective*, Michael Gordon, ed. (New York: St. Martin's Press, 1973).
246. R. J. Trall, *Sexual Diseases* (New York: Fowler and Wells, 1858); Dr. Hey-

wood Smith, *A Handbook of the Diseases of Women* (Philadelphia: Lindsay and Blakiston, 1878); E. H. Hare, "Masturbatory Insanity; The History of an Idea," *Journal of Mental Science,* CVIII, No. 452, pp. 2-25.
247. Literature concerning the changing status of women and childhood from the mid to late nineteenth century is of course extensive. The following citations are representative materials from which the described synthesis was drawn: G. Ackerly, *On the Management of Children* (New York: Bancroft and Holley, 1835); William A. Alcott, *Young Mother* (Boston: Light and Sterns, 1836), *Young Wife* (Boston: George W. Tright, 1838); G. P. Bayer, *Maternal Impressions: The Study of Child Life* (Winoka: Jones and Kroeger, 1897); Catherine E. Beecher, *Evils suffered by American Women and Children* (New York: Harper and Bros., 1846); *The Parents' Magazine;* Arthur W. Calhoun, *A Social History of the American Family from Colonial Times to the Present* (New York: Barnes and Noble, 1945); Lydia Child, *The Mother's Book* (Boston, Carter, 1831); Fleetwood Churchill, *Diseases of Females, Including Those of Pregnancy and Childbirth* (Philadelphia: Lea and Blanchard, 1843); Edward H. Clarke, *Sex in Education* (Boston: James R. Osgood, 1875); F. H. Davenport, *Diseases of Women* (Lee Bros., 1892); William Davidson, "A Brief History of Infant Feeding," *Journal of Pediatrics,* XLIII, No. 1 (1953); John Demos, "Developmental Perspectives in the History of Childhood," *Journal of Interdisciplinary History* II, No. 2 (1971); Edward Dixon, *Woman and her Diseases from the Cradle to the Grave* (New York: Charles H. Ring, 1847); Al Donne, *Mothers and Infants, Nurses and Nursing* (Boston: Phillips, Sampson, and Co., 1859); Dorothy Canfield Fisher, *Mothers and Children* (New York: Holt and Co., 1914); S. Fowler, *Amativeness, or the Evils and Remedies of Excessive Sexuality* (Edinburgh: H. Robinson, 1850); *Godey's Lady's Book;* Philip J. Greven, *Child Rearing Concepts, 1628-1861* (Itasca: F. E. Peacock, 1973); Joseph W. Howe, *Excessive Venery: Masturbation and Continence* (New York: E. B. Treat, 1907); Ellen Key, *Century of the Child* (New York: G. P. Putnam's Sons, 1909); Stephen Kern, "Explosive Intimacy: Psychodynamics of the Victorian Family," *History of Childhood Quarterly,* I, No. 3 (1973); Joseph Kett, "Adolescence and Youth in Nineteenth-Century America," *Journal of Interdisciplinary History,* II, No. 2 (1971); *The Mother's Assistant, The Mother's Magazine;* Pracilla Robers, "Home as a Nest: Middle Class Childhood in Nineteenth-Century Europe," paper made available by Lloyd deMause; D. Rosch, *Chronic Diseases* (New York: Fowler and Wells, 1849); Carroll Smith Rosenberg, "Beauty, the Beast and the Militant Woman: A Case Study in Sex Roles and Social Stress in Jacksonian America," *American Quarterly,* XXIII, No. 4 (1971); C. S. Rosenberg and C. Rosenberg, "The Female Animal: Medical and Biological Views of Woman and her Role in Nineteenth-Century America," *Journal of American History* LX, No. 2 (1973); C. Rosenberg, "Sexuality, Class, and Role in Nineteenth-Century America," *American Quarterly* (May, 1973); L. H. Sigourney, *Letters to Mothers* (Hartford: Hudson and Skinner, 1838); Robert Sunley, "Early Nineteenth-Century American Literature on Child Rearing," in *Childhood in Contemporary Cultures,* ed. by Margaret Mead and Martha Wolfenstein (Chicago: University of Chicago Press, 1955); Ann Douglas Wood, "Fashionable Diseases: Women's Complaints and their Treatment in the Nineteenth Century," *Journal of Interdisciplinary History,* IV, No. 1 (1973); *The Child at Home;* Caleb Ticknor, *A Guide for Mothers and Nurses* (New York: Taylor and Dodd, 1839); *Child Study Monthly; The Advocate and Family Guardian;* Bernard Wishy, *The Child and the Republic: the Dawn of American Child Nurture* (Philadelphia: University of Pennsylvania Press, 1968); The following periodicals of the nineteenth century contain articles frequently concerning motherhood and childhood: *Unitarian Review; Eclectic Magazine; North American Review; Monthly Religious Magazine; Nineteenth Century; Pedagogical Seminary; Contemporary Review; Littell's Living Age; International Journal of Ethics; Dial.*
248. Robert H. Wiebe, *The Search for Order, 1877-1920* (New York: Hill and Wang, 1967), p. 14.

249. *Ibid.,* xiv.
250. Samuel P. Hays, *The Response to Industrialism, 1885-1914* (Chicago: University of Chicago Press, 1957), p. 4.
251. John Garraty, *The New Commonwealth, 1877-1890* (New York: Harper and Row, 1968), p. xiii.
252. George M. Fredrickson, *The Inner Civil War: Northern Intellectuals and the Crises of the Union* (New York: Harper and Row), p. 112.
253. Samuel Haber, "The Professions and Higher Education in America: A Historical View," in *Higher Education and the Labor Market,* ed. by Margaret S. Gordon, p. 246.
254. James R. McGovern, "David Graham Philipps and the Virility Impulse of Progressivism," *New England Quarterly,* XXXIX, No. 3 (September, 1966), 335.
255. *Ibid.,* 341.

CHAPTER 10

Psychohistory and Psychotherapy

LLOYD
deMAUSE

The following speech was delivered to the Psychiatric Conference of the Tufts-New England Medical Center, Boston, Massachusetts, on March 7, 1974.

During the long summer of 1973, as the Watergate hearings began to reveal the full extent of the illegal activities of Richard M. Nixon, I would often have lunch with associates in the mental health field, and invariably our discussions turned to the personality of Nixon. Surprisingly, my friends each described for me quite similar profiles of his character. Previously, they said, it had seemed that Nixon was a typical obsessive-compulsive personality, reasonably well integrated, warding off a great deal of repressed hostility through typical defense mechanisms, chiefly overcontrol of himself and others, and through a variety of over-moralistic projects. In short, he had seemed little different than, say, the average compulsive businessman who was so frequently seen in psychotherapy.

But, with Watergate, it was becoming more and more evident that this appraisal of Nixon was superficial, that his compulsive traits were only protective coloration which allowed him to blend in with the predominant American personality-type. Instead, it was becoming apparent that he was closer to the psychopathic personality-type, making paranoid lists of enemies and ordering their illegal surveillance and persecution, tape-recording secretly on a wholesale basis, and so on down the familiar list of Nixon-directed activities. Every one of the character-traits familiar to those who regularly treat psychopathic personalities began to be revealed: the shifting moral standards and patchy superego, the continuous confusion between what is right and what is narcissis-tically needed, the paranoid insecurity and compensatory grandiosity, the shallow inter-personal attachments, the lack of the capacity for guilt or even regret, the overcontrol combined with an increasingly unpre-dictable impulsivity.

Sometimes our lunch-table discussions went further, and we would speculate on whether a real analysis of Nixon's childhood would con-firm this diagnosis, since psychopathic personalities generally could be traced to a great deal of emotional abandonment and even violence in the family, whereas the family patterns of obsessive-compulsive per-sonalities usually centered more on the problem of parental overcon-trol and excessive demands. But regardless of the different turns our discussion took, we usually ended our luncheon with a weak joke, which usually ran something like: "Well, with all these awful things now coming out about Nixon, I sure hope he doesn't feel he has to show he still has balls by pushing the little red button or something!"

Since at that time I had just started a scholarly journal of psycho-history, I made it a point to ask each of these psychotherapists if they would write up some of their professional opinions for publication, in-cluding the possibility that there was a danger of Nixon, like other psychopathic personalities, reacting to exposure and ridicule by having to prove his potency, and that this might take the form of precipitating an international nuclear crisis solely for personal interpsychic reasons. As you might suspect, all of my friends refused to commit their opinions to writing. It was not just that they were reluctant personally to state their opinions; beyond this, they appeared to believe that psychothera-pists *should not be allowed* to express professional opinions on political problems, that somehow the professional status of the psychotherapist *prohibited* him or her from analyzing political behavior. "I'm a specia-list," was the feeling. "Let the social scientists handle political events."

A few months later, on October 23, 1973, what we joked about, what we most feared, happened. Using as a pretext a completely insig-nificant political event, the Russian demand that they be allowed to include some Soviet troops in the U.N. Middle-East peace-keeping force, Nixon pushed the Red Alert button, and two million American soldiers went into a state of war-time readiness, including the arming of 15,000 nuclear bombs. I don't know what your personal response to this Red Alert was, but my own reaction was to go home, put my family and dogs into our car, and head north toward Canada. Luckily, as in the

Cuban missile crisis, the Russian leaders recognized a case of *machismo* as well as my psychoanalytic friends did. They quickly backed off on their demand, and for a second time in a decade we all narrowly escaped being blown off the face of the earth.

The reaction of my friends in psychotherapy to the October Red Alert, like the reaction of the rest of the country, was a studied silence. Their analysis of Nixon's personality and his need to prove his potency had been proved spectacularly accurate, to the extent of achieving that much-desired scientific goal of prediction. Yet, unbelievably, I now found I could no longer get anyone to discuss anything about Nixon's personality, nor about the Red Alert. It was if an unspoken agreement existed which considered the topic "bad manners," "unprofessional" in the extreme. Now when a gap in logic appears in the thinking patterns of a patient undergoing psychoanalysis, the therapist is trained to suspect the existence of a powerful unconscious fantasy. Let us call a shared fantasy of similar effect a "Group-fantasy," and, further, let us call that Group-fantasy shared by the mental health community which strenuously denies the direct application of the insights of psychotherapy to history "The Group-fantasy of Specialization."

This Group-fantasy of Specialization has at least three subordinate beliefs. The first is that there exists a separate group of individuals called "social scientists" who have a body of knowledge somehow beyond psychology which better explains an individual's public behavior than depth psychology does. The second belief is that there exist entities called "social structures" and "political institutions" which are something over and above the individual psychological mechanisms which psychotherapists are used to dealing with in their patients. And the third belief is that there exist places called "universities" which house these "social science" specialists, who are alone qualified to describe and explain these "social structures" and "institutions."

Now, let us for a moment imagine that, through a process similar to that of the lifting of repression in individual psychotherapy, this Group-fantasy of Specialization were one day to be rationally examined, and, like all infantile fantasies, to disappear, and psychotherapists were all to realize that their psychological science and their ability to explain, weigh and predict the motivations and behavior of individuals is *identical* to that science which the "social scientists" had long dreamed of constructing. Let us suppose that psychotherapists were suddenly to realize that the 75-year split between the academic and the mental health community was in fact a reflection of two opposing attitudes, one admitting and one rejecting the existence of unconscious mental activity; that psychoanalytic psychology had been minimally tried and then vigorously rejected by every department in the university over the past four decades; and that, further, most of the theories of the "social sciences" have been motivated by a *flight from psychology,* a vast defensive response to the growing discoveries of depth psychology.

The concrete result of such a destruction of the Group-fantasy of Specialization, I would argue, would be for every unit within the mental health field to set up a psychohistory section. This psychohistory section would assume an obligation to accomplish research toward the construction of a new science of psychohistory, which would include everything from political psychology and group psychohistory to the history of childhood and psychobiography. One of these new psychohistory sections might want to examine contemporary political leaders; another might want to reach out into the community and construct a taxology of family types, with generalizations on the kinds of personal and political behavior which result from childhood in differing kinds of families; a third might attempt to reconstruct the Watergate hearings as a kind of group-process, examining its group-unconscious determinants, and so on. But each unit within the psychotherapeutic community would assume some research project of fairly long-term commitment, and would publish their research results as contributions to the new psychohistory.

This assumption of responsibility would be similar to the dual responsibility historically assumed by the universities for both teaching (for which they receive money) and research (for which they have to find the money). It may be argued that money for psychohistorical research is not currently available to psychotherapy centers. In response, I would suggest that if the Federal government were to propose a law requiring all mental health clinics to report the content of all their therapy sessions to the F.B.I., there would be little difficulty among psychotherapists in finding the money and the time needed to organize the defeat of such a clear and present danger to the professional existence. I would further suggest that it is only the Group-fantasy of Specialization which prevents psychotherapists from similarly seeing events like last October's Red Alert as equally clear and present dangers. History is indeed happening all around us, and the tools necessary to understand public behavior and motivation are identical to those used to understand private behavior and motivation. A separate social science does not exist; we must yet create it as an extension of psychotherapy. And the name we shall give this new science shall be psychohistory.

Let me describe briefly one such research project in psychohistory which has already produced several unexpected results. For the past five years, I have headed a research project investigating children's lives in the past for the Association of Applied Psychoanalysis. What we found in examining diaries, letters, autobiographies, pediatric and pedagogical literature back to antiquity was that good parenting appears to be something only historically achieved, and that the further one goes back into the past the more likely one would be to find children killed, abandoned, beaten, terrorized and sexually abused by adults. Indeed, it soon appeared likely that a good mother, one who was reasonably devoted to her child and more or less able to empathize with and fulfill its needs, was nowhere to be found prior to modern times. In the book which resulted from the project, entitled *The History of Childhood*, I wrote that it seemed to me that childhood was one long nightmare from which we have only gradually and only recently begun to awaken.

Now it is no secret to you as psychiatrists that childhood in many homes even today remains a nightmare, but what is most fascinating is that each type of family with which you are familiar from your practice was once the predominant type of family in the past. When you arrange parenting modes on a scale of decreasing health, from empathic down to the most destructive child-battering parents, you have also listed historical modes of child care reaching back into the past. It is as though today's child abuser were a sort of "evolutionary arrest," a psychological fossil, stuck in a personality mode from a previous historical epoch when *everyone* used to batter children.

Parents in antiquity, for instance, were found to have murdered their newborn children, regardless of economic situation, and in many other ways to have transmitted powerful death wishes to their children. Only when the strength of the infanticidal mode is recognized does it become understandable why early religions focused so exclusively on sacrificial themes. Early Christianity, for example, directly acted out the killing of a Son under orders of his Father. Believers were "buried with Christ" and then resurrected as first a repetition and then a denial of infanticide, were baptised as a repetition of the washing of those newborn babies who were going to be allowed to live, and anticipated a Last Judgment which was as real to them as the First Judgment which every newborn experienced, laying on the ground and waiting for the father to lift it up into life or to cast it into Hell (which the Jews named Gehenna, after the Valley of Hinnom, where children were sacrificed to Moloch). By joining in Christ's death, believers avoided being killed by the Father, as they in their childhood watched their real-life siblings being killed by their fathers after being born, joining the millions of infants who filled the rivers and latrines of antiquity and medieval times.

During the medieval period, the infanticidal wishes of parents toward their legitimate offspring decreased, and the emotional reality of childhood began to evolve more around the fear of abandonment, either emotional or actual, to wet-nurse, monastery, nunnery or foster family. As in badly abandoned and abused children today, who have never had a stable relationship and who from their earliest years have been forced to take care of themselves, the average medieval child grew up to be a psychopathic personality, unable to develop mature attachments, developing instead personal dominance-submission patterns known to historians as feudalism. The feudal bond of personal loyalty, an attempt to deny the possibility of abandonment, combined with the typical psychopathic need for violence, gives medieval Europe its restless, marauding character, centering on the psychopath's world view of everything as consisting solely of exploiting or being exploited.

The Renaissance and early modern period was one of enormous ambivalence toward children, the child being more highly cathected than previously, but also, because emotionally closer, more dangerous, a container for parental projections, a devil or animal which had to be beaten into human shape, molded at every step, and generally made to feel that he or she was essentially bad inside. The result, again like contemporary highly ambivalent families, was a manic-depressive personality, continuously guilty and often self-destructive, under the attack of a severely rejecting superego. The paradigmatic depressive character, Hamlet, provides the characteristic list of depressive symptoms; but what is most interesting is his feeling that his melancholy is an *achievement,* an advance on the psychopathic medieval personality. And, of course, he is right—in the sense that being loved and hated by ambivalent parents is indeed a step higher than being abandoned by unloving and uncaring parents, even today.

The eighteenth century saw a new kind of parent, closer than ever before to the child, but over-controlling and intrusive to a degree only rarely seen in today's families. The child, it is true, was no longer swaddled, nor was it usually sent out to a wet-nurse, but was instead made an active part of the mother's ongoing interpsychic defense system. It began to be both toilet-trained in its earliest months and severely punished for masturbation for the first time in history, and, as with the children of intrusive and overdemanding parents today, the predominant personality type which resulted was the obsessive-compulsive character, Freud's "anal personality," Eric Fromm's "hoarding character." It is this compulsive personality which has dominated the modern world, with its Faustian drive to control nature and its massive need to displace interpersonal aggression onto the social sphere. Only in the twentieth century are we slowly beginning to overcome the compulsive personality through a less intrusive, more helpful and empathic mode of parenting for some of our children.

Perhaps my brief summary of some of the findings of our little project in psychohistory will convey to you a taste of the excitement we have felt in using the tools and concepts of modern psychotherapy in a wider context. New kinds of questions have been generated at every turn, questions which can only be asked and answered within the conceptual framework of psychotherapy: Exactly what causes changes in parent-child relations over a series of generations? Why do some family lines show progress and others seem to stagnate? Why do some areas seem to lag far behind others? How can we better describe childhood modes and resulting personality-types? How might these concepts better explain our social problems? And, finally, merging into the field of contemporary family therapy, how can we facilitate those life-enhancing factors in childhood which further its evolution, applying our leverage for change where it is most meaningful, to childhood? Until we can extend our psychotherapy into a new science of psychohistory which can begin to give us answers to questions like these, we will no doubt continue our habit of giving highly destructive weapons to infantile leaders, who may yet use them to solve their personal problems and thereby end both our psychohistory and our psychotherapy together in one big bang.

Subscriptions to *History of Childhood Quarterly: The Journal of Psychohistory* may be purchased by sending your check for $14.00 to History of Childhood Quarterly: The Journal of Psychohistory, 2315 Broadway, New York, N.Y. 10024.